THE WASHINGTON LOBBYISTS

THE WASHINGTON LOBBYISTS

by

LESTER W. MILBRATH
Northwestern University

GREENWOOD PRESS, PUBLISHERS
WESTPORT, CONNECTICUT

Library of Congress Cataloging in Publication Data

Milbrath, Lester W
   The Washington lobbyists.

   Reprint of the ed. published by Rand McNally, Chicago,
in series: Rand McNally political science series.
   Bibliography: p.
   1. Lobbying--United States. I. Title.
[JK1118.M5 1976]   328.73'07'8   76-5789
ISBN 0-8371-8802-4

Originally published in 1963 by Rand McNally & Company,
Chicago

Reprinted with the permission of Lester W. Milbrath

Reprinted in 1976 by Greenwood Press,
a division of Williamhouse-Regency Inc.

Library of Congress Catalog Card Number 76-5789

ISBN 0-8371-8802-4

Printed in the United States of America

328.38
M638

TO KIRSTEN AND LINDA BEATE

Preface

Although the academic literature is replete with studies of pressure groups in politics, very little has been written about lobbyists as a special political skill group. Because lobbyists are important links between organized interests and government, it is important to know something about them. Careful examination of the roles of lobbyists may also enhance understanding of the process by which groups participate in the making of public policy.

Following the introduction of this study in Part One, Part Two will focus on lobbyists as persons and on their roles as political actors. Part Three will examine the communication process by which the policy desires of groups are fed into the governmental decision process. Part Four will apply certain findings to some of the problems of the role of lobbying in American democracy.

Data for this study were gathered primarily through lengthy personal interviews with a random sample of Washington lobbyists. These were supplemented by interviews with persons in Congress who are the customary recipients of lobbying—congressmen and congressional staff members. The interviewing occupied the better part of a year of research at The Brookings Institution in Washington, D.C.

This book is essentially a research report, and, as such, it is primarily addressed to professional political scientists, though college students of social science and general readers curious about government and politics have been addressed as well—thus, academicians may regret the exclusion of full reports of statistical tests and levels of significance in the interest of readability.[1]

[1]*All statements of tendency or relationship can be taken as statistically significant unless otherwise stated. Two major variables are exceptions to this: When the sample is analyzed by the type of organization a lobbyist represents and by the lobbyist's role to his employer, the categories are so discrete and the sample so small that tests of significance are precluded. Tendency statements for these variables should be accepted with more caution. Many tables are presented in full cross-tabulation form to enable the reader to determine for himself the confidence he wishes to place in the tendencies and relationships.*

vii

Although The Brookings Institution supported the study, it is not a project of the Brookings staff and should not be considered an official statement of that organization.

Both Duke and Northwestern universities supported the study. The Social Science Research Council provided money for research assistance and for subsistence during the summer of 1959.

I am fundamentally indebted to the 101 lobbyists and 38 persons in Congress who gave so generously of their time for interviews. I am grateful for the many helpful suggestions for the design of this study from the staff and fellows of The Brookings Institution, especially Paul T. David, Stanley Kelley, Jr., and Merton Reichler. Herbert Kelman and Richard Christie provided welcome suggestions for the design of a short personality test. Robert Kaufman then of *Congressional Quarterly* offered many helpful suggestions for finding my way around the lobbying scene.

The analysis of the data was facilitated by several faithful and enterprising student assistants: Jenny Marshall, Julian Juergensmeyer, Emilie Smith, Jack Jensen, Dave Lee, Dale Neuman, Ita Ekanem, Walter Klein, Ann Sembower, and Barbara Schadt. Michael Durkee, a Fulbright student in Norway, reviewed and criticized the manuscript. Mrs. Jane Taylor was a key person in preparing the manuscript for publication, offering to take upon herself a large share of the typing, editing, and correspondence.

My professional colleagues at Duke and Northwestern Universities were generous with advice and encouragement: David Minar reviewed some early stages of the manuscript and bibliography; Harold Guetzkow provided cogent advice on analyzing the personality data; and James A. Robinson, out of warm friendship and far beyond the call of duty, read and carefully criticized the entire manuscript; much of whatever merit the book has is due to his endeavors.

Alexander Heard, whom I assisted in a study of money and politics, contributed my basic understanding of research design and execution. Richard Snyder added abundantly to the broadening of my horizons on the study of social science and to my appreciation of the relevance of social scientific knowledge to the problems of life in the twentieth century.

L.W.M.
Oslo, Norway
June, 1962

Table of Contents

ix

PART THREE   *Lobbying as a Communication Process*

PART FOUR *Lobbying in American Democracy*

List of Tables

Part One

Introduction

CHAPTER I

LOBBYISTS AND LOBBYING

On February 3, 1956, Senator Francis Case (R.–S. D.) rose on the floor of the United States Senate to announce that a lobbyist for the natural gas interests had approached his campaign manager in South Dakota on January 25 and left a $2,500 contribution for his political campaign. This occurred just a few days prior to the Senate vote on the natural gas bill. When informed of this matter, Senator Case was so distressed by the bribery-like action, which indicated to him an abnormal financial interest in the outcome of the bill, that he ordered the money returned and announced his intention to vote against the bill even though he formerly had favored it.

This dramatic statement stimulated a chain of events. Presented as front-page news around the country, it gave many people the impression that this was normal lobbying procedure. News commentators and cartoonists wrote "exposés," implying that lobbyists were buying and stealing public decisions. An old political problem—what to do with lobbyists—surged into prominence again.

Members of Congress were convinced that they must do something about the Case incident—though they knew that it was

3

'All Right, You Guys—Line Up'

— from *Herblock's Special for Today* (Simon & Schuster, 1958).

atypical. On February 6, the Senate appointed a select committee to investigate the contribution. This committee uncovered several other contributions by the natural gas interests to various senators, adding to the clamor for remedial action. To head off pressures for immediate legislative action, a bipartisan "Special Committee to Investigate Political Activities, Lobbying, and Campaign Contributions" was appointed, with Senator John McClellan (D.-Ark.) as its chairman. The "McClellan Committee" made such deliberate preparations that the public furor had largely subsided by the time its first hearings were held on May 1, 1956—perhaps as intended by the congressional leadership. Hearings were held intermittently and were not completed until March 14, 1957. The final committee report appeared sixteen months after the committee's formation. Though it was a useful study of lobbying, it disclosed no startling findings; it only recommended minor changes in the lobby regulation act.[1] The lack of interest shown in this unsensational report was almost as striking as the surge of concern about Case's sensational announcement; the press had turned to other more "news-

"You Fellows Haven't Seen Any Undue Influence Around Here, Have You?"

— from Herblock's *Special for Today* (Simon & Schuster, 1958).

[1]*U.S. Congress, Senate (1957). This report also summarizes past investigations and studies of lobbying. For complete references, consult the Bibliography.*

worthy" items. Even the changes recommended for the lobby regulation act have not, by 1962, been enacted by Congress.

Case's disclosure had other more immediate ramifications. Two natural gas lobbyists and their employer, the Superior Oil Company, were indicted for violation of the Lobby Regulation Act of 1946 (they were charged with improper attempts to influence and with failure to register); they pleaded guilty and were fined. The natural gas bill they were attempting to promote was later passed by Congress but was vetoed by President Eisenhower, who personally favored it, on the ground that the public believed improper methods had been used to promote it. Similar natural gas bills were introduced in subsequent Congresses, but so vivid was the memory of the public reaction to the 1956 incident that the new bills were held in committee.[2]

This incident reveals that the public and the press have a very lively distrust of lobbying.[3] So colored is the emotional charge on this topic that few public servants would defend lobbying publicly during the uproar. Yet evidence gathered for this study suggests that the public is misinformed about lobbyists and lobbying.[4] The press tends to focus on the sensational and to expose the unsavory aspects of lobbying. Though newspapers perform a service in exposing evil, they seldom indicate that the evildoers constitute only

[2]*The oil industry in Texas held an appreciation dinner in 1958 for Representative Joseph Martin (R.–Mass.), minority leader of the House. The interpretation of this gesture as special favoritism by the press and political opponents probably abetted the efforts of the opponents of the natural gas bill.*

[3]*Although the writer cannot cite a public opinion poll evidencing distrust of lobbying, the attitude is probably well known to all readers. DeVries (1960, pp. 8–9) collected ninety-five newspaper articles on Michigan lobbying during 1958 and 1959; only two were favorable to lobbyists. An example of the attitude of the popular press is Velie (1949). Other evidence comes from the reactions of lobbyists and public officials. Lobbyist respondents in both this study and the DeVries Michigan study disliked being called lobbyists. Business representatives in Washington who participated in a round-table conference held by The Brookings Institution were extremely wary of being labelled as lobbyists; they objected to the connotations carried by the term and reported that their corporate employers were reluctant to have them register as lobbyists for fear of tarnishing the corporate image. Cherington and Gillen (1962, pp. 13, 46, 50). Members of Congress interviewed for this study were reluctant to admit that lobbyists have any influence on their decisions. A questionnaire sent out by Redbook picked up the same attitude. Toffler (1962).*

[4]*While conducting this study, the writer gave several lectures and speeches on lobbyists. Audience reaction invariably disclosed great information gaps. Lobbyist respondents in this study frequently mentioned that the public does not understand what they do. See also Cherington and Gillen (1962, pp. 46, 50).*

a small percentage of the persons engaged in lobbying and that lobbyists often provide valuable services to the political system.

DEFINITION OF LOBBYING

The words "lobbyist" and "lobbying" have meanings so varied that use of them almost inevitably leads to misunderstanding. Of "lobbying" the "McClellan Committee" report says:

It is a word that denotes and connotes different things to different people. As is the case with all such words, its lack of precision results in faulty communication of ideas among people. One man thinks of lobbying as the factual presentation of useful data to legislators. To another, it means sinister influence peddling by pressure groups with reckless disregard for the general welfare. Indeed some state statutes limit the definition of lobbying to attempts to exert *improper* influence. . . . All recent studies confirm that the emphasis of pressure groups has changed in recent years, from the old style of "buttonholing" legislators in the Halls of Congress to new techniques . . . more and more reliance is being placed on mass media campaigns, which result in inspired letter-writing campaigns and other manifestations of interest in legislation by the voters.[5]

Despite the imprecision of the term "lobbying," some boundaries can be defined. First, lobbying relates only to governmental decision-making. Decisions made by private organizations or corporations may be influenced by special interests within those organizations or from without, but they do not affect the entire body politic. Second, all lobbying is motivated by a desire to influence governmental decisions. Many actions and events affect the outcome of governmental decisions, but if they are not accompanied by an intent to influence, there is no lobbying.

Third, lobbying implies the presence of an intermediary or representative as a communication link between citizens and governmental decision-makers. A citizen who, of his own volition and

[5]*U. S. Congress (1957, pp. 64–65).*

by his own means, sends a message to a governmental decision-maker is not considered a lobbyist—though he is attempting to influence governmental decisions. Some may not agree with this stipulation. However, if all citizens are potential lobbyists and if all voters are lobbyists (since voting is, in a sense, a message sent with intent to influence), the word "lobbying" would lose its usefulness.

Fourth, all lobbying involves communication.[6] Without communication, it is impossible to influence a decision. On the other hand, not all communication—only that which attempts to influence governmental decisions—is lobbying. Broadly defined, then, lobbying is *the stimulation and transmission of a communication, by someone other than a citizen acting on his own behalf, directed to a governmental decision-maker with the hope of influencing his decision.* Though this definition does not identify persons called "lobbyists," it does spell out the essence of the lobbying process.[7]

THE VARIETY OF LOBBYISTS

If one adheres to this definition, one can still find a considerable variety of persons who might be deemed to be lobbyists. Briefly, several kinds of lobbyists may be distinguished, some of which would be excluded by any narrower definition of lobbying. It was necessary for the operational research purposes of this study to adopt a narrower definition, but that fact need not restrict a broader discussion here.

There are lobbyists at all levels of government. There are Washington lobbyists, state capital lobbyists, county lobbyists, and city lobbyists. There are even United Nations lobbyists called non-governmental representatives. We shall see that traditions, role expectations, and other functional relationships in an interdepen-

[6]*See Chapter IX for a full theoretical statement of the basis for the proposition.*
[7]*It is not necessary for the purposes of this study carefully to define groups that lobby or to distinguish lobby groups, special interest groups, and pressure groups. For a recent discussion of this question, see Eckstein (1960, chap. i). Lobbying is only one means of the exertion of influence by pressure groups. The reader should be aware that the two are not equivalent. For a further discussion of the term "lobbyist," see the next section.*

.dent system are important determinants of lobbyists' behavior. Since the setting in which lobbyists operate determines their behavior to a considerable extent, it is possible to distinguish lobbyists on the basis of governmental level. System controls seem to be much more powerful at the federal than at the state level; for this reason, one finds less special privilege lobbying in Washington.

Most lobby regulation laws cover only legislative activity, and it is popularly believed that a man is a lobbyist only if he attempts to influence legislators. Yet it is indisputable that many important governmental decisions are made in other branches and that representatives of interest groups attempt to influence those decisions.[8] Even judicial decisions are sometimes the target of lobbyists, although barriers to such pressures are imposed by the deliberate isolation of the judiciary from the political process and by the aura of impartiality surrounding it. Pressure groups and lobbyists consider executive branch decisions so important and accessible that most registered lobbyists spend as much time and energy lobbying before the executive branch as before the legislative branch. Normally lobbyists divide their attention between the two branches of government, but some groups have a sufficiently large staff to assign some lobbyists exclusively to the legislature and others exclusively to the executive branch. Other lobbyists who are not members of large staffs also give exclusive attention to executive decisions. Thus, in certain circumstances one can reasonably talk about legislative branch lobbyists and executive branch lobbyists. Under present federal law, only persons lobbying before the legislative branch are required to register as lobbyists.

Some of the most powerful attempts to influence decisions are directed by government officials against other government officials. This is generally not considered lobbying; and by our definition, it would not be lobbying if the influencing official acts on his own behalf. If the official acts as an intermediary or spokesman for an interest, however, he is lobbying by our definition. Lobbying by government officials assumes various forms. One form comes from "built-in" lobbyists who have seats in Congress. They are

[8]*More decisions of interest to lobbyists may, in fact, come out of the executive branch than the legislative branch. See Eckstein (1960, pp. 78–91). The business representatives at the Brookings round-table discussion said they spend most of their time dealing with executive decisions. Cherington and Gillen (1962, passim).*

spokesmen for certain interests and, being governmental decision-makers, they are in advantageous positions to make their influence felt. Sometimes such persons lead and direct comprehensive influence campaigns which may involve several supporting pressure groups. According to one congressman:

> The built-in lobbyist is one of the most effective kinds because he can be on the floor itself and represent a specific point of view. I myself am a built-in lobbyist for the welfare interests. Of course there are built-in lobbyists for railroads and petroleum and that kind of thing; you know those people as well as I do.

A former congressman turned lobbyist admitted to having been a built-in lobbyist for labor while he held his seat in Congress. The built-in lobbyist is even more common in countries were the parties more closely reflect the class and economic divisions of society than do those in this country. West Germany, for example, does not have as many special lobbying actors because groups have spokesmen on the floor of the house.[9] A similar situation exists in Britain; there are always some members of the British Parliament who draw salaries from and are spokesmen for interest groups.[10]

Lobbying also takes place between officials of the executive and legislative branches. Most executive departments have a full-time congressional liaison staff whose major concerns are to protect the appropriations for the department and to faciliate a great variety of communications.[11]

Legislators are equally likely to communicate with decision-makers in the executive branch. Often they call on behalf of constituents or strong local pressure groups. Sometimes they check on the administration of various legislative enactments. A large proportion of the communications between officials of different

[9]*From a graduate seminar of Professor Osmond K. Fraenkel, University of North Carolina, August, 1955.*

[10]*Potter (1961, pp. 272–80).*

[11]*For further information on Congressional Liaison Officers see Freeman (1955 and 1958). The entire issue of the* Annals *in which the latter item appears is devoted to pressure groups and lobbies. On the State Department Congressional Relations Office, see Robinson (1962, chaps. v, vi).*

branches of government is motivated by a desire to influence the recipient, and whenever communications are made on behalf of a third party, they may properly be considered lobbying.

Officials within the same branch of government also try to influence one another. Legislators have strong influence relations among themselves. Each is dependent on others to get bills passed, and therefore each must be prepared to help others accomplish their goals.[12] Staff aides in all branches of government are also active influence agents. Their strategic positions enable them to urge office-holders to adopt policy positions; they are frequently asked for advice, and they have immediate access if they volunteer recommendations. They also can influence policy choices through their positions as communication links; a part of their job is to intercept, sort, condense, and transmit messages. Since they also carry out investigations and research, they are in a position to write their own policy views into conclusions and findings. Whatever they attempt to influence policy-makers on behalf of others, they may properly be considered to be lobbying, even though they certainly are not considered as lobbyists under present law.

People who register as lobbyists play a considerable variety of roles. Salaried agents who lobby for a single organization may be contrasted with those who lobby for many clients. Some lobbyists are staff employees; others are consultants—such as attorneys, public relations consultants, or other specialists. Salaried lobbyists may be officers of organizations or staff members. Some are motivated by a messianic zeal to do good; others merely consider lobbying a pleasant and well-paying way to make a living. Some are experts in a certain subject; others have a broad competence and perform a variety of tasks. Some spend most of their time doing research; others are primarily occupied with advocacy before decision-makers. Some are consulted by other lobbyists—they might be called "lobbyists' lobbyists." Some lobby for foreign governments or firms; but most represent some aggregate of American citizens. Some are "hobby lobbyists," who, on their own initiative, spend their days on the Hill trying to influence legislators; however, since they represent only themselves, they should not be considered lobbyists by our definition.

[12] *A more complete discussion of this point can be found in Chapter IX.*

THE CONSTITUTIONAL RIGHT TO PETITION

Lobbying is probably as old as government; in fact, Congressman Celler suggests that lobbying probably preceded government, since the establishment of a governmental system implies the accommodation of conflicting demands of participating groups.[13] The king or dictator is probably subject to as many lobbying messages as are congressmen or the President of the United States. However, the democratic governmental decision-maker is more obliged to listen and respond to lobbying messages. His power is sufficiently limited and his position sufficiently vulnerable that he feels obliged to receive and consider messages from the people. Presumably, even the dictators must listen to certain key supporters (e.g., the army and the party); but compared to the elected official, he has much greater power to close off lobbying messages from many segments of the population. Autocrats can deal with much potential lobbying by simply refusing to listen.

In the United States, the likelihood that officials will receive lobbying messages is further guaranteed by the First Amendment to the Constitution which forbids the government to make any law abridging the freedoms of speech, press, peaceful assembly, or the right to petition the government for redress of grievances. This is not the place for a full legal and philosophical examination of the right to petition;[14] however, the right forms a completely honorable

[13]*Celler, (1958, p. 5).*
[14]*Robert A. Horn has thoroughly examined the constitutional right to petition and has set forth five principles of the right of association:*
Principles of the Law of Association: First: The rights of individuals to associate must be protected from unlawful governmental infringement. Second: Government may promote the opportunities of individuals to associate by appropriate means, and may grant appropriate privileges and powers to associations when the public interest will be fostered by doing so. Third: Government may when the public interest requires it forbid private persons to interfere with the rights of individuals to associate and may even require private persons to enter into legal relations with associations. Fourth: An Association must not without adequate reason infringe upon the rights of other persons: and government must define the interests entitled to legal protection of these other individuals and groups, whether they are members or nonmembers of the association. Fifth: Government may prevent the use of the rights of association to do serious injury to society as a whole or to the organized political institutions of the society.

Reprinted from Groups and the Constitution *(pp. 18–19) by Robert A. Horn with the permission of the publishers, Stanford University Press. Copyright 1956 by the Board of Trustees of the Leland Stanford Junior University.*

and legal basis for lobbying in the United States system of government.

While no one seriously argues that the right to petition should be abridged, some maintain that lobbying is not protected by that right or that lobbying can be curbed without infringing on that right. There can be no doubt that lobbying as defined in this study or in the Federal Regulation of Lobbying Act of 1946, is protected by the right to petition. The Supreme Court in the Harriss case[15] restricted the application of the 1946 Act so that it would not violate the right to petition. It is very difficult to draft laws which do not compromise or damage a right but do correct an abuse of it. A law which forbade persons to hire spokesmen (in effect requiring persons to speak for themselves when contacting officials) would eliminate many lobbyists and lobby groups, but it would also put at a disadvantage those persons who are not well-educated or skilled in the art of communication and those who are busily engaged in other pursuits. As one senator points out, "Every farmer can't leave his plow and come to Washington." Furthermore, if everyone tried to speak for himself, officials would be drowned in a babel of voices. Combining many messages reduces the total load and increases the chances of favorable reception.

There seems to be no way, in fact, to curb or eliminate lobbying without infringing on the right to petition. Abuses of the right can be controlled, and legal controls and system controls already seem to do a respectable job.

VARIOUS PERSPECTIVES ON LOBBYING

Several perspectives have been taken by earlier students of lobbying. The most general approach has been that of the writers on the group theory of politics. Any society that does not have autocratic decision-makers must make political decisions by a group process. The decision-making body is a group (a legislature, for example), and it must organize and focus its energies to make a decision. Almost inevitably, interested citizens want to

[15]347 U.S. 612 (1954).

influence the actions of official decision-makers and organize into groups to focus more effectively their energies and influence. The universal nature of this grouping or coalescing process in open societies leads group theorists to say that politics consists mainly of the contention of groups for power and privilege. The contention of groups is not expressed solely as a raw power struggle; in recent years we have seen many refinements in group conflict. Government is the most crucial battleground for groups, not only because government can establish or eliminate public programs, but especially because government writes and enforces the rules of the game within which the group process must be played. Three prominent writers on the group theory of politics are Arthur F. Bentley (1908), David B. Truman (1951), and E. E. Schattschneider (1961).[16]

Other scholars have looked at lobbying as an aspect of the legislative process. The legislative process is just one part of the total group process in politics, and not necessarily the most central part. It has, however, been given the most attention relative to lobbying. Some scholars have taken a total view of the legislative process. Prominent examples are: E. Pendleton Herring (1929); Bertram Gross (1953); and Roland Young (1957). Other scholars have studied the legislative process through case studies of the decision process on single bills or policies. Prominent examples are: Stephen K. Bailey (1950) and Earl Latham (1952).

Still others have investigated the group process by studying the evolution, structure, and behavior of specific groups or types of groups. Prominent examples are: Harwood L. Childs (1930); Philip Taft (1954); Andrew Hacker (1958); Orville M. Kile (1948); Oliver Garceau (1941); and Luke Ebersole (1951).

Legislators, as targets of lobbying, generally take a perspective different from those of scholars. They investigate what lobbyists and pressure groups are doing so that they can decide how to control them. The first congressional investigation of lobbying took place in 1913, and since then, investigations have been held periodically.[17] Despite the numerous investigations, it was not until the Seventy-ninth Congress that a Federal Regulation of

---

[16]*This list is illustrative, not comprehensive; consult the Bibliography.*
[17]*Citations to all of the hearings and reports from these investigations can be found in Dorothy C. Thompkins (1956).*

Lobbying Act was passed as Title III of the Congressional Reorganization Act of 1946. Several articles have been written about the performance of that statute. The most recent, by George Galloway, was published as an appendix to the McClellan Committee report. Prior to the McClellan Committee, a Select Committee on Lobbying Activities was created by the House in 1949; it was chaired by Representative Frank Buchanan (D.–Penna.). The Buchanan Committee, as it was popularly called, held extensive hearings which were released in ten parts or volumes; it also issued eleven separate reports. All in all, it was probably the most comprehensive investigation of lobbying that Congress has conducted. The hearings, and especially the reports of these committees, are valuable sources of information about specific lobby groups and lobbying in general.

Finally, lobbyists and special interest groups are viewed by some persons as threats to our system of government which should be exposed from time to time to the restraining glare of publicity. Many articles and some full-length books are written in this vein. Two such books are: Kenneth G. Crawford (1939) and Karl Schriftgiesser (1951). Much of the information in the latter book is derived from and summarizes the findings of the Buchanan Committee.

This quick overview of perspectives on lobbying is not intended as a comprehensive review of the literature on the subject. It should, however, map the terrain within which the lobbying literature is located and help to pinpoint this study.

CHAPTER II

A NEW PERSPECTIVE ON LOBBYING

We have seen that past work on lobbying can be grouped into studies of the group process, of the governmental decision process, and of groups as political entities; congressional investigations; and journalistic exposés.

This study is designed to help to fill some of the gaps still remaining in the information available. Research that focused on groups has slighted or ignored the impact on the political process made by the individual political actors. Studies that focused on political actors have often contained evaluations couched in terms of good or bad, moral or immoral—implying that the behavior of the actors is determined primarily by personal moral convictions. A close look at the decision process leaves considerable doubt that individual morality is the primary behavioral determinant. It seems, rather, that government is a system of functionally related actors whose behavior is very much confined by the demands of the system and the behavior of the other actors. No actor in the system is free to behave as he wishes so long as he accepts or desires the role he plays; the penalty for misbehavior is ejection from the system. He is free only to reject the system and leave it.

This study is an analysis of one set of actors—the lobbyists —in the political system. One can take two perspectives in role analysis: one can examine the characteristics of the actors who play the roles, and one can examine the situation or system within which the actors function (analogically the play or the plot) which largely determines the boundaries of the roles.[1] Both perspectives will be taken in this study: Part Two will consider the characteristics of the actors, and Part Three will be devoted mainly to the system within which they operate. Data were gathered for the most part through lengthy structured interviews, conducted solely by the author, with a random sample of Washington lobbyists. These were supplemented by interviews with persons in Congress who are targets of heavy lobbying.

Several important questions about lobbyists and lobbying could be answered only partially, if at all, from data previously available: Why do groups select personal envoys as a means of representation? What are the characteristics of those envoys? How are they selected? How do they relate to their employers? How do they relate to and communicate with governmental decision-makers? How do they communicate among themselves? How do they communicate with and mobilize the public? What is the nature and extent of their influence on governmental decisions? Under what conditions do they have a decisive impact? When do they have very little impact? What boundaries and controls does the system place on lobbying activities? For which goals or values is lobbying functional, and for which goals is it not functional? On balance, is lobbying functional to, or even necessary to, the goals and success of the political system?

The study was designed to provide more data for answering these questions. Because of inevitable design limitations, the data produced do not provide completely satisfying answers, though the new facts lead to a deeper understanding of many questions.

FOCUS ON LOBBYISTS AS POLITICAL ACTORS

No scholar has systematically studied the Washington lobbyist as an individual before. The information lobbyists provided

---

[1] *For a general discussion of role theory and a review of the relevant literature, see Gross, Mason, and MacEachern (1958). For the point that roles are engendered by the system in which they occur, see Nadel (1951, pp. 57 ff.).*

about themselves as persons and about their activities served as material with which to reconstruct the system in which they operate. Lobbyists were not expected to understand the system fully, since each has a necessarily limited perspective. The governmental decision system is so complex that even observers striving for a detached perspective have difficulty describing it adequately; thus, descriptions will be imperfect for some time to come. Some lobbyists, however, have remarkably perceptive insights into the system, and the aggregation of these observations appreciably advance our knowledge of it.

Several kinds of information about individual lobbyists were gathered. To discover how people became lobbyists, information about their career backgrounds and the circumstances surrounding their selection as lobbyists was sought. The lobbyists were asked how they liked lobbying work and how they thought the profession compared to other possible career choices. We asked about their social and economic backgrounds and their experiences in politics. Personality characteristics of lobbyists were explored through asking lobbyists to evaluate their fellows and to fill out short personality tests. Other questions elicited a picture of the routine tasks of the lobbyists—where they spend their time, whom they see, how they go about their tasks. The relationship between the lobbyists and the organizations they represent and the roles they see themselves playing in relation to the government were investigated. Finally, lobbyists were asked to evaluate their own activities and the performance of lobbying in the over-all governmental process.[2]

The information on the lobbyist as political actor is largely contained in Part Two. These facts can be compared to those gathered by other scholars on various other political actors and skill groups, such as public relations men, senators, political bosses, campaign workers, state legislators, and lawyers.[3]

[2]For wording and placement of specific questions, see the complete interview schedule in the Appendix.

[3]See, for example, Kelley, Jr. (1956); Matthews (1960b); and Milbrath (1956). Some of the findings from the last study appear in Heard (1960). Several studies have been made of state legislators: the most comprehensive is Wahlke, Eulau, Buchanan, and Ferguson (1962); see by the same authors (1959a, 1959b, 1960). See also Silverman (1954) and McConaughy (1950). Agger (1956a) and his associates are studying lawyers in politics. Also see Kuroda (1962) and Derge (1959). There are also some studies of lobbyists in other settings; see Millett (1957) and DeVries (1960). Not to be overlooked are the various biographies and autobiographies of political bosses, such as Flynn (1947) and Curley (1957).

FOCUS ON LOBBYING AS A
COMMUNICATION PROCESS

If the political process is made up of actors who are functionally related in a system, one method for tracing out their relationships would be to follow the flow of communications from actor
to actor.[4] An ideal research method would enable one to follow
every communication, map a complex network of connections, and
finally assess the influence relationships tying the actors together.
Unfortunately, social science is far from the attainment of such
a refined and complex method, and we shall have to be content
with a much less ambitious goal.

To narrow the inquiry to manageable size, communications
flowing from lobbyists to governmental decision-makers, especially members of Congress, were focused upon. General and
evaluative rather than specific and detailed information was
sought: Under what conditions are direct or indirect communications preferred? What specific methods of communication are
preferred over others? Why? What special touches or nuances
help to make certain communications especially effective? What
techniques do lobbyists employ to keep open their channels of
communication to public officials?

To place lobbyist–decision-maker communications in context,
several peripheral, yet relevant, communication patterns were
investigated: How do officials receive and evaluate all messages
intended to influence their decisions? What are the patterns of
communication between officials and their staffs? Between officials of the same branch of government? Between officials from
different branches?

To learn what factors lobbyists consider as they make decisions concerning how and when to send messages and to which
decision-makers, communications between lobbyists and their
employers, patterns of communication and policy-making within
organizations, communications between organizations, and communications between lobbyists for different organizations were
investigated. Questions were also asked about the flow of communications between political party officials and lobby organizations and representatives.

---

[4]*See Chapter IX for a more complete discussion of government as a
communication network.*

To complete the information about communication patterns and to appraise the influence of various communications on governmental decisions, persons in Congress were asked how they receive various kinds of communications, how they evaluate the communicated information as they make their decisions,[5] what their role is in sending communications and initiating action, and how they evaluate lobbying in the context of other influences in the policy-making process.

Examining lobbying as a communication process not only reveals the perceived relative effectiveness of different types of communications, it also illuminates the pattern of relationships binding several kinds of actors into a decision-making system. Further, it furnishes some of the best evidence we have about the impact of the lobbyist on governmental decisions and, thereby, provides a basis for evaluating public policy toward the activities of lobbyists. Both legislators and lobbyists report that the public holds erroneous views of lobbying. Thus, gathering such information is a proper prelude to developing reasonable controls of the process.

DEFINITION OF LOBBYING FOR THIS STUDY

"Lobbying" was defined as the stimulation and transmission of a communication, by someone other than a citizen acting on his own behalf, directed to a governmental decision-maker with the hope of influencing his decision. The term "lobbyist," as it applies to this study, remains to be delimited. The meaning of a word in any language is a social, not an individual, product, and anyone desiring to be understood is well advised to use the most common meanings of words. Yet interviewing for this project did not uncover any commonly accepted definition of lobbyist.

The one common thread running through the variety of defi-

---

[5]*Analysts of the impact of groups on governmental policy have been criticized for ignoring the role and the behavior of the recipients of influence as they try to explain and evaluate the influence process; see Odegard (1958). See also the critics of the group theory cited in note 1, Chapter III. Some scholars have analyzed the role of officials with respect to pressure groups; see Wahlke et al. (1960a), Millett (1957), Garceau and Silverman (1954), and Key, Jr. (1943).*

nitions of lobbyist was that all lobbyists try to influence governmental decisions in some way. Another standard to which many observers repair is the definition given in the Federal Regulation of Lobbying Act of 1946. This act requires spending reports to be filed quarterly by anyone who

> directly or indirectly, solicits, collects or receives money or any other thing of value to be used principally to aid, or the principal purpose of which person is to aid, in the accomplishment of any of the following purposes: (a) the passage or defeat of any legislation by the Congress of the U. S.; (b) to influence, directly or indirectly, the passage or defeat of any legislation by the Congress of the U.S.

This definition is far from precise, and judicial interpretation in *U. S.* v. *Harriss* limited the law's applicability to "direct communication with Members of Congress."[6] This interpretation still leaves much ambiguity. *Congressional Quarterly*, which regularly compiles and publishes summaries of lobby spending reports, also expresses dissatisfaction with the law: "The Act's vagueness on what constitutes lobby spending permits pressure groups to decide for themselves what they shall report as lobby expenditures."[7]

This confusion has a salutary result for this study since persons who are in doubt as to whether or not to register find safety from possible penalties of the law by registering.[8] Consequently, the registration list kept by the Clerk of the House and the Secretary of the Senate includes persons in a variety of roles who anticipate that by one definition or another someone might consider them to be lobbyists. This public list, compiled via the threat of criminal penalties, is perhaps the best means available of identifying lobbyists without resorting to the means and powers of an agency such as the Federal Bureau of Investigation. There-

[6]U.S. *v.* Harriss, *347 U.S. 612 (1954), p. 633.*
[7]Congressional Quarterly Weekly Report *(March 11, 1960, p. 407).*
[8]*A story based on a* Congressional Quarterly *compilation of lobbyists' reports appeared in the* Washington Post, *January 13, 1957. Harold E. Fellows, then president and board chairman of the National Association of Radio and Television Broadcasters, was said to have written on his report, "The Federal Regulation of Lobbying Act is not applicable to me or this organization. I file in order that I may be free to consider and discuss legislation without question."*

fore, a random sample of lobbyists was drawn from the list of persons with Washington addresses who registered in compliance with the Act during the first two quarters of 1956 (the time period immediately prior to the beginning of the study).[9] There were 614 persons in the study universe, and a random sample of 114 names was drawn from it; eventually 101 of these persons were interviewed.

The definition of lobbyists for this study, then, is as follows: *Washington lobbyists are persons with Washington addresses who registered in compliance with the Regulation of Lobbying Act during the first two quarters of 1956.* The data and interpretations in this book apply only to lobbyists so defined. However, the unavoidable arbitrariness of this definition may cast doubt upon the capacity of the sample to inform of the total picture of lobbyists and lobbying in Washington. As mentioned above, the vague meaning of the law encourages persons in doubtful categories to register to be safe; 16 per cent of those interviewed did not believe they were lobbyists. Self-definition, of course, is not a very reliable criterion. Only one person in the sample said he had not acted in any way to influence legislation, and he had attempted to influence decisions in the executive branch. The point is that a great variety of lobbyists do register; this increases the likelihood that the sample is actually representative of Washington lobbying.

Certain kinds of persons were systematically excluded by the definition. Persons without Washington addresses (about 30 per cent of those registered) were excluded because time and money would not permit interviewing them. Thus, the lobbyist universe from which the sample was drawn contains a somewhat higher than normal proportion of persons who live in Washington year round and give sustained attention to lobbying. Because of this, figures showing the percentages of lobbyists who want to make a career in lobbying or to build a reputation in lobbying are probably somewhat inflated.

The law excuses from registering persons who are not paid

[9] *Under the law, both organizations and individuals must register. The simple random sample was drawn from a composite list of all the individual registrants who had Washington addresses. Law firms which registered as representing clients were telephoned to determine which partner or employee principally handled the case; that person was then made a part of the study universe.*

and, presumably, are acting in their own behalf. However, such persons are not considered to be lobbyists by our definition in Chapter 1. Persons who contact decision-makers only in the executive or judicial branches are not required to register. Although this is a deficiency in the law,[10] executive branch lobbyists are not systematically excluded from the sample. Fully 77 per cent of the lobbyists interviewed normally contact decision-makers in both legislative and executive branches. If lobbyists contacting executive officials were required to register as well, the total number of registered lobbyists might rise appreciably, and our estimate as to whether lobbyists concentrate more on the executive branch or the legislative branch would be better informed. Because most registered lobbyists try to influence decisions in both branches, we know something about lobbying in both branches, although we could certainly wish to know more about executive branch lobbying.[11]

The narrowed interpretation given the law by the Supreme Court in the Harriss case mentioned above produced a drop in the number of registrants. Presumably, then, certain persons who never communicate with members of Congress but who concentrate instead on communication through intermediaries do not register. Again, this omission probably is not serious since nearly all the lobbyists interviewed use communications through intermediaries as well as direct communications with officials. It is doubtful that indirect communicators use any tactics not disclosed by respondents in this sample.

One disquieting unknown is how many people who would qualify under the law simply do not register. One respondent argued that perhaps persons who engage in illegal or unethical activities try to evade the law entirely. Naturally, such people would not be picked up by the means used to select the universe for this study. This omission is serious only if there are considerable numbers of these persons or if there are a few who have great influence. There are no data available to provide a decisive answer

[10]*The McClellan Committee submitted a draft for a new Legislative Activities Disclosure Act which would focus on disclosure of communications and communicators rather than on the regulation of spending and would apply to decisions in the executive branch as well as the legislative branch. To date such a bill has not passed Congress. See U.S. Congress (1957).*
[11]*Some information about corporations and executive branch decisions can be found in Cherington and Gillen (1962).*

to this problem. It would seem difficult, however, for an influential person, who is certain to be visible at least to some officials, to evade the registration requirement. An alert opposition and a sensation-hungry press corps would probably unearth such people if they existed. Practically no inkling of "backdoor lobbying" was uncovered in the interviews with people who are constantly involved in decisional activity. One respondent, a former state legislator, member of Congress, and lobbyist, rocked back in his chair and thought for a full minute before answering when I asked him about the influence of "backdoor lobbying." Finally he said slowly:

> I don't think it has much influence. Maybe I'm naïve, but I don't think so. I am thinking here of Congress—not the state legislatures. The state legislatures are a horse of another color. Of course, pressures come up in Congress, and if by that you mean backdoor lobbying, then I suppose there is some of that. But there is none of this petty venality around here that one finds in the state legislatures. There is just none of this petty venality in Congress. I don't say that campaign contributions are not important or anything like that, but there is none of the goofy stuff that goes on in the state legislatures.

Congressmen and congressional staff members were interviewed to find out whether the lobbyists' beliefs about their own activities and effectiveness are shared by the recipients of lobbying. Since this aspect of the research design did not call for statistical treatment of the data, no attempt was made to draw a random sample. Instead, persons who were most likely to be heavy targets of lobbyists—including majority and minority leaders in both the House and Senate, chairmen of most of the important committees, and all members of the special bipartisan committee to investigate lobbying, were contacted. If a member was too busy, an interview with his chief assistant was requested, since the latter probably had the most direct dealings with lobbyists anyway. This substitution would not be admissible in a survey intended for statistical treatment but is acceptable and even useful in this context. Some letters were also sent directly to the chief staff persons serving various committees.

Interviews were conducted with thirty-eight people. Four were senators; ten were members of the House; eighteen were chiefs of staff to committee; and six were staff assistants to members. The interviews followed a structured schedule, but only the most appropriate questions were asked of respondents who were pressed for time.[12] These interviews varied from five minutes to two hours in length and averaged about forty-five minutes.

INTERVIEWING LOBBYISTS

Lobbyists, whom the public generally view as little better than underworld characters, might be expected to be reluctant to be interviewed. Yet only four persons in the sample refused to be interviewed; one other evaded repeated appointments; and another, the president of a large labor union, was so busy that after about ten phone requests for an appointment, the interviewer finally gave up. The remainder of the non-respondents, seven in all, had moved out of the city permanently. This 90 per cent response rate is equivalent to that demanded by strict survey standards.[13]

There are several reasons for the generally excellent cooperation by the respondents. First, many lobbyists are actually eager to be interviewed. Often lobbyists are sensitive about public disapproval of their job. They think that the press plays up the sensational and unsavory aspects of lobbying, which comprise a tiny fraction of the total effort, and ignores the ordinary men who are doing an honest job. They wish to redress this imbalance.

Another very important reason is that the approach to the respondent was designed to assure him that the project was a serious, scholarly work and that he could speak his mind freely. An advance letter, written on stationery of The Brookings Institute, alerted the respondents and gave them time to think the matter through. Several of them took the opportunity to investigate the interviewer and the study. A few reported that they made such a check and found everything to be satisfactory. When word spread within the lobbying community that it was all right

[12]See the congressional interview schedule in the Appendix.
[13]Stephan and McCarthy (1958, p. 262).

to cooperate with the study, formal checks dropped off. Another reassuring factor was the high prestige and reputation for objectivity of The Brookings Institution, under whose auspices the investigation was conducted. A third factor was that the respondents were repeatedly assured that all the information given by them would be kept confidential.

The persistence of the interviewer and his willingness to accommodate his own schedule to the time schedule of the respondent was essential to the high response rate.

Some lobbyist respondents believed they had so little experience lobbying that they requested to be excused from the interview. Most people are unfamiliar with a study which selects respondents by a random procedure and do not realize that no substitutions are allowed for individuals so selected. Generally, careful explanations of systematic sampling procedures and the assurance that all types of persons were needed in the sample sufficed to obtain a respondent's cooperation.

Some respondents were puzzled and hesitant about the interview. Familiar only with group studies of lobbying, they had to be reoriented to questions about their personal behavior and to the relevance of such questions. In addition, many respondents, acquainted only with the unstructured journalistic type of interview, resented having to follow a specified list of questions.[14] In summary, the interviewing task was not as formidable as it might appear to be at first glance, and the data gathered are quite extensive and reliable.

Do the lobbyists tell the truth? Let us look at the motives for lying. The major one is fear of revealing something damaging. In an effort to counterbalance this, many assurances were given that all information would be held in confidence. In addition, respondents had ample opportunity to check up on the study and the interviewer. Backing this up was the impeccable reputation of The Brookings Institution.

A second possible motive for lying is fear of unfair or biased treatment. The fact that the study director and Brookings had no self-interest to serve by giving preference to one person or group over another, or by giving any special interpretation to the data,

---

[14]*For a discussion comparing survey interviewing with journalistic interviewing, see Robinson (1960) also reprinted as an appendix to Robinson (1962).*

helped to allay this fear. It was also reassuring that the data were to be collated in general categories and treated statistically; thus, there would be little opportunity in the report for the discussion of specific persons or groups.

Those respondents who had engaged in clearly illegal activities, such as bribery, probably did conceal them. It is likely that there was very little of this (see Chapter XIII), but it is not absolutely certain. More important, most of the questions did not ask for information that respondents might wish to conceal. General knowledge, not specific information about incidents or persons, was sought. This factor, plus careful procedures, makes it very likely that almost all the information received was truthful. Certainly it is far more reliable than an estimation made without interview information.

The interviews produced both quantitative and qualitative data. Many of the questions were "open-ended" and encouraged respondents to talk freely within their own frame of reference. To preserve these extended remarks in the respondents' own words, the interviewer dictated full notes at the conclusion of each day's interviewing. These notes contain interpretive data which help to explain many of the statistical relations disclosed by the study.

Interview responses were also coded into categories which could be counted for statistical treatment (see the code in the Appendix). All of the interviewing, coding, and data analyses were conducted by one man. This produced a high level of consistency in gathering, translating, and interpreting data. Thus, although the sample is small, the data are probably less subject to error than data from a large survey.

CHAPTER III

CHARACTERISTICS OF PRESSURE GROUPS

Lobbyists are group representatives almost by definition. A person who represents only himself is merely a citizen exercising his constitutional right; he is not paid, and he is not required to register, although he may try to influence the decisions of officials in much the same manner as a lobbyist. Lobbyists represent someone—usually more than one person—other than themselves before governmental decision-makers. Only one of the 101 lobbyists interviewed for this study represented a single individual; all the others represented one or more organizations. The nature of the group base from which lobbyists operate will be explored—but briefly, since groups in politics have been thoroughly discussed elsewhere.[1]

[1]*See Bentley (1908), Truman (1951), Schattschneider (1961, 1935), Latham (1952), Gross (1953), Herring (1929), Bailey (1950), Riggs (1950), Hardin (1952), Ebersole (1951), and Blaisdell (1957). Blaisdell also edited an issue of the* Annals *of the American Academy of Political and Social Science (1958) devoted entirely to pressure groups and lobbies. The* Annals *has also devoted many past issues to lobbying and pressure groups. See the Bibliography.*

The group approach to politics has also been thoroughly criticized. See Garceau (1951, 1958), Odegard (1958), Stedman (1953), Taylor (1952), Monypenny (1954), and Rothman (1960).

The groups that lobbyists represent are often called "pressure groups," implying that they pressure governmental decision-makers to follow certain policy courses. Sometimes they are called "special interest groups," implying that they have an interest in adopting a policy which will benefit a certain segment of the public but which may not be beneficial for the general public. They aim to obtain or maintain this special privilege by law or other governmental activity. These groups are also sometimes called "lobby groups," implying that they hire lobbyists to communicate their wishes to governmental decision-makers. It will not be necessary, for our purposes, to maintain a distinction between the types of groups; the different names will be used interchangeably.

All of these implications are more or less true of the groups that the lobbyists in this study represent. The number of such groups to be found in Washington would depend on the particular definition adopted. Groups, like individuals, are required to register by the Regulation of Lobbying Act, but, in this case, too, there is considerable ambiguity about which groups must register with Congress. In 1957, 269 groups registered with Congress; in 1958, 262; and in 1959, 275. These figures show a remarkable stability of groups on the legislative scene in Washington. In recent years these groups have shown aggregate spending on lobbying of about $4 million.[2] However, as the law is written, the definition of what expenditures fall under lobbying is decided by the groups themselves and, therefore, varies so greatly from group to group that figures on spending are almost meaningless except as an indication of the bare minimum.

TYPES OF GROUPS

There is probably no one best scheme for classifying lobby groups. All classifications force certain groups into somewhat ill-fitting categories. The classification reported in Table III–1 combines the categories of "interest" and "size of membership." It is familiar to readers of pressure group literature, and it will be

[2]Congressional Quarterly Weekly Report (March 11, 1960, p. 405).

shown that differences in interest and size do affect group behavior.[3]

The greatest number of respondents (forty-three) in this sample represent small trade associations; nine represent large trade associations. These trade associations may represent a single industry or profession—e.g., the margarine industry, the pottery manufacturers, the osteopaths—or they may be agents for a somewhat larger group of industries. For example, the American Mining Congress represents various kinds of metal mines as well as the producers of mining equipment. At the apex of these trade associations are the nationwide representatives of business, such as the National Association of Manufacturers and the United States Chamber of Commerce. The executives of trade associations, many of which have their national headquarters in Washington, also have their own trade association—a luncheon group called the Washington Trade Association Executives Club.

The possible divisions among trade associations are well illustrated by the transportation industry. At the basic level are several transportation corporations—specific airlines, for example —represented in Washington. At the next level are associations for various modes of transportation—the Air Transport Association, three railroad associations, three shipping associations, the Committee for Oil Pipelines, the American Trucking Association, and so forth. At a still higher level is the Transportation Association of America which attempts to speak for and provide services for all types of transportation.

[3]*The thirteen persons who were sampled but not interviewed are counted in these tables. Generally, they will appear in the no-response category, especially if the question being coded calls for a personal belief or observation; however, it was possible to code some variables for these non-interviewed persons on the basis of data available elsewhere. For example, data on type of organization represented and other organizational information could be obtained without a personal interview. Sometimes basic data on personal background (age and training, for example) could be obtained from Who's Who or other biographical sources. The no-response category, then, will generally contain the thirteen persons not interviewed but may vary above or below that figure. An additional variant for this category arises from the fact that certain questions in the schedule were not asked of all respondents. The schedule was so long that certain questions were designated as second priority and were not to be asked if a respondent was pressed for time. In practice, nearly all of the questions were asked of most respondents, but a few of the designated questions that did not seem to be pulling very valuable information were dropped for respondents who were in a hurry. This accounts for a high proportion of no response for a few items in the code (see the Appendix). No data from these items will be used to characterize the entire sample.*

TABLE III–1
Type of Organization Represented and Percentage of Respondent's Income from Lobby Clients

TYPE OF ORGANIZATION	PERCENTAGE OF INCOME FROM LOBBY CLIENTS								
	Not Appropriate	Less than 20	20 to 35	35 to 65	65 to 80	80 to 95	Above 95	No Response	Total
Large labor				1	2	2	4	1	10
Small labor							7	1	8
Large farm						1	1		2
Small farm					1		2		3
Large trade				1	1	1	5	1	9
Small trade	1	3	3	3	3	6	19	5	43
Corporation		5	1	2		1	5	3	17
Large citizens			2	1			3		6
Service or veterans			1					1	2
Church and humanitarian		1					2	2	5
Foreign government or firm		1	1						2
More than one type		2		2			1	2	7
TOTAL	1	12	8	10	7	11	49	16	114

Some of the other categories shown in Table III–1 are a little more straightforward. In the sample, there are seventeen representatives of specific business corporations, eighteen representatives of large and small labor organizations, and five representatives of large and small farm organizations.

Citizens' organizations include such groups as the NAACP, the Japanese-American Citizens' League, and the Washington Home Rule Committee; there are six representatives of this type. There are only two representatives of such service or veterans' organizations as the American Legion and the Retired Officers' Association. Church and humanitarian groups include The National Woman's Christian Temperance Union, the American Friends Legislative Committee, and the American Parents Committee; five representatives of this type appear in the sample. There are two representatives of foreign governments or firms. In addition, seven respondents who represent more than one type of group are in a residual category.

In Table III–1, the type of group represented is cross-tabulated with the percentage of income the respondent receives from lobby clients. Most of the representatives of labor, farm, and church and humanitarian organizations receive nearly all of their income from the group they represent. Representatives of business and citizens' groups, however, are much more likely to get only part of their income from lobbying. Many of the latter are lawyers or Washington representatives who have several clients, only some of whom require lobbying services. Twelve respondents receive less than 20 per cent of their income from lobbying clients or groups.

PURPOSES AND FUNCTIONS

The nature of these groups is further illuminated by an examination of their goals. The groups work to advance the welfare of their members. Since this can be accomplished in a number of ways, it is necessary to examine more specific functions and purposes. Nearly all perform a liaison function. They gather information about the activities of government and dispatch it to their members; the members can then take action or not as they see fit.

A few claim they perform only liaison functions with respect to the government.

Lobbying is most clearly associated with the attempt to influence legislation. Government in modern times is so deeply involved in the regulation of business, agriculture, labor, and general citizen activities that many groups believe that they must have a lobby representative in Washington to protect their interests. One of the inherent difficulties of regulation is that any given law may favor one group at the expense of another. Thus the battles between groups frequently focus on the writing of the rules. A group at a disadvantage because of a given law may draft a new bill, find a member of Congress to introduce it, and press for it in committee and with the members. The group favored by a current law will push equally hard to get this proposed legislation defeated and preserve its favored position. Generally, the group fighting to defeat a bill has an advantage because new bills can be stopped at any one of several legislative hurdles.

Some groups are concerned only with legislation before the national Congress. Others—especially industries or activities in which legislative regulation is left primarily to the states (e.g.,) the regulation of liquor or insurance—are also concerned with business before the state legislatures.

Lobbyists and lobby groups are not concerned exclusively with legislation, however. All legislation must be put into effect by some part of the executive branch of the government, where detailed interpretation of its meaning occurs. Some agencies, such as the independent regulatory commissions, possess rather sweeping rule-making powers. Thus, nearly all lobby groups attend closely to the activities of the executive branch. They confer regularly with officials charged with the administration of regulations that apply to their members. They attend or testify at hearings very similar to those held by Congressional committees. They peruse the *Federal Register* just as carefully as the *Congressional Record*. In fact, some lobby respondents say they find it more efficacious to influence the interpretation of a bill than to participate in the drafting and passage of it. Most lobbyists try to influence decisions at all stages.

Lobbyists do not depend exclusively on direct communications with governmental decision-makers to accomplish their purposes. They also think it is important to stimulate their members and the general public to communicate the group's desires to decision-makers. To accomplish this, they disseminate information, sponsor advertising and public relations campaigns, publicize voting records, organize letter-writing and telegram campaigns, and stimulate their members to participate in political party activities and election campaigns. All this activity at the grass roots is designed to communicate the desires of the group and the power that lies behind those desires.

Some lobby groups have very narrow and specific programs; some programs are limited to the passage or defeat of a specific bill. Other groups have very broad programs going far beyond the specific economic interest of the members. Broad programs often include foreign as well as domestic policy. Organizations with broad programs sometimes spread their resources too thin. Generally, they emphasize specific aspects of their wide program at given times, while devoting the major share of their resources to the narrow central interest of the group.

In addition to concern with public policy, many lobby groups, especially trade associations, advance the welfare of the members in other ways. For example, they conduct research which helps the members to produce more efficiently or sell more readily. They generally publish an industry magazine which disseminates information of use to the members. Trade associations sometimes provide or sell a variety of other services to members. One large transportation association raises most of its funds, including its lobbying expenses, from the sale of its services. The collective bargaining and welfare activities of labor unions are other examples of non-lobbying concerns of pressure groups.

ORGANIZATION, MEMBERSHIP, FINANCING

The differing organizational structures of lobby groups reflect and vary with differences in purpose, membership, financing, and subject matter. Yet discernible general patterns, though they vary in specific detail, serve to characterize a number of groups.

MASS ORGANIZATIONS

The organizational structure adopted by most mass organizations with thousands of individual members is generally analogous to the levels of governmental organization in the country. At the grassroots level, members are organized into local clubs which usually meet regularly for the dissemination of information, the discussion of policies, and social interaction. Delegates are elected periodically by these locals to state or regional conventions which, in turn, usually elect delegates to the national convention of the organization. Organization at the state and national levels is usually more permanent, having officers who stay in office for long periods and a permanent staff. Mass organizations are increasingly tending to establish national headquarters in Washington so that the officers and staff can be on hand continually to represent the group before government. Organizations with headquarters in another city usually establish a branch office in Washington, customarily headed by their chief lobbyist.

TRADE ASSOCIATIONS

Some trade associations are also organized on governmental-like levels, especially those with many small firms as members. (Usually firms, rather than individuals, are members of trade associations.) Associations with relatively few members—from 10 to 200—seldom have local and state levels of organization. Instead, all the firms send a representative to the board, or, if that is too cumbersome, the firms elect a board from leading men in the industry. Officers of trade associations generally do not give full time to running the association, as do officers of mass organizations; instead they hire a general manager or executive secretary to handle the administration of the organization and (usually) supervise the lobbying operation. Trade association officers, since they do not manage the associations, usually rotate in office periodically.

Another form of trade association structure was mentioned in the previous section—the federative structure. Several trade associations with a common interest, such as participation in the same general industry, may band together in an association of trade associations (e.g., the National Retail Federation).

CORPORATIONS

Little need be said about the organizational structure of corporations who send lobbyists to Washington; corporations follow a standard pattern. The people who man the Washington offices of corporations generally are integral members of the corporation structure who are sent for a tour of duty in Washington just as they might be sent to any other branch office.[4] Corporations sometimes also retain an attorney or other expert consultant, but usually these men are retained for a specific bill or task. Long-range representation of the whole corporation is performed by someone inside the organization.

LOBBYIST ENTREPRENEUR

A curious kind of organization is occasionally encountered in the lobbying field that is not generally encountered elsewhere. It is built around one man, a lobbyist entrepreneur. He builds a reputation as an expert on a certain topic and pursues a given policy line on that topic. As this becomes known, he collects clients who agree with his point of view and are willing to support him in his lobbying activities. Generally, the clients share few interests other than their concern for the one policy. The only formal structure is likely to consist of a board of directors, but actually the little policy that is made (the point of view is well-established) is almost completely in the hands of the lobbyist entrepreneur. If he should be removed from the scene, the entire organization would probably disintegrate. (See Chapter VII for further details.)

SPECIAL COMMITTEE

Another type of organization is the temporary special committee; this organization is formed to press for a particular policy. Money is solicited, and a staff is hired to lobby for the policy. If the objective is achieved, the committee and the staff are disbanded. However, policies, even if achieved, have a tendency to be under attack for quite some time; thus, a temporary committee may become more or less permanent. The Committee for a National Trade Policy is a good example. In 1953 the President's Commission on Trade Policy, headed by Clarence Randall and known as the "Randall Commission," urged the gradual lowering of tariffs and the renewal of the reciprocal trade agreements program. Certain prominent businessmen who agreed with this re-

[4]*Corporate representation is more thoroughly treated in Cherington and Gillen (1962).*

port perceived that some lobby support would be helpful to the eventual realization of these policies. About four thousand telegrams were sent out to the heads of American business firms around the country appealing for funds for a Committee for a National Trade Policy. In six weeks they had raised $100,000, and the committee was underway coordinating lobbying activity on behalf of the President's program. Even after achievement of the initial objectives, the fight on trade policy developed into a continuing battle. In 1957 one of the leaders indicated that ways were being sought to make the committee permanent and give it a more stable financial undergirding. The committee is still active today.

ORGANIZATION IN WASHINGTON

The organization of the Washington office of a group is partially dependent on the size of the staff. Members of a small staff must become Jacks-of-all-trades, so to speak. Members of a larger staff can become more specialized. The division of labor may be along subject-matter lines, enabling staff members to become well-informed, or even expert, in a given area. Specialization may also be related to the skills possessed by staff members. In one two-man organization, one man, skilled in the preparation of documents and the development of strategy, handles those tasks, while the other man, skilled in social relationships, handles the contacts with people. Labor may also be divided in terms of the offices or persons that must be contacted. Some men may be assigned to Congress, and others, to various executive agencies. If the staff is large, those assigned to Congress may each be assigned a certain number of congressional offices to cover. Moreover, since many Washington offices of lobby groups perform functions other than lobbying, labor is divided on an additional basis in these organizations.

STAFF CONTROL

The control exercised over the staff also varies from office to office. Some staffs are ruled by an iron-handed administrator, and all actions are dictated and supervised by him. Most staffs, however, have considerable freedom of action and can exercise discretion and initiative. Freedom of action is especially characteristic of those lobbyists who are paid by fee rather than salary; the client, in a sense, hires the man's judgment and does not expect to dictate his activities to any great extent.

POLICY-MAKING

In most organizations, general policy is made by the board of directors and the officers, but the development of strategy is left to the staff. Committees are often used to maintain contact between the lobby staff and persons in the industry. Committees even may be set up in certain subject-matter areas; the staff member who lobbies in that policy area meets regularly with the committee to discuss policy and strategy and, if necessary, to enlist their aid in communicating with governmental decision-makers.

MEMBERSHIP

Membership varies considerably from group to group, not only in number of members but also in the variety of units considered members. Members may be persons, firms, industries, states, state organizations, foreign governments, Indian tribes, labor unions, or federal employees. (Federal employees are separated from labor unions because they can bargain with their employer only through lobbying activity.) Large membership is important to an organization because it means more financial support and communicates more voting power to governmental decision-makers.

FINANCING

Table III–2 reports the various methods by which the lobby activities of the respondents in this sample are financed. More than half of the lobbyists are supported by dues of some sort. These dues may be the same for each member of the organization or graduated according to a formula, such as the volume of business of each member. A few organizations are supported solely by contributions. Some, mainly corporations, finance lobbying by appropriation from their general budget. Others simply pay a fee to a lobbyist who is not a part of their regular organization. One lobbying organization sells subscriptions, but this amounts, in effect, to the solicitation of contributions.

Organizations financed by fees or contributions have much more difficulty maintaining support. They continually must con-

TABLE III–2

**Financing
Lobby Operations**

MEANS OF FINANCING	NUMBER USING
Solely by contributions	5
Solely by dues	48
Combination of dues and contributions	4
Combination of dues and other money-raising functions	4
Lobbyist charges a fee to clients	17
Budgetary appropriation	14
Sale of subscriptions	1
Other	1
No response	20
TOTAL	114

vince their members or clients of the need for their continued existence. This is called "farming the membership." Even dues-financed organizations with a long history of lobbying have to worry to a certain extent about maintaining membership support.

Table III–3 shows the ways in which various types of organizations pay their lobbyists. About 69 per cent of the respondents are paid an annual salary; another 29 per cent are paid by fee; and 2 per cent are paid by a combination of fee and salary. Farm and labor organizations pay their lobbyists only by salary; much the same is true of church and humanitarian organizations. Some business and citizens organizations pay their lobbyists by fee, others pay them a salary. Trade associations emphasize salary; corporations pay more often by fee. Foreign governments or firms pay their lobbyists by fee only.

LEADERSHIP AND POLICY FORMATION

How lobby groups are led, the extent to which members actually make the policy their lobbyists proclaim, and whether

TABLE III–3

Method of Paying Respondent for Services by Type of Organization

TYPE OF ORGANIZATION	Annual Salary Only	Salary and Expenses	METHOD OF PAYMENT Fee Only	Fee and Expenses	Fee and Salary	No Response	Total
Large labor		9				1	10
Small labor	4	4					8
Large farm		2					2
Small farm	3						3
Large trade	1	5		1	1	1	9
Small trade	14	15	8	3	1	2	43
Corporation	4	2	7	2		2	17
Large citizens	2	1	2	1			6
Service or veterans	1					1	2
Church and humanitarian	1	2	1			1	5
Foreign government or firm			1	1			2
More than one type	1		3	1		2	7
TOTAL	31	40	22	9	2	10	114

leadership and policy formation are the same thing, are considered in this section. This analysis is not detailed or exhaustive, but these topics have been thoroughly examined elsewhere.[5]

POLICY

To take the last question first, it might be useful to distinguish between formal policy-making power, which usually is lodged with an organ responsive to the desires and votes of the membership, such as a board or convention, and policy leadership, which often is not centered in the formal policy organ. To be blunt, policy leadership is generally exercised by the officers and staff of the group; only ratification occurs in the formal policy sessions.

An understanding of the formal pattern for policy-making in lobby groups is necessary to the examination of the shifting relationships that actually produce policy. It would be wise, first, to distinguish policy, strategy, and tactics. *Policy* consists of the relatively long-range purposes and objectives of a group; *strategy* is the plan by which those objectives are to be achieved; and *tactics* are the specific actions taken to fulfill the strategy plan.[6]

Mass Organizations. In mass organizations, formal theoretical policy formation begins with the local organization. Local organizations are supposed to discuss the issues, arrive at policy decisions, elect delegates to county or state conventions, and instruct the delegates to push for acceptance of the local policies at the convention. At the convention, the policies received from the various locals are considered, and out of the political interchanges of the delegates a compromise statement of organization policy is arrived at. Delegates are elected to the next higher level where the process of politics and compromise is repeated. The statement of policy by the national convention is generally the highest authority until the next convention is held. In the meantime, certain policy decisions may have to be taken; therefore, the power to make policy adjustments usually is delegated to the national board. However, since the national board is usually very large and cumbersome

---

[5]*McConnell (1953); Odegard (1928); Garceau (1941); Eckstein (1960); Dearing (1952); Lipset, Trow, and Coleman (1956); Taft (1954); Lorwin (1933); Kile (1921 and 1948); Brady (1943); Bonnett (1922); Hacker (1958); Hamilton 1957); Duffield (1931); Gray (1948); and Rutherford (1937).*

[6]*These definitions most closely conform to lobbyists' usage and not necessarily to academic usage; for a different definition of policy, see Robinson (1962, chap. i).*

and often meets only two to four times a year, the power to make policy decisions is delegated to the executive committee of the board whenever the full board is not in session. Occasionally the staff has too little time to consult even the executive committee on a policy decision, and must make the required choice itself.

Generally in mass organizations the real policy leadership lies with the executive committee, which usually consists of the top elective officers of the organization. One evidence of this is the long tenure in office of most national leaders of mass organizations. Their grasp of the political machinery and policy leadership of the organization is so firm that in most instances only senility, ill health, or death can dislodge them.

Trade Associations. In most trade associations the formal system of policy-making is less complicated, mainly because they have fewer members to consider. Most trade associations hold a national convention or "show" each year which provides an occasion to elect new members of the board. Generally, few policy decisions are taken at these conventions. Instead, policy-making is delegated to the board or the executive committee of the board. After laying down the broad outlines of policy, the board may turn details of policy-making over to the staff; or, what is even more likely, the chief staff officer may sit on the board and provide most of the policy leadership. The officers of most trade associations do not give as much time to organization affairs as do the officers of most mass organization and therefore do not exercise the same degree of policy leadership.

Corporations. Policy-making in most corporations or firms is even less complicated, perhaps because the formal policy machinery fits more exactly the actual policy decision process. In most corporations the chairman of the board or the president is charged with policy determination. However, the executive frankly depends heavily on staff for policy ideas and recommendations, and the staff frequently takes the initiative on policy. Though the staff participates quite actively in the creation of decisions, final policy comes from the top. Since corporations generally do not try to maintain any semblance of a democratic decision process, the pattern of communications within the organization can be relatively informal. Many lobbyists for corporations are not required to make any formal reports, as the lobbyists for mass organizations and

TABLE III—4

Locus of Policy Leadership by Type of Organization

PRIMARY LOCUS OF POLICY LEADERSHIP

TYPE OF ORGANIZATION	Not Appropriate	Respondent	Staff	Board	Executive Committee	Annual Meeting or Convention	Staff and Board	Board or Executive Committee and Annual Meeting	No Response	Total
Large labor						1		8	1	10
Small labor			3		1			4		8
Large farm								2		2
Small farm								3		3
Large trade	1		1	1		1	2	3		9
Small trade		2	1	13	3		4	18	2	43
Corporation	5	1	4	1			3		3	17
Large citizens				4	1			1		6
Service or veterans								2		2
Church and humanitarian		1					1	2	1	5
Foreign government or firm	1			1						2
More than one type	3	1		1					2	7
TOTAL	10	5	9	21	5	2	10	43	9	114

trade associations must do. The corporate leadership is generally content with a letter or a phone conversation.

Table III–4 shows the locus of policy leadership for the organizations represented by respondents cross-tabulated with the type of organization. Over 70 per cent of the respondents report that the organization's board participates in policy-making in one way or another. Of these, most (about 40 per cent) report that policy-making is accomplished by the board and an annual meeting. These respondents represent mainly labor, farm, and service and veterans organizations. Only 2 per cent of the respondents claim that primary policy leadership comes from an annual meeting or convention. About 20 per cent report that the staff participates significantly in policy-making; another 5 per cent claim policy leadership for themselves. Staff leadership on policy seems most characteristic of trade associations and corporations, although three representatives of small labor unions report that staff makes most policy in their unions. The question of policy leadership is not appropriate for 10 per cent of the respondents; in most of these instances the lobbyist had been assigned a specific task which he performed for a fee, and the question of participation in general policy was irrelevant.

Characteristically, then, policy decisions are made by the board or the executive committee of the board. Generally these boards are responsive in some way to the membership of the organization, but in some instances they are self-perpetuating: the sitting members of the board choose the replacement when a vacancy occurs. If an organization covers a wide range of specific interests—as does a federation of trade associations—the representative function of the board can become very significant. Each segment of the industry is usually represented on the board, and, generally, acquiescence from all must be achieved before a policy stand can be taken.

Although policy decisions usually must be taken by the board or annual meeting, policy leadership regularly comes from the staff. In fact, many board members expect initiative from the staff. They feel that the staff is closer to the scene of action, has better information, is better qualified by training and, especially, experience, has more time to think about the problems of the organization, generally has a longer history of service with the organization, and may even be more closely identified with the organization.

Although they are thoroughly involved in policy-making for the organization, most staff members are cognizant of the boundaries of their policy-making activities. They realize that they must propose policies that the membership actually wants or lose support. Wise staff members seldom make recommendations which might be turned down. Some are clever enough to have their ideas proposed by a more prominent and less vulnerable person in an effort to make them more acceptable:

My personal recommendations on policy are always followed, but this is because we all know what we want to do. Essentially, all I do is prepare the documents that the board and the president pass on. If I dream up an idea of something I want done, sooner or later it seems to happen. Sometimes it is better to act as though it were presented by the president of the association, or sometimes I can get a senator to present it for me. It helps to cover up my footprints and act as though someone else had originated the idea.

Another respondent prefers to operate without the supervising presence of a board:

On that . . . thing we ran wild and handsome; there were only two of us up there, and we could do what we wanted to. Those associations where they have an active board, they tend to hamstring things. I much prefer to act without a board.

The roles of lobbyists in policy-making vary with the type of organization represented.[7] Lobbyists for citizens groups, veterans' groups, and humanitarian groups often have an important role. Representatives of large trade associations generally are more active in policy formulation than representatives of small ones.

[7]*The findings from various cross-tabulations are summarized from time to time to avoid an excessive number of tables. If the sample is broken down by "type of group" or "role of respondent to his employer," there are too many categories to enable statistical tests of significance; further, the categories are too discrete to allow the combination of categories, as can be done with single-dimension variables. When two single-dimension variables are compared in a statement, the relationship can be taken as statistically significant unless otherwise specified.*

And lobbyists for corporations and for more than one type of organization take the least responsibility for policy.

Trade association executives, officers of organizations, and lobbyist entrepreneurs make the most policy; free-lance lawyers make the least. Respondents who travel and speak to the grassroots membership have a greater role in policy than those who do not. Moreover, lobbyists who play major policy roles are more personally committed to organization policy.

STRATEGY

As indicated earlier, making policy and planning strategy are related but generally occur at different conceptual and organizational levels. (See Table III-5.) Most policy responsibility is located in the board, but the responsibility for planning strategy generally is given to the staff; all but nine respondents report that the staff is involved in planning strategy. Where strategy was planned exclusively by the board, the board was also highly involved in making policy. Sixteen respondents say they personally map strategy; ten of these either make policy too or find the policy question inappropriate.

About 20 per cent of the respondents report that they generally consult other lobby groups in mapping strategy. Groups very commonly work in concert on specific bills or policy areas. They exchange information, plan joint strategy, and divide up the chores.[8] Interestingly, most of the groups which consult with others on strategy receive their policy from the organization board and the annual meeting. These include mainly large membership groups which tend both to discuss policy at annual meetings and to be interested in broad policy problems requiring the collaboration and assistance of other groups.

The reasons given earlier for staff leadership in policy-making are even more appropriate for staff strategy-planning. One respondent put it this way:

> Strategy is usually mapped by us, and that means me. Our people have no concept of how legislation is carried on here, and they can't plan strategy, so they ask us what we think. For this reason we also play a very significant role in

[8]*This practice is discussed further in Chapter VIII.*

TABLE III-5

Locus of Policy Leadership and Strategy Planning

PRIMARY LOCUS OF POLICY LEADERSHIP	LOCUS OF STRATEGY PLANNING						
	Respondent	Staff	Board or Executive Committee	Staff and Board	Consultation with Other Lobby Groups	No Response	Total
Not appropriate	6	4					10
Respondent	4				1		5
Staff		6		2	1		9
Board	2	5	3	10	1		21
Executive committee		1	3	1			5
Annual meeting or convention		1		1			2
Staff and board		6		2	2		10
Board or executive committee and annual meeting	2	16	3	6	16		43
No response	2					7	9
TOTAL	16	39	9	22	21	7	114

making policy for the organization. I'll bet the other people you have interviewed haven't been as honest about that as I have been.

An additional reason for keeping strategy in the hands of the staff is that the legislative scene can change rather quickly. Only the persons on hand can act with appropriate dispatch. Some offices have master strategy planners who order subordinates about, but typically strategy is hammered out in conference with the full staff.

The locus of strategy planning varies with the type of organization represented. In labor organizations, strategy is designed by the staff alone or in collaboration with other groups; corporations usually leave strategy to the staff. Among trade associations, small associations assign their boards a greater share of strategy planning than do large trade associations partly because many small associations have only one lobbyist representative and he needs someone to confer with.

Close examination of the respondent's personal role in planning strategy discloses that every respondent has some role in planning; fifty have primary responsibility for developing strategy. Primary responsibility for strategy depends mostly on the size of the lobby staff: members of large staffs more often share in strategy sessions with other staff members, while lone representatives must of necessity take primary responsibility. The member of a small staff communicates with his superiors by reports to board meetings or via a newsletter; he does not simply report to a staff meeting.

TACTICS

Respondents were also asked if they determine their own tactics. All report that they have at least some freedom; ninety-four have at least considerable freedom; and fifty-seven claim complete freedom. Respondents or staff members who determine policy, also have complete freedom to determine tactics. Size of staff and role in strategy partially determine the respondent's freedom on tactics: those on small staffs have complete freedom, and those on larger staffs generally must consult superiors or colleagues. Clearly, boards and membership play no role in the choice of tactics. Choosing tactics is uniquely the lobbyist's task; tactical skill is one of the major reasons many lobbyists are hired.

THE FUNCTION OF OPPONENTS

Groups generally send lobbyists to Washington because a policy objective is in possible jeopardy. Usually another group with an opposing interest is pushing for the other side. Do opposing lobbyists and groups frequently confront one another over long periods? Do the antagonists know one another well? Does opposition to lobbyists come only from opposing groups?

Although some groups have long-standing disagreements and appear in opposition on specific bills time after time, more normally, groups encounter shifting opposition as one policy after another comes up. Despite the changing panorama of opposition, respondents were asked to identify the type of opposition they encounter most of the time. The results are reported in Table III–6. Notice that fifteen respondents say they have no single major opponent.

Most opposing groups are economically self-interested. They may be competing businesses, union groups, or opposing economic forces—as labor against management. Usually economic contention is within a broad industry: for example, railroads against truck lines, medical doctors against osteopaths, real estate boards against savings and loan associations, Railway Labor Executives Association against the Association of American Railroads, Farm Bureau against Farmers Union, and so forth. Each group strives for economic advantage and uses the area of public policy as one battleground. Each tries to write the rules to its own advantage. Sometimes a clash results in a standoff; sometimes a compromise is reached. When some astute lobbyists realize that a conflict is inevitable, they try to work out a compromise in advance; others have difficulty reconciling themselves to taking half a loaf.

Once in a while, in order to convince someone that they ought to go along on a compromise measure, we will completely block a thing. We will get some friend of ours to just

TABLE III-6

Major Opponents by Type of Organization

TYPE OF ORGANIZATION	MAJOR OPPONENTS								
	Few or no Opponents	Competing Business or Union	Opposing Economic Forces	Executive Department	Congress	Members of Congress Opposite Political Faiths	Vary from Case to Case	No Response	Total
Large labor	1		5	2		1		1	10
Small labor		1	4		1	1	1		8
Large farm		2							2
Small farm			3						3
Large trade		3	3			1		2	9
Small trade	5	14	2	3		7	8	4	43
Corporation	2	2	2		1	2	3	5	17
Large citizens	2					2	1	1	6
Service or veterans	2								2
Church and humanitarian						4		1	5
Foreign government or firm		1					1		2
More than one type				3		1	1	2	7
TOTAL	12	23	19	8	2	19	15	16	114

nail up something tight in committee. Then when the fellow realizes what has hit him he will come around and say, "All right, let's talk, I understand now what you mean, so let's go to work on this thing." We may not always have the power to get something through, but, if we can't win, we have the power to keep the other side from winning. Seldom do we come into a head-on clash with other organizations on legislation, and one reason is that we will put our muscle into a thing to work out a compromise.

Nineteen respondents (Table III–6) say that their major opposition comes from groups who differ from them in basic political philosophy: Isolationists oppose internationalists on foreign policy; the "lib-lab lobby"[9] (liberal and labor coalition) opposes conservatives; "spenders" oppose advocates of economy in government. These philosophical differences come into direct conflict when the ideas are embodied in specific legislative bills or other specific policy decisions.

About 10 per cent of the respondents report that their major opposition comes from persons or agencies in government—from specific members of Congress or officials of an executive agency whose program would be affected by the legislation or decision. Much opposition from within government is in reaction to proposals which would add more costs to government or reduce tax revenues, but opposition also occurs because an agency thinks that a proposal might diminish or at least would not further its program. The natural opponents for unions of governmental employees are the agencies that employ them.

Returning to Table III–6, we see that labor representatives consider that most of their opposition comes from opposing economic forces—mainly management groups. Farm representatives find that their opposition is from competing kinds of farm production (e.g., dairy products against oleomargarine) or that it shifts. Trade association lobbyists see a variety of opponents, but a slight majority see their major opposition from competitors. Citizens and veterans groups have little steady opposition. Opposition to various church and humanitarian groups seems to come from those with differing political philosophies.

[9] *Bailey (1950) popularized this phrase.*

Respondents also were asked how they evaluated the strength of their opponents. No generally accepted method of evaluation appeared, and, in fact, many respondents groped for an answer. There simply seems to be no consistently good method for evaluating the strength of the opposition. The "yes" and "no" votes in Congress are one visible test of legislative strength, but evaluation after the decision has been taken is of little strategic value for that decision. Many observers base their appraisals primarily on the past voting records of members; a few lobbyists keep a detailed card file of the past performance of members. They may keep estimates of the money available to the opposition, of the size of their membership, and of the vitality of opposition commitment to the proposal. When the vote in Congress is quite near, the whips and other key people know quite well how each member will vote; the lobbyist who can get close to these key people at this time (few can) may receive a valuable advance estimate of how his cause stands and of whether anything can be done at the last minute to change things. One former member of Congress claims that in making evaluations of voting potential one has to consider seven political parties in Congress instead of the usual two.

Generally, we simply can't win on a strict party vote. I generally make the point up on the Hill that we don't have to try to get one party to work together, or two parties to work together, but we are dealing with seven political parties. First of all, there are the real New Dealers; secondly, there are the run-of-the-mill western and northern Democrats; thirdly, there are the liberal southerners; and fourthly, there are the Dixiecrats on the Democratic side of the aisle. On the Republican side, there are a handful of liberal Republicans; the great bulk of what I call the "stand-still Republicans"—they don't take much action; they are a great mass that have to be pushed here and there; and then there is a small group of ultra-reactionary people. The coalition that generally rules the situation now are the Dixiecrats, the stand-still Republicans, and the reactionary group. This is a pretty tough coalition to lick although we have licked it on occasion.

Curiously, many lobbyists find opponents useful; without opposition, the lobbyists might be unemployed. It is occasionally said that a certain group wishes to keep an issue alive long after it is necessary, just to have something to do. Once a major program is agreed to—for example, the St. Lawrence Seaway—the contending groups remain—and fight about the appropriations to carry out the program. One female lobbyist reports that her opponent credits her with helping him to win a raise—since he based his request on the fact that he has had to work so hard. Another curious result of opposition is a tendency for some lobbyists to claim that their opponent is very strong. This is probably an ego defense against possible defeat: it is no disgrace to be defeated by a very powerful lobby group. Fifteen choose their major opponent as the most successful lobby in Washington.

SUMMARY

In this chapter, some of the more characteristic aspects of lobby or pressure groups have been reviewed. Different types of pressure groups were noted. In addition to the usual labor, farm, and business bases of distinction, there are veteran, citizens, church and humanitarian, and foreign organizations. Groups can also be distinguished by their size, wealth, and pattern of organization.

Lobby groups have many purposes and functions. They attempt to influence legislative and executive decisions either by direct communications or by manipulation of public opinion. They provide many kinds of non-lobbying functions and services for their members. Most are financed by dues, but many other means are used as well—such as contributions, fees, sale of services, and so forth.

Policy leadership for a group is not always found where the formal structure suggests. Most groups are led and managed by a small oligarchy of staff and officers. As a general rule, lobbyists are thoroughly involved in making policy for the group. Decisions about strategy and tactics are given over almost totally to the lobby staff.

Most groups confront a shifting pattern of opponents rather than a single consistent opponent group. The anticipated behavior of opponents is an important determinant of a group's lobbying strategy.

Part Two

The Lobbyist
as Political Actor

One of the major purposes of this study is to examine the lobbyist as an individual. In Part Two, the questions of how specific people become lobbyists, what kinds of persons they are, what their day-to-day jobs are like, and what their roles are in relation to their employers and to the government will be considered.

Fundamentally, lobbyists are much like other people. In a complex society with great division of labor, some inevitably are assigned the role of lobbyist. Although they were selected because they possessed certain skills, most lobbyists did not plan and prepare for their role. The role, however, is the most important factor determining their behavior and setting them apart from similar persons playing different roles.

CHAPTER IV

RECRUITMENT OF LOBBYISTS

The average person probably never considers making a career of lobbying. Colleges and professional schools do not prepare students specifically for this position. If a youngster announced that he would like to be a lobbyist, his parents would probably vigorously discourage him. Public disapproval of lobbyists and lobbying is so strong that most present practitioners admit to being lobbyists only reluctantly and qualifiedly.

Considering these psychological barriers, how are lobby positions filled? Many superficial observers believe that money alone is sufficient to surmount the psychological barriers of public disapprobation; yet money is seldom the sole or even the major motive attracting people to lobbying. Motivation is usually much more complex; generally, entering lobbying is just one of a long series of related steps; the career patterns of certain individuals have so developed that lobbying is the natural next step. Some persons gravitate to lobbying; some simply wander to it. Only one reports that he carefully considered the various career opportunities open to him (he already had a law degree) and decided that a career in lobbying was best suited to his temperament. All of the others went into lobbying as a result of the unintended consequences of several earlier career opportunities and decisions.

Although nearly all respondents became lobbyists as a result of a series of career choices, some differences in the factors leading directly to their employment remain. Most give at least two reasons for becoming lobbyists. Table IV–1 shows a cross-tabulation of the first and second reasons. Examination of the marginal frequencies shows that sixty-seven respondents report that "the requirements of the job" was their first or second reason for becoming a lobbyist. The reason next in importance is "best use of one's talents," mentioned by fifty-one respondents.

Seventeen respondents insist that they are not really lobbyists —that they registered as such only to be safe from possible prosecution. As a second reason, most of these claim that they have their positions as a result of the requirements of their jobs. It should also be noted that many who report "requirements of the job" or their bosses' belief in their qualifications as the first reason choose "best use of their talents" as the second reason. Many of those who choose "best use of their talents" first give "monetary reward" as second choice. Most people say, then, that lobbying was the next natural development in their careers. Even among the ten who say that the promotion of some policy was their most important reason (a non-career-oriented motive) for becoming a lobbyist, eight give "requirements of the job" as the second reason.

Persons who represent large citizens organizations or church and humanitarian organizations tend to say that they became lobbyists to promote a policy. Representatives of small trade associations and of foreign firms usually say that job requirements were important. Labor lobbyists have a variety of reasons for having become lobbyists. Most respondents who claim they are not really lobbyists represent small trade associations or corporations; usually these persons perform tasks in addition to lobbying.

Further study of Table IV–1 suggests that the sample could be recombined into two groups: (1) those who feel that they were pressured into lobbying (the first two categories under primary reason); and (2) those who in a minimal way sought a lobbying position (the remaining categories under primary reason). Interestingly, less than half of the registered Washington lobbyists can be said to have sought a lobby position. The difference in approach

TABLE IV–1

**Reasons for
Becoming Lobbyists**

SECONDARY REASON	PRIMARY REASON (Same as 1–9 left)									
	1	2	3	4	5	6	7	8	9	Total
1. I am not a lobbyist — I register only to be safe.		1								1
2. The requirements of my job led me into it.	12			4	8	1				25
3. My boss thought I was especially qualified.		8	6		1					15
4. It was the best way I could use my talents.	3	16		6						25
5. I wanted to promote certain policies.	1	8		3						12
6. The monetary reward was very good.		5		10						15
7. I just enjoy this kind of work.		2	1	2	1					6
8. Other.		1								1
9. No response.	1	1		1					11	14
TOTAL	17	42	7	26	10	1	0	0	11	114

to lobbying is related to the way lobbyists feel about belonging to a "profession"; respondents pressured into lobbying more often say that they feel no sense of profession; those who sought lobbying positions tend to think that professionalism is developing.

The skills or knowledge that a person brings to his work affects how well he accepts the lobbying role. Those who believe they were hired because of their knowledge of law or of a special subject matter feel that they were pressured into lobbying. Those who believe they were hired for their knowledge of the legislative and the political process usually sought lobby positions. A related finding is that members of legislative relations staffs, who spend most of their time working on legislation, usually sought lobby positions. In contrast, trade association executives and lawyers in large law firms who work on other tasks in addition to legislation, feel that they were pressured into lobbying.

The difference between those seeking lobbying and those urged into it is related to over-all career interests. Respondents were asked to imagine that they could start over and make any career choice they desired without considering any lack of talent or training on their part. They were presented with a list of fifteen occupations. Lobbyists who sought their positions choose careers close to politics and humanitarian service. Those who were involuntary lobbyists choose careers in business or law. People who have been active in politics or who have had experience on the Hill often seek lobbying positions, and persons with public policy concerns and political experience are more likely to seek lobby positions than those with business concerns and experience.

In summary, all lobbyists accepted their positions in order to advance something of importance to themselves, usually their careers. Contrary to the expectations of many observers, their great concern is not to increase their wealth, although this may be a factor. Also, only a few of them chose lobbying in order to battle for a policy or philosophy of government, although this, too, is a factor. For most, lobbying is a career step; it is the final or culminating step for some, but a way-station leading to the realization of some further ambition for others. Some large corporations groom their rising young executives by sending them to Washington for a tour of duty; if they perform well in this assignment, they may be promoted to higher, decision-making levels. Persons enter lobbying for a variety of motives, but nearly all of the motives seem to be related to career progression.

HIRING OF LOBBYISTS

How do organizations evaluate a man for a lobbying position? The ideal man would have a variety of qualities. First, he would have knowledge of and experience with four subjects: (1) the legislative and political process; (2) law and the legal process; (3) the subject matter of concern to the organization; and (4) an understanding of public relations techniques. He would possess verbal facility both in speaking and writing and would be able to interact well with people. He would have "contacts" with decision-makers who are important to him and with people who know how to get things done. He would be enthusiastic, optimistic, patient, and imaginative. For certain kinds of jobs he should also have administrative ability. Many of these are the same qualifications required for any demanding professional position.

Obviously, only rare persons possess all of these qualities, and it is unlikely that all of these traits would be equally prized for a particular lobby job. Most respondents say that they were sought on the basis of at least two qualities. The first and second qualities mentioned are cross-tabulated and shown in Table IV–2. The marginal totals indicate that knowledge of the subject matter of the industry, knowledge of the legislative and political process, and knowledge of law and the legal process are considered the most important qualities. Knowledge of the legislative and political process is mentioned by 58 of the 101 respondents, and knowledge of the subject is mentioned by 50 of them. It is interesting that knowledge of the political process is mentioned more frequently as a second than as a first response, and that knowledge of subject receives only twelve second but thirty-eight first responses. Although specific data to substantiate this interpretation cannot be cited, it seems that many respondents believe knowledge of the legislative and political process to be an obvious prerequisite for the job and do not mention it first.

Referring to Table IV–2 again, the reader will note that all six of the persons mentioning possession of a wide circle of contacts as their primary quality mention knowledge of the legislative and political process as their secondary quality. Mentioning contacts and knowing the political process are characteristic of people who have been active in various aspects of partisan politics or who have served in one capacity or another in the legislative branch. In contrast, those coming from the executive branch or

TABLE IV–2

Qualities Desired in Persons Recruited for Lobby Positions

SECONDARY QUALITY DESIRED	PRIMARY QUALITY DESIRED (Same as 1–X left)									
	1	2	3	4	5	6	7	8	X	Total
1. Knowledge of legislative and political process		9	13	1	3	6	2	1		35
2. Knowledge of law and legal process	2		6				2			10
3. Knowledge of subject	7	1		2	2					12
4. Ability to interact well with people	3		4		1					8
5. Ability to communicate effectively	4	2	4	1						11
6. Possession of wide circle of contacts	4	1	6	1	1					13
7. Reputation for success	3		1							4
8. Other		1	2		1					4
X. No response		1	2						14	17
TOTAL	23	15	38	5	8	6	4	1	14	114

from business emphasize knowledge of the subject matter of their industry.

The qualities desired in lobby recruits can also be evaluated from the point of view of the hiring organization. Labor organizations generally pick men for their knowledge of the legislative and political process; they also place some emphasis on knowledge of the subject, ability to interact with people, and having contacts. Farm organizations place major emphasis on knowledge of the subject and a little emphasis on knowledge of the legislative and political process. Large trade associations value most a knowledge of the legislative and political process; small trade associations, which are more specialized, are most interested in knowledge of the subject. Corporations place greatest stress on knowledge of the subject and knowledge of law. Generally, one can discern a tendency for organizations with a wide range of policy interests to select lobbyists who are knowledgeable about the political process and who function well within it. On the other hand, those organizations with narrower policy interests tend to pick men primarily because of their intimate knowledge of the subject with which they will be dealing.

The reader familiar with the popular lore on lobbyists may wonder why so little emphasis is placed on having a wide circle of contacts in the selection of lobbyists. Respondents were asked specifically about how important their circle of contacts seemed to the hiring organization. In addition, more than half of the respondents were asked if men were generally considered valuable for lobbying because of their circle of contacts. A cross-tabulation showing responses to these two questions is reported in Table IV–3. The marginal frequencies on the importance of contacts in respondent's case show that almost half of them believe that contacts are of no importance at all and that only fifteen think they are of considerable or major importance. On the other hand, respondents answering the second question tend to rate the value of contacts for "lobbyists in general" higher than they rate their own case. The two categories for "lobbyists in general" with the highest marginal frequencies are "some importance" or "considerable importance." Interestingly, even when speaking generally about lobbying, very few respondents say contacts are of major importance; in fact, three out of the seven who say they were of major importance in their own selection do

TABLE IV–3
Importance of a Circle of Contacts to Lobbyists

GENERAL IMPORTANCE OF CONTACTS*	IMPORTANCE OF CONTACTS IN R's CASE						
	Not at All	Minor	Some	Considerable	Major	No Response	Total
Not at all	3		1				4
Minor	4	2	1		1		8
Some	11	4	14				29
Considerable	8	3	4	4	2		21
Major					4		4
No response	17	9	5	4		13	48
TOTAL	43	18	25	8	7	13	114

*This question was not asked of all respondents (see page 30).

not think they are of major importance generally. Table IV–3 discloses a slight positive correlation between the rating of contacts in one's own case and the general rating; those who rate it high in their own case tend to rate it high generally.

It is easy to understand why there is a correlation between the two judgments; it is more difficult to understand why it is not higher. Why do some respondents rate contacts of little importance in their own case but of greater significance for lobbyists in general? One possible reason is that even lobbyists believe the folklore about lobbying. They are inclined to discount first-hand knowledge which contradicts the folklore, thinking that their own case is atypical. Operating within the system, they are in a poor position to get an over-all perspective such as can be provided by a study of this kind.

A second reason for the discrepancy is that, while contacts may be a valuable asset, they often are actually not as important as other qualities in recruiting new lobbyists. The man who has no contacts when recruited, but who is skilled in human interaction, can readily build up a circle of contacts. One respondent summed up the utility of contacts in this way:

> Oftentimes a circle of contacts is considered more important by people who are not really close to the situation. Anybody who thinks that a fellow goes up to the Capitol and gets something done because he has fed a lot of cocktails to people is crazy. The main advantage of having contacts is that you don't have to qualify yourself every time that you approach someone. If you know people well enough, you may be able to get a hearing without delay; of course, if they know you well enough and don't like you, you may never get a hearing.

The importance of contacts in recruitment varies with the kind of organization represented and with the position held in the organization, but the variations are small. The representatives of farm organizations and small trade associations place the least emphasis on contacts—75 per cent say it is of no more than minor importance. Trade association executives and lawyers in large law firms are more likely than others to say that contacts were of little importance in their selection. A greater than average percentage of those having experience on Capitol Hill believe that contacts were important in their selection.

In short, contacts are not emphasized at the time of recruitment, and their value is limited primarily to saving time and more readily gaining access to decision-makers. It is thought highly unlikely that a contact will give a lobbyist an advantage in obtaining a favorable decision. (See Chapter XIII.) Several respondents even said that a friendly contact may be a disadvantage, explaining that they prize their friendships highly and hesitate to jeopardize them by pressing a friend for a favorable decision. Friendships also affect decision-makers; they are sometimes extremely determined to avoid seeming to make a decision on the basis of friendship; thus they inadvertently place the friend at a disadvantage.

How do persons attain the qualities that will enable them to fill lobby positions? There is no training in the formal schooling sense. On the other hand, many respondents believe that working in Washington in a position involving some phase of policy-making is a valuable training experience. Several say it was helpful to have been the recipient of lobbying, since the experience helps the lobbyist to avoid behaviors likely to be resented and to choose tactics that are most effective. One respondent likened this experience to an old journalist, saying, "If you have been a newsman you can always talk to newspaper people." The recruiters of lobbyists seem to give some credence to this general point since 57 of the 101 respondents came to lobbying directly from jobs either in the executive or legislative branch of the government.

How important is legal training for lobbying? Forty-five respondents had legal training. Many think it is helpful but do not believe it is nearly as important as experience in Washington. Certain characteristics of the policy process in Washington must be learned before a person can operate effectively in that setting. Knowledge of the communications network and the unofficial centers of decision-making is particularly important. As with legal training, experience in politics outside of Washington, while helpful, is not considered particularly valuable.

Organizations with specialized subject matter tend to seek lobbyists who are technically competent in their fields. For many types of problems, the expert is more valuable than the political operator. This is especially true of organizations with tax problems that require correction by legislation; such groups seek out lawyers or consultants specializing in taxation. Tax consultants have very lucrative practices in Washington. In most of their work, they deal directly with the Treasury and other executive agencies. If a problem cannot be corrected there, it is sometimes taken to Congress in the form of proposed remedial legislation; then the tax consultant must register as a lobbyist. Several men engaged in this type of practice are former clerks of tax-writing committees in Congress, especially the House Ways and Means Committee. Service on a tax committee is apparently considered excellent qualification by prospective clients. Persons who are highly trained in complex and technical subjects sometimes have difficulty simplifying presentations so that members of Congress or other laymen can understand them. One respondent is so dissatisfied with the necessity of simplifying that he is thinking of quitting his lobbyist position.

There is an aura of impermanence and non-professionalism about lobbying. This is perhaps reflected by the fact that only one respondent followed his father in becoming a lobbyist. In this case, the father had many years' experience as a Washington representative for a small trade association and several other clients. When the son completed college (a normal liberal arts education), he decided to go into partnership with his father, in much the same manner as a son joins his father in a law partnership, except in this case neither father nor son had specialized training. We may see more cases like this in years to come. Sons following fathers in the profession might lead toward more permanence, prestige, and higher professional standards.

The selection of a lobbyist by an organization is very important since a wrong choice could ruin an organization's reputation and effectiveness for years. Where does an organization look to find lobbyists? Through the folklore of politics proclaims that many lobbyists are former members of Congress, this is largely untrue. Only three former members appear in the sample.[1] To be sure, having been a member means one has useful knowledge and skills, but so does having performed other jobs. Several heads of lobby organizations report that former members of Congress have come around seeking positions but that the organizations have

[1]Congressional Quarterly *counted 11 former members among 579 persons who registered as lobbyists in 1955.* Congressional Quarterly News Features (*January 11, 1957, p. 58*).

been reluctant to hire them. The defeated member is probably not strikingly capable; also, he is unlikely to have the technical skills and knowledge that many lobby jobs require.

It is often thought that former members are valuable because they have access to the floor of their former chamber. This is true only so long as they are disinterested in legislation. Former members of the House of Representatives are denied the floor if they are personally interested in legislation or are in the employ of organizations interested in legislation. Former members who are admitted are forbidden to manifest approval or disapproval of the proceedings.[2]

The Senate is somewhat more liberal in allowing admission to the floor, not specifically denying entrance to ex-senators who are interested in legislation.[3] However, the former member is not highly sought after as a lobbyist even though he may know many persons in Congress and possibly have access to the floor of his former chamber. These assets tend to be relevant only if he possesses other talents as well.

TABLE IV—4
Position Held Immediately Prior to Becoming a Lobbyist

PRIOR POSITION	NUMBER
Never did anything else	2
Lawyer	9
Journalist	1
Elective public official	3
Businessman	18
Government job-holder — executive branch	41
Government job-holder — legislative branch	16
Other professional	4
Labor union employee	5
Other	7
No response	8
TOTAL	114

[2]For details on admission to the floor of the House, see Lewis Deschler, parliamentarian (1953, pp. 486–87).

[3]For details on admission to the Senate floor, see Charles L. Watkins, parliamentarian (1958, p. 325).

TABLE IV–5

Experience on the Hill
Prior to Lobbying

TYPE OF EXPERIENCE	NUMBER
None	79
Committee staff	8
Staff of member of House	3
Staff of member of Senate	6
Member of House	3
Member of Senate	0
More than one type	3
General congressional staff	1
No response	11
TOTAL	114

The major source of lobbyist recruits is government service, either in the legislative or executive branch. Preliminary conversations with lobbyists and knowledgeable people in Washington lead to the expectation that half of the lobbyists will have formerly served on the Hill in one capacity or another. The survey discloses, however, that more than twice as many (forty-one) lobbyists come from the executive branch as from the legislative branch (sixteen). Table IV–4 shows only the position immediately prior to becoming a lobbyist; it does not indicate previous experience on the Hill or elsewhere. Table IV–5 shows persons who have worked on the Hill at any time in their careers. Even under this criterion, only twenty-four persons had served on the Hill. The evidence is very clear—the executive branch is by far the most important source for recruiting persons for lobbying positions.

Why is the executive branch the most highly favored source of lobbyists? First, the executive branch has more staff members than the legislative branch; therefore, there is a much larger pool from which to recruit. Experience in the executive branch is just as valuable as legislative experiences. The executive branch is subject to lobbying activity as much as is the legislative branch. In addition, executive officials are accustomed to attempting to influence legislation. Staff persons in the executive branch are observed in action by lobby organizations, and this performance is recalled when a lobby position opens. In modern times, when most forms of economic activity are affected by governmental regulation, the person who has administered a regulation can be an extremely knowledgeable and valuable employee for an organization affected by that regulation. This expertise and acquaintance with the details of a subject often make the staff member of an executive agency or congressional committee more valuable as a lobbyist than the official decision-maker whom the staff member served. Almost one-fourth (nine) of the lobbyists coming from the executive branch took positions as trade association executives. In addition, many persons moving from the executive branch to lobbying had training as lawyers; seven became free-lance lawyers, and four joined large law firms.

Business is also an important source for recruitment. Eighteen persons were businessmen or employees in business immediately prior to lobbying. Eight of these became trade association executives, and four became Washington representatives for one or more business organizations. These people are inclined to have very little sense of identification with lobbying as a profession; many find performing their lobbying duties repugnant. In contrast, those coming from government are likely to have a sense of an emerging lobbying profession. Persons moving from business to lobbying are usually oriented toward their own organization or industry and aspire to move up in that structure. Their major skill is a broad and thorough knowledge of the industry they represent.

What is the role of the practicing lawyer in lobbying? The legal profession is not as important a source for lobbyists as is popularly supposed. Table IV–4 shows that only nine persons came to lobbying directly from law practice. Most of these are persons whose law practice involves them in problems requiring correction by legislation. Most Washington lawyers and large Washington law firms, as they perform general legal services for clients, have, from time to time, problems that can be solved only by legislation. If they successfully promote legislation, their reputation grows, and they attract more and more legislative work. Much of the legal work of Washington lawyers is concerned with the federal government. However, most lawyers are such purists in interpreting the law that they will not admit to lobbying when they are in contact solely with persons in the executive branch;

they register and admit to lobbying only when their problems lead them into legislative activity. Twenty-four respondents in this study carry on their lobbying activities from the base of a legal practice. This should be contrasted with forty-five respondents in all who have legal training. The legal profession, then, is a significant source of lobbying manpower—but perhaps not as important as has been supposed.

Persons with wide political party experience are seldom chosen as lobbyists. Although they have a thorough knowledge of partisan activity, they do not necessarily know the legislative process and over-all decision-making processes in Washington. They seldom have the technical knowledge required in some lobby jobs. And clear identification with one of the political parties presents difficulties; it sometimes puts a lobbyist at a disadvantage when he calls on a person of the opposite party. Some lobbyists who have been previously highly involved in politics diminish or discontinue their partisan political activity. On the other hand, this concern can be overemphasized; many recipients of lobbying say they do not resent dealing with persons of the opposite political faith so long as they can be confident that their conversations will not be used for partisan political advantage.

The recruiting process is not very clearly defined in most organizations, and different organizations use different methods. While many people seek lobby positions, top quality candidates are scarce. Employers are wary of persons who circulate from organization to organization asking for a job; they immediately suspect those who are out "beating the bushes." Most organizations are willing to pay enough to get highly qualified persons. On the other hand, most well qualified men are already employed in fine positions at good salaries. The offer of a substantial increase in salary frequently is not sufficient to dislodge them. The recruiting person or team must sell the organization to the prospective employee. Some respondents report that they were spotted years in advance by an organization which made repeated attempts to persuade them to accept employment. Some organizations try to avoid this costly competitive bidding by searching for a relatively unknown man who has the potential to develop into the kind of person they want. A few organizations throw out a dragnet, requiring applicants to take personality tests and give speeches; this technique is not widely used, however.

CAREER BACKGROUNDS

Each respondent was requested to recount his occupational history from the time he completed his formal education. Nearly all responses are very detailed. Each individual has a unique background which is best understood in its own context; yet it would be impossible to recount each story here. No background can be described as characteristic of most lobbyists. Still, there are some regularities. Not all career backgrounds would be equally likely to lead to lobbying. Several categories were set up, and data were coded first into career preparation and then into over-all career pattern. These two variables are cross-tabulated in Table IV-6.

Although there is some correlation between career preparation and over-all career pattern, there is perhaps less uniformity than one would expect. Less than half of those trained in the law have followed law careers. Only two of nine trained as journalists have followed journalism careers. Only four of eleven trained for business have followed business careers. On the other hand, people who become lobbyists are probably not very typical of the persons trained for their professions. The fact that they have not stayed in the main stream of the profession indicates dissatisfaction with the initial career choice.

Surprisingly few registered lobbyists can be said to have an over-all career pattern in lobbying. Even if careers in association work, which includes more than lobbying activities, are considered to be lobbying careers, less than one-fourth of the respondents have had over-all careers in lobbying. Those who have had predominantly lobbying careers received their training in a variety of professions.

Less than half of the legally trained respondents have spent most of their careers in law practice. Many went into governmental service, association work, business, or politics. Reference to Table IV-4 discloses that only nine respondents came into lobbying directly from law practice. Lobbyist-lawyers are not necessarily disenchanted with the legal profession, however. When asked what their choice of profession would be if they had their lives to live over again, twenty-eight of the law-trained respondents say their first choice would be either attorney or judge.

TABLE IV–6

Career Preparation and Career Patterns of Lobbyists

OVER-ALL CAREER PATTERN	No Specific One	Law	Journalism	Politics	Business	Governmental Service	Teacher, Professor, Researcher	Skilled Labor	Other	No Response	Total
						CAREER PREPARATION					
Law		22	1								23
Journalism	2		2								4
Politics	1	2		1			1				5
Business	4	2			4						10
Governmental service	3	10	3		1	2	8			1	28
Association work	1	5	2		3	1	5		1		18
Labor union work	1		1				1	4			7
Lobbying		2			3		1				6
Other							3		1		4
No response		2								7	9
TOTAL	12	45	9	1	11	3	19	4	2	8	114

Moreover, it seems likely that the wide variety of jobs open to people with legal training is one of the attractions of that training. Several respondents report that they came to Washington and were employed full-time, usually in government, while they studied for a law degree in a local law school.

Journalism schooling also leads to a variety of careers; more respondents so trained had careers in government than in journalism. Two other persons without journalistic training developed careers in journalism. No one with journalism training gives journalist as his first-choice career if he could start afresh.

Very few persons train specifically for careers in politics or governmental service; yet twenty-eight had over-all careers in governmental service, and five had careers in politics. These people had a wide variety of career preparation. Legal training and academic training prepare many for governmental work.

Eleven persons prepared for a business career. Ten had previous careers primarily in business; yet only four who trained for business had business careers. The others with business training went mainly into association work or into lobbying. Considering that 52 of the 114 in the sample represent trade associations, most of which are business associations, it is interesting that more of the lobbyists do not have business backgrounds. This is another indication that legal and political skills are more useful in lobbying than business skills.

Most of the respondents who have academic training for teaching or research did not follow academic careers. Instead, they usually developed careers in governmental service or association work. Often they were drawn into lobbying because of their expert knowledge of a subject. There also seems to be a tendency among persons who select this kind of training to be attracted to careers with policy-making potential. When asked for their first choice of profession if they could start over again, many pick senator, corporation executive, or legislative representative.

The only way a person trained as a skilled laborer can become a lobbyist is by working his way up through the ranks of the labor union. In effect, each of the labor representatives also developed political and social skills before being moved into lobbying. Manual skills per se have very little use in a lobbying role. Persons with careers in labor union work need not come from the ranks of labor, although that is the general pattern. Incidentally, most of the people with labor backgrounds choose legislative representative as their first choice of profession if they could start afresh. Since this is their present job, they know it concretely and know it is attainable; they do not aspire to more prestigious positions, such as attorney, physician, or senator.

Of those respondents who have come to lobbying with career backgrounds in the legislative branch, many were trained in the law, but some were trained for journalism or academic life. Interestingly, none of those prepared for business or labor careers has had Hill experience. Lobbyists whose over-all career patterns have emphasized politics are also very likely to have had experience on the Hill.

Those who left the Hill for lobbying were frequently sought by large trade associations for their legislative and executive relations staffs. About 60 per cent of the respondents who represent large trade associations have had experience on the Hill; whereas only 23 per cent of the full sample have had this background. Persons with Hill experience generally hold staff rather than executive roles with these large trade associations; the officers or executives usually have been drawn from inside the industry or the executive branch. Officers and executives apparently need a specialized knowledge of the industry that is not likely to be developed in legislative work.

Men with experience on the Hill also have often become freelance lobbyists. Half of the fourteen respondents classed as freelance lawyers have had Hill experience. They apparently rely on their thorough knowledge of the legislative and political process to attract clients.

People with experience on the Hill say they were able to move into lobbying with little psychological strain. Nearly all of them like their jobs and plan to continue their careers in lobbying. Lobbying tasks are in many ways similar to legislative tasks; they involve considerable interaction with other persons and a concern with policy problems. Most of them mention these factors when asked what features of their work appeal to them the most. When asked to choose the job or profession they would most like to have if they could start over, respondents with Hill experience are significantly more inclined to pick senator or representative than are other respondents. In fact, all three of the respondents who choose representative (eighteen select senator) have worked on the Hill.

Men coming from careers in law, politics, or labor organization work are likely to have been active in a political party; whereas those coming from business or association work are unlikely to have been active.

Those with career patterns in business, association work, and lobbying are somewhat more likely to identify themselves as Republicans. On the other hand, those with career patterns in politics, governmental service, and labor organization work tend to be Democrats. We would expect from our knowledge of the bases of support for political parties in the United States that business lobbyists would usually be Republican and labor lobbyists would usually be Democratic. Also, since the Democrats controlled the White House for twenty years prior to the Eisenhower administration, one could expect that lobbyists coming from careers in government and politics would be Democrats.

To summarize, the career backgrounds of lobbyists do not follow a neat pattern. Only a limited number of careers can prepare one for lobbying: law, politics, journalism, business, governmental service, association work, and labor union work. The nature of the particular lobbying job largely determines the appropriate career background.

POLITICAL CHARACTERISTICS

Since lobbyists must be concerned with political decisions, every lobbyist is somewhat active in politics. One of the hypotheses of this study is that this concern with policy decisions would lead many lobbyists to become involved in political party activities. The political activities discussed relate only to political parties and elections, not to the politics of Washington policy-making.

It was rather surprising to discover how infrequently lobbyists participate in partisan political activities. Almost half of them have never been active in a party, and only about one-fourth continue to be active. Only eight have ever held an elective office, and only thirteen have ever been a candidate for elective office.[4] We will return to this general point after discussing specific types of political behavior of lobbyists.

[4]*For a detailed breakdown of political activities engaged in by respondents, see Milbrath (1958).*

PARTY PREFERENCE

Respondents were asked if they generally think of themselves as Republicans, Democrats, Independents, or what, and whether they are strong or not very strong partisans. Those saying initially that they were Independents were asked if they lean toward one party or another. The breakdown of these responses is shown in Table IV–7. Southerners who said that they were Democrats locally but Republicans nationally were classified as presidential Republicans.

TABLE IV–7

Party Preference by Type of Organization Represented

PARTY PREFERENCE	Labor	Farm	Large Trade	Small Trade	Corpora- tion	Other	Total
Strong Democrat	6			7		4	17
Weak Democrat	5	2		5	5	5	22
Independent — Democrat	3			4			7
Independent — no leaning	2	1	1	3			7
Independent — Republican		1	2	4	3	2	12
Weak Republican		1	2	8	3	4	18
Strong Republican			3	8	2	2	15
Presidential Republican					1	2	3
No response	2		1	3	2	5	13
TOTAL	18	5	9	43	17	22	114

The column headers under *TYPE OF ORGANIZATION* span Large Trade, Small Trade, Corpora-tion.

Democratic leanings = 46
Republican leanings = 48
Independents = 7

Strong partisans = 32
Weak partisans = 69

The party with which a man identifies appears to be relatively unimportant in lobbying. Forty-six respondents lean Democratic and forty-eight lean Republican. Party preference does relate to the type of organization a lobbyist represents. (See Table IV-7.)

Among labor representatives fourteen lean Democratic, two are Independent, and none is a Republican. Business representatives (trade associations and corporations) on the other hand, include thirty-eight Republican preferences to twenty-one Democratic. The other types of groups show almost an even split between the parties. These labor-business differences probably reflect the political leanings of the members of the groups. A man need not belong to the "right" political party to be chosen as a lobbyist; however, organizations have policy positions and are reluctant to hire men who disagree with them.

As noted earlier, lobbyists characteristically play down their partisan preferences. There are more than twice as many weak as strong partisans. Although this ratio is not very different from that of the general population, the general population is much less concerned with politics than are lobbyists. Some lobbyists believe they must play down their partisanship to avoid antagonizing persons who might be making decisions of importance to them. This fear is easily inflated; most members of Congress do not resent a person of the opposite party; they resent only a partisan who tries to use a contact for partisan advantage. As one lobbyist put it: "I don't want to get labeled too heavily. I don't want to get the people in Congress to feeling that I am sticking my nose into their election activities."

Voting surveys of the general population have repeatedly shown that people of higher socio-economic status (SES) are more likely to vote Republican.[5] Lobbyists, however, tend to fall almost uniformly in the upper-middle SES category; consequently, the SES variance in the sample is too small for factors such as education, occupation, income, and self-class identification to show any relationship to partisan preference. Even income, which covers a considerable range among lobbyists, is not related to party preference.

One curious relationship did develop: Republicans are significantly more likely to believe unqualifiedly that lobbying is healthy for our democracy. Whether a person is a strong or a weak partisan is unrelated to this question. There is no hint from the data to explain why Republicans and Democrats should differ in this respect. One can only speculate that Democrats are gen-

[5]*Campbell et al. (1960, chap. xiii).*

erally more concerned with reform and change and may be less inclined to give blanket approval to existing institutions.

Strength of party preference is highly correlated with having been active in a political party. Voting surveys of the national electorate show this same general relationship. Strong party preference is probably a psychological prerequisite for a person to invest precious time and energy in a campaign unless he is being paid for it or it is an essential aspect of his job. Rather clear evidence indicates that party activity is not an essential aspect of a lobbyist's job.

PARTY ACTIVITY

We hypothesized that lobbyists would become active partisans because they would conceive of party activity as a means to preferment for the groups they represent. The data refute the hypothesis; lobbyists are not very active. Groups may seek preferment by assisting candidates in their campaigns, but that usually is the job of men other than the lobbyists. Lobbyists also do not have a very high opinion of the role of political parties in making public policy. Only about one-third of the respondents believe parties have "considerable importance" in making public policy. Nearly all of them think that the President, the executive branch, and the Congress are much more important than parties in making policy. Fifty-eight per cent of the respondents report no contact whatsoever with political party officials as they carry on their lobbying activities. Sixty-two per cent of the respondents say that the organization they represent has never presented its views before a platform committee of one of the national party conventions.

As indicated earlier, prior political activity is related to recruitment for a lobbying job and to the duties a man performs in his organization. Among those who think they were recruited for their knowledge of the legislative or political process or for their wide circle of contacts, about 80 per cent have been active in a party; among those recruited for other reasons less than 50 per cent have been active. The party actives are also slightly more likely to have sought their lobby jobs.

A concern with politics and party activity seems to arise from something more fundamental and earlier in time than performance in a lobbying job. Evidence presented in Chapter V shows that personality traits affect the level of a man's activity in politics.[6] Persons who have been active in politics often report that their interest in public affairs was stimulated at home or in school, whereas persons who have never been active in a party tend to report that they developed their interest while working at lobbying. If they could start all over, respondents who have been active in politics pick occupations that are closely tied to law and politics—such as senator, congressman, attorney, and judge. Those who have not been active more often pick jobs relating to business—such as corporation executive and proprietor.

The position held before becoming a lobbyists is also related to being active in politics: Former labor union employees, political officeholders, practicing lawyers, or those who have worked on the Hill are the most likely to have been active in politics. Those working on the Hill have generally engaged in political activity of all kinds as a normal part of their jobs.

The role the respondent plays for his employer is only slightly related to party activity: Trade association executives and lobbyist entrepreneurs are not likely to be active; however, those in other roles are not necessarily extremely active. This lack of pattern supports the point that likelihood of party activity depends more on upbringing and personality that on holding a lobbying job. Once again, there is not enough variance in socioeconomic status among lobbyists for party activity to be related to SES variables.

Party activity affects the way lobbyists evaluate the effectiveness of campaign work and money contributions as lobbying tactics. Active party members rate these two tactics higher. They may do this to justify their activity, but they may also be in a better position to see the impact of these tactics. The data do not enable us to determine which explanation is most accurate.

OFFICE-HOLDING

The seeking, winning, and holding of public and party office is the height of political activity. Only those most involved in politics try to become office holders. Only thirteen respondents have ever been candidates for public office: eight have held elec-

[6]See also Milbrath and Klein (1962).

tive public office, and five of the eight have also held appointive office. Twenty-nine have held appointive public office, nineteen of them at the federal level. The predominance of appointive office in the political backgrounds of lobbyists recalls an earlier finding that lobbyists are more likely to be recruited from the executive branch than from the legislative branch.

Twenty-four respondents have also held an official party position at one time or another, but only seven held such a position at the time they were interviewed. About two-thirds of these positions (seventeen) were at the local or state level. Curiously, the representatives of small labor, farm, and trade associations are more likely to have held a party position than the representatives of large organizations in each of these categories. Conversely, the representatives of large organizations and corporations are more likely to have held appointive public office. The data are not adequate to explain the origin of this difference. One might conjecture that large organizations are in a position to offer sufficient salary and prestige to attract lobbyists from appointive office. On the other hand, no plausible explanation comes to mind for the fact that representatives of smaller organizations are more likely to have held a party position.

It was noted above that persons with experience on the Hill are more likely to have been active in a party. They are also more likely to have been a candidate for public office and to have held public office. Six of the eight people who have held elective office have had experience on the Hill; only three are former members. Curiously, there is no relationship between working on the Hill and holding a party position. This finding, plus the one showing that party positions are more likely to be held by representatives of small rather than large organizations, suggests that there is little relationship between holding a position in a party and being selected for public office, especially appointive office. Further testing of this proposition on other populations is needed to spell out its limitations more fully; it may only be an artifact of this particular sample.

Another clue to the puzzle is supplied by a finding that those who have held a party position are significantly more likely to seek a lobby position than to be pressured into it. Those who have held public office also tend to have sought a lobby job, but the difference is not significant. These bits of evidence reinforce the conclusion that people who are well acquainted with politics find it congenial to move into lobbying.

CONTRIBUTING AND FUND-RAISING FOR PARTIES

Political contributing is the most widely participated in of all the political activities reported by the lobbyists—aside from voting. Only twenty-nine have never made a political contribution; most of these represent business or farm organizations. More than half of the lobbyists report having made three or more contributions in the past five years. The average size of the contributions is rather modest. Almost half average less than $50. Only twenty-four have contributed an average of $100 or more, and only three give an average of $500 or more. Considering the fact that the median income for the lobbyists is in the $15,000 to $19,999 category, these contributions are not very large. Size of income shows no relationship to the likelihood of contributing or to the number of contributions. For example, nine people with incomes in the $25,000 to $49,999 category have never made a political contribution. Size of income, however, correlates (.40) with size of contributions. Only lobbyists making more than $25,000 a year give average donations of $500 or more.

The representatives of labor organizations tend to make the greatest number of contributions, but the average size is rather small. Labor lobbyists are unique in that they alone give to a political fund set up and run within their own pressure group. Business lobbyists tend to make fewer contributions, but the average size is larger than that of labor lobbyists. Business lobbyists spread their contributions over all levels of government; whereas labor lobbyists focus theirs on the national government. The representatives of farm organizations are unlikely to make any political contributions. Representatives of other types of lobby organizations do contribute, but there are so few cases in each type that it is difficult to generalize further.

Lawyers who lobby for a fee and who generally have the highest incomes, also make the largest contributions, although they do not make a larger number of contributions. Officers of organizations, many of them labor union officers, make the greatest number of individual contributions. Other than these expected relationships, the role of the lobbyist as he relates to his employer shows little relationship to political contributing.

What is the difference between lobbyists who contribute to parties and candidates and those who do not? Generally, those lobbyists or lobby organization who are close to a political party contribute. Lobbyists reporting personal contact with party officials are particularly likely to contribute. Labor lobbyists are usually more active in politics; all of the labor lobbyists make contributions. Nearly all of the non-contributors work for business or farm organizations; they are also completely uninvolved in partisan politics.

Second, a political contribution is viewed by some persons as a weapon of political battle. All but one of the persons who went into lobbying to promote a policy have made political contributions. Labor lobbyists tend to be policy-oriented, and all of them contribute. Persons with messianic personality traits are also more likely to make political contributions; however, this relationship is not statistically significant.[7]

Third, some persons' moral scruples forbid participation in certain 'types of political activities, especially the contribution of money. One of the personality scales discussed in Chapter V is a scale of moral rigidity. It measures how strongly and rigidly persons feel about their moral principles. Although some who score "very moral" on this scale do make political contributions; persons inclined toward "amorality" are significantly more likely to contribute and to contribute more often.

In addition to the three variables mentioned, other factors may distinguish contributors from non-contributors; for example, some persons may use contributions to assure access to decision-makers.[8] We do, however, have reasonably reliable information on these three factors, and they were found to relate to political contributing in another study.[9]

About 42 per cent of the lobbyists have assisted in the raising of political funds. The task of raising funds generally falls upon persons who are highly involved in a political party or campaign. For example, having raised funds is significantly related to experience on the Hill. Helping to raise funds is part of the job of many staff aides to members of Congress. Persons not closely

---

[7]See Chapter V.

[8]See Chapter XIII.

[9]For a more elaborate discussion of the motivations of political contributors, see Heard (1960, chaps., iii, iv). Also see Milbrath (1956).

involved in a party or a campaign, such as most trade association executives, seldom are drafted for fund-raising.

Like political contributions, fund-raising may be used as a weapon or tactic in political battle. Eighty per cent of those who became lobbyists to promote a policy have raised funds for a political party. People who wanted to be lobbyists are more likely to have raised funds than those pressured into the job. Some respondents use the contacts and facilities of their pressure group to help raise money. These include not only the labor representatives, who make it a regular practice, but also certain business representatives. Business lobbyists are careful to solicit on an ostensibly personal basis—not in the name of the organization. Nevertheless, it is clear that the raising of campaign war chests is the most popular means of unofficial participation by lobby groups in political campaigns.

To get a clearer indication of the concern of lobby organizations with political campaigns the organizations were reclassified on the basis of their power at the polls. They were rated on the size of their membership, their monetary resources, and their concern with the election outcome. The scores on these three variables were then added to create a single score called "power at the polls."[10] There was a discernible but not significant correlation between power at the polls and most of the political activities of respondents. However, contributing money and raising funds are strikingly and significantly correlated with power at the polls. Lobbyists for groups with considerable power at the polls are more likely to contribute, to contribute often, and to raise funds. Again, the provision of funds appears to be the major way that lobby organizations participate in campaigns, and fund-raising is the only activity which most lobbyists are expected to perform in campaigns. The division of labor in most pressure groups is such that lobbyists need not engage in other types of political party activity; if lobbyists do participate in other ways, they do so of their own volition.

The impact on public policy, if any, of these political activities, especially the fund-raising activies, is elusive. The data needed to determine the effects are not available; we have no tools to measure the impact of factors going into public policy. How-

---

[10]*For details, see the last item in the code reproduced in the Appendix.*

ever, certain evidence gleaned from interview notes sheds some light on this question. For one thing, most organizations urge their members to concentrate their contributions on specific candidates for office instead of on party committees. One respondent urges his membership to make contributions mainly to candidates in primary elections on the ground that they are more likely to be remembered:

A $50 contribution in the primary is of more value than $1,000 in the general election. The prospective congressman is going to be much more likely to remember the contribution which was made when he really needed it, when all of the assurances were not already there that he would win. I urge my people to get in on this primary angle even if they have to give to people on both sides.

Another respondent argues that it is more economical to give money to candidates for the House than for the Senate or the Presidency. "A group with limited resources can more likely be remembered by a congressional candidate who is generally forgotten in the scramble for campaign funds. It is from the congressmen that we get our favors, too." This respondent solicits funds in his own name rather than in the name of the organization. "We make [register] contributions in our own name for some of our people [members] who don't want to be recorded as contributing."

Some respondents contribute in the hope of gaining timely access to decision-makers. One respondent reported:

Every congressman's secretary has a list of people who can always call or get in contact with the congressman. Whenever you phone that office the secretary says, "Oh, yes, the congressman is in," or if you send a letter, the secretary puts it on the congressman's desk. If you come in to make a personal call, instead of saying, "The congressman is on the floor" or "the congressman is busy," she will go in to the congressman and put your card in front of him. At least in that way you have entree when you need it. The point of the contribution in the primary is that one has set his entree up in advance so that whenever he wants to get something done he does not have to tear down a barrier first.

As much as the foregoing appears to be expected lobbyist behavior, this point of view is not shared by many lobbyists. This particular lobbyist is of "the old school" that believes that entertainment, parties, and campaign contributions are the major devices effective in winning the cooperation of governmental decision-makers. Actually, there are many alternatives, and most lobbyists are not highly in favor of the use of campaign contributions.[11]

One is so accustomed to thinking that campaign contributors want their gifts known to the recipient that it is somewhat surprising to discover that some groups build war chests and donate them anonymously. The actual words of a respondent are perhaps most adequate to convey the rationale for this practice:

> Every once in a while people in Congress whom we respect get in difficulty during an election and need money. In such a situation we will generally contact our members in the district and ask them to contribute. We also ask each of them to call five other people and try to get them to conribute. We start the thing rolling and then we walk away from it. In most cases the member does not even know we have gone in to help him. [Why don't you tell him?] We feel that he might be embarrassed and we don't want to embarrass him. Generally, we feel that we are in a stronger position if he is not embarrassed. If he gets the impression that whenever we come down to talk to him that we are trying to take advantage of the $2,000 we put into his campaign, he is going to say to us, "Well you can't own me just because you gave me $2,000," and probably in the long run we would lose more than we would gain by this kind of activity.

The words of the respondents have given us an understanding of what many lobbyists think they are accomplishing through contributions. Another bit of evidence appears in the cross-tabulations of contributing and the answers to a question about whether decision-makers consult lobbyists about policy. Contributors are more likely to be sought out for advice on a wide range of policy issues; whereas non-contributors are usually asked

[11]*See Part Three, esp. Chapter XIII.*

only about views relating to their own organization. These data suggest that contributing is but one part of a larger and very complex pattern of interpersonal relationships between lobbyists and governmental decision-makers. The lobbyist who is, or manages to become, a confidant of a decision-maker has a multitude of personal ties. In such an instance, campaign contributions are likely to be the outgrowth of the relationship rather than the major factor setting up the connection.[12]

SUMMARY

In evaluating the political activities of lobbyists it is necessary to reiterate the distinction between the political behavior of lobbyists as individuals and the political activities of the groups they represent. In general, lobby groups are concerned about the outcome of election campaigns and the policy orientations of the parties. Some groups with large membership and monetary resources regularly do their best to affect the outcome of elections. Most lobby groups, however, prefer to avoid involvement in elections, primarily on the ground that there are more efficacious means to achieve their objectives. For example, less than 20 per cent of the lobbyists said their groups regularly present their views to the platform committees of the parties.

More than 50 per cent of the individual lobbyists have been somewhat involved with political parties, and a few of them were picked for their jobs because of this experience. The striking fact, however, is that nearly half of them have had little or no experience in party politics, and many of those with prior experience dropped their political activity when they became lobbyists. As one formerly very active respondent put it, "The more I get into heavy lobbying, the less I stay in politics." Even those who continue their political activities do so primarily because of their interests as citizens rather than as a result of their lobbying job or in hopes of achieving something related to their job. The conclusion is inescapable that political party activity generally is not a necessary part of a lobbyist job.

[12]*For a full discussion of this problem, see Heard (1960, esp. chap. ii). The topic of the impact of political money-giving will be examined further, along with a variety of other influences, later in the book, especially in Chapters XIII and XVII.*

There are several reasons for this, some of which have been alluded to previously. For one thing, most lobbyists believe that political parties, as institutions organized to conduct political campaigns, have little influence on public policy. Some of them think that the congressional parties have some influence on certain issues, but they attribute practically no influence to the national committees of the parties. More than half the respondents reported no contacts whatsoever with party officials. Even where lobbyists believe that it is important for the members of their group to become active in political campaigns and to elect men favorable to the policy of the group, they usually do not feel personally compelled to be active. In other words, lobbyists do not think that personal political activity pays off in the kind of influence they are seeking.

Even if a lobbyist desires to become or remain active, the demands of his job make this difficult. In our system of fifty state political parties, a base inside a state is generally essential to maintaining effective activity; the full-time lobbyist in Washington finds it difficult to be on his state base enough to maintain his influence. Some large lobby organizations introduce division of labor to handle more adequately the many aspects of pressure politics; they may have one staff for legislative activities, another for relations with the executive branch, and another for political action. The national AFL-CIO is a good example.

In contrast to those lobbyists who feel that their personal political participation has only a minor relationship to their job, some think that partisan political action will hurt them in their jobs. We noted above that most members of Congress are broad-minded and fair in dealing with persons belonging to the opposite political party. However, most lobbyists are careful not to give the impression that they are intensely active in a party or that they might be using their lobbying contacts and activities for partisan advantage.

From the lobbyist's point of view, then, they deliberately choose not to become or remain active in a political party either because there is little to be accomplished by doing so or because the activity might defeat their purposes. Those who engage in political action do so for personal reasons.

CHAPTER V

PERSONAL ATTRIBUTES OF
LOBBYISTS

This chapter examines the social, economic, and personality characteristics of lobbyists—whether they are different from ordinary people, and, if so, in what ways. In some respects, lobbyists show the same variety of characteristics as the general population. They are male and female, old and young, extrovert and introvert, successful and unsuccessful, and so forth. As a special political skill group, however, they differ in important respects from the general population. The differences may be better illuminated if we show what lobbyists in this sample are not. None of them is a blue-collar worker; only one respondent placed himself in the lower or working class; most placed themselves in the upper-middle class; none in the sample is Negro; none ended his education at the elementary level; only two have incomes of less than $5,000.

Respondents were asked if they could think of a group of traits that seem to characterize most lobbyists they knew. They generally had difficulty with this question. Many of them had never thought about it before, and their on-the-spot reflections did not produce anything approaching a majority view. Typical responses pointed out very superficial characteristics and were not insightful or introspective. In fact, the interviewing experience disclosed that lobbyists, on the whole, are not very introspective people.

About 33 per cent of the respondents could think of no traits whatsoever that characterized most lobbyists; another 33 per cent mentioned the ability to interact well with people; and the remaining group listed such scattered characteristics as manipulativeness, skill with words, intelligence, patience, and ability to "roll with the punches." One particularly perceptive respondent gave the following answer:

> I would say that the I.Q.'s of most lobbyists are approaching or just short of genius. Most of them would be able to maintain a high B average in a college of mathematics. Most desire to participate in making news that winds up on the front page the next day. This is not quite the same thing as Reisman's "inside dopesters." Lobbyists are extremely knowledgeable from an educational and experience standpoint; in other words, they are pretty sharp guys. Almost invariably, they are people of pretty high social intelligence and of pretty low mechanical aptitude. They are much higher than the average in their ability to communicate, and this is more than simple articulation; it is an ability to form ideas and words so that they get across in the most telling manner. Many of them also have a contagious enthusiasm. On the other hand, I can think of successful exceptions to all of these various characteristics. I know people who do not have certain of these traits and yet they have been very successful lobbyists.

As the respondent pointed out, very few lobbyists live up to the ideal characterization. We shall turn now to a more specific examination of the personal qualities of lobbyists.

SOCIO-ECONOMIC CHARACTERISTICS

SOCIO-ECONOMIC STATUS

Since our sample is confined to persons in a narrowly defined occupational group, most belong to the same socio-economic class.

(Class here is a combination of income, education, and occupation.) Two measures of class were used: respondents were asked to select the one of four classes to which they thought they belonged, and the interviewer also observed the class of respondents. The results of these two ratings are reported in Table V–1. The table reflects the class uniformity that a single occupation imposes. By either measure, the vast majority of lobbyists are in the upper-middle class. The interviewer's judgments show even less variance than respondent's self-choice; this probably reflects the interviewer's more constant standard.

TABLE V–1

Comparison of Class Status Selected by Respondent
and Class Status Assigned by the Interviewer

CLASS STATUS	R's Choice of Class	Interviewer's Judgment of Class
Upper	11	6
Upper-middle	77	103
Lower-middle	12	4
Lower	1	0
No response	13	1
TOTAL	114	114

These measures of class are positively and significantly related to actual income and education. The correlations fall in the .40-to-.50 range. Another cross-tabulation shows that income and education are positively and significantly related to each other (see Table V–3), but the correlation is sufficiently low (.27) to indicate that each makes an independent contribution to class status. Further evidence that income and education are only partial indicators of class is shown by the fact that persons who place themselves in the upper-middle class have incomes ranging from $4,000 to above $50,000, and educations ranging from some high school to the Ph.D. Persons who place themselves in the upper class do not have incomes of less than $10,000 or less education than college. Persons who place themselves in the lower-middle class have incomes as high as $20,000 and educations as high as graduate or professional training; most, however, have not finished college.

Class status shows little relationship to the nature of the organization represented or to the role of the lobbyist to his employer. Labor representatives tend slightly to place themselves in the lower-middle class, and lawyers in large law firms and lobbyist entrepreneurs frequently place themselves in the upper class. Class status does not correlate significantly with certain other variables in the study because there is so little class variance in the lobbyist sample.

A closer look at the income characteristics of respondents is represented in Table V-2, where the annual income of respondents is cross-tabulated with the percentage of income they receive from lobbyist organizations or clients. First, the marginal frequencies show that respondents' incomes range from less than $5,000 to nearly $100,000. The median income falls in the $15,000 to $19,999 category. About 29 per cent have incomes above $25,000, and 5 per cent have incomes above $50,000. About 50 per cent of the respondents receive nearly all of their income from lobby clients. More than 75 per cent of those with incomes of less than $15,000 receive at least 80 per cent of their income from lobby clients. People in the higher income brackets tend significantly to receive less of their income from lobby clients. Seventy-five per cent of those with incomes above $50,000 receive less than 20 per cent of their income from lobby clients. Those receiving only a small percentage of income from lobby clients are usually lawyers who have a variety of clients. Lawyers also tend to rank high in over-all income. This relates to another finding that those who were paid fees instead of a salary generally had higher incomes.

Only a few respondents obtained a small proportion of their income from lobby clients; in fact, only six received less than 5 per cent of their incomes from lobby clients. Yet, thirty-nine respondents had registered as receiving no salary or fee with the Clerk of the House and the Secretary of the Senate. These data strongly suggest that the Lobby Registration Act which requires reporting of income from lobby clients either is interpreted differently from organization to organization or is being regularly violated. Those receiving a small percentage of their income from lobby clients tend to report no salary or fee at all on their regis-

TABLE V-2

Annual Income Compared by Percentage of Income from Lobbyist Clients

PERCENTAGE OF INCOME FROM LOBBY CLIENTS	INCOME BEFORE TAXES								Total
	Under $5,000	$5,000 to $9,999	$10,000 to $14,999	$15,000 to $19,999	$20,000 to $24,999	$25,000 to $49,999	$50,000 and Over	No Response	
Less than 20		2	2	1	1	4	3		13
20 to 49		1	1	3	2	3			10
50 to 64		1		1	1	4	1		8
65 to 79				4	2	1			7
80 to 95		1	5	2	1	2			11
Above 95	2	8	14	10	5	10			49
No response		1			1		1	13	16
TOTAL	2	14	22	21 ↑ median	13	24	5	13	114

tration forms. Fourteen additional respondents who get nearly all of their income from lobby clients report no salary or fee whatsoever on the official forms. This wholesale failure to report, combined with the fact that many respondents receive only part of their income from lobby groups, explains why there was no correlation (.0047) between respondent's income and his reported salary or fees on the lobby reports.[1]

The size of a respondent's income was related to the kind of organization he represents. Representatives of church and humanitarian organizations are the lowest paid, and lobbyists for large citizens' organizations are next lowest. The highest incomes (all of them over $25,000) belong to those who represent more than one type of organization. Generally, the business representatives are paid more than labor or farm representatives: the median income for business representatives is a little above $20,000; whereas that for labor and farm representatives is between $10,000 and $15,000.

Income also varies with the role a respondent plays for his employer. Lawyers and lobbyist entrepreneurs, who are usually paid fees for their services, generally receive the highest incomes. Trade association executives are also quite well paid; three-fourths of them earn over $20,000 per year. The lowest incomes are generally earned by Washington representatives of small organizations which cannot afford either a large staff or high salaries.

The size of a respondent's income affects his judgment concerning his success as a lobbyist. Respondents with incomes above $15,000 are significantly more likely to say that their personal success had been good. On the other hand, size of income is not related to a respondent's appraisal of whether lobbying is good or bad for society.

As mentioned earlier, income is positively and significantly related to education (see Table V–3). Most of the respondents who earn more than $20,000 received some training beyond college. High education, however, does not guarantee a high income; some of the lowest-paid lobbyists have very good educations. Lawyers are uniformly well-educated. Although respondents playing other roles are not uniformly as well-educated, the lowest median education rank for any role is graduation from college. Clearly, extensive education is a virtual prerequisite for lobbying.

[1]*See Chapter XVI for further development of the enforcement problem.*

TABLE V-3
Education Compared with Income

EDUCATION	Under $5,000	$5,000 to $9,999	$10,000 to $14,999	$15,000 to $19,999	$20,000 to $24,999	$25,000 to $49,999	$50,000 and Over	No Response	Total
				INCOME BEFORE-TAXES					
Some high school			3	1	1				5
Finished high school			4	1	1	1			7
Some college	1	3	2	4		4			14
Finished college		4	2	3		2			11
Graduate or professional training	1	1	5	1	2	5	1		16
Professional degree		4	4	11	9	9	4	4	45
Ph.D. or equivalent		1	2			3		1	7
No response		1						8	9
TOTAL	2	14	22	21	13	24	5	13	114

r = .27

OTHER PERSONAL CHARACTERISTICS

Table V–4 shows the ages of the lobbyist respondents; they vary from twenty-eight to eighty-seven. Almost 75 per cent of them are between forty and sixty. The oldest are often officers of lobby organizations; the youngest are frequently legislative and executive relations staff members. In general, however, age does not significantly separate respondents into various roles. Most

TABLE V–4

**Age of
Lobbyists**

AGE	NUMBER
20–29	1
30–39	8
40–49	38
50–59	35
60–69	15
70–up	5
No response	12
TOTAL	114

Median = 50–59

lobbyists are men; only 7 of the 114 in the sample are women. Women tend to be paid less than men, some of them working only part-time. Women are more likely to work for humanitarian and moral causes.

Since only one Oriental and no Negroes were found in the sample, race could not be used as a variable in the analysis. There undoubtedly are some colored lobbyists, but these few generally represent a racially identified cause. Religion, marital status, and size of family apparently are not important variables affecting the roles lobbyists play. Religion is not related to family size, but it is slightly related to party preference. Baptist and Jewish persons seem to prefer the Democratic party, Catholics tend to be Independent, and Episcopalians seem to prefer the Republican party. These relationships accord with findings from voter surveys. It is also interesting to note that persons who had no religious identification were usually weak partisans.

Another related finding is that Independents are decidedly

less active in non-political groups than are partisans. Respondents with careers in politics or business prior to their lobbying careers are more active in groups than those with other careers. Generally, however, depth of activity in non-political groups shows little relationship to lobbying activities. One exception was a finding that lobbyists who are quite active in non-political groups are solicited significantly more often for their views on policy by governmental decision-makers than are lobbyists who are not very active in groups.

The socio-economic characteristics of lobbyists can be summarized rather briefly. There is considerable uniformity of SES; nearly all are upper-middle. Lobbyists have very high incomes and educations compared to the general population. Most are middle-aged, white, male, and Protestant. People of this type in the general population tend to be quite active in the group life of their communities; the same seems to be true of lobbyists. The wide variance of general group activity among lobbyists suggests that group interaction outside the immediate working situation has little relationship to the lobbyist job. In general, one can say that socio-economic characteristics do not go very far in explaining how lobbyists differ from other segments of the population.

PERSONALITY CHARACTERISTICS

Is there something distinctive about the personalities of persons who are selected to be lobbyists or of those who are especially successful in their lobbying jobs? Two methods of gathering information on this point were used. First, respondents were asked what traits characterize lobbyists, especially successful lobbyists. Second, respondents were asked to fill out a 100-item personality test which was left with them at the conclusion of the interview. The test was designed to measure certain traits hypothesized to be distinctive about lobbyists. The completed form was returned by 89 of the 101 respondents.

We noted at the beginning of the chapter that questioning lobbyists about traits characteristic of lobbyists was not very productive. Their answers were not particularly introspective or insightful. One respondent trained as a psychologist gave the following (paraphrased) response. One common trait of lobbyists, he observed, is a need to identify with social change or to attempt to influence the course of events in some way. This trait is related to the lobbyist's desire to enhance his own appraisal of his self-worth. Many lobbyists need to see an appreciation of themselves reflected in the people they encounter. They need to be constantly reassured that they are doing a useful and desirable job and that people like them. "Lobbyists need to have a continuing validation of their adequacy as a human being in our culture." This is probably especially important because the profession is disapproved by the public at large. The common cliché that lobbyists are gregarious probably stems in part from the lobbyists' need to be well-liked. This respondent also thought that certain lobbyists tend to be reluctant to accept responsibility for decision-making. They prefer to work through other people, to influence their decisions but not take full decision responsibility.

Respondents' insights and the personality test indicate that there is no universal or general trait shared by *all* lobbyists. For every generalization one can find many exceptions. The same traits that lead to success in many professions tend to lead to success as a lobbyist. In summary, the successful lobbyist has traits such as these: He is honest, agreeable, capable, well-informed, gregarious, manipulative, communicative, and persistent.[2]

The personality test provided more systematic information relevant to our query. It contained part scales from certain scales in Harrison Gough's California Psychological Inventory (CPI)[3] plus a few additional scales and items to be discussed later. The data produced by this test are too voluminous to be fully reported in this chapter and are not all relevant to the topic; the discussion here will be confined to summaries of the findings.[4] Even this summary discussion must, of necessity, be somewhat technical; those

[2]*The characteristics of successful lobbyists will be discussed in detail at the conclusion of Chapter VI.*

[3]*The copyright on the 1956 version of the CPI is owned by the Consulting Psychologists' Press, Inc., Palo Alto, California. Permission to use the part scales was granted by Professor Gough and the Consulting Psychologists' Press. The part scales were drawn from the dominance, social presence, sociability, self-acceptance, self-control, and intellectual efficiency scales.*

[4]*Readers wishing a more detailed inventory of the findings should write the author for a copy of his "Measuring the Personalities of Lobbyists" (1960b). Also see Milbrath and Klein (1962).*

readers not interested in technical problems might skip ahead to the summary at the end of this section.

The CPI scales are especially useful because the CPI has been administered to many other groups; thus comparisons between lobbyists and these other groups are possible. Scores on the part scales used were obtained for a group of professional males, a group of college males, and a group of high school males. Part-whole correlations were computed for the part and full scales on the criterion groups; the correlations were sufficiently high (from .70 to .95) to indicate that the part scales measured substantially the same thing as the full scales. The CPI scales contain both negatively and positively scored items to control for response set bias.

Generally, the mean for the lobbyists on the CPI part scales is not very different from the means for the three criterion groups. The lobbyists rank higher than the high school male group and about the same as the college males and professional males on most of the part scales. Only on the dominance and the self-control scales do the lobbyists rank significantly higher than the three criterion groups. One general conclusion, then, is that lobbyists are not very different in their personalities than persons in other professional pursuits.

On a trait like sociability, which is important in the pursuit of their job, the lobbyists actually rank lower than professional males (mean score, 6.91 for professional males and 6.08 for lobbyists—significant at the .05 level of confidence) and about the same as college males (mean 5.94). This does not mean that sociability is not important to lobbying activities but rather that many of the people in lobbying are not exceptionally sociable when compared to other professional persons.

Lobbyists also rank lower on intellectual efficiency than professional males (mean score 7.22 for professional males and 6.44 for lobbyists—significant at the .05 level of confidence). On this trait as well, lobbyists are not exceptional.

Lobbyists do score higher than the other groups on dominance (mean score 14.75 for lobbyists compared with 12.82 for professional males—significant at the .05 level of confidence). Gough says that men with high scores on dominance are aggressive, confident, out-going, planful, self-reliant and tend to take initiative.[5] These characteristics would certainly be helpful in the execution of lobbying tasks, and many of the persons in the lobbyist sample rank high on this test. In contrast, however, lobbyists score higher on the so-called self-control scale than any of the criterion groups (mean score 6.49 for lobbyists and 5.62 for professional males—significant at the .05 level). These two findings are especially extraordinary because dominance and self-control are negatively correlated (−.37) for the lobbyist sample.[6] People who rank high on self-control tend to lack confidence and be conservative and withdrawn. How could lobbyists rank significantly higher than criterion groups on each of these two negatively correlated scales? Possibly the lobbyist sample contains some persons who score exceptionally high on dominance but low on self-control and still others who score exceptionally high on self-control but low on dominance. If this is correct (comparison of the lobbyist scores with the criterion groups suggests that it is), it is but another bit of evidence that lobbyists' personalities are considerably varied and divergent. Another possible explanation is that the measuring scales involved have low validity and do not measure what we think they measure.

It is difficult to interpret the meaning of psychological scores because the name given to a scale by the researcher may or may not convey to the reader what the researcher had in mind. Also, it may or may not be closely related to what the scale actually measures. For example, the researcher may call a trait self-control, whereas it may actually constitute withdrawal by the respondent into safe and routine behaviors. The latter explanation more closely fits all the facts on the lobbyist sample.

Several of the CPI scales on the lobbyist sample highly intercorrelated. The correlation matrix shown in Table V–5 shows intercorrelations sufficiently high to suggest that the sociability, social presence, self-acceptance, and self-control scales could be combined into a single score.[7] We might call this new broad dimension the "Sociality" syndrome. It does not distinguish lobbyists from persons in other professions, but it does distinguish lobbyists

---

[5]*For a more complete description and the presentation of validating information on this as well as other CPI scales, consult Gough (1957).*

[6]*Gough (1957, p. 33) reports a .01 correlation between the two full scales.*

[7]*Application of Guilford's correction for attenuation creates estimates of intercorrelation close to unity for all four scales. See Milbrath and Klein (1962).*

TABLE V–5

Intercorrelation Matrix on Five Gough Subscales

| | | SUBSCALE | | |
SUBSCALE	Dominance	Socia-bility	Social Presence	Self-Acceptance
Sociability	.51			
Social presence	.53	.71		
Self-acceptance	.49	.66	.64	
Self-control	—.37	—.56	—.64	—.67

who are active in partisan politics from those who abstain from political activity. The political actives seem to be more at ease socially, to have more social skills and greater ego strength, to like themselves better, and to participate more in social activities. Evidence from other studies suggests that this set of relationships characterizes other populations as well as lobbyists.[8]

Summing up the findings from the CPI scales, lobbyists apparently are not much different in the personality traits measured than other professional persons. The lobbyists score higher on dominance and self-control and lower on sociability and intellectual efficiency than a professional criterion group. The measuring scales are sufficiently fallible that one cannot be confident that similar results would be obtained in a repeat study. Several CPI scales were so highly intercorrelated that they were recombined into a single scale called Sociality, which effectively distinguishes political actives from non-actives; it does not, however, distinguish lobbyists from other professionals.

In addition to scales derived from Gough's scales in the CPI, two additional scales were administered to the respondents: the F scale and a "Mach" scale developed by Christie. The F scale was originally developed by researchers on the authoritarian personality,[9] but the version used on the lobbyists was revised by Christie and his associates to avoid problems of response-set bias.[10]

[8]*Milbrath and Klein (1962). Also see Milbrath (1960c).*
[9]*Adorno et al. (1950).*
[10]*Christie, Havel, and Seidenberg (1958).*

The newer version is a more reliable measure of authoritarian tendencies.

Christie reports that college students rank slightly lower on this version of the F scale than the lobbyists.[11] On the other hand, lobbyist F scale scores do not vary significantly from the scores of the college-educated portion of a national sample of voters.[12] Most lobbyists do not score particularly high or low on the F scale, and the variance in their scores is sufficient to suggest that members of the profession cannot be characterized as particularly authoritarian or equalitarian. Probably lobbyists vary to the same extent on this trait as the general population.

This F scale, however, does correlate with some interesting differences within the lobbyist population. Persons ranking high on F are disinclined to participate in a variety of ordinary political party activities. They are less likely to be active in a political party, less likely to campaign, less likely to make a political contribution (if they do contribute, they do so less often), and less likely to raise political funds; all of these differences are statistically significant.[13] In addition, high F lobbyists are less likely to rate the use of political contributions and campaign work as effective lobbying tactics.

Not only does this scale help to distinguish political actives from non-actives, it also separates lobbyists who are highly involved in and concerned about policy from those who are less so. High F lobbyists are significantly less likely to have considered policy an important factor in their decision to represent their organization; they are less committed to their organization's policy; and they are much less likely to have their policy views solicited by governmental decision-makers.

Ranking on the F scale is also related to the respondents, ratings of various tactics and techniques of lobbying. Orthodox tactics are accepted and used by all lobbyists, while other tactics are rejected by some lobbyists. Orthodox tactics (personal presentation of arguments, presenting research results, and testifying at

[11]*Personal letter to the author dated May 28, 1957. Also see Christie, Havel, and Seidenberg (1958).*
[12]*Based on scores derived from combining the positive and negative F scale items (Christie's version) administered by the Survey Research Center of the University of Michigan to a national sample of voters in the 1956 election.*
[13]*For further details, see Milbrath and Klein (1962).*

hearings) are rated higher by those scoring high on F than by those scoring low; unorthodox tactics (publicizing voting records, campaign work, giving political money, contacting decision-makers through a constituent or a friend) are rated lower by those scoring high on F than by those scoring low on F. Fear of the unorthodox fits our general knowledge of the personality dynamics of authoritarians.

The Mach scale developed by Christie has items based on concepts drawn from the writings of Niccolo Machiavelli. Christie is reluctant to call it the Machiavellian scale because of the load of connotations carried by that word. Here is how he describes what the scale measures:

> The items in the scale express a conception of human nature as fallible and weak, a lack of affect (i.e., the value of detachment in dealing with other people), and the use of expedient procedures in social relations. Those making a high score on the scale endorse such items and reject items of opposed kinds, such as those portraying human nature idealistically, emphasizing the need of warmth and affective involvement with other people, and holding that social relations should always be governed by strict adherence to ethical norms.
>
> The dimension appears to vary from a tough-minded philosophy of life (in William James' sense) to a tender-minded one, verging on a sentimental *Weltanschauung*.[14]

The items drawn from Christie's pool and used in the lobbyist study can be divided into two subscales: Mach tactics and Mach views. The two subscales do not always show relationships to the same variables, suggesting that they measure somewhat different things. Combining the two subscales into a total Mach scale produces a measure that does not seem to be as unidimensional nor as powerful as the separate subscales. This scale, as well as the F scale, contains both positively and negatively scored items for protection against response-set bias.

Experience with the Mach scales in the lobbyist study sug-

[14]*Christie and Merton (1958, p. 134). The development of the Mach scale is described by Christie (1956).*

gests that they are not powerful instruments for explaining the differences in lobbying roles exhibited by respondents or for indicating why people go into lobbying. The low correlations between Mach and other variables could arise because the scales are poor tools or because there actually is little relationship between political behavior and the Mach personality trait; unfortunately, the data do not indicate which interpretation is correct.

We have only preliminary comparisons between lobbyists and other populations on Mach; contrary to expectations, lobbyists tend to rank slightly lower on Mach than college students, especially medical students. This is another suggestion that lobbyists probably cannot be distinguished very readily from the general population by their personality traits.

The Mach scales were run against a variety of lobbyist behaviors to see whether they would differentiate among lobbying roles. The tactics scale correlates slightly with certain evaluations of tactics. Those ranking high on tactics tend to rate orthodox tactics lower than those scoring low on tactics. High scorers on tactics tend to rate unorthodox tactics higher than low scorers. These findings conform with theoretical expectations.

We would also expect that those scoring high on Mach would more likely be active in a political party than those scoring low; yet Mach shows no significant relationship to party activity. Either the scales are weak or there actually is no relationship to party activity.

Another set of cross-tabulations produces expected results. Those scoring high on tactics spend more time with members of Congress, more time entertaining, and more time talking with people in the localities. Perhaps something like a Mach trait does affect lobbying behavior; unfortunately, the Mach scales used in this study seem to be too weak to enable reliable investigation.

In addition, the author attempted to create some new scales by Guttman techniques using some of the Gough items and ten new items. Five of these scales produced sufficiently interesting results to be worth discussing briefly here.[15] A "Messianic-Cynical" scale shows that lobbyists who were oriented toward doing good are significantly more likely to say that they are strongly committed to the policy of their organization and that the

---

[15]*For details of method and item content, see Milbrath (1960b).*

policy is an important consideration in their decision to represent the organization. Messianics tend to play a significantly greater role in making the policy of their organization. They are also more likely to have their personal views on policy solicited by governmental decision-makers. Another group of cross-tabulations indicate that messianic lobbyists are more eager to use unorthodox partisan political tactics such as making political contributions and working in campaigns to achieve their lobbying objectives.

A "Morally Rigid-Amoral" scale is both similar to and different from the Messianic-Cynical scale. The cynics seem to be much like the amorals, but the messianics act differently from those who score morally rigid. The messianics are eager to use partisan political tactics, but the morally rigid are significantly less likely to make political contributions or to raise political funds than the amorals. Certain people commonly refuse to contribute to parties out of a sense of moral righteousness. Publicizing the voting records of members of Congress is also considered morally wrong by many lobbyists. Morally rigid respondents are significantly more likely to rate this tactic low than are the amoral lobbyists. It is also interesting to compare these two scales when each is cross-tabulated with the F scale. The cynics tend to score higher on F than the messianics, but the morally rigid score higher on F than the amoral. This is exactly the pattern to be expected if all three scales are measuring what they are intended to measure.

The "Esteem" scale seems to measure self-esteem as well as a desire to receive esteem from others. Lobbyists who score high on esteem are significantly more likely to have sought their lobbying position, to desire to stay in lobbying, and to say that their success as a lobbyist has been good. Those desiring esteem are much more likely to use political tactics and to be spirited participants in political and other group activities. Lobbyists scoring low on esteem are much more likely to prefer orthodox tactics of direct communication to decision-makers than are those scoring high on esteem. The esteem scale is about as effective as the Sociality syndrome and the F scale in separating political party participants from non-participants among the lobbyists. It is highly correlated (.64) with the Sociality syndrome and seems to measure much the same thing. It is often suggested that lobbyists probably have a "passion for anonymity" because they like to "pull strings" behind the scenes. Results from the Esteem scale suggest exactly the opposite interpretation; persons holding lobbying jobs want esteem—not anonymity.

It was hypothesized that lobbyists have a high tolerance for frustration since so many of their objectives cannot be obtained or must be postponed. A "Tolerance of Frustration" scale produces a bit of evidence tending to confirm the hypothesis. Those scoring high on tolerance of frustration tend to find lobbying more congenial; they are more likely to have sought a lobbying position; they more frequently report that they intend to stay in lobbying; and they are more likely to feel a sense of professionalism. Scores on this scale are also correlated with the way lobbyists spend their time. Those who are more tolerant of frustration spend less time in the office, less time on research, more time on the Hill, and more time calling on members of Congress. Calling on people on the Hill may result in considerable waiting and disappointment; thus, the person who has difficulty tolerating frustration is somewhat more likely to retreat to the security and manageability of work in his own office.

It was mentioned earlier that lobbyists tend to resist introspection and that possibly this might be functional for continuation in their jobs. Since this generalization developed out of the interviewing experience, specific introspective items had not been devised or selected for the personality test. A short, three-item scale adapted from the Gough items performs reasonably well. Introspective lobbyists (as measured by this scale) are significantly more likely to play a major role in the policy decisions of their organization, to be more strongly committed to organization policy, and to report that policy figured importantly in their decision to represent the organization. Introspectives are also more likely to see something bad in lobbying. These results accord with theoretical expectations. Since we do not have scores on this scale for other groups, we do not know whether lobbyists are more or less introspective than the general population. It does seem, however, that lack of introspection might serve a useful function in the psychic economy of certain lobbyists.

From time to time, we have noted that lobbyists with certain personality traits are more likely than others to play special roles. We find, in this connection, that lobbyists who are active in partisan politics, for example, are more likely to be sociable, equalitarian (opposite of F), dominant, desirous of esteem, and intellectually efficient. Another role differentiation is a concern with policy. Some lobbyists are very interested in policy matters; they consider carefully the policy of their organization before they agree to represent it; they participate very actively in the formation of policy in their organization; and they tend to be consulted on policy matters by governmental decision-makers. Such persons are very much like the persons who are active in a political party; they tend to be dominant, sociable, self-accepting, messianic, and introspective. They tend to rank low on the self-control and F scales, just as the political actives do. There is probably a functional connection between activity in partisan politics and role in policy formation.

Respondents' evaluations of certain tactics and techniques for communicating with governmental decision-makers are also affected by personality traits, although in this instance there is no general pattern one can point to. We saw earlier that high F persons rate orthodox tactics higher than unorthodox; much the same is true of morally rigid persons. Sociable lobbyists tend to emphasize and rate highly those tactics that require social interaction, such as collaboration with other groups and campaign work; they rate lower certain non-sociable tactics, such as testifying at hearings and the presentation of research results. Personality, then, can be an important factor in determining how a lobbyist evaluates tactics he might use.

Personality also affects the way lobbyists spend their time, but the differences here are not as great as those examined above. We saw earlier that persons with a high tolerance for frustration spend less time in the office and more time on the Hill. Those ranking high on social presence spend less time in the office than those ranking low. High Machiavellians spend more time entertaining than those ranking low. The amorals spend more time entertaining and traveling at the grass roots. All of these findings fit theoretical expectations and illustrate the point that personality inclinations affect time allocations.

SUMMARY

Lobbyists do not seem to have personalities very different from the general population and certainly not much different from persons in other political skill groups. Lobbyists rank significantly higher on Gough's dominance and self-control scales than a professional male criterion group. (Dominance and self-control are negatively correlated.) Contrary to some initial expectations, lobbyists do not score significantly differently from professional males and college males on sociability, social presence, self-acceptance, and intellectual efficiency. Lobbyists seem to desire esteem rather than anonymity; they seem as moral and as messianic as ordinary persons; they seem to excel slightly in their ability to tolerate frustration; and they seem disinclined to be introspective. However, there are no similar measures on criterion groups with which to compare these impressions.

The pattern set forth above does not form a well-rounded picture. The measuring instruments used are not perfect or comprehensive; thus there are many gaps in the data. Personality does not seem to be a crucial factor in selecting persons from the general population to become lobbyists. Past experience, especially in politics and in the industry represented, is probably much more important than personality in recruitment. Personality does, however, affect the style with which a lobbyist goes about his job. Personality affects patterns of time allocation, tactics pursued, role in policy-making, role in a political party, and the lobbyist's conception of his profession and his success in it. It is impossible at this time to assess accurately the role of personality in the success or failure of a lobbyist in his job, although it may be great. The major difficulty arises from the fact that success, like personality, is not easily measured. The goals of lobbying are constantly shifting; they are usually much broader than securing the passage or defeat of legislation. The means for pursuit of goals are not static or well-defined. Even if a given end is achieved, there is no certainty about which means or pattern of means were most instrumental in that achievement.

Respondents show little insight or widespread agreement about traits characterizing lobbyists. Qualities such as being agreeable, honest, gregarious, capable, manipulative, persistent, and having a facility for expression were often said to aid a man in his lobbying role. However, these same qualities would help him to succeed in many other professions as well, especially those requiring cooperation in pursuit of common goals.

SINCERITY OF COMMITMENT TO AN ORGANIZATION OR CAUSE

Lobbyists are commonly thought to be men with few principles and personal convictions who will represent any well-paying cause. Is this true? To what extent are lobbyists committed to the principles and policies of the clients or organizations they represent? Which lobbyists are highly committed and which are less committed? To measure commitment, these questions were asked: "Do you consider your relationship to the organization you represent to be like that of a lawyer to his client: that is, presenting your client's case in the best possible light without necessarily committing yourself personally to your client's position?" "Would you describe your commitment to your organization's policy position as strong, mild, or weak?" "Was the policy position of your organization a very important factor in your decision to represent it?"

Table V–6 reports a cross-tabulation of the responses to the last two questions. About 60 per cent of respondents are weakly or mildly committed to their organization's policy, and about 40 per cent are strongly committed. In slight contrast, only about 30 per cent report that policy was an important factor in their decision to represent the organization, and more than one-fourth claim it was not important at all. The second question elicits less policy commitment than the first because many lobbyists feel that it is important to appear to be sincerely committed to what they are doing if they expect to be trusted and listened to. Therefore, respondents are probably inclined to overreport their commitment. They may not, however, feel the same social compulsion to report that organization policy was important in their decision to represent their organization. A second reason is that some persons who were unconcerned about policy at the time of employment subsequently became involved as they participated in the decision process within their own organization. Many persons enter lobbying through chance-like developments of their careers and are not guided by policy aspirations. One respondent expressed a change in his attitude in the following way:

TABLE V–6

Lobbyist's Commitment to
Policies He Espouses

POLICY AS A FACTOR IN R's DECISION TO REPRESENT	Just a Job, No Commitment	Weakly Committed	DEGREE OF COMMITMENT				Total
			Mildly Committed	Strongly Committed	R makes the Policy	No Response	
Not at all	4	4	18				26
Yes, partially	2	5	28	12			47
Yes, very much			2	23			25
R makes the policy					3		3
No response						13	13
TOTAL	6	9	48	35	3	13	114

As I got to know the people and educated myself to the issues, I discovered that I really had not had a full opinion on the thing. I grew up to the issues—in a sense I matured. I became convinced that the organization is sound, that it has made a tremendous contribution.

Despite the differences in the percentages showing a strong concern about policy on the two questions, Table V–6 shows a high correlation between the two answers. Clearly some lobbyists personally are much more concerned about policy than others, and for many, this concern predates their acceptance of a lobbying job. What factors lead to high commitment on policy? An important one is the involvement of the lobbyist in the policy decision process of his organization. Those who are highly committed are, generally: those who are paid by salary (rather than by fee); those who are officers or staff members of the organizations (not hired from outside); those whose first choice of a career is legislative representative; those chosen as lobbyists primarily because of their knowledge of subject matter; and those who have major roles in making policy in their organization. Two respondents said: "I would have to [be committed]. I just about make the policy; there could not possible be any strong difference of opinion." "It's my position they adopt, why shouldn't I feel strongly about it."

The other side of the coin is that those who lobby for a fee, and perhaps represent several clients, feel less strongly about policy. Others who are less committed include: those who came to lobbying from careers in law or association work; those who were chosen for lobbying primarily because of their knowledge of law; and those who represent business groups or foreign governments. Attorneys tend to say that lobbying is just a job they take with little personal conviction; this is a direct carry-over from law practice in which attorneys represent clients whether or not they may be guilty. One respondent reported:

My commitment is as strong as my sense of honor; I am bound to deliver them what I have to offer. I think this is the best kind of incentive there is; it is like being in business for oneself. I often wonder about the moral questions involved here. In a way it is like a lawyer who feels that his client is entitled to the best possible presentation of his case. On the other hand, I suppose if you didn't do it, someone else would. And yet, if they asked me to do something I really do not believe in, I would have to decide. I have, on occasion, told them I would not do such-and-such a thing. It is quite a luxury to be able to do that. Few men, especially if they have a family to support, can stand up against the economic pressure.

Although some lobbyists accept the lawyer's role, others make what appears to be a fundamental distinction between the role of the lawyer and that of the lobbyist:

In lobbying more than in law, you identify yourself with the policy of the organization you work with. In part, this is inevitable because you have to make that policy, and therefore you become identified with it. You make policy democratically, of course, in that you don't win every time, but in this process you become identified with the policy. There is another reason why a lobbyist can't be completely detached from the policy he is presenting. The individual member of Congress won't let you take a lawyer's view. I was at a hearing recently where a member of Congress asked a lawyer if he personally believed in the testimony he was giving. When he answered that he was merely trying to present his client's position in the best possible light, it inevitably weakened his testimony. Most lawyers are used to a situation in court where they are not subject to cross-examination, but a lawyer who testifies before a committee of Congress is obviously going to be cross-examined, and if he is not prepared, he is in a hell of a shape. For this reason we never let anyone testify who is not convinced about the rightness of the policy. If I cannot agree with a policy, and yet the president and the board insist on it, usually one of the other boys in the legislative department can agree with it and will carry the ball. I, myself, will not do it because I couldn't stand up under cross-examination.

Another respondent presented a third reason for distinguishing the roles of the lawyer and the lobbyist:

It is different in this respect. A lawyer may stretch every point almost to breaking in order to win a case, but when a person is appearing before a congressional committee, he doesn't stretch points; instead he leans over backwards to be sure he is right with his facts. I have to be up there next year and the year after that, and if the members don't trust me, I am sunk. I have seen some people go up there and try to mislead them, but over the long pull the members catch up with them and they get what is coming to them. If you get four or five senators jumping down your throat on something, you've lost your case and you are finished.

Conviction about policy also arises out of a need for conviction. Many people need to feel that what they do is important and that it will lead to public good. One respondent said, "I would not work for an outfit whose policy I would feel uncomfortable about. Life is too damn short for that, one has to believe in what he is doing." In fact, highly committed lobbyists like lobbying more and also are more likely to have sought a lobbying position. More highly committed lobbyists come from careers in governmental service and labor organizations than other careers. More highly committed lobbyists represent labor unions, large citizens organizations, and church and humanitarian organizations. Generally, too, persons working for such organizations or having such careers demand less salary. Perhaps high commitment on policy mobilizes talents and energies and reduces the mobilizing attraction of money.

Committed lobbyists spend more time with members of Congress and other people on the Hill; they also spend more time traveling at the local level stirring people to take action. Committed persons tend to think that the publication of voting records of members of Congress is an efficacious tactic that will lead members to follow popular desires on policy. Highly committed lobbyists are less inclined to be content with their personal record of success; less committed lobbyists significantly more often report that they have good records of success.

In general, then, most lobbyists are committed to some degree to the policy they present; about 40 per cent are very strongly committed. Commitment is important to performance on the job; a highly committed lobbyist is a better advocate, and he tends to put more of his energies and talents into his job. Some lobbyists, to be sure, fit the popular stereotype, have no commitment, and perform only because they are paid to do so, but this is certainly not characteristic of all, and in extreme form is characteristic of only a very few.

CHAPTER VI

LOBBYING AS AN OCCUPATION

Chapters IV and V have indicated several tasks of lobbyists. This chapter will focus directly on the lobbyist's job and will discuss how the lobbyist spends his time, whom he sees, how he likes his job, and what makes him successful at the job.

Definition of what the job of lobbying requires is by no means clear. Lobbyists engage in a great variety of tasks. The tasks not only vary from lobbyist to lobbyist but also among the working days of any given lobbyist. The variety of tasks was considered an asset of the vocation by many lobbyists. An onerous chore can be readily borne if one can look forward to a more interesting task to be done at the next moment.

The most general way to state the nature of the lobbyist's job is to note that he must in some way communicate with governmental decision-makers. This may be done in many different ways and will be examined closely in Part Three. Lobbyists have considerable latitude in choosing how they shall spend their time. As a result, they tend to specialize and to allocate time to activities they like or at which they are skilled.

Despite the variety of tasks and tendency to specialize, nearly all lobbyists engage in certain activities. Most call on members of Congress and other governmental decision-makers. Most read and study in their offices. Most prepare written communications. Many testify before committees; many travel to contact constituents; many spend a small part of their time entertaining. We asked respondents how they generally allocate their time, and the resulting information is discussed in the next section.

ALLOCATION OF TIME

Respondents estimated the percentage of their time they allocated to each of several specific activities. Since the estimates are based on recall, they should not be interpreted too literally. Table VI–1 reports the number of respondents saying they give a certain proportion of time to each of seven activities. Working in one's own office is by far the most time-consuming activity. In fact, ten respondents report spending more than 90 per cent of their time there; and more than 70 per cent spend half or more of their time in the office. According to folklore, lobbyists spend much time entertaining and calling on members of Congress; yet, Table VI–1 shows that these activities consume very little time for most lobbyists (less than 10 per cent for calling on members and less than 5 per cent for entertaining).

OFFICE WORK

The office work of the lobbyist is quite similar to office work in other professions. Most of this time is spent receiving and sending communications. Many communications are channeled over the phone, a much more expeditious method than personal visits or written communication. Some office time is spent reading reports, official documents, publications, and correspondence. Additional time is spent writing correspondence, testimony for hearings, reports, and articles and columns for publication. Some office time is usually spent in conferences; frequently these are with the lobbyist's fellow staff members, but they may also be held with staffs from other organizations who are collaborating on a bill or project.

Executives and lawyers spend slightly more time in their

TABLE VI–1

Lobbyists'
Allocation of Time

PERCENTAGE OF TIME R's SPEND ON A GIVEN ACTIVITY	ACTIVITY						
	Working in Own Office	Doing Research	Calling on Members of Congress	Calling on Other Governmental Officials	Chatting with People on the Hill	Traveling at the Grass Roots	Entertaining
Zero		39	7	5	21	31	32
1– 5	1	17	50	40	48	21	50
6– 10	1	11	18	32	13	16	9
11– 25	12	17	20	17	15	24	7
26– 40	13	11	5	6	2	5	2
41– 60	34	4			1	3	
61– 75	17	1					
76– 90	12						
91– 95	9						
96–100	1						
No response	14	14	14	14	14	14	14
TOTAL	114	114	114	114	114	114	114

offices than do other types of lobbyists. Since executives carry a greater administrative burden than other staff persons, they need more time in the office. Lawyers spend much time doing research and preparing briefs. It is also relevant to note again that persons who feel less secure and less sociable tend to spend more time in their offices.

RESEARCH

Doing research is part of office work for many lobbyists, but since research is specialized, we asked about it specifically. Many lobbyists (39 per cent) report that they do no research whatsoever, but most of these say they need and use it. Many organizations have a special research staff which provides the information used by the legislative relations staff in communications with governmental decision-makers. Some lobbyists for organizations with limited financial resources and overworked staffs complain that they do not have sufficient time for research. In general, though, those who believe in the efficacy of research spend more time at it. Also, people who have previously held legal or governmental positions are the most likely to do research; former career politicians are least likely to do so. Consultants to organizations, such as lawyers, do more research than organization staff members.

DIRECT CONTACT WITH OFFICIALS

It is curious that lobbyists report spending relatively little time calling on members of Congress and other governmental decision-makers. This is so because, for one thing, these visits must be carefully prepared for; this consumes some time in the office. Also, lobbyists must not "carry their pitchers to the well too often," as one congressman put it.[1] Most lobbyists perceive that they will increase their effectiveness by saving good will and access for very important matters. "I figure I am doing them a favor by not inviting them out to dinner and by not calling on them until I really need them." For this reason, most lobbyists

---

[1]This notion of storing up good will in order to obtain access and attention is similar to Banfield's idea that political actors have influence accounts with one another. No actor can draw on his influence account with another actor indefinitely; influence can be cultivated, conserved, and invested as well as spent. See Banfield (1961, esp. chap. xi, p. 312).

are content to conduct their business with staff assistants or to confine routine communications to brief letters or phone calls.

Despite this general limitation on time available for personal calls on decision-makers, the amount of time lobbyists spend with officials is related to certain perceptions and past experiences. Table VI–2 shows that representatives of organizations with high power at the polls spend more time with members of Congress than do representatives of organizations with little power.[2] Persons

TABLE VI–2

Influence of Power at the Polls of Organization on Lobbyist's Time with Members of Congress

PERCENTAGE OF TIME SPENT WITH MEMBERS	POWER AT THE POLLS OF ORGANIZATION	
	Little Power at Polls	Great Power at Polls
5 or less	35	22
More than 5	15	28

Chi-square test of significance shows $p < .01$
$r \varphi = .26$

involved in partisan politics also spend more time with members. Those who believe that personal presentation of arguments is the most effective way to get a point across to a decision-maker clearly spend more time with members than those who rate personal calls lower. Those who work full-time on legislative concerns tend to spend more time with members than those who spend only part-time on legislative matters.

According to lobbying folklore, the lobbyist spends most of his day on the Hill stopping members or congressional employees in the corridors or lobbies and dropping into their offices for friendly chats. However, 21 per cent of the lobbyists spend no time whatsoever at it, and about 70 per cent spend 5 per cent or less of their time at it (see Table VI–1). Those who believe that personal calls are the best way of developing contacts spend a little more time on the Hill, and public relations consultants and

[2]*See p. 84 for a discussion of the measurement of power at the polls.*

legislative staff members spend a little more time than those in other roles. Curiously, those who have formerly worked on the Hill, those with somewhat more sociable personalities, and those who are more highly involved in group activity, are no more likely to spend time informally conversing on the Hill than other lobbyists.

TOURING AND SPEAKING

Recent lobbying trends emphasize communication with governmental decision-makers through the intermediation of the people at the political grass roots. Communications from constituents often are stimulated by lobbyists stationed in Washington. The flow of communication from lobbyist to the grass-roots constituents and thence back to decision-makers is sometimes facilitated by personal tours and speeches by lobbyists to local groups. Visits help to clarify what the lobbyist is doing and the role the local members can play in achieving the goals of the group. From the lobbyist's point of view, these visits also help to insure that the membership continues to be interested in and ready to maintain financial support of the lobbying operation. Among lobbyists, this latter activity is called "farming the membership" and is considered essential to the maintenance of some organizations. Thus, most lobbyists spend at least some of their time touring at local levels: about 70 per cent spend some time there; and 50 per cent spend more than 5 per cent of their time there; a few even spend as much as 50 per cent of their time in the hustings. Lobbyists who emphasize communication through intermediaries, who have important roles in organization policy, who believe in the efficacy of partisan political tactics, who have had past political careers, and who represent organizations with power at the polls tend to spend slightly more time with local groups than other lobbyists.

GIFTS AND ENTERTAINMENT

Another folklore concept of lobbying is that lobbyists win their way with governmental decision-makers through gifts and entertainment. Much evidence shows that such a picture is greatly overdrawn. Very little time is devoted by lobbyists to entertaining. About one-third do no entertaining of officials whatsoever, and over 80 per cent spend less than 5 per cent of the time entertaining. None spends more than 40 per cent of the time at it. Despite the rather low general emphasis on entertaining, some lobbyists do place more confidence in and spend more time at it than others. Those who entertain more tend to rate it higher as a tactic of lobbying. Lobbyists who are skilled at meeting people and at entertaining also tend to spend more time doing so. Executives of organizations and legislative relations staff members might be expected to devote more time to entertaining than lobbyists in other roles, but this was not borne out by the data. There was no difference in the amount of entertaining done by persons in various lobbying roles.

SUMMARY

In summary, lobbyists spend most of their time receiving and sending communications. Most of this they do from the seclusion of their own offices. Some communications are passed via personal conversation with members of Congress or other governmental decision-makers, but these consume little time. Very few are transmitted or facilitated through entertainment.

Most lobbyists spend at least some time traveling about visiting local groups attempting to improve communication with the people who support them and to stimulate a flow of communications from the grass roots to governmental decision-makers. A particular lobbyist's allocation of time is determined partly by the demands and the boundaries of the political influence system within which he operates and partly on his personal predilections, skills, and the demands of the moment.

WHOM THE LOBBYIST SEES

It is in the nature of his job that the lobbyist sees and communicates with governmental decision-makers. Usually people think that members of Congress are the only targets of lobbying. In actual fact, however, most lobbyists are as concerned with decisions made in the executive branch as with those made in the legislative branch. This is especially true of groups or firms whose activities come under the jurisdiction of independent regulatory commissions. Lobbyists must develop contacts and carry on communications with persons in any branch of the government making decisions of importance to them or their groups.

We noted above that lobbyists spend only limited time with officials; they tend to spend more time with the staff aides to decision-makers: administrative assistants, legal counselors, legislative counselors, clerks, private secretaries, and so forth. In many instances, such aides are very close to official decision-makers and participate significantly in their decision processes. Aides have more time to listen to the pleas of lobbyists. The lobbyist frequently presents his case in full to a staff assistant first and later covers only the high spots in the few minutes allowed for personal conference with the official. In many offices, the various aides each concern themselves with a specialized subject matter area. A lobbyist with a problem in a given area—e.g., agriculture—works most closely with the aide who is responsible for that area. So useful are these aides, these brokers in communication, that many lobbyists say that in certain cases they prefer to confer with a trusted aide than with the decision-maker himself.

Another group of aides are the staff assistants to congressional committees. Staff members carry on the administrative and clerical functions of the committee, conduct research, and indirectly participate in the decision process. Their power comes from their ability partly to control the flow of information and communications to the committee: they do research, plan and administer hearings, question witnesses, write committee reports, give advice, and listen to lobbyists. So absorbed are these staff persons in the committee's decision process that they cannot be considered impartial; therefore, most committees have both a majority party and a minority party staff. The chairman of the committee appoints the majority staff, and the ranking minority member appoints the minority staff. The lobbyist's most useful and open point of access to the committee's decision process is through the committee staff. Many staff persons also realize that they can get useful assistance, information, and advice from lobbyists. It is not uncommon to find close personal relationships between lobbyists and staff members. Although no figures directly indicate this, it appears that committee staff members have more communication with lobbyists than any other set of political role-players on Capitol Hill.

Lobbyists are not concerned solely with communications to decision-makers or aides close to them. They also interact frequently with fellow lobbyists, persons in political parties, members of the press, or ordinary voters. Lobbyists often act in concert to try to influence governmental decisions. Several groups interested in the same policy may regularly exchange information and plot joint strategy. Each organization may send a delegate or the entire staff to a conference. Groups may work in harmony on some issues and go separate ways on others. For example, the railroad brotherhoods and the Association of American Railroads may cooperate on a policy that affects the over-all prosperity of the railroad industry, but may oppose each other on labor-management questions. Regular working sessions create close personal relationships between individual staff members of different organizations and facilitate a great variety of informal communications.

Most lobby organizations have regular staff sessions. Some staffs meet daily in the morning to check signals, exchange information, and plan their activities for the day. In addition, many informal conferences are held to clarify points, pass on information, agree on the wording of a draft, plan strategy, and so forth. Some staffs are as small as one or two persons; others are as large as ten or fifteen.

Lobbyists also interact regularly with the members and officers of their own organizations. Some of the officers may live in Washington or visit there regularly; some organization members visit Washington; some lobbyists take trips to the local units. The above is not a total cataloging of persons lobbyists see, but it covers the types of persons with whom they regularly interact.

EVALUATION OF THE VOCATION

The kinds of things that lobbyists like best and least about their jobs and whether they would like to continue as lobbyists or aspire to some other employment were examined. When asked, "What features of your work appeal to you the most?" many lobbyists found several features attractive. The aspects mentioned as most important are reported in Table VI-3.

Most lobbyists like the sense of accomplishing something im-

TABLE VI–3
Most Appealing Features
of Lobbyist Work

FEATURES	NUMBER
A sense of accomplishing something important — sense of mission	35
Interacting with people	16
Preparing an argument	11
Being close to important people and decisions	9
Variety of work	7
Freedom of schedule	3
Matching wits with opponents	3
Monetary reward	1
Entertainment and parties	0
Other	11
None stand out as appealing	5
No response	13
TOTAL	114

portant. Lobbyists who believe this is the most appealing part of their job tend to have deep personal convictions about the cause they fight for. Some took their jobs at a personal financial sacrifice; the sense of the importance of the task helps to compensate for this. One was offered a lobbying job for an industry at five times his present lobbying salary. He says he refused because "arguing for a tariff is not like lobbying for human rights. Every time I think of leaving this job I reconsider because of the useful services I can perform for my people." This same respondent at another time was asked to run for Congress, but he again refused because he believed he could do more for his cause as a lobbyist. Persons who report that a feeling of accomplishment is the most appealing part of lobbying tend to represent small labor groups, citizens organizations, and church and humanitarian groups—although a few from other groups also are attracted by a feeling of accomplishment. Officers of organizations are also slightly more likely to report this motive than are others.

Many lobbyists like the constant opportunity for interacting with people offered by their work. For many, interaction is stimulating, exciting, and satisfying. Lobbyists who have legislative relations staff roles or who formerly worked on the Hill tend to pick this as the most satisfying part of their job. Two respondents spoke of their jobs in this way:

> I love every minute of it. The thing that appeals to me the most is going out and speaking to people of influence. Another thing that appeals to me is the possibility of stimulating a damn good legislative battle. It is stimulating, but it also gives you ulcers.   * * *

> What appeals to me most is just being with people and accomplishing something. In fact, my mind is always being stimulated on this job. The Hill is a very stimulating place; I don't stagnate up there.

Eleven respondents very much enjoy preparing an argument or a brief; this is especially true of lawyer lobbyists. It is a stimulating exercise in logic and the marshalling of facts. This factor is somewhat related to the enjoyment of matching wits with opponents, which a few other respondents mentioned. Lobbyists who enjoy preparing arguments and matching wits generally play important roles in making policy in their organizations. One said, "In lobbying you meet unique problems that the ordinary lawyer doesn't ordinarily get into. There is an aspect of it that is almost like playing a game in imparting your ideas and trying to get them across."

Another 9 per cent mentioned that they enjoy being close to important people and important decisions. They find a vicarious thrill and sense of self-importance in contact with famous people and important events. Persons in other walks of life, as well as lobbyists, are motivated by a desire to be close to fame and importance. The difference is that the lobbyist regularly meets and works with important people. This particular satisfaction is often mentioned by executives of small trade associations.

About 10 per cent of the lobbyists like their working conditions—variety of work and freedom of schedule. In general, lobbyists have a heavy load of work, but they can come and go as they choose so long as the job is completed. They also engage in a variety of tasks.

I like best the fact that it is a job that is never the same. There is something new all the time. This presents a challenge to my ingenuity, and I like it very much. I don't know of anything that I actually dislike. I am one of the few people in the world who actually likes his work.

Persons who know only the folklore of lobbying might suppose that high pay, an expense account, and frequent parties and entertainment would be the most satisfying aspects of the job. Yet only one person finds monetary reward to be the most appealing part of the job, and none mentions entertainment and parties. A few respondents mention as a second or third factor that they like the pay, but very few think it is the most appealing part of lobbying. One respondent, who could have earned much more money in another job, answered that he would like to continue in lobbying:

Yes, I think it's a pleasant activity. There may not always be sufficient inducement in a financial way, but I am satisfied now and wouldn't want to change. I would not accept offers from other firms just because they were offering more money. I would only work where I would like to work. There are many bastards in this business and I do not want to get into a situation where I have to work with any of them. I have the best set-up that I know of. They have been very good to me around here in that they let me cut the whiskey drinking and social activities to a minimum. When I go home at night I want my time for myself.

On the whole, lobbyists find more things that they like about their jobs than that they do not like. Sixteen can find nothing disagreeable about it (Table VI-4). Those preferring careers in government or as legislative representative for an organization tend to find everything about the job agreeable. One respondent put it colorfully:

It's congenial with nearly everything I'm expected to do, jumps with my inclinations. I'm pretty much an unfrustrated person. Nothing stultifies my convictions in the work that I'm doing. There is not a great deal of income involved in my job, but I would rather have less income and more satis-

TABLE VI—4
Least Appealing Features
of Lobbyist Work

FEATURES	NUMBER
Preparing detailed briefs or research results	21
Having to be nice to people to win their favor	8
Approaching people who disagree with or oppose you	8
Getting clients to understand job and requirements of the situation	8
Working conditions: long or odd hours; low pay; travel	7
Discouraging to fail or be frustrated	3
Having to state only one side of an argument	2
Public disapprobation of job	2
Too much entertainment and parties	2
Other	22
Nothing disagreeable about it	16
No response	15
TOTAL	114

faction. My boys are not ashamed of me, and I understand that's not too usual these days.

The detailed preparation of briefs, reports, or research results is the most disliked activity of twenty-one respondents. Though eleven like this aspect of the job, more lobbyists find it onerous. Curiously, many of those who dislike it would still like to be attorneys or judges, so it is not a preference that falls along preferred occupation lines but a manifestation of a personality trait. People who like interaction with others frequently do not care for detailed pedestrian activity.

It drives me nuts to have to sit down to a time-consuming effort of putting names together with something that we

need to relate them to. What I usually do is set it up and
turn it over to my secretary. But it is even the setting up
that I hate—files and records and that [junk.] I don't do very
much of it; I turn as much of it over to her as I can.

Some lobbyists find having to curry favor distasteful. To say
things that one does not really mean, to withhold things that one
would like to say, or, especially, to try to convince someone of
something one knows he opposes seems undignified and weak to
some respondents. To ask people for favors and constantly to
worry about losing their support is humiliating. "The thing that
I dislike the most is having to be extremely politic with people
who are not really interested and whose motives I have good
reason to doubt."

Some lobbyists must be concerned not only with currying
favor with governmental decision-makers but also with those who
support them. This seems to be especially true of lobbyists who
represent small trade associations and who must "farm the membership" if they hope to keep the association going. "I dislike
the not very constructive things that one has to do in order to
maintain the membership and solicit them to maintain their activity. But you have to eat, too." Another is frustrated in communicating with his clients: "To try to make a record of all the things
you do to satisfy those who pay you is very difficult because so
much of what one does is intangible. A little request may take
hours of time to fulfill, and yet when you put this down on a
report, it somehow doesn't come across in its importance. You can
never express the value of what you are doing in a cold report."

Related to this is the difficulty for the specialist in simplifying a complicated problem for a client or governmental decision-maker. One respondent considers it a kind of intellectual
dishonesty.

Lobbying to me is all work—no legal skills are needed,
and there is no intellectual challenge in it. In lobbying you
have got to make sure that you get to the proper ear and
explain intricate problems to members of Congress. This is
very difficult when you have to be very simple about a very
technical matter. You can spend all day on the Hill just see-
in two people, and it is very slow and drudgery-like. I don't

find it intellectually stimulating. This may be one of the reasons that so many people like lobbying; they don't have to think hard in lobbying. It is financially rewarding, and we don't discourage people from coming to us, but we do not seek it either because it is not intellectually exciting.

On the whole, the working conditions of lobbyists are rather congenial. Table VI–3 reports that ten respondents mention the working conditions as the most appealing aspect of their job. Others find their working conditions difficult. They most frequently complain that lobbyists must put in long and irregular hours. Most put in much more than forty-hour week, much of the time during the evening hours, and they very frequently work under considerable pressure.

Toward the end of the session the day-to-day constant haunting of the halls of Congress and office buildings of the members in order to urge them to take a position on a critical vote is the think I like the least. We always have such days of pressing legislative work, especially on . . . bills toward the end of the session, and in these urgent situations there is sometimes a shift in strategy, and you need to contact the members and change what you told them the day before. In these situations, months of work is at stake. You also realize that the members of Congress are very busy and you hate to press them for time, and yet you feel that you have got to do everything that you can do. Perhaps it would not change the vote one bit if I just sat up in my office and did nothing, and yet I feel that I must go down and do everything I can. That is the real drudgery of lobbying.

Some also complain about having to travel frequently; some dislike their low pay; but both groups are relatively small. The most frequent complainers about working conditions are the representatives of big labor organizations. Considering the standard of excellence that they have been able to obtain in their staffs, the labor organizations pay their lobbyists considerably less than do business organizations.

Several lobbyists mention the frustration and disappointment of failure to obtain a desired policy decision, but only three think this the most prominent liability of their job. The poignancy of this frustration is evident in this respondent's words:

> You can work your legs off for something and really not know what you are eventually going to get out of it. You can have done all that you wanted to and can do and then you have to sit around and wait for the decision. In a court room you know that eventually you are going to get a decision one way or the other—but this is not true in lobbying. Sometimes a project can get caught up in the end of a session log jam and you get no decision at all; it dies on the calendar. Success or failure can depend on factors over which you have no control or influence.

Another respondent lamented:

> You work for eighteen months before you find out if you have been working on the right road; 35,000 people depend on you, and you don't really know if you are doing your job right or not. Working on legislation is strictly a pressure problem all the way.

Some rebel against having to state only one side of an argument. This kind of intellectual dishonesty also pricks at their self-respect. Only two respondents selected it as the most disliked aspect of their job perhaps because many persons, especially those trained in the adversary system of the common law, are accustomed to this kind of behavior and find it completely justified in the nature of the system. They are confident that the adversary will expound his side of the argument. This same justification is given by many for the belief that lobbying is good for the political system. Another reason that more respondents did not choose this factor as bothersome is that many lobbyists actually are not required to state only one side of an argument. Some have discovered that it helps their presentation to state both sides of an argument. A balanced presentation carries an aura of objectivity and self-restraint that appeals to the decision-maker. Thus, in actual fact, only a minority of lobbyists feel compelled to state only one side of an issue.

A few respondents are strongly aware that the public disapproves of lobbying. Nearly all recognize that the public has little respect for lobbyists, but many have made peace with the situation. Some rationalize that the public judgment is wrong; some believe that they personally are good lobbyists and not the type the public disapproves of; still others insist that they are not lobbyists at all. Only two respondents find that public disapproval is the greatest drawback to their job.

Two respondents think that lobbying entails too much entertaining and parties (and, again, no one picked entertaining as a desirable part of his job). The fact that only two mentioned entertaining as an unfavorable factor is evidence not so much that lobbyists dislike it, but rather that it is not a very large part of Washington lobbying. It probably plays a much smaller role in Washington lobbying than in private business or in lobbying at state capitols—according to several respondents who have served in both state and federal settings.[3]

Is it possible that lobbyists were drawn into their present jobs by circumstances and have resolved their frustrations by deciding that they like their work? In fact only one respondent reported that he consciously and deliberately set out to enter. lobbying because he believed it would be congenial. If they had it to do over again, would lobbyists choose lobbying? Respondents were handed a card listing fifteen different jobs or professions and were asked: "If you had a perfectly free choice, and without considering any lack of talent or training on your part, which of the jobs or professions listed on this card would be your first five choices." A cross-tabulation of their first and second choices is reported in Table VI–5.

The professions are shown in rank order according to their frequency as first choices. Attorney was clearly the most favored choice. In part, this reflects the fact that some respondents considered themselves attorneys first and lobbyists second. Second, many respondents think that being an attorney provides access to a large variety of jobs.

United States senator was second rank of the first choices and first rank on the second choices. To many respondents, senators hold positions of power and prestige which enable them to

[3]*See Chapter XIV.*

TABLE VI–5

Lobbyists' First and Second Choices of Profession

SECOND CHOICE	FIRST CHOICE (Same as below)															No Response	Total
	1	2	3	4	5	6	7	8	9	10	11	12	13	14	15		
1. Attorney		1		1	2	3	2		1								10
2. Senator	3		4	2	1	1		1				1					13
3. Legislative representative for an organization	4			1	1		1	1			1			1			10
4. Corporation executive	4	2			1			2	1	1							11
5. College professor	3	2															5
6. Judge	9	2					1										12
7. Physician	1	1		1													3
8. Proprietor of small business			2	1													3
9. Congressman	1	9					1										11
10. Public relations counsel	1		1										1				3
11. Government agency head	2									1							3
12. Journalist	2	1	2			2			1								8
13. Administrative assistant to senator			3							1							4
14. Sales representative			1	1			1				1						4
15. Realtor																	0
No response												1				13	14
TOTAL	30	18	13	7	6	6	7	4	3	3	2	2	1	1	0	13	114

accomplish many things. Half of those who named senator as their first choice named congressman as their second, indicating a strong desire for any seat in Congress. Such people tend to have had experience on the Hill. Some readers might be surprised that the number of choices for congressional seats is not higher. One reason is that not all people desire power and responsibility. Another is that lobbyists are in a good position to observe the frustration and tension involved in winning, holding, and discharging the responsibilities of a congressional seat. The necessity for members of the House to run for their seats every two years is the major reason that congressman was not chosen as often as senator by the lobbyists. One respondent, quoted above, thinks he can accomplish more for his cause in his present position than he could in Congress. Being a member certainly does not permit single-minded attention to a cause.

TABLE VI–6
Lobbyists' Total Choices for Each Profession

CHOICE	NUMBER
Attorney	63
Legislative representative for an organization	48
Senator	43
Public relations counsel	41
Judge	39
Corporation executive	39
Congressman	34
Journalist	32
College professor	30
Proprietor of small business	24
Government agency head	20
Physician	17
Administrative assistant to senator	13
Sales representative	8
Realtor	4
No response	108
TOTAL	563

Legislative representative, or lobbyist, ranked as the third most frequently mentioned first choice. Table VI–6, which reports the total choices given for each profession when all five choices are summed without regard to priority of choice, shows that legislative representative slightly outranks senator. This suggests that lobbyists generally do like their work and would be reluctant to exchange it for anything except some of the finer positions in the land.

Careful perusal of Tables VI–5 and VI–6 indicates that the three top-ranking professions are also frequent second, third, fourth, and fifth choices. The second choices are more widely and evenly distributed than the first and fall into some interesting patterns. Respondents who pick attorney as the first choice tend to pick judge as the second. Judge receives a total of thirty-nine choices. The frequent selections of attorney and judge reflect the importance of legal training for the kinds of professions listed in Tables VI–5 and VI–6. Another curious fact in these tables is that "public relations counsel" received only three first choices and three second choices, but forty-one choices in all to give it fourth place ranking on Table VI–6; this results from twenty fourth choices. Public relations consultants do work that is very similar to lobbying, and some lobbyists would naturally make it a third or fourth choice. Interestingly, realtor received no first or second choices and ranked at the bottom in the total choices. Sales representative was also considered relatively less desirable.

Cross-tabulations of these choices with other variables provides some clues to motivations behind these fanciful career choices. Not surprisingly, lawyer lobbyists usually pick attorney as first choice. Lobbyists on legislative relations staffs choose senator or legislative representative first. Trade association executives and Washington representatives spread their choices over a wider range.

When these choices are compared with whether or not a respondent approves of lobbying, we find that would-be attorneys, public relations consultants, and sales representatives are slightly more likely to approve of lobbying; would-be judges are less inclined to approve. A larger than normal percentage of those inclined to be college professors do not like lobbying very well. Persons who like promotional or advocacy jobs believe lobbying is good more often than do persons inclined toward scholarly and dispassionate positions.

Part of a lobbyist's evaluation of his vocation is his sense of identification with the profession. Most do not have such a sense of identification. Seventeen say there is a slight sense of profession among those who collaborate on a bill or a project. Sixteen have a general feeling of goodwill toward other lobbyists, even among opponents. Three think that a sense of profession carries over from the legal field. A few also believe it would be wise to adopt professional standards. But, fifty-three feel no sense of profession at all. Most lobbyists are more identified with the career they had before they became lobbyists. Only those who had no specific career preparation are eager to adopt professional standards.

Two respondents explained why it is difficult to develop a sense of profession in lobbying in these terms:

> Among lobbyists, their primary affiliation is with their employer, and a lobbyist has to preserve his detachment from the other lobbyists with whom he works. You may have to work with the guy one day and fight him the next. Therefore, you can't develop a very close affiliation. The successful lobbyist is one who lives his job for twenty-four hours a day. One cannot be palling around too much. It would be similar to generals of opposing armies belonging to the same officers' club. Yet there is still an unexpressed feeling among lobbyists of doing the same thing. These are people; even though they would be working against each other at times, they are still engaged in the same kind of endeavor and activity, and they feel this. Although lobbyists get together in groups to discuss tactics on specific problems, they do not exchange their personal techniques or approaches to the solution of problems. The best that I can express it is that lobbyists seem to recognize the close similarity of their various activities in the sense that they are all following pretty much the same kind of life endeavor.

* * *

There is to some extent a sense of profession among lobbyists but not as strong as in the professions which require exams and registration and that kind of thing. There is a lot of resentment by the old-time lobbyists toward the newcomers, and also a lot of jealousy, throat-cutting, and character assassination. This is done in all professions, however.

The most stringent test of a lobbyist's liking of his job is the question of whether he wants to continue in this type of work for the rest of his professional life. Answers are reported in Table VI–7. Three-fourths of the respondents are ready to make their

TABLE VI–7

**Desire to Continue
in Lobbying**

DEGREE OF DESIRE TO LOBBY	NUMBER
Unqualifiedly not	2
Probably not	1
Undecided or maybe	2
For a while, but not entire career	7
Hope to continue or make a career	76
Like job in general and will continue but dislike lobbying aspects of it	13
No response	13
TOTAL	114

careers in lobbying. Only two unqualifiedly oppose long tenure in their jobs. Thirteen, who are part-time lobbyists, dislike the lobbying aspects of their total job. Seven perceive lobbying as a phase in their careers which may lead to a more desirable position. Usually these people aspire toward high corporation executive positions. Some firms place aspiring young executives in Washington for a tour of duty to provide training in the ways of government and to test their mettle.

On the basis of the findings reported in Table VI–7, the sample can be divided into those who desire to stay in lobbying and those who prefer not to continue. The ones who want to stay like the variety of their work and the continual opportunity to interact with people. Those who do not want to continue like the contact with important people (which might help them to advance); they also particularly dislike detailed preparation of briefs.

The respondents who like and want to continue in lobbying are: slightly more active in groups; significantly more likely to approve unqualifiedly of lobbying as a part of our political system; more likely to have previous experience on the Hill; usually receive a large percentage of their income from their clients, probably being on a full salary basis in their organization; came from careers in law, journalism, and lobbying.

Respondents who do not want to continue in lobbying tend: to have come from labor organization work, work in a trade association, or no special career; presently to represent small labor organizations, trade associations, or corporations; to be more inclined to question the value of lobbying in our political system.

Respondents' own words give added insight into their reasons for wanting to continue or discontinue lobbying:

> I would be quite satisfied to stay in this kind of work for the rest of my professional life. One of the reasons is that in this job the world is the limit. Our program covers the entire range of things our people would be interested in; thus there are many different ways I can move. I am very content being the biggest frog in a small puddle.
>
> * * *
>
> It is just becoming interesting now after ten years. I am developing a sense of continuity and of long-range thinking. Now I can play a tune and not just a note. At the present time I think in terms of ten to fifteen years. I especially want to develop a good grass-roots organization of forty to fifty thousand members which would be working in the public interest.
>
> * * *
>
> This is a pretty satisfying job. Lobbying is not the kind of thing that one is likely to be in unless one likes it. A person must be pretty well sold on it in order to find his way into it.
>
> * * *
>
> Nope, the main reason is that in this job I have to fulfill the role of a spokesman. In other words, I am somewhat of a front man. I don't like that sort of thing. Fortunately, in

the job I am in at present I can be my own front man 90 per cent of the time. I do much of my own thinking, and therefore I don't need to constantly feel I am being a spokesman for someone else. A spokesman does not do his own thinking and creating; he is only selling.

In summary, most lobbyists like their jobs quite well. Most feel that they are making an important contribution to our way of life, that they are well paid, that their working conditions are reasonably good, and that they do stimulating and exciting things. Lobbying, of course, is not congenial for certain kinds of personalities, and those who do not fit the requirements tend to drift on to other employment. Most of the present incumbents would like to continue in their lobbying activities for the rest of their careers. If they had it to do over, many of them would go into lobbying again or into a similar occupation, such as senator or attorney. Despite the general liking for the job, most lobbyists do not feel identified with lobbying as a profession; they more often identify with their career prior to lobbying.

THE SUCCESSFUL LOBBYIST

This section summarizes personal qualities that tend to lead to success as a lobbyist. Lobbyists were asked to evaluate their success in two ways: "How do you appraise the record of success of your own organization?" and "How do you appraise your personal record of success?" The answers to these two questions are crosstabulated and reported in Table VI–8. It is immediately clear from the table that most respondents consider both their own and their organization's success to be quite good. The two appraisals are also quite highly correlated, reflecting the fact that it is difficult to separate organizational and personal success.

Respondents were expected to have a high opinion of their success. Psychologically it is very difficult to continue in a task if one feels that he is failing; thus, in order to maintain self-respect, persons tend to convince themselves that they are succeeding. Persons with high incomes were much more likely to appraise their personal success highly. Lobbyists, then, like many

TABLE VI-8

Appraisal of Success at Lobbying

APPRAISAL OF PERSONAL SUCCESS	APPRAISAL OF SUCCESS OF OWN ORGANIZATION							
	Failure	Poor Results	Moderate Results	Good Results	Resounding Success	Cannot Measure	No Response	Total
Failure								
Poor results		1	1					2
Moderate results			17	9	1	1	2	30
Good results		3	6	42	1		2	54
Resounding success					3			3
Cannot measure		1	1	1		5		8
No response		1			1		15	17
TOTAL	0	6	25	52	6	6	19	114

other Americans, look to their salary figures as a gauge of their success. Appraisal of personal success was not correlated, however, with the means of payment.

Representatives of different types of organizations were substantially similar in their rating of success. However, lobbyists for citizens organizations are inclined to rate their success moderately, while those representing more than one type of organization all rate their success as good. The following trends appear, but none of these differences is statistically significant: Those who appraise their success as good are more likely to feel a sense of profession and to play a greater role in making policy for their organization; they also tend to be specialized, a little more active in groups, a little less active in a political party, and a little more inclined to emphasize direct communication with decision-makers rather than communication through intermediaries. These findings should be interpreted cautiously since the differences were not statistically significant.

An additional, and indirect, measure of success was the frequency with which respondents were solicited for their views on policy by governmental decision-makers. Lobbyists aspire to be consulted on policy, so the frequency of their consultation can be taken as a partial measure of success. Some of the findings are related to those just reported for personal appraisal of success: More highly paid lobbyists tend to be solicited oftener; those having a greater role in making policy in their organization are asked for their views more frequently; specialists on a certain subject tend to be consulted for information and views on that subject; those chosen for their jobs because of competence in the political process, legal process, and for their ability to meet people, tend to be consulted more frequently than those chosen for other reasons.

Some information on the subject of what makes a successful lobbyist derives from a question put to lobbyists about traits that characterize lobbyists. In addition, congressional respondents were asked what kinds of traits or skills they thought made lobbyists successful. The discussion that follows is a synthesis and summary of the answers to these questions by the two groups.

The qualities most frequently mentioned by both lobbyists and congressmen were honesty and integrity. Many, especially in Congress, went so far as to say that if a lobbyist did not possess these qualities, he was completely ineffective. It was assumed that persons of integrity had a general concern for the public welfare in addition to the special concern of the organization represented. Another aspect of integrity was a rigid expectation that lobbyists must respect the confidences of the people they talk to. This code of behavior is strictly enforced through sanctions.[*]

Almost as essential to success is the requirement that the lobbyist be very capable and well-informed. An incapable or poorly informed person is visible almost immediately. One respondent said that many lobbyists "operate on the brink of their information" and thus are unable to convince a decision-maker when pressed with questions. Such persons soon become pegged as incapable and are shunned. It is especially important that the lobbyist be well-informed on the subject of concern to his organization, but he should also know a great deal about the legislative and political process and should be widely read and well-informed on the major problems of contemporary society. It is also desirable that the lobbyist be analytical, incisive, and articulate. As might be expected, only a minority of lobbyists attains this high standard.

A third general quality can be summed up by the term "agreeableness." The lobbyist is basically dependent on the actions of others, and as such he dare not offend. One respondent said, "Lobbyists must be careful to hold their tempers; they dare not explode. In our outfit we have three cardinal rules: first of all don't threaten; secondly, don't beg; and thirdly, don't assume you are 100 per cent right." Congressional and lobbyist respondents were probed further on the agreeableness dimension. These kinds of characteristics were said to lead to success in lobbying: extrovertiveness, gregariousness, confidence, sincerity, enthusiasm, energy, forthrightness, thick skin, slowness to frustration and anger, patience, persistence, determination, physical attractiveness. In addition, the successful lobbyist does not bluff, act all-knowing, or order people about. Probably no one person possesses all these qualities, but each is considered an asset for an operating lobbyist.

Manipulativeness was not mentioned as a trait leading to success by congressional targets of lobbying, but it was mentioned by some lobbyists. The lobbyist must manipulate others in order to succeed. One respondent put it this way: "You develop a turn

[*]*See the end of Chapter XIII and the end of Chapter XVI.*

of mind which is trying constantly to think how the hell can I get so-and-so to do such-and-such. You are trying to shape and sell ideas, which is much more nebulous than selling pencils. Many lobbyists tend to think in terms of 'who the hell' rather than 'what the hell.' " This same respondent thinks it is necessary to have an inherent urge to sell ideas and to create (to manipulate). "You can develop finesse, friendliness, a pattern of contacts, but you cannot develop the basic urge which is necessary in order to do a good job."

Closely related to manipulativeness and agreeableness is a facility for expression. Lobbyists must use words to convince, and a facility in their use is important. Some lobbyists are extremely skilled with words, but others are only mediocre at best. To convince others one must be, or appear to be, completely convinced of the rightness of the cause one is pleading. A communication conveying anything less will surely be interpreted as partial invalidation of the argument.

Persistence, mentioned above, should be emphasized a bit more. Many of the tasks of lobbyists stretch on for months, years, sometimes decades. A lobbyist needs to be long-suffering and tolerant of frustration. It is especially important that frustration not be vented in anger, which could alienate important people.

One final point is that a lobbyist generally must like his job if he is going to succeed in it. As noted earlier, most lobbyists do like their jobs. Some few who do not are not particularly successful lobbyists either.

Some respondents reflected upon the qualities they would seek in a man they might hire as a lobbyist. Their remarks are not all-inclusive, but the reader will be interested in the way two of them phrased the problem.

Those that impress me as effective have an ability to articulate ideas well. They are able to control their anger and maintain a semblance of a high boiling point. They are able to discuss matters with equanimity. If I were to advise a client who wanted to get a lobbyist to do a job for him, I would suggest that he try to get a fellow with a quick mind who could think on his feet, so to speak. He should be a man with a great depth of intellectual ability and perception if possible. Also, I would want a man who has got the willingness and physical stamina to work hard for long hours. Of course, a fellow who has had enough experience to have acquired a reputation for ability and integrity would have more effect than a person who was unknown.

* * *

There has to be some of the same characteristics that a politician has. A successful lobbyist should enjoy meeting people and talking to them. He has to be a little of the lawyer, and he has to be something of an expert. I would not want a person who repelled people or who created ill will. Such a person should have sufficient judgment not to make unfortunate statements or to give away a confidence or to be a message carrier—talk too much or talk out of turn, be a gossip. I would want him to talk on one issue and be professional in that particular issue and not mingle in other affairs. . . . I would want him to keep the record straight, say the same thing to everybody, not something different to a Republican congressman and a Democratic congressman. . . . I would want people who talked with him to get a sense of reliability. I would not want him to get out on a limb or to give faulty facts. . . . Never go wrong on behalf of someone who places confidence in you, because if you do, you are sunk, not only in terms of that person, but all the other people you might deal with. On the other hand, if over a period of time you do not let anybody down and you have been faithful and constructively worked for the cause of your people, then the members of Congress will have confidence in you and put themselves in your hands. That should be one of the highest aims of a lobbyist.

SUMMARY

In this chapter we have examined some of the major characteristics of the day-to-day job of the lobbyist: most lobbyists spend more than half of their time in their offices; they devote less time to calling on officials than is generally supposed; they normally interact more with staff aides and committee staffs than with officials; they also regularly deal with fellow lobbyists and the officers and members of their own organizations.

On the whole, lobbyists like their positions rather well and believe that they are doing important things; most would like to continue as lobbyists for the remainder of their careers. They feel very little sense of profession, however.

They evaluate their personal and organizational success highly. They believe that several characteristics are likely to contribute to success at lobbying. Some of them are: honesty, integrity, capability, agreeableness, manipulativeness, facility for expression, and persistence. Congressional respondents generally agree with this list.

CHAPTER VII

LOBBYISTS AS THEY RELATE TO THEIR EMPLOYERS

Lobbyists as they relate to their employers are categorized here by their position titles. These titles are familiar to observers of the political scene, and provide immediately recognizable labels around which a set of charactertistics can be sketched. As with all categorical schemes, the distinctions are not clear-cut; the categories tend to blend into one another (the people in different categories are all engaged in the same general occupation). Yet an economy of language and understanding can be gained by developing them.

Table VII–1 shows the categories of roles and the types of organization represented. The table itself gives some indication of the meaning of the classification. For example, most trade association executives represent small trade associations; most officers of organizations represent labor unions. Most representatives of large trade associations are on legislative and executive relations staffs. Representatives of small trade associations have a variety of positions. None of the persons who play lawyers' roles represents labor or farm organizations; instead these people tend to represent small trade associations, corporations, citizens organiza-

TABLE VII–1

Role to Employer by Type of Organization

ROLE TO EMPLOYER	TYPE OF ORGANIZATION												
	Large Labor	Small Labor	Large Farm	Small Farm	Large Trade	Small Trade	Corporation	Large Citizens	Service or Veterans	Church and Humanitarian	Foreign Government or Firm	More Than One Type	Total
Trade association executive	1	3		1		14							19
Officer of organization	3	1		1	1	2		1					9
Legislative relations staff	5		2			1	2		1	1			12
Legislative and executive relations staff		3		1	7	7	1		1	1			21
Washington representative	1	1				8	3	2		3			18
Lawyer in large law firm						3	2	1				4	10
Free-lance lawyer						4	6				2	2	14
General counsel in organization						3	1	2					6
Public relations counsel					1	1							2
Lobbyist entrepreneur							2					1	3
TOTAL	10	8	2	3	9	43	17	6	2	5	2	7	114

tions, foreign governments, or more than one type. Lobbyists who are concerned primarily with relations with the legislative branch usually work in organizations with large staffs and considerable power at the polls—mainly labor unions. Washington representatives, on the other hand, most often represent organizations with smaller memberships and staffs—small trade associations, corporations, citizen groups, and church groups. As the description of the various roles in relation to employers proceeds, the reader may wish to refer back to this basic table.

Table VII-2 shows the lobbyist's methods of reporting to their employers cross-tabulated with their roles with relation to the employers. Trade association executives and officers of organizations tend to report directly to the board of the organization or to the annual meeting. Staff lobbyists usually report to a supervisor or a staff meeting. Officers and staff employees are usually closely identified with their organization; they tend to be much more involved in the policy of the organization and to have their views on policy matters solicited by governmental decesion-makers more often than those not so closely identified. Lobbyists who report to the board play a much greater role in organizational policy than those who report to a supervisor or who report only informally. Outside consultants (lawyers) are more likely to be allowed to report informally by phone or by letter. Those who report informally are usually allowed greater freedom to determine their own strategy and tactics. Lawyers almost never report to a supervisor or staff meeting. Washington representatives use a variety of methods for reporting to employers.

Table VII-3 shows the methods by which persons in various roles are paid for their services. Executives, officers, and staff are paid almost exclusively by annual salary, in many instances with an added expense account. Lawyers and other outside consultants are paid almost exclusively by fees, with additional expenses in certain instances. Two of the three lobbyist entrepreneurs pay themselves; they set their own figures since they create and run their own organization.

These three tables help to clarify the basis for the role classification to be developed in this chapter. It is taken as a given that a major and basic function of all lobbyists is communication. All must pick up information and pass it along to others; all play

TABLE VII–2

Method of Reporting to Employer by Role to Employer

ROLE TO EMPLOYER	METHOD OF REPORTING					
	Informal Reporting Only	To Supervisor or Staff	To Board or Annual Meeting	To Board and Supervisor or Staff	No Response	Total
Trade association executive	2		16	1		19
Officer of organization			6	1	2	9
Legislative relations staff	2	3	2	5		12
Legislative and executive relations staff	1	11	3	3	3	21
Washington representative	3	4	5	4	2	18
Lawyer in large law firm	6		2		2	10
Free-lance lawyer	11		3			14
General counsel in organization	1	1	2		2	6
Public relations consultant	1		1			2
Lobbyist entrepreneur	2		1			3
TOTAL	29	19	41	14	11	114

liaison roles. As one respondent phrases it, "It is my job to spot the threats and the opportunities." Since communication and liaison are universal, these tasks will not be replaced over and over again as we discuss the various roles.

OFFICERS AND EXECUTIVES

TRADE ASSOCIATION EXECUTIVES

Most trade associations have a chief of staff or executive officer who gives full-time attention to the affairs of the association and is usually a staff servant with long tenure and experience. He resembles a permanent civil servant, staying on through many changes in the officer personnel of the organization. He usually is not an operating member of the industry and is not formally charged with making policy for the organization. Just the same, by a variety of informal techniques, not the least of which is his strategic position at the center of communication in the industry, he has a great deal of influence over organizational policy. In most instances, he is the chief policy architect for the organization. As such, he also is usually the chief spokesman for the industry to the press and to the country at large.

There is a growing trend for trade associations to locate their national headquarters in Washington, although by no means all of them are located there. Trade association executives located in Washington commonly contact members of Congress from time to time; thus they are required to register as lobbyists; nineteen in this sample are classified as such. Their lobbying task is to represent their organization before both the legislative and executive branches of the national government. Most national trade associations confine their concern to decisions of the national government, leaving representation before state governments to the state units of the association or to firms operating in given states. For the few small trade associations which do not have state units, the national association may take charge of representation before state governments whenever and wherever the need arises. Representation is a process by which information and points of view coming from industry are transmitted to governmental decision-

TABLE VII–3

Method of Payment for Services by Role to Employer

ROLE TO EMPLOYER	METHOD OF PAYMENT							
	Annual Salary Only	Salary and Expenses	Fee Only	Fee and Expenses	Fee and Salary	Contract	No Response	Total
Trade association executive	11	8						19
Officer of organization	3	4					2	9
Legislative relations staff	1	11						12
Legislative and executive relations staff	7	11			1		2	21
Washington representative	6	6	2	2			2	18
Lawyer in large law firm			6	1	1		2	10
Free-lance lawyer			10	4				14
General counsel in organization	1		1	1		1	2	6
Public relations consultant				1		1		2
Lobbyist entrepreneur	2		1					3
TOTAL	31	40	20	9	2	2	10	114

makers. This information is intended to persuade the decision-makers to accept the point of view of an industry. Such messages may be channeled directly, but alternative message routes also are used.

Trade association executives seem to favor collaboration with other groups with similar policy concerns; this helps distribute the communication load and adds power and influence to the request. Another means of message transmission is the stirring of the membership at the grass roots to send messages to governmental decision-makers. Although, as chief lobbyist, the trade association executive has responsibility for exhorting the people back home, he is personally unlikely to be involved in politics Many trade association executives believe that they must stay clear of politics if they hope to work with people on both sides of the aisle in Congress; some must also avoid alienating partisans within their own organization. Most are weak partisans or independents, even in their private lives.

Most trade association executives dislike lobbying though they realize that it is important. Many are grateful that it occupies only part of their time; the major portion of their time is devoted to the administration of the association's affairs. Most associations act as information clearing houses and perform other services, such as research or training, for the industry. They generally distribute a trade publication which includes a section dealing with governmental and lobbying activities. If financial support is uncertain, the executive must "farm the membership" and use other methods to raise money. In addition, he may feel compelled to do favors for members or clients. He might help one member with a government contract and take the daughter of another sightseeing. Many of these small services are similar to those provided for constituents by members of Congress.

Most trade association executives are recruited from their own industry or from the executive branch of the federal government. Certain executive branch officials are uniquely qualified because they have managed programs or administered regulations that apply to the industry; thus, they are intimately acquainted with both government and the industry. Trade association executives generally receive better salaries than do government employees. Trade association executives report that they prefer to have contacts in the executive branch, that they have developed those contacts by having worked together on problems, and that they depend on contacts in the executive branch and in the industry to keep them informed of developments. This is additional evidence that, for many trade associations, more governmental decisions crucial to them are made in the executive branch than in the legislative branch.

OFFICERS OF ORGANIZATIONS

The elected officer of an organization who registers as a lobbyist is somewhat similar to the trade association executive. Both administer the organization and represent it before the government and the press. Both handle errands and grievances for members. Yet certain differences warrant placing them in separate categories.

Many officers represent labor unions. In business, when a man is elected to an office in his trade association, he usually continues to run his own business and devotes only partial attention to the affairs of the association. In labor organizations (and, to a certain extent, farm organizations), however, when a man assumes high office in his union, he quits his job in the factory and devotes full time to the affairs of the union. From this basic distinction flow many related factors. Most officers who register as lobbyists have long tenures; they are older than most lobbyists; they are generally paid less than trade association executives (their salaries cannot be too much higher than those of members on the assembly line). Three officers believe they belong in the lower-middle class, whereas most lobbyists consider themselves in the upper-middle or upper class. Some officers are relatively poorly educated. They are more likely to be Democrats than are other lobbyists.

Moreover, officers generally represent organizations with considerable power at the polls. As such, they place more emphasis on grass-roots political activity and devote more time to stirring up and manipulating the local membership. Unlike trade association executives, most officers have been or are now involved in partisan politics; most have campaigned at one time or another; and most have made political contributions. In fact, they contribute more frequently than any other lobbyist group. They also place slightly greater emphasis on collaboration with other organizations in their lobbying activities than do trade association executives. In part, this results from the fact that labor organization often advocate broad programs which require and attract collaboration from a variety of groups; but lobbyists for organizations with considerable power at the polls also favor pooling the resources and influence of several groups.

Officers of organizations, more than trade association executives, are charged formally and explicitly with policy development, though the board of directors generally has the final word on policy. It would be erroneous, however, to conclude that these officers have more impact on policy in their organizations than trade association executives have in theirs. Undoubtedly both types of role-players are centrally concerned with policy development.

STAFF

Any lobbying undertaking that requires dealing with more than one bill or more than one branch of the government is too large for one man. In fact, one could argue that any *effective* comprehensive lobbying job must have more than one man working on it. Still, there are many one-man lobbying operations. Some single lobbyists partially lessen their limitations by collaborating with lobbyists from other organizations. However, if money is available, organizations prefer to hire a staff to share the burden. Organizations with large memberships and considerable power at the polls are generally more able to afford a supplementary staff. The larger the staff, the more elaborate the division of labor. Some organizations have a staff such that one division can handle representation before the legislative branch, and another, before the executive branch. It is also possible to assign each man responsibility for a certain set of bills or group of governmental decision-makers.

However, very few staffs are large enough to enable a very elaborate division of labor. A large majority of registered lobbyists is responsible for representation before both branches of government. Lobbyists who work only with the legislative branch have more time available for services to the legislators and their staffs. They can help write speeches or reports and do research.

Lobbyists who work with both legislative and executive branches must give more attention to problems of administrative regulation of their industry and to trouble-shooting problems for members or clients. Generally they are members of smaller staffs than are those who work only with the legislative branch; therefore, they are likely to have more personal responsibility for program development.

Staff members generally have less influence on organization policy than do officers or executives. They are also less likely to play a dominating role in strategy planning and have slightly less freedom to determine their tactics; nevertheless, most still have considerable freedom to determine strategy and tactics. Although staff members generally do not have the administrative responsibilities that their supervisors have, all have some minor administrative tasks and a considerable amount of correspondence. Staff members tend to be the youngest (in their forties) of the lobbyists. They are also very well educated. Many were drawn into lobbying from jobs in the legislative and executive branch of the government. They prefer contacts in the legislative branch, especially committee staffs. Most are strong partisans and view political contributions and campaign work as efficacious.

WASHINGTON REPRESENTATIVES

These lobbyists are Washington envoys for organizations that have headquarters in another city. The Washington representatives in this sample represent a variety of organizations. Usually they are of a small or a single-man staff, or a single man may represent several organizations.[1] Since the headquarters and

[1]*The Brookings Institution sponsored round-table conference of representatives of corporations in Washington indicated that the corporate representative has a more specialized role than do the variety of Washington representatives discussed in this section; Table VII–1 shows that only three Washington representatives represented corporations. Most of the corporation representatives studied by Brookings focused their attention on executive decisions, especially on the allocation of defense-related government contracts. Much of corporate representation is thought of as sales work; in fact, several representatives said they report to the corporate vice president in charge of sales. Only a small minority participating in the round-table conference registered as lobbyists; most were anxious not to be labeled as lobbyists. See Cherington and Gillen (1962).*

officers of the organizations are in other cities, the Washington representatives take part in organizational policy-making less than persons in the roles discussed above. They are more like envoys than ambassadors.[2] As experts on the scene, their views receive careful attention, but their ties with the organization are somewhat tenuous compared to officers and staff.

As members of a small staff or perhaps as the sole person on the staff, the Washington representatives tend to become "jacks-of-all-trades." They handle representation before both Congress and the executive agencies; they do trouble-shooting, settle grievances, function as "listening posts," and supply favors for their clients. Since persons in this role have so many tasks, they virtually cannot carry on comprehensive lobbying campaigns. Generally, they restrict their role primarily to that of watchdog for the interests of their clients. When trouble appears, they sound the alarm; it is then up to the clients themselves to communicate with governmental decision-makers.[3] Naturally, they stand by to offer advice and assistance. Washington representatives use a variety of methods for reporting to their clients, but since the organizations they represent are usually small, they can be more informal (usually letters and phone calls suffice) than representatives of large organizations. To reduce the burden of their many tasks, they collaborate with the representatives of other organizations that have similar problems.

Although it is common for Washington representatives to operate alone—with perhaps a secretary to assist with correspondence—some men develop a reputation which attracts more clients then they can handle by themselves; they may then add staff to share the load. This staff differs from the type discussed earlier in that it is employed by and responsible to the Washington representative rather than to the organization he represents. Typical clients of Washington representatives are small trade associations, corporations, and church and humanitarian organizations. Despite the conglomeration of tasks and clients they represent, Washington representatives tend to be the least well paid of the lobbyists.

[2]*Cherington and Gillen (1962, p. 112) found that though corporate representatives like to think of themselves as ambassadors, their home office supervisors think of them as envoys.*

[3]*Corporate representatives performed the same liaison function. Cherington and Gillen (1962, p. 12).*

Some, though by no means all, consider lobbying as a temporary phase of their careers. There is considerable variety in their vocational backgrounds. All these factors indicate that there is greater variety in this lobbying role than any other discussed in this chapter; a glance at the tables presented earlier will confirm this.

CONSULTANTS

Some organizations prefer to handle lobbying problems by hiring salaried, full-time employees; others prefer to hire a consultant to do a specific job. Generally, consultants are not concerned with over-all policy for the organization or even with the total lobbying effort; their charge is more specific. They make decisions relating only to the specific task and usually have complete freedom to plan the strategy and choose the tactics for following through on the job. Consultants are generally chosen on the basis of expertise and success; thus, they are in a position to insist on a completely free hand in execution.

Lawyer-consultants come to mind when organizations have problems relating to government. The tables in the first part of this chapter show that thirty of thirty-two consultants in the sample are lawyers; the other two are public relations consultants. Lawyer-consultants can be further subdivided into "inside" and "outside" counsel. Inside counsel generally have offices in the headquarters of the employers and are considered members of the staff. Outside counsel generally have separate offices as attorneys in private practice. Outside counsel can be subdivided further into partners or employees in large law firms and free-lance lawyers in practice on their own. Before these types are discussed in detail some general comments about lawyer-lobbyists are in order.

Most lawyers consider themselves lawyers first and lobbyists second. Lobbying positions come to them in the course of their general legal practice. Some do not care for lobbying and do it only because an old and favored client has a problem that requires legislative action and might take his business elsewhere if refused assistance. Other lawyers enjoy lobbying and seek to expand that aspect of their practice. Even these, however, do mainly legal work. Comprehensive lobbying efforts, typical of large organizations, are usually not given to lawyer-consultants.

Because most lawyers are concerned with building a practice and a general reputation, they examine prospective cases rather carefully. They prefer to take cases with which they feel they have a good chance for success. Desiring to be known for honesty and integrity, they avoid cases that might require them to take contradicting points of view. It is considered bad form on the Hill to profess one point of view one day and take the opposite position the next. This factor, and the desire to focus their energies cause many lawyer-consultants to develop a specialty—such as tax legislation or communications cases. Moreover, the technicality of many problems makes specialization essential. Many lawyers are so specialized that they speak for only one point of view (i.e.) management's) on a single problem. In taking a case, lawyers also consider whether they will have complete freedom in handling the case. Most insist on this. One described his decision process in this way:

> You have to decide on three things. First of all, does the problem have merit; can it stand on its own feet? Secondly, is it enough of a problem so that Congress would seriously consider it? Thirdly, is it enough of a problem that the client feels that he can afford to pay me to do anything? In addition to deciding if it is meritorious, I also try to find out if it is likely to succeed soon or whether it would take a period of years. It would also be important to see if it would be acceptable from the executive point of view. Once the decision has been made, the client expects you to take care of the entire matter; that is why it is not satisfactory to simply have a congressman introduce a bill. Most members of Congress can't give the detailed attention that is required to get these things through Congress. Most members are just rushed to death. The person who is plugging for a bill has to check frequently with the committee to see if hearings are coming up and when. He must prepare testimony for hearings. Proceeding before these hearings is much like appearing in court; the members of the committee act very much like judges on the bench.

One might guess that some clients have difficulty finding a good lawyer to take their case. Some clients who are unsure of their own cases agree to pay the lawyer only on the contingency that he succeeds. Most top lawyers will not accept contingency cases. Other cases are so desirable that several lawyers or firms compete for them. In such instances, the client's choice may turn on the contacts, reputation, and background of the lawyer.

It is interesting that none of the labor or farm organizations has lawyer-consultants; they hire their own staff. Since many lawyers dislike lobbying, a small percentage of their personal income comes from lobby clients; this is especially true of lawyers in large firms. Lawyers are generally minimally involved in the policy decisions of their clients; as a result, they are not usually consulted on policy matters by governmental decision-makers.

Lawyers join a large firm because it has a reputation and an established practice. The younger men in the firm are employees; if they are capable, they may be admitted to partnership in due time. Some very large firms have as many as ten, twenty, or even fifty partners. Some have branch offices in several cities. Several large New York firms have branch offices in Washington. Out-of-town firms with problems requiring attention in Washington may hire Washington lawyers or firms to act as "Washington counsel."

Usually the entire firm registers as officially representing a lobby client; however, the actual handling of the case is generally delegated to one individual. If the pressure for action becomes heavy, he calls on his colleagues for assistance; this manpower pool is one reason that large firms are attractive to prospective clients.

The client is billed on the basis of the total time devoted to the case, and payment goes into the general firm account. At the end of the year, the profits are disbursed equally to the partners. However, this is not always the case; in some firms, each partner has his own clients, and income from them is his own. (Such an arrangement is not too dissimilar from situations in which lawyers practicing for themselves share offices, secretary, and telephone.) Lawyers in large firms have the highest incomes and best educations of all lobbyists. Several place themselves in the upper class. They also often give large political contributions. They are the least inclined to identify with lobbying as a profession, identifying totally with the legal profession instead.

The free-lance lawyers perform tasks similar to those of lawyers in a large firm, but they operate from a different base. They are generally their own entrepreneurs. Usually the office consists of one or two men. Clients are smaller or poorer and greater in number. They may share offices, but they handle their own accounts. They are paid a retainer and also for the time devoted to the case—just as is a firm. Most free-lance lawyers are able to go into business for themselves because they have built a reputation before they begin. The reputation may have been gained in larger firms, or, more likely, in government—on the Hill or in the executive branch. Experience gives free-lance lawyers special competence in subject matters and contributes to their general reputations for integrity and ability. Free-lance lawyers have to compete a little harder for cases than do the large firms; they are not usually in a position to bid for the really big jobs. Their income generally is lower than that of large-firm lawyers. Still, the free-lance lawyers give the largest political contributions—perhaps in the interests of reputation-building.

General counsel, or inside counsel, in organizations are members of the legal staff. They give legal opinions, draft legislation, and plan strategy. They generally work for annual retainers which are, in effect, salaries. They have the lowest incomes among the lawyers. Some supplement their income with other clients—so long as it does not interfere with their primary responsibility to the organization. Their offices are generally in the organization suite. Most work for business organizations and lean toward the Republican party.

The two public relations consultants are the only other outside consultants in the lobbying sample. Both are trained as journalists and are lone or free-lance operators. In many respects their operations resemble those of free-lance lawyers; they have many clients, and most of their tasks are rather specific. Because of their training and background, they are not asked to perform specifically legal tasks. Instead, they are hired to run public relations campaigns, prepare literature, ghost-write books, write speeches and reports, and so forth. In a word, they are consulted for their communication skills.

LOBBYIST ENTREPRENEURS

Since entrepreneurship plays such a large role in American life, it is not surprising to find it in lobbying. However, only three respondents in this sample were classified as entrepreneurs. Lobbyist entrepreneurs differ from business entrepreneurs in that they invest no risk capital; in most other respects, the two are similar, however. The entrepreneurs have ideas and make arrangements to bring them to fruition—like going into business for oneself. Entrepreneurship differs from a legal or other consulting practice (which is also a business) in that the entrepreneur does not consult on clients' problems but has his own special policy area.

Two variations on the entrepreneurial theme were discovered. In the first type, a man develops expertise and a reputation in a certain subject-matter area; he speaks and writes on the subject; from time to time he testifies before Congress on it, usually from a specific and consistent point of view. Persons, organizations, or firms who agree with that point of view believe, or can be convinced, that the voice should continue to be heard and that therefore they should contribute to his support. He receives contributions or sells subscriberships and lists his clientele as the people he represents. Usually a board is set up for appearances' sake, but it makes no policy decisions. The policy is already quite clearly defined, and if any changes are to occur, they will be made by the entrepreneur. The client can control policy only through the acceptance or rejection of membership. "They have retained me, in a sense, as an attorney to represent my own thoughts. If they are in disagreement with the way I do things, they drop their membership." Some entrepreneurs also collect information and conduct research relevant to their topic and distribute this to their clientele. Lobbyist entrepreneurs, then, sell their special know-how and, at the same time, retain fairly complete control of policy and strategy.

The second type of lobbyist entrepreneur is the "lobbyist general contractor." These men are alert and knowledgeable about the lobbying scene and spot situations in which governmental action might be used for the benefit or detriment of some group and for which there is no existing lobby organization. They then go to the people who might be affected and tell them, "I will protect your interests if you will get together and support me." They sometimes propose to secure the introduction and passage of bills in Congress which will solve their problems or promise to block unwanted bills. Meanwhile, though they have no organization or staff to do the job, they know where to get talent if they are given the money. When money is received, they still cannot make long-term staff commitments since they work on only one bill at a time. They, like general contractors, subcontract various aspects of the assignment. One subcontractor drafts the legislation; another plans the strategy; another prepares literature; another researches and writes a report; another helps contact members of the relevant committees, and so forth. If he knows Washington well, the general contractor can obtain highly qualified talent in this fashion—having each subcontractor work at what he does best. Successful efforts often produce sizeable remunerations for all concerned.

Lobbyist entrepreneurs find their roles ideal in many ways. Their greatest problem is raising money; they often spend much time maintaining the clientele. They must keep their issues alive, for a dead issue or a resolved issue will certainly eliminate support. (It was said facetiously that if the St. Lawrence Seaway ever passed, half the lobbyists in Washington would lose their jobs. When it passed in 1954, a few did lose their support, but protagonists on both sides were still on hand in Washington in 1957 to fight about the size of the appropriations.) They must stay clear of partisan politics, for political action can alienate clients as well as members of Congress. Most of the lobbyist entrepreneurs manage to solve their money problems very well and are able to pay themselves handsome salaries. It is a role, however, in which few can succeed, and opportunities for entrepreneurship very rarely present themselves.

CHAPTER VIII

LOBBYISTS AS THEY RELATE TO THE GOVERNMENT

The tasks and roles of lobbyists vis-à-vis the government are varied. This chapter is a systematic discussion of those roles. Many people wrongly believe that lobbying is confined to the legislative branch. The Federal Regulation of Lobbying Act of 1946 encourages such a narrow interpretation by requiring registration only by persons paid to influence the passage of legislation by Congress. Though the term "lobbying" antedates the regulatory act by many decades, the legal definition in the act has narrowed the use of the term. This chapter will be concerned not with a legal description of lobbying (legal prescriptions will be discussed in Chapter XVI), but with an examination of the full range of lobbyist roles as they relate to the government.

Nearly all of the relationships between lobbyists and government take place through means of communication. Lobbyists communicate to their clients what is happening or is likely to happen in government. They communicate to government what is happening or is likely to happen to their clients. They advocate policies and points of view before both Congress and the executive agencies. They stim-

TABLE VIII–1

Role to Government
by Type of Organization

TYPE OF ORGANIZATION	Liaison Only	Liaison and Advocate before Congress only	ROLE TO GOVERNMENT Liaison and Advocate before Congress and Executive Agencies	Strategist Lobbyist	No Response	Total
Large labor		5	5			10
Small labor		1	6	1		8
Large farm		1		1		2
Small farm			3			3
Large trade	1	1	5	1	1	9
Small trade	2	3	37		1	43
Corporation	1	4	12		1	17
Large citizens		1	4			6
Service or veterans			2			2
Church and humanitarian		2	3			5
Foreign government or firm			2			2
More than one type			6		1	7
TOTAL	4	18	85	3	4	114

ulate others to communicate with government. Yet only advocacy before Congress is defined as lobbying by federal law. Table VIII-1 shows these various roles cross-tabulated with types of organization represented. Strikingly, the vast majority of lobbyists play both liaison and advocacy roles before both Congress and the executive agencies. Only four (mainly trade association representatives) are concerned only with liaison; eighteen focus their advocacy exclusively on Congress. Some representatives of large labor organizations can focus advocacy exclusively on Congress because they work on staffs large enough to allow this division of labor; other staff members represent the union before the executive agencies. A larger than normal proportion of church and humanitarian representatives can give exclusive attention to Congress because fewer decisions of importance to them are made in the executive agencies. Church and humanitarian groups are not regulated by government to any appreciable degree, and they tend to be concerned with broad programs and policies requiring wide public support.

LIAISON MEN

Liaison between clients and the government is an important part of every lobbyist's job even though many persons do not believe this constitutes lobbying. Several lobbyists describe their positions as "listening posts." Viewed from this perspective, lobbyists can be conceptualized as communication channels picking up information about government from the press, government publications, and personal contacts, screening it for items of interest to their clients, and transmitting these items to appropriate persons among their clientele. In much the same way, items of information from the clientele are picked up by the lobbyist, screened, and then transmitted to appropriate persons in government. This information is transmitted to members of the executive or even judicial branches just as readily as to the legislative branch. Liaison communications are strictly informational and do not constitute advocacy.

Some clients or groups expect their representatives to act only in a liaison capacity.

They figured I could get information; they thought I had a lot of contacts and knew where to find information. A lobbyist is not so much a doer as he is a receiver of information. It is his job to find out what's in the wind. If one could do this well, one was performing his job as a lobbyist. I will use my friends to get information for me; they are always calling me up about things I ought to know; but I will not ask favors of them. You can lose friends if you keep imposing on them.

Other clients expect their representatives to go only one step further and give them advice about how to utilize the information and meet the new situations. They want the lobbyists not to be their advocates but to advise them how to be their own best advocates. Many sophisticated observers of lobbying believe that if a client is skilled at communication, he is well advised to be his own advocate, keeping his lobbyist representative in the background.

ADVOCATES

Many clients lack the skill at communication or the time to plead their own cases before governmental decision-makers. They expect their lobbyist representatives to play the roles both of advocate and liaison man. Table VIII-1 has indicated that some lobbyists carry advocacy to the legislative branch only, while most also go before the executive branch.

Advocates are those who plead a case or make a request on behalf of others; they are spokesmen. They are selected for the ability to communicate persuasively. They communicate not only facts and information but also the clients' reasons for desiring the adoption of various policies. These reasons usually include statements of how the proposed policies will benefit or harm the clients, how they will benefit or harm the nation, and how they will benefit or harm elected officials in their bids for re-election. The lobbyist's task is facilitated if he can point out that thousands of members in his organization will be watching closely for the decision of the government official.

Advocacy arguments may be made through a variety of means: face-to-face conversations with a governmental decision-maker (perhaps in his office or another congenial spot); open or closed hearings either in Congress or before an executive agency; face-to-face conversations with a staff assistant to a decision-maker; telephone communication to an official or staff-member (especially if there has been frequent personal contact in the past); and letters or proposals for the decision-maker to study at his leisure.

Sometimes lobbyists, as chief advocates, think that messages that appear to come from other sources will be better received. They arrange to have the message come from someone to whom the decision-maker is receptive. Thus they write testimony to be delivered by clients at a hearing; they ask friends or constituents (thousands, if possible) to call or write the decision-makers; they also use colleagues of the decision-maker or officials of another branch of the government as the "source" of the messages.[1]

Advocacy is naturally carried to legislators, for they are officially charged with making policy. It is also carried to executives and administrators since they, too, make policy decisions. Executive officials very often draft proposed legislation. Executive agencies are almost always consulted by congressional committees on bills related to that agency. Many bills give broad grants of power to an agency which is then directed to make specific rules or specific arrangements for execution.

In addition, the mere execution of programs and the enforcement of laws involve many decisions with which lobbyists and their clients are concerned. For example, many agencies let contracts or make purchases from private businesses.[2] Many trade associations spend thousands of hours on behalf of their members contacting executive officials over such matters as contractual negotiation, interpretation, renegotiation, and enforcement.

Some trade associations work in close collaboration with executive agencies or regulatory commissions on the enforcement

---

[1] *These methods are discussed in detail in Chapter XII.*

[2] *The corporate representatives at the Brookings round-table discussion were primarily interested in contracts and sales. Cherington and Gillen (1962, esp. chap. iii).*

of regulations. Enforcement officials sometimes call trade association executives to inform them that one of the members is "getting of the reservation." The trade association executive passes the word to the member to "get back in line" or suffer the consequences. Not only is the delinquent member likely to conform, but the experience serves as a warning to the other members of the industry. Such communications must be kept out of the public record and out of the press to protect both the official and the offender. On the whole, it is quite an effective law enforcement device: it relieves the agency of the burden of pressing charges; it relieves the courts of the burden of another case; it saves the offending firm damaging publicity; it is a preventive rather than a retributive approach to law enforcement.

Since numberless decisions are made in hundreds of agencies, bureaus, and commissions, it is little wonder that lobbyists spend as much or more time in liaison and advocacy with the executive branch as with the legislative branch. It is curious, then, that advocacy before the executive branch is not considered lobbying by many individuals and by the law.

STRATEGIST-LOBBYISTS

Although nearly all lobbyists have liaison and advocacy tasks, which usually include some kind of strategy, a few lobbyists specialize in the development of strategy. Some lead sizeable staffs and work out grand strategic designs; some advise other lobbyists about strategy, acting as "lobbyist's lobbyists," as one respondent put it. Strategist-lobbyists with reputations for sound advice make handsome incomes just advising other lobbyists how best to do their jobs.

Strategist-lobbyists are rare—only three appeared in the sample. Such men must have an impressive array of talents: they must be exceptionally intelligent and perceptive; they must have an accurate and broad grasp of the political and governmental system; they must have intimate and detailed knowledge of the formal and informal rules of the policy-making process; and, perhaps most important, they must know the habits of thinking, quirks of mind, and patterns of action of the major players in the drama that they attempt to influence. With such requirements, it is not surprising that strategist-lobbyists are few.

Strategies naturally differ from situation to situation, and strategists with different backgrounds and perspectives would plot different strategies in the same situation. Thus, it would be pointless to discuss abstractly the details of strategy here. One respondent, however, has a general strategy perspective that deserves paraphrasing. He assumes that persons or groups who insist on all or nothing will get nothing. Almost all proposals have opposition, and the opposers have an advantage in that it is easier to block legislative proposals than to secure their passage; thus, one must be prepared to compromise. Compromise must be proposed at the most advantageous stage of development, however. In the opinion of this respondent, the most propitious time is before the participants' thinking has jelled and positions have become frozen. His general strategy is to "explore areas of agreement." When working on a project, he has exploratory conversations with all members of the congressional committee which would handle the bill. In these discussions he seeks out areas of maximum agreement. He then drafts a bill to spell out that agreement. He carefully clears the bill in advance with members of the committee, the committee staff, interested parties in the executive agency who would administer it, and representatives of the pressure groups likely to be interested in it. If the opposition can be dissipated in advance, the bill usually has clear sailing. The various interested parties think that they have participated in developing the policy and are unlikely to oppose the bill for personal or other extraneous reasons. The strategy heads off the introduction of extreme and conflicting bills that raise problems of pride or authorship and public commitment to extreme positions. It is conceded, of course, that this compromise procedure works only in certain policy areas where the protagonists do not have inherently conflicting interests.

This general strategic perspective applies as well to bills authored by non-strategists. If they are alert to happenings in Washington, all lobbyists know the persons or agencies likely to draft legislation that might interest their clients. They go to these people and confer with them about the language of the bill. A change of a phrase here or there will often satisfy the needs of their clients and readily will be agreed to by the bill's authors. If they were to wait until the bill was introduced in Congress to try to have it amended, the effort might easily be interpreted as an attack on the bill itself and be firmly resisted. Personal motives such as pride of authorship are also likely to enter at that point. One of Washington's unwritten rules is that any effort to amend a bill must be cleared with its authors and sponsors to avoid incurring anger and resentment. The effectiveness of this strategy depends on the strategist's ability to spot prospective legislation before it is "dropped in the hopper."

Many other basic strategies could be described, and several will be alluded to at various points in the volume. The point here has been to describe the special role of those few lobbyists who have the position and the skills to be able to devote most of their time to strategy.

THE UNITED FRONT: COLLABORATION

One other role, or posture, toward government should be discussed. That is the posture of a united front among lobbyists as they approach the government. Why do lobbyists collaborate? What does collaboration communicate? What are the advantages and disadvantages of collaboration?

Collaboration "gives the impression that it's part of the majority of people," as one respondent put it. It is an indication that more than just one self-interested minority favors a policy. It usually communicates augmented power behind a proposal. Nearly all governmental decision-makers hesitate to decide against a strong coalition. One staff member in Congress commented on this with relation to the lobbying behind the natural gas bill: "That was probably the biggest lobbying effort ever made up here. Effectiveness of the lobby campaign was greatly assured by the joint effort of several organizations. When they all get together, you sort of are swept off your feet—you just can't resist." If the groups presenting a united front previously disagreed, the achievement of the front is in itself impressive. Collaboration among groups that traditionally are in agreement and have worked together in the past usually is less impressive.

There are two main varieties of collaboration: "log-rolling" collaboration and "common-interest" collaboration. One respondent said, "Washington is one big nest of back-scratchers." Many lobbyists, especially those representing small organizations with little power at the polls, realize that they have little chance of getting any bill through Congress without the assistance of other groups. Therefore, they seek out alliances with other groups where mutually advantageous cooperation can be achieved. When log-rolling is the cement of the alliance and policy concerns are marginal, the cooperation is sometimes looked upon with skepticism by governmental decision-makers. They doubt the integrity and sincerity of lobbyists or groups who lobby on behalf of something peripheral to the central interests of the groups.

Collaboration among groups with common policy interests is more readily accepted. Governmental decision-makers are more inclined to believe that each group is sincerely and deeply concerned. Some of these groups collaborate so regularly that they have set up semi-permanent machinery to facilitate their frequent interaction. In a sense they become lobby groups for lobby groups. Moreover coalitions may be formed to combat coalitions. Coalescence occurs to so great an extent that some respondents characterize the Washington lobby scene as whirlpools of groups. One pattern of whirlpools will take shape for a battle, and once it is over, the pattern breaks up, shifts, and reforms for the next battle. Some coalitions are virtually permanent and institutionalized; the names of some help to illustrate the variety of topics around which coalitions may focus: Council for the Preservation of the Robinson-Patman Act; Point Four Information Committee; Luncheon Conference on HEW; Electric Consumers Information Committee; Small Business Anti-Monopoly Conference; Housing Legislation Information Service; Committee on Federal Aid to Education; Civil Liberties Clearing House; Transportation Association of America; Committee on a National Trade Policy. Some of these coalitions are sufficiently permanent to have their own staff, some of whom are registered as lobbyists; however, group representatives commonly merely meet regularly on an informal basis, exchange information, and plan strategy.

Some advantages of collaboration have already been suggested. A broadened base of support facilitates the passage of some policy proposals through the governmental decision process. Several groups working in concert in support of a public relations campaign can stimulate thousands of communications from the grass roots of governmental decision-makers. The exchange of information in joint sessions increases the total knowledge that any one lobbyist has to guide his tactics. The joint strategy is informed by this increased information and holds greater promise of success. Joint strategy planning also enables a more efficient division of labor. The task of any given lobbyist becomes more manageable. Some groups, especially the smaller ones, plan nearly all strategy in joint session with collaborators; and for some, collaboration becomes the very essence of their effectiveness and survival.

Although collaboration has many advantages, it is not adaptable to all situations and can be overrated as a general approach. It seems to work most effectively on specific bills or policies in which several organizations have a common interest which is central to the *raison d'être* of the respective organizations. There seems to be an optimum level of problem generality suitable for collaboration ; problems that are too specific or too general do not benefit as much. If the problem is general but confined to a single industry, the chances for success by a united front are very good; however, if a given industry appears to be asking for special consideration on a problem that is common to many industries, the chances are less good. A broad general policy that affects many kinds of groups is less likely to be advanced significantly by a united front because such policies generally attract strong opposing coalitions. And some policy proposals are so specific in application that a coalition would look unnatural and forced.

Collaboration is also put at a disadvantage when a group is brought into a coalition which, because it is offensive to certain decision-makers, detracts from the total influence of the coalition. In such instances, separate strategies and separate presentations are more effective. Another disadvantage arises from the difficulty of coordinating and managing a coalition. Timing may be poor on the part of some collaborators; a foolish statement or tactic by one may reflect on the total effort. The many meetings required for effective collaboration can also be very time-consuming.

For somewhat different reasons than those held by lobbyists, collaborative lobbying is usually welcomed by governmental decision-makers. Groups commonly bring their quarrels to Congress or an executive agency and ask the government officials to arbitrate or choose between conflicting policies. A decision that helps one group may hurt another. In a sense, members of Congress sit as judges deciding between contending interests. This is an uncomfortable position because members must stand for election, and they would rather not be put in a position of having to decide against one group and for another. "No senator wants to get in a buzz saw." The united front is a welcome way out of this dilemma. "It dispels worries about conflicting viewpoints." "It takes it out of the realm of controversy," said members of Congress when asked for their reaction to joint lobby efforts. If the conflicting viewpoints are very intense, a congressional committee may shove the problem right back to the contending groups and tell them to compose their differences before they bring new policy proposals to the committee. A united front on a proposal by several groups, especially if they had been in disagreement in prior times, can be used as evidence to recommend the bill as the committee pilots the bill through the full house.

Legislators also appreciate united fronts because they save time. Congressional committees generally hold hearings on the same issue year after year. One congressman said, "We do a lot of spinning of our wheels up here." In such instances, the hearings produce very little that is new, and it is a real chore to listen to one group after another say much the same thing. As a result, many committees urge groups with the same general viewpoint to select one spokesman. The spokesman testifies in full for all the groups on his side; each of the representatives for the other groups signing the joint statement is given a minute or two to go on the record endorsing the statement and perhaps to point out some special facet of his own situation. Some committees extend the courtesy of allowing each lobbyist to go on the record because they think it is one way the lobbyist can prove to his clients that he is earning his pay. In this writer's opinion, people in Washington overplay the importance and value of appearing on the record. Washington folklore insists that there is something sacred about getting on the record and that great benefits will follow. Those who believe this seem to assume that masses of people (as well as congressmen) read the record or that they listen to persons who do read the record; neither assumption is justified by the evidence available.

Although collaborative lobbying is generally welcomed by

governmental decision-makers, some united efforts are pushed too hard and create resentments. A case in point is the natural gas lobby performance in 1955-56. A united front which produces a solution to a problem is welcome, but a united front behind a policy that may hurt a member at the polls is very unwelcome. One respondent stated, "It depends on whether the congressman is with them or agin them." The common everyday occurrence of coalitions also detracts from their effectiveness: "Everyone tries to be in on a coalition," said one congressman.

Some observers fear that coalitions may become near monopolistic combinations that will sweep government officials along irresistibly.[3] This danger would possibly become quite real if equally powerful coalitions were not formed in opposition; therefore, citizens should be alert to this possibility. It is easy to over-dramatize this danger, however; no historical examples come to mind of officials who were overwhelmed by irresistible combinations of private groups. Such occurrences seem especially unlikely if officials are supported against private combinations by an alert citizenry.[4]

Coalitions are usually oriented toward influencing governmental decision-makers, but sometimes governmental officials are very active participants in the coalitions. Members of Congress, congressional staff members (committee staffs usually remain neutral unless the committee chairman involves them), and officials in the executive branch very frequently participate in the strategy planning of a coalition; they sometimes even help to organize the collaboration. They are as likely to be partisans for a particular viewpoint as are lobbyists. They support and work through the coalition in the hope of influencing the decisions of their fellow officials. They use lobbyists to arrange trades on votes that, for reasons of protocol, they could not readily arrange themselves. They work closely with lobbyists in writing, polishing, and amending bills as well as in helping to push them through Congress. The most important service that lobbyists and their governmental collaborators perform for each other is the mutual

---

[3]*This argument is made in the General Interim Report of the Buchanan Committee. U. S. Congress (1950b, pp. 47–51).*
[4]*See the discussion p. 346. Matthews suggests that although tightly knit coalitions may have awesome power, the natural internal strains of the coalition prevent its reaching its full power potential. See his excellent discussion of coalitions, Matthews (1960, pp. 186–88).*

exchange of information. They help each other to keep in touch. A member's office often trusts a lobby group to keep track of a bill that the member is interested in. The group stands by to provide the member with facts for use in the battle; sometimes it even does special research for him or writes his speeches and reports.

Lobbyists were asked to rate the importance of collaborative lobbying for the purposes of their group. They generally rate it quite high. The results of that rating, cross-tabulated with type of organization, are presented in Table VIII-2. This table shows that corporation representatives place the least emphasis on collaboration, while labor and farm representatives place the greatest stress on it. Small trade association representatives show little agreement; some value it highly and others rarely use it. About 80 per cent of the respondents think collaboration is at least moderately important, and 12 per cent consider it more important than any other factor in their success.

Unions collaborate a good deal with other unions as well as with other types of organizations. Collaboration is especially characteristic of federal employee unions which achieve gains for their members only through legislation and other governmental decisions. Lobbyists close to organizational policy and leadership, especially officers, are slightly more likely to value collaboration highly than are lawyers and other consultant lobbyists. Those responsible for planning strategy value collaboration slightly more highly than persons without responsibility. Representatives of organizations with large memberships and considerable power at the polls rate collaboration highly. These large organizations tend to have staff members who can give exclusive attention to Congress; congressional relations staff members value collaboration more highly than lobbyists in other roles.

To sum up, collaboration seems to be valued most highly by organizations with large memberships (usually farm or labor), with considerable power at the polls, and with staffs which work exclusively with Congress. Collaboration is valued both by lobbyists and governmental decision-makers because it saves time and signifies the resolution of conflict. It is also clear, however, that collaboration is useful only in certain settings and that it is unwise where the conditions are not appropriate.

TABLE VIII-2

Ratings of Collaborative Lobbying by Type of Organization

RATING OF COLLABORATIVE LOBBYING

TYPE OF ORGANIZATION	No Importance	Probably Important But We Do Not Use It	Slight Importance	Moderate Importance	Considerable Importance	Most Important Factor	No Response	Total
Large labor				2	5	2	1	10
Small labor		1		1	6			8
Large farm					1	1		2
Small farm					2	1		3
Large trade				2	6		1	9
Small trade		4	3	5	22	7	2	43
Corporation	1	3	5	3	3		2	17
Large citizens	2				4			6
Service or veterans		1					1	2
Church and humanitarian		1			2	1	1	5
Foreign government or firm	1				1			2
More than one type	1		1	3			2	7
TOTAL	5	10	9	16	52	12	10	114

Part Three

Lobbying as a
Communication Process

IN PART Three the study of lobbyists as individuals is abandoned
for the examination of the setting in which lobbyists operate and
the methods they use. To cut through the mass of detail characteristic of the Washington scene, the influence process (another
way of talking about the policy-making process) has been ab-
stracted into a communication process.

Chapter IX presents a model of government as a communication network which is intended as a guide to thinking about the
influence of lobbying on governmental decisions. Chapter X
focuses on patterns of communication within and among lobby
groups. Chapters XI, XII, and XIII concentrate on specific methods
used by lobbyists to communicate with government officials from
the perspective of their effectiveness in obtaining favorable
attention.

CHAPTER IX

GOVERNMENT AS A
COMMUNICATION NETWORK

Several functions are performed in all civil
societies. Two of these functions, as listed by Gabriel Almond, are
"interest aggregation" and "interest articulation."[1] In every society some people attempt to influence the decisions of government
officials; therefore, lobbying exists in every society. The way in
which influence is transmitted and lobbying is conducted varies
with the environment and institutions of a given society.

Understanding influence—and such related concepts as authority, control, and power—has always been of central concern
to political science. Presumably, if one fully understood influence,
he could explain why governmental decisions develop as they do.[2]
Political analysts have recently used several different approaches
and developed different models to aid in the understanding of in-

[1] *Almond (1958, pp. 270–82). Almond's notions are developed further in
Almond and Coleman, eds. (1960, chap. i).*
[2] *Robinson (1962, p. 4) suggests that in certain instances one can substitute
the term "influence" for "explanation."*

fluence.[3] The approach or model employed depends mainly on the kind of influence one is trying to explain and on the way in which the analyst asks his question. For example, some ask which actors in a given group or institution are most influential.[4] They have generally found that no set of individuals is most influential but that influence varies with the issue under contest, the roles of the actors, the tactics employed, and the diligence with which goals are pursued. Other analysts have tried to explain the factors producing given policy decisions.[5] Still others have attempted to weigh the relative influence of different branches of government or of different groups.[6]

The design of this research project leads to a slightly different set of analytical questions. We want to know what the goals or objectives of lobbyists are. We want to know the basis or rationale for choosing means or tactics to achieve those goals. We want to evaluate the effectiveness of lobbying tactics. Finally, we want to form a general estimate of the influence of lobbying on the policy-making process. A communications model seems to be the most serviceable means for clarifying relationships and providing a basis for evaluation.

A COMMUNICATIONS MODEL OF GOVERNMENT

The diagram in Figure I illustrates a useful model for thinking about the relationships among political actors as they function in the governmental policy-making network. A constitution usually specifies the formal power relationships, tying together the actors

[3]*A good theoretical orientation can be found in Lasswell and Kaplan (1950). See also March (1955). Hunter (1953) developed a sociometric model to study influence in a community and later extended his model to the nation (1959). Mills (1956) and Lundberg (1937) are in a similar vein. The elite approach has been severely criticized; see Dahl (1958), Polsby (1959a, 1959b, 1960), and Wolfinger (1960). A game theory model was suggested by Long (1958). Banfield (1961) developed a new model for studying community influence that is difficult to characterize by a short term. Also see Dahl (1961).*

[4]*For a convenient summary of such studies, see Matthews (1960a). Also see Matthews (1960b, chap. v); Dahl, March, and Nasatir (1956); MacRae, Jr. and Price (1959).*

[5]*Bailey (1950), Amrine (1959), Riggs (1950), and Latham (1952). Also see Banfield (1961) for several case studies of influence on policy decisions.*

[6]*Chamberlain (1946) and Kendall (1960). Refer also to Robinson (1962).*

FIGURE 1.

Government As A Communication Network

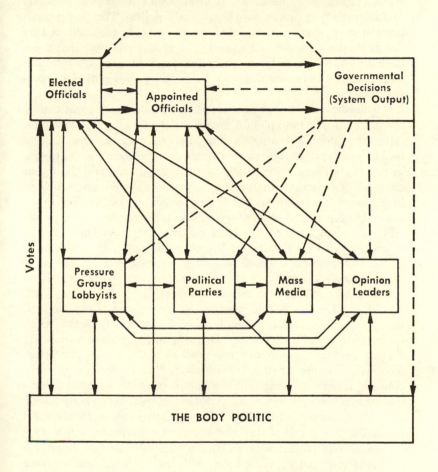

Legend

Power relationship ——————————————▶

Message transmission ◀———————————▶

Feedback loops — — — — — — ▶

in a political system or government. The outputs from such a system are authoritative governmental decisions (laws, executive orders, judicial decisions, etc.). These decisions are produced by elected or appointed officials who are placed in their jobs (directly or indirectly) by the votes of the body politic. The power relationships connecting these actors in the system are indicated by the broad dark arrows in Figure I. The reader will note that these dark arrows run in only one direction (as befits a power relationship), while the message arrows indicate a two-way flow of communications.

The formal power relationships, as specified in a constitution, are not sufficient to explain a government's functioning, however. All such systems develop sets of auxiliary actors who are tied into the formal system by an elaborate communications network. Types of auxiliary actors, their institutional bases, and the major channels of communication tying them into a system are indicated in Figure I. The auxiliary actors can be thought of as intermediaries. They transmit and interpret messages coming from public officials and directed to the body politic. They also transmit and interpret messages flowing in the other direction from the body politic to the officials. These auxiliary actors, of course, are more than intermediaries; very often they initiate communications carrying information and influence attempts.

Figure I indicates that a considerable amount of message exchange takes place within each level of the system (governmental, intermediary, and body politic). Government officials communicate a great deal with one another as well as with citizens and intermediaries. Actors at the intermediary level (lobbyists, party officials, reporters, commentators, etc.) carry on extensive communication among themselves. Also, at the level of the body politic there is an enormous complex of message transmission from citizen to citizen. One result of this vast complex of messages is that cognitions become sufficiently stabilized that officials can make the decisions required by their roles with the more or less accurate perception that they will be supported for doing so.

Although all of the actors in the system probably have some influence in shaping the decisional outputs of the system, we shall be mainly concerned with two sets of actors: the officials and the lobbyists. The lobbyists are the auxiliary actors whose role demands most forthrightly that they try to influence the decisions of the officials. In order to understand the specific objectives of lobbyists and the means they choose to realize those objectives, it is necessary to examine more closely the position and role of the officials they are trying to influence.

The very designation "official" is a formal recognition by all the members of a civil society that a designated individual, or set of individuals, has the right and the power to make and enforce authoritative decisions that are binding on the entire society. Even if a given official cannot make a decision by himself, his assent or denial may be requisite to the completion of the decision (e.g., majority rule). The right to make authoritative decisions is usually granted only for a specified period of time; therefore, all officials are more or less vulnerable. This vulnerability is the main key to understanding their behavior as decision-makers.

Although it may not be true of all officials, it is certainly generally true that their most persistent and pervasive motivation is to maintain or enhance their positions. Officials who do not consciously or unconsciously try to maintain or enhance their positions generally will be ejected from the system. Officials, then, have authority, but they are not autonomous.[7] Elected officials generally want to be re-elected; this usually means that they must please their constituents and satisfy those persons who might support or oppose them in election campaigns (colleagues, party workers, contributors, etc.). Appointed officials want to avoid being discharged and generally also want to be promoted. Not only must they please the official who appointed them and the officials who appropriate money to pay their salaries, but they must avoid situations or behavior which will make their official supporters more vulnerable (e.g., a scandal arising from corruption or a serious error in judgment). A related motivation, characteristic of both elected and appointed officials, is that all want to make a "good record" of performance. Not only does a "good record" lead to maintenance and advancement in the system; it also satisfies the ego needs of the official.

As a general rule, the necessity of maintaining his position in the system does not completely confine the behavior of an

---

[7]Banfield (1961, p. 310) defines autonomous actors as those who cannot be controlled.

official (reduce his decision latitude to zero). On some issues his decision latitude may be very broad; on others it may be rather narrow. Within the decision latitude allowed by his supporters, other motives may come into play. Evidence from the congressional interviews for this study (see Chapter XVII) suggests that the most important of these secondary motives is the desire of the official to have society ordered the way he believes it would be best. Nearly all officials have a so-called political philosophy they would like to see fulfilled. Fulfillment of a political philosophy is in most cases compatible with the motivation to maintain and enhance a position, but the two motives may possibly conflict. Other motives, too, may enter an official's decision. He may, for example, desire pleasant relationships (to be good friends with) his colleagues and may bow to pleadings from a friend. Some officials may like to have a good time, or earn more money, and they may comply with the wishes of persons who can provide those items. The particular combination of motives producing the decision of an official will vary from issue to issue. It will also vary from one individual to another and one role to another.

Understanding something about the role and motives of officials (the discussion above is only a skeletal outline) is essential to understanding the nature of the challenge to any actor who tries to influence an official decision. It is also important for evaluating the success of influence attempts and for understanding the role of non-official actions in the governmental decision process. It is obvious that decisional outputs from the system can be affected only by influencing the decisional processes of officials. The challenge to the lobbyist, or any other would-be influencer, is to affect the decisional process of officials.

There are no objective (real) connections that tie men into a political system;[8] all connections must be perceived by minds. An official's political world is the world that he perceives. A decision by any given official at any given moment will be consonant with his perception of his political world.[9] His perception objectively may well be wrong; in fact, most, if not all, officials operate on the basis of imperfect information. The point here is that all offiicials arrive at decisions on the basis of what they perceive and

[8]The terms "objective" and "real" are used in a physical rather than a metaphysical sense.
[9]"Perception," as used here, may be conscious or unconscious; the term is used broadly to include a system of beliefs and values.

not on the basis of what is objectively true or real.[10] The only way to influence a decision, then, is to influence the perceptions of official decision-makers. Communication is the only means of influencing or changing a perception; the lobbying process, therefore, is totally a communication process.[11] Governmental decisions may also be altered or influenced by substituting one official for another, but that is, by definition, a process different from lobbying.

Congressman Emanuel Celler also thinks of lobbying as a communication process:

> We may define lobbying as the total of all communicated influences upon legislators with respect to legislation . . . After thirty-six years as a target of such messages, I still regard them as the bloodstream of the democratic process and a *sine qua non* of effective legislation. It is true that these messages come to us in a Babel of tongues . . . But fundamentally, I believe, we all recognize that the touchstone of "good" lobbying and "bad" lobbying is not whether the objectives of persuasion are selfish or altruistic, liberal or conservative, prolabor or probusiness, but solely and simply whether the message conveyed is intelligible, accurate, and informative, or cryptic, deceptive, and obscure. . . . The task of the Congressman is arduous enough without being complicated by apocryphal or spurious messages.[12]

If all influences on the perceptions of officials come via communications, it follows that any communication received by an official is potentially influential. An official may be influenced by a message even if the sender had no intention to influence. Officials also actively seek information and thereby, in a sense, influence themselves. We shall not be very concerned with these last two kinds of influence, except as residual categories; our main concern is with deliberate attempts to influence the perceptions of officials. Not all influence attempts are so simple as dispatching a message to an official. It is possible to change the perception of an official by changing the objective reality to which he attends. For example, a lobbyist might convince a strong contender to file

[10]*It is not necessary for this argument to decide how close perception is to reality, nor even carefully to define reality.*
[11]*Milbrath (1960a).*
[12]*Celler (1958, pp. 3, 6).*

against an elective official in a primary election in the hope of influencing the official's perception of his political world. All of the influence in such a sequence of events is transmitted via communications, but the route is much more circuitous than a direct message from lobbyist to official.

With the above considerations in mind, it should now be possible to state more specifically the challenge that faces a lobbyist or any other would-be influencer. The strongest influence an individual or a group could have over an official would result from having the official perceive that his would-be influencers have the power to keep him in office or remove him from office. Strong influence would also result if an official perceived a lobbyist or a lobby group as having the ability to make him look good or bad in the eyes of the other actors in the system and the public-at-large. A good public image is important to the ego of the official as well as to his endeavors to maintain or enhance his position. It shall be apparent later that both of these influence challenges are very difficult for influencers to carry out.

A lobbyist might also try to convince an official to change his political philosophy, but this, too, is considered almost hopeless by lobbyists. Since all officials operate with more or less imperfect information, and they are aware that their information is imperfect, the lobbyist's best means of influence is to try to affect the stream of information that flows to officials. They may challenge the veracity of information he has tentatively accepted; they may supply new information or more reliable information; they may try to structure the way that he processes and assimilates information; they may try to obstruct the reception of competing information; and they may try to formulate new policy alternatives which hopefully are more acceptable. Lobbyists also stand ready to supply personal rewards to officials, but motivations to maintain position and make a good record generally are more important to officials than personal pleasure.

COMMUNICATIONS CONCEPTS

Communications theory, or information theory as it is sometimes called, is finding increasing application in social science.[13]

[13]*This trend was stimulated by the writings of Weiner (1948, 1956).*

Many of the terms and concepts are borrowed from theories of electricity, radio, and electronics. It would be extraneous to our purpose to give a full explanation of communications theory here; however, the concepts borrowed and used in this volume will be defined. Any analysis requires a choice of a unit of analysis. Information theorists use the "bit" as their smallest unit of analysis. There may be several bits of information in a word and many more in a sentence. It will suffice for our purposes to use *message* as our unit of analysis. A message may be as short as one sentence or it may contain many sentences or even paragraphs. We shall define a message as *any thought that is complete or stands by itself.*

Messages are not only *sent* or dispatched, they must also be *received.* A message is received when its intended recipient accepts and ingests the thought it conveys. Messages may fail to be received because they have been *intercepted* and *blocked* by someone other than the intended receiver. Many officials have staff assistants who *sort, code, condense,* and sometimes *block* incoming messages. This coding and condensing is a *translation* process and may introduce *distortion.* A message may also fail to be received if the intended receiver *screens it out.* Every individual (especially a busy public official) is bombarded with many more stimuli than he can possibly attend to. The organism attends selectively to *competing messages* and screens out those that are not wanted. This *selective attention* is often a conscious choice, but it may also operate more or less automatically and unconsciously. A very important behavioral rule here is that the organism receives stimuli that it is *predisposed* to receive and screens out stimuli that it is not predisposed to receive. We recognize this in everyday life when we say that people hear only what they want to hear. A significant fact about officials, simply because they are human, is that they attend only to those messages to which they want to attend. Officials may also seriously distort a message by accepting only part of it and screening out the rest.

In the relations between officials and would-be influencers, it is the official who decides whether communication *channels to* himself will be *open* or *closed.* (A channel is a transmission medium over which messages flow.) An official will not decide to open or close a channel on a whimsical basis; he will naturally be sensitive to keeping channels open to those who can determine his position and advancement in the system. The power of the vote is the best insurance that the governmental communication network will stay relatively open. With this qualification in mind, it is still an important fact that officials can easily stop listening (they can always plead that they are too busy to attend to every message directed to them). This latitude of decision to give or withhold *access* provides a significant power advantage to officials vis-à-vis those who try to influence them. We shall see in Chapter XIII that lobbyists spend considerable time and energy trying to keep open their communication channels to officials.

Messages follow what are usually called *paths* or *routes*. A message coming via one channel or path may be more acceptable than the same message coming via another channel or path. The knowledge of the sender about the predispositions of the receiver may determine the path he chooses for transmitting the message. The path taken by a message may also affect *transmission time*. The sender with a more direct route or who can make faster *connections* (this is the crucial importance of contacts) sometimes gains an advantage by getting his message through first. Channels may carry messages in only one direction, but generally they can carry messages in both directions. All the message channels shown in Figure I carry messages in both directions.

Channels have a certain *capacity* which, if exceeded, creates a condition called *overload*. A slight amount of overload will distort messages; a serious overload will make them completely unintelligible. Lobbyists recognize this when they use several alternate channels for transmitting messages. Chapter XI will indicate that lobbyists prefer direct conversations with officials as a means of conveying their message, but they realize at the same time that this channel can be easily overloaded (an official can see only a limited number of callers in a day); therefore they try to reserve their access via this channel for problems that they consider very important. In addition to messages, channels may carry a certain amount of extraneous matter that is called *noise* or static. Noise is any stimulus that detracts from the clarity of the message. To recapitulate, there are four kinds of distortion that a sender must worry about: (1) distortion arising from any translation or condensing process, (2) distortion arising from the predispositions of the receiver who hears only what he wants to hear, (3) distortion arising from overloaded channels, and (4) distortion arising from excessive noise in the channel.

Most communication systems incorporate *feedback loops*. A feedback loop is a stimulus arising from the output of the system which feeds back and becomes a new input to the system. A system that is dynamic must be closed by one or more feedback loops or else it may react erratically (oscillate) or come to rest for lack of a new stimulus.[14] In the model shown in Figure I, the new laws or orders produced by the system become a part of the environment for actors in the system. The changed environment stimulates new perceptions in the actors which become new factors guiding their behavior.

Keeping these concepts in mind, the task of the lobbyist can now be stated in communication terminology. *It is the lobbyist's job to create messages and choose means of transmission which are most likely to insure clear and favorable reception of the message by the intended receiver.* This means that the lobbyist must anticipate the predispositions of his intended receiver(s) and so act that the message will be favorably received with as little distortion as possible. He must take care that the message is not intercepted or blocked. He must choose a transmission channel which is open (has access), is not likely to be overloaded, and has a low noise level.

MASS MEDIA, PARTIES, AND OPINION LEADERS IN THE UNITED STATES POLICY-MAKING NETWORK

Perhaps the most important intermediaries between officials and the body politic are the mass media; they certainly carry the greatest load of communications. Citizens learn about the behavior of officials primarily through the mass media, and officials learn about citizens largely through the mass media. Transmission of such information involves selection, condensa-

---

[14]*In electronic applications, feedback loops are designed into systems to make them more stable and to prevent oscillation.*

tion, and distortion by the persons who operate the mass media. The power that accompanies control of information may tempt media workers to try to influence governmental decisions. Although professional codes pressing for objectivity tend to suppress this temptation, many workers in the mass media field work just as diligently as lobbyists to influence governmental decisions. Reporters and commentators who have large public followings, or who have close confidential relationships with certain public officials, can have considerable impact on official decisions.

The Washington press corps deserves special comment here. The hustle of the Washington scene and the weightiness of the decisions made there attract many of the best reporters in the country.[15] This group of political actors has a high reputation with public officials in Washington. Officials and reporters are tied in a close working relationship.[16] Reporters need information, tips, and gossip — in Washington most of these come from public officials. Meanwhile, officials need information about movement and change in their environment — especially about the behavior of other officials. Reporters give and collect information as they make their rounds. In return for giving news to reporters, officials expect to be speedily informed of developments important to their own endeavors. Many officials (and lobbyists) report that they obtain a great deal of valuable information from the Washington press corps. In a sense, Washington reporters are circulating gossip-mongers who do much to link together the various parts of the government into a functioning political system. They are so essential that if they were not present, their role would have to be invented to make the system work.[17]

Political parties and party officials are another set of actors in the system. American parties are oriented primarily toward election campaigns and have less force in shaping policies and governmental decisions than do parties in other democracies such as Britain and Scandinavia. Nevertheless, parties and party officials do try to influence the behavior of public officials (sometimes, of course, party officials are public officials also). A party

[15]Cater (1959), Rosten (1937).
[16]Matthews (1960b, chap. ix). Although he wrote a novel, Allen Drury (1959) describes this relationship rather well.
[17]In developing a simulation of international relations, Guetzkow (1959, 1962) found that reporters and newspapers were a necessary part of the system.

official may contact a public official about a problem of personal interest; more frequently, however, party officials contact public officials on behalf of other citizens or constituents. Members of Congress report few contacts by party officials for personal or ideological reasons but report regular contact about constituent problems. Sometimes a party official uses an elected official as an intermediary in an attempt to influence the decision of an appointed official. It is common for a party official and a member of Congress to call jointly on an appointed official in the administration who is making a decision of concern to their district.

Opinion leaders also enter the communication system. Their institutional base is less clearly definable than those of the other sets of actors in the system. The concept of opinion leader used here is largely that developed by Lazarsfeld, Katz and associates.[18] Lazarsfeld first described the two-step flow of communication from officials or the mass media to opinion leaders and thence to the wide citizenry.[19] Opinion leaders give much more sustained attention to the political process than the average citizen. They have read and learned more about politics, and they often have well-developed opinions which they urge upon their friends and neighbors. An implicit division of labor occurs in society such that citizens who are not well informed and who do not have clearly formulated ideas look to opinion leaders for guidance on political problems. Persons not reached in any other way may be reached via opinion leaders. This central position in the communication network gives opinion leaders more than ordinary influence. Officials, especially elected officials, realize that they need the support of opinion leaders to win re-election and to organize support for policies and programs. This enables opinion leaders to make demands on officials and even to influence their decisions.

The persons who occupy these other intermediary roles (in addition to lobbyists) in the communication network are in as strong a position as most lobbyists to influence government decisions. In nearly all influence attempts, the lobbyist is competing with numerous other would-be influencers; it is important to remember this fact when evaluating the impact of lobbying on democracy.

[18]*Katz and Lazarsfeld (1955); Lazarsfeld, Berelson, and Gaudet (1948); Berelson, Lazarsfeld, and McPhee (1954); and Katz (1957).*
[19]*Lazarsfeld, Berelson, and Gaudet (1948, pp. 150–58).*

COMMUNICATIONS AND INFLUENCE
ATTEMPTS AMONG OFFICIALS

Officials are often conceived of as mere pawns in the political game who are pushed hither and yon by the contending forces trying to influence governmental decisions. This is but a half-truth (see footnote 8, Chapter XVII). To be sure, officials do receive and react to influence attempts (in fact, they expect them as a normal part of their role); however, most officials also have issue positions and ideas of their own that they wish to see enacted into policy. Government is intentionally structured in the United States and in many other countries so that no one official has the power to make policy decisions all by himself. Therefore, an official must convince other officials to go along with him if he hopes to have his policies officially enacted. Officials, then, are advocates and influence senders as well as the recipients of influence attempts.

How do officials transmit influence attempts directed at fellow officials? The most obvious and frequently used method is to send a direct personal communication, usually in a face-to-face conversation. The heaviest flow is within an official's own branch or department. If the sender has a well-established working relationship with the receiver, messages are highly credible and are likely to be influential. Members of Congress interviewed for this study report that they most frequently consult their own colleagues for information and advice. In addition to the frequent interaction required by the formal institutional relationship, there is a network of informal social relationships outside the work situation which not only provides opportunity for additional interaction, but also establishes standards of communication credibility. For example, one congressman reports that the wives of the freshmen members of each new Congress form a club. The social relationships established at this time often continue through many succeeding Congresses. Also, the freshmen members of one House committee formed a card-playing group that met once a week. They have continued to meet and play cards even though the members have dispersed to permanent positions on more important committees.

In addition to the easy communication and confidence created by everyday working relationships, quid-pro-quo relationships are encouraged by the necessity of gaining the acquiescence of other officials to make governmental decisions. Official B, in return for going along with official A on something A desires, can demand that A vote with him on something that he desires. Quid-pro-quo relationships are more effective on minor unpublicized matters than on major well-publicized matters. On well-publicized matters, the official's concern with the maintenance of his public image and support from constituents outweighs and more or less precludes the operation of individual quid-pro-quo relationships. These reciprocal relationships also tie an official to his reference group. The members of a political party in Congress constitute such a reference group. It is often made clear to a member that he must vote with the party or the leadership if he hopes to find cooperation for matters that he wishes to accomplish. Reference groups also exist in executive agencies and even across different branches of the government; for example, Republicans often invoked the team concept during the Eisenhower administration.

The necessity for all officials to maintain support if they hope to continue in their decision-making role makes them vulnerable to pressure from outside the government. This is true of both elected officials, where the main pressure is exerted through votes, and appointed officials, who must maintain the support of the elected officials. Officials also try to wield outside pressure upon one another. Members of Congress and other officials work intimately with lobby groups to exert pressure on fellow officials and to excite public sentiment in support of desired policies. Officials have even been known to create lobby groups to pressure other officials to support a proposal. It was mentioned earlier (page 36) that the Committee for a National Trade Policy was formed by the White House to lobby the Congress for renewal of the Reciprocal Trade Agreements Program. Occasionally an elected official who is receiving many letters in opposition to his personal position on a matter will ask a lobby group friendly to his personal position to stimulate an equal number of letters supporting his position — leaving him free to vote his personal convictions. In particularly hard-fought battles in Congress, a member who is highly involved and committed on the issue may allow his office to be used as a command post or general clearing house for all lobby groups supporting his position on the matter.

Officials try to use the press as well as lobby groups in fighting their battles. The quid-pro-quo information exchange between reporters and officials was mentioned previously. Officials also cultivate a favorable relationship with the press so that they may use it to maintain or create a favorable public image. They also want the cooperation of the press in publicizing their views on policy matters. Wide publicity for a given view and its clash with alternative views stirs up a variety of communications from the public designed to influence other officials. No officials, especially elected ones, can afford to neglect relationships with the press. The greater their concern to get their policy views adopted, the more important are their press relationships.

Although message flow is heaviest within the branches of the government, many messages are also transmitted between the branches. Direct personal communications (phone calls, meetings, letters, social encounters) are most frequent, and many are purely informational. The executive branch has an enormous variety of experts which legislative officials regularly call on for information. Executive officials also have the most direct and relevant information about the way a given piece of legislation functions.

In addition to exchanging information, officials try to influence the decisions of officials in other branches. They may work with lobby groups; they may utilize the press; they may try to stimulate letters from the people. The formal governmental structure also gives officials of one branch power to wield against officials of another branch. Congress has powers to appropriate, legislate, and investigate with which to operate against the other branches. Many citizens recognize these powers when they use the intervention of their congressman to secure favorable action from administrative officials. Administrative departments react to this power by setting up congressional liaison divisions to cultivate smooth relationships between the department and Congress. These liaison officers try to avoid being thought of as lobbyists, but they are often spoken of as executive bureau lobbyists.[20]

[20]*Dorothy C. Tompkins (1956) has a chapter on "The Federal Lobby" containing many references to articles, hearings, and reports on the subject. See also Freeman (1955, 1958).*

From time to time, Congress investigates the activities of these congressional liaison divisions[21] to remind them to act properly but allows them to continue performing what is generally considered a useful function.[22]

Executive officials, in turn, have power to wield against Congress. They possess detailed information and expertise. In addition, the executive appoints persons to fill many jobs, especially at the local level. Any member of Congress who needs patronage to strengthen his local political organization becomes sensitive to the executive's power of appointment. Further, significant policy choices are sometimes entrusted to executive officials, and these can be used to bargain with members of Congress. The Secretary of Agriculture (both Brannan and Benson were mentioned) has been accused of using his power to establish support prices for certain commodities as leverage to obtain support for his farm program. For example, high support prices for cotton might be promised to cotton belt senators in return for their favorable votes on the secretary's farm program. In another case, the Eisenhower administration is reputed to have agreed not to submit to the Senate for ratification the United Nations Covenant of Human Rights (which was opposed by southern senators) in return for southern support of the President in his opposition to the Bricker amendment.

Another set of actors in the communication network are the staff members who support government officials. These people have their own ideas and policy positions. They are not in a position to wield great power (unless they are acting for their bosses), but they have an advantage in their strategic position in the communication network. The official overloaded with messages turns the processing of information over to assistants. The assistants can allow information which supports their personal preferences to pass on to the officials and cull out that which opposes their preferences. More important, they can give valuable information and advice to lobbyists and the press when they know it will be used to support their policy position. In addition, they often are more knowledgeable on a given subject than their

---

[21]See Dorothy C. Tompkins (1956) for references.

[22]Robinson (1962, pp. 158–67) found a heavy flow of communications between Congress and the State Department passing through the Congressional Relations Office of the State Department.

employers—which inclines the bosses to accept the advice of their assistants.

The total network of influences and communications has a circular character; it was described by several respondents as a whirlpool. The comment of one staff member to a Senate committee suggests again the variety of messages and influences at work in the governmental decision process:

> You must think about this as a set of circular pressures. Private groups can help a Senator get a friend named to a judgeship. There is plenty of lobbying by Congress of the executive too; and there is much lobbying within the House and Senate; we call this intramural lobbying. There is even more lobbying by the staffs of the members and the staffs of the committees. This is probably the most potent and most hidden kind of lobbying. Generally it is healthy; there is no way to prevent it, and where there are abuses, the best cure is to get a counter-lobby. Countering one pressure by another pressure is the best way to control it.

THE POLICY PROCESS IN WESTERN DEMOCRACIES

The model of the governmental policy process set forth in Figure I is abstract and general enough to apply to any system of government with popularly elected officials and a relatively open communications system. One would expect to find all of the kinds of actors shown there playing more or less the same general roles in any such system. On the other hand, different structural characteristics and national heritages lead to differences in emphases. It may be instructive to look at some similarities and differences in emphases with respect to our understanding of influence and the functions of interest aggregation and articulation.

POLICY INITIATION AND LEADERSHIP BY THE EXECUTIVE

Every American school child learns that there is division of labor in government—that the legislative branch makes the laws, the executive enforces the laws, and the judicial branch interprets them. From this it is easy to leap to the conclusion that the legislative body has the most influence in initiating and developing policy. Yet it seems to be ever more obvious in the modern world that the executive takes the leadership in policy development. This trend is quite pronounced in countries with cabinet-led parliaments, but the generalization clearly holds also for the presidential system in the United States.[23] The pre-eminence of the executive in policy formation is attested to by both congressional and lobbyist respondents.[24]

One reason for this trend is that so many of the major problems of modern government have their roots in foreign policy and international relations.[25] In matters of foreign policy the executive is both constitutionally charged with leadership and better equipped to take leadership.[26] Another reason for executive initiative is that executive staff members can become more specialized and give problems more sustained attention. Since they can dig deeper into problems, they are more likely to come up with ideas and take the policy initiative. The executive is in a better position to take advantage of the "information revolution" of the twentieth century.[27] The executive can accumulate, store, and process a great amount of data; whereas legislative bodies, as presently constituted, are not equipped for the task. One particularly thoughtful leader of Congress lamented the inability of Congress to compete with the executive in creativity and lay the blame primarily to inadequate staffing for Congress:

> If Congress is going to assume a leadership position, it is a problem of staff. We need to be equal to the executive branch in the ability to create—that means ability to do research. We need time to think about ideas, and that means a larger and more capable staff.

[23]*Truman (1959, pp. 1–7) and Acheson (1957, p. 26). On Britain, see Eckstein (1960, pp. 16–18).*
[24]*See Chapter XVII.*
[25]*The pressure by the executive to keep the steel companies from raising prices in the spring of 1962 was justified as in the national interest because of the challenge of the cold war and international trade.*
[26]*Robinson (1962, esp. chap. vii).*
[27]*Boulding (1960).*

On the other hand, some members do not believe that Congress should even attempt to compete with the executive in hiring staff and conducting research.

LEGISLATURES SIT IN JUDGMENT

As the executive has assumed policy initiative to a greater and greater extent, legislative bodies have adopted a role that looks increasingly like that of a judge. Although the analogy should not be pushed too far, it is fair to say that on many questions Congress performs like a court. It is common for points of dispute between two or more contending interests to be brought to Congress for ruling. Congress hears testimony from both sides and then writes a rule (passes a law). The rule may favor one side or the other, but will probably be a compromise between the contending points of view. Interests that fail to obtain satisfaction through administrative or judicial decisions often bring their case to the "court" of Congress. Many members of Congress are trained in the law and find it natural to sit in judgment; they often speak of "using their judgment" or "deciding on the merits of the case."[28]

Congress naturally operates by different rules than do judicial courts: standards for the admissability of evidence are more liberal; members (unlike judges) can actively seek information and may totally alter the character of the case; Congress may postpone decision indefinitely or decide not to hand down any decision at all; it need not decide for or against any of the parties; it can decide on the basis of public sentiment rather than restrict itself to the merits of the question; and it is not bound by precedent. Despite these differences, it is analogically correct to say that Congress sits in judgment; this is especially true of its role vis-à-vis interest groups, but it also tends to be true of its role on any policy question. Proposals are generally brought to Congress, and Congress sits in judgment. Its primary role is as a legitimator of policy. Parliaments and other Western legislatures also seem to have assumed the primary roles of judges and legitimators. On the other hand, parliaments are less frequently called upon to settle disputes between private contending interests than is the United

[28] *The court analogy for Congress vis-à-vis interest groups is also used by Truman (1951, p. 394) and Key (1961, pp. 192–93).*

States Congress; in other countries, the resolution of conflicts between contending interests seems to be handled more routinely through the executive bureaucracy or political parties.[29] Perhaps this difference will become clearer through examination of why lobbying as a role is more elaborately developed in the United States than in other Western democracies.

WHY MORE LOBBYISTS IN THE UNITED STATES?

Only in the United States are large numbers of special political actors designated to play the role of lobbyist on a full-time professional basis. It is difficult to give an adequate explanation of this because the subject has not been adequately studied. This is not at all to say that European pressure groups have not been studied; actually quite a number of studies of European pressure groups have been made in recent years.[30] The presence of many more lobbyists does not mean that there are many more pressure groups in the United States; neither does it mean that pressure groups have a greater impact on policy-making here. The evidence comparing pressure group impact in various countries is not sufficiently clear or complete to enable generalization. The question here is, why has the United States political system developed so elaborately the role of the lobbyist? The following are only suggestions for explanatory factors. Further research may disclose additional factors and suggest emendations to these.

It is characteristic of interests that they seek representation in governmental decision-making; if they cannot find adequate representation through formal governmental or semi-governmental channels, they will seek other channels. In most western European governments, decision-making is highly concentrated in the cabinet executive, and interests are given more or less direct representation in the making of decisions. Interest groups are given seats on advisory boards or are consulted as a matter of course

---

[29]*Eckstein (1960, pp. 17, 18).*

[30]*There has been a recent flurry of academic interest in British pressure groups: Eckstein (1960); Finer (1958); Stewart (1958); and Potter (1961). Potter cites many recent articles on the subject (pp. 13–15). Pressure groups in other countries are not so thoroughly studied, but considerable work is in progress. The best available summary of work to date is Ehrmann, ed. (1958a). Also see Ehrmann (1958b, 1961). The Christian Michelson Institute of Bergen, Norway, has launched a long-range study of interest representation in Western governments.*

by ministers or bureau chiefs.[31] It is also more common in Europe than in the United States for interest groups to succeed in electing one or more of their own men to seats in the legislative body. Representation of interests is not so clearly built into the United States system, although advisory committees are widely used in the executive branch. Groups must generally take the initiative if they want to be heard at decision time—hence the hiring of special envoys to spot opportunities and challenges and make certain that the group is heard.

In the United States decisions are shared to a greater extent between coordinate branches of the national government and also to a certain extent among the national, state, and local governments. The governmental decision process in the United States is so diffuse that groups must hire lobbyists to give them eyes and ears at the seat of government—as necessary insurance.

Differences in the political party system also seem to affect lobbying. European parties are more closely allied with and based on interest groups (especially in multi-party systems). Generally, they are also more "responsible" (able and required to carry out their program when given power) than American parties. European interest groups, then, are somewhat more likely than American interest groups to find political parties a useful means of representation.[32] American parties are so heterogeneous that they must compromise group interests rather than clearly speak for them.[33] Furthermore, American parties cannot be counted on for firm policy leadership. This study shows that interest groups in the United States have almost abandoned working through parties and instead have hired lobbyists to secure policy representation.

It has often been suggested that a more responsible party system in the United States would decrease the influence of pressure groups. That proposition seems doubtful; at most, such a development would shift the clash of interests away from the congressional battlefield to the party battlefield and might leave the net impact of pressure groups substantially the same. Not only is

[31]*For a case in Britain, see Eckstein's (1961, pp. 78–91) description of the relations between the British Medical Association and the Ministry of Health.*
[32]*Beer (1958, p. 138).*
[33]*Eckstein (1961, p. 162), in discussing parties in two-party systems, says, "They do not so much aggregate opinions as reduce them to their lowest and vaguest denominators, sometimes distorting the perspectives and goals they seek to mobilize out of all recognition."*

it highly unlikely that we shall ever have significantly more responsible parties in the United States, but, according to Harry
Eckstein, interests probably could never be represented adequately through parties:

In democratic systems parties must perform simul-
taneously two functions which are, on the evidence, irrecon-
cilable: to furnish efficient decision-makers and to represent
accurately opinions. The best way to reconcile these functions
in practice is to supplement the parties with an alternative
set of representative organizations which can affect decisions
without affecting the positions of the decision-makers. This
is the pre-eminent function of pressure groups in effective
democratic systems, as the competition for power is the
pre-eminent function of the parties.[34]

---

[34]*Eckstein (1961, p. 163).*

CHAPTER X

PATTERNS OF COMMUNICATION WITHIN AND AMONG LOBBY GROUPS

Within organizations, communications flow from lobbyist representatives to the membership of the groups they represent. They also flow in the opposite direction—from the members and officers of organizations to their lobbyists. In this chapter, the flow of communications between different lobby organizations and between lobby organizations and political parties also will be briefly explored.

FROM LOBBYISTS TO SUPPORTING ORGANIZATIONS

Each respondent in the study was asked how he reports back to his organization. Most have several methods. The method selected depends on the content of the message, the type of organization, the respondent's role in the organization, and the size of the organization's lobby staff. The method that figures most prominently for each respondent's role is shown in Table VII–2.

Every lobbyist must report to his group on the day-to-day progress of governmental decisions important. These reports include information about recent developments and estimations about possible tactics. They are usually made in staff meetings if the lobbyist is a member of a staff of several persons. The staff members pool their information and substantially increase the total information available to the group. In the absence of a staff meeting, the staff member usually reports to the chief staff person. Table VII-2 shows that about 20 per cent of the respondents report primarily to a supervisor or staff meeting.

The lobbyist who works alone has no occasion to pool or coordinate information; therefore, daily reports are not necessary. However, he probably reports regularly and fairly frequently (e.g., once a week) to the legislative leaders of his organization; these may be officers, an executive committee, a legislative committee, or a "strategy committee." His reports may be transmitted in face-to-face conversations, or, if the headquarters are in a distant city, the lobbyist probably reports by phone or letter. One respondent reports confidential matters only by phone or in conversation; he does not want any written memos circulating that could be traced back to him. He is a bit naive not to reflect that a phone call could be recorded or that the recipient might take notes, but it is interesting that some lobbyists are so elaborately cautious in reporting.

Lobbyist-consultants and attorneys often are selected for specific and limited jobs. As experts, they are given a rather free hand. They are not expected to report to their employers as regularly as are staff members, and they report more informally. A letter or phone call often will suffice. Further, when the job is completed, they usually do not write a lengthy report; a letter explaining the outcome is all that is expected. Table VII-2 shows that a little more than one-fourth of the respondents report by these informal methods.

Lobbyists pass much important information on to the membership: appraisals of the political and legislative situation as it affects the interests of the members or clients and data and economic studies focusing on the particular product or subject matter interest of the membership. Lobby organizations usually have a regularized medium for disseminating this information, such as their own newspaper or magazine. The lobbyist himself may edit the paper or write a column or section. Some organizations put out weekly newsletters on the legislative and political situation; still others issue special legislative bulletins dealing with one or two matters at a time. Usually these are published only when Congress is in session.

Appeals to the membership for action usually are handled separately. Special action bulletins call on the membership to communicate with government officials. Sometimes these are sent to only a select list of interested and involved members who can be relied upon to take the initiative in reaching officials. Organizations with locals or community-based clubs often have one person who receives the action bulletins; he is responsible for stimulating his fellow members to take appropriate action. Since it is important that the communications not appear to have been "ground out" by the leadership, many organizations print pamphlets or otherwise instruct local leaders to send communications to officials which appear to be spontaneous.[1]

Many lobbyists, especially the salaried ones, are required to make formal summary reports each year to the board or the annual meeting of the membership. These are usually carefully prepared and may even be printed and widely distributed. One lobbyist says that his report to the annual meeting usually presents a rosy picture, but his report to the board dwells on problems. Over half of the respondents say they are required to report formally to the board or annual meeting.

One additional type of communication flowing from lobbyist to membership deserves special mention. In many lobby organizations, continued support by the membership is by no means a foregone conclusion. From time to time, the membership may consider eliminating the lobbying activity, and it is up to the lobbyist or lobby staff to make a case for continuation of the work. About one-third of the respondents must make a case from time to time for the continuation of their activities. This is especially true of lawyers, consultants, and others who lobby for a fee, but even a few salaried staff members must convince the membership. Organizations financed by dues seldom question their lobbying activ-

[1] See Chapter XII.

ities, but those financed by fees or contributions are more likely to examine the continuation of lobbying.

Related to having to make a case for continuation is the tactic of "farming the membership." Most officers and lobbyists realize that written, impersonal communications are not sufficient to keep the members well informed and to maintain their support. Therefore, whenever possible they tour at the grass roots, conferring with local leaders and speaking to local membership meetings. They encourage enthusiasm and develop in the members the conviction that lobbying performs useful functions. Lobbyists of all types participate in this activity; some are active even though the elimination of lobbying activities is never considered by the organization. In fact, lobbyists on a salary (they are probably more closely identified with the organization) spend more time at the grass roots than those lobbying for a fee. About 33 per cent of the lobbyists report spending more than 10 per cent of their time at the grass roots and another 37 per cent spend up to 10 per cent of their time there.

FROM MEMBERS OR CLIENTS TO LOBBYISTS

Messages flowing from members to lobbyists are not as frequent as those from lobbyists to members—mainly because of division of labor. Lobbyists are generally chosen for an expertise which precludes the necessity of day-to-day guidance by the membership. In addition, they are guided by long-range programs or policy statements. These programs are usually approved, at least *pro forma*, by the membership, though lobbyists often have considerable influence in the formation of the program or policies. In sum, it is not necessary for the members, or even the leaders, to give daily guidance to the activities of their lobbyists.

Other kinds of communication come up from the ranks, however. The members are sometimes important sources of information relevant to the lobbyist's job. Inside tips and other useful bits of information are passed on to Washington. This is especially true of trade associations of large and significant firms. A few trade association executives and officers say that their own industry is their major source of inside information. In addition to tips and "inside dope," association members usually send information about production and employment to association headquarters, where it is compiled and distributed.

In some organizations, most communications from members to lobbyists are requests for help of one kind or another. A lobbyist for a federation of government employees is asked to handle a considerable number of grievances for members. Industrial members of trade associations often want help with government contracts or the interpretation of regulations. Lobbyists for farm organizations are requested to clear up various members' difficulties with the Department of Agriculture. Because government reaches intimately into the lives of so many people, lobbyists receive a substantial number of these requests. Sometimes simply advice rather than assistance is sought. Since the lobbyist is on the Washington scene daily, he is naturally turned to for advice on how to get things done.

BETWEEN LOBBY ORGANIZATIONS

Collaborative action is the main occasion for message flows between organizations.[2] When organizations have interests and goals in common, the communication flow between them is likely to be rather heavy. If they are collaborating in a hot policy battle, they may be in daily or hourly contact.

Communications also pass between competitive organizations, though probably less directly and less frequently. All lobbyists try to keep informed about the activities of their competitors. They read one another's publications, gather information about each other from neutral sources (mutual acquaintances, for example), and often take time for a friendly talk when they meet. Organizations that are neither competitive nor collaborative may also exchange messages. Whether communications move between cooperating, neutral, or competitive organizations, they serve to tie the various groups into the governmental decision-making net-

[2]See Chapter VIII for a discussion of collaboration.

work. Only by being well informed about each other's activities can each organization function adequately in pursuit of its own interests.

BETWEEN LOBBY GROUPS AND POLITICAL PARTIES

It was hypothesized that lobbyists would try to utilize political parties to further the goals of their groups; therefore, they were asked specifically about their contacts with political party officials. Lobbyists do not try very hard to utilize political parties in their work. The volume of communications between lobbyists and party officials is quite low; fifty-eight respondents have no contact at all with party officials; another thirty-nine say they have only a few contacts; and only four have many contacts. Only about a third of the respondents report that their organizations make any presentations before the platform committees of either party.

The hesitancy to build contacts with parties seems to derive from two factors. First, most lobbyists believe that political parties per se have little influence on governmental decisions. Only about 20 per cent of the respondents believe parties have considerable importance in shaping public policy; whereas about 60 per cent think parties have very little importance (the remaining 20 per cent think they have moderate importance). The perception that parties have little influence over policy arises from several historical and institutional factors that need not be detailed here.[3] The widespread belief that party platforms are almost useless as guides to future governmental decisions is but one commonplace evidence.

The second factor leading to little party contact is lobbyists' belief that since they must work with elected officials from both political parties (nearly all respondents report that they work "both sides of the aisle"), they try to avoid becoming too closely identified with one party. This is true even of those who have, over the years,

[3]For a discussion of several of these factors, see Key (1958, pp. 727–41) and Truman (1951, chap. ix).

generally supported candidates from one party at election time. Fear that too close contact with party officials may cut them off from elected officials of the other party leads some lobbyists to shun all contact with party officials. On the other hand, there can be little doubt that lobbyists would have much more contact with party officials if they believed that these officials had important power to influence governmental decisions.

Whether or not a lobbyist communicates regularly with party officials seems to be a function of his past political experience and also of the type of organization he represents. Persons who were active in party politics before becoming lobbyists continue to have party contacts and communicate more frequently with party officials. Lobbyists from large membership organizations, which generally are more inclined to get involved in election battles, are more likely to have contacts than those from small membership organizations. Large membership organizations are more likely to present their views before platform committees of the parties. These relationships reflect the recognition by these organizations of their power at the polls (and, therefore, their ability to utilize political parties to attain their objectives). Finally, lobbyists who are politically active are more likely to suggest that parties are important in determining public policy.

In addition to communication with party officials, lobbyists can learn about political party activities from the mass media and from elected public officials. This, too, is a type of communication with political parties. On the whole, however, overt and direct communication between pressure group representatives and political party officials is rather limited. The flow of communication would probably be much heavier if lobbyists perceived party officials and organizations as having considerable power over governmental decisions. Lobbyists representing groups with sufficient power at the poles to affect the nomination and election process (the limited province of American parties) may try to affect that process by utilizing party institutions to affect governmental decisions. Lobbyists representing groups with little power at the polls generally ignore political parties.

CHAPTER XI

LOBBYISTS APPROACH GOVERNMENT — DIRECT PERSONAL COMMUNICATION

In discussing the methods lobbyists use to communicate with governmental decision-makers, it might be wise to emphasize that lobbyists must not only send communications, they must also design them so that they will be favorably received. The only *effective communications* are those which penetrate the perceptual screen of the receiver. The concept of *effective communication* is close to David Truman's use of the word *access* to describe the prime motivation or purpose of lobbyists and lobby groups.[1] Truman uses *access* in a slightly broader way to imply that persons or groups with high access have sufficient power and status to insure that the receiver will more or less comply with the behavior pattern suggested by the communication. *Effective communication* here means only that the receiver gives the message a considered hearing. Both of these concepts are somewhat stronger than the word *entree*, which connotes merely obtaining an appointment.

There are several barriers to effective communication that

[1]*Truman (1951, Part III).*

lobbyists must overcome. Each governmental decision-maker has a set of predispositions which derive from a variety of sources: heredity, environment, conditioned learning, current role constraints, physiological needs, etc. These personal predispositions are enduring rather than transitory and provide long term guidance for behavior. An individual's predisposition complex can be called his personality. The important thing about predispositions for our analysis is that they not only guide behavior but also provide a perceptual screen allowing some stimuli to pass through while arresting or shutting out others. It is well known that different people viewing the same event may perceive it quite differently. Anyone reading congressional hearings, for example, must conclude that most members of Congress hear what they want to hear from witnesses. The most significant barrier to effective communication facing the lobbyist, then, is the perceptual screen of his intended receiver.

There are other barriers as well. Officials suffer from a serious overload of communications. It is physically impossible for any government official to attend to all the communications directed to him. Officials use their personal perceptual screen to protect themselves from some of this overload. They also have devised some institutional means, such as staff assistants and data coding, to help them sort, condense, and comprehend as much of the incoming information as possible. In the scramble for limited attention, the lobbyist must plan carefully and seize a rare moment of receptivity to drive home a communication.

Another condition to be met is that the lobbyist must make his communication credible. In some ways the credibility barrier is similar to the perceptual screen—except that the perceptual screen is unconscious, whereas decisions about credibility are usually conscious. Government officials receive many messages containing conflicting or contradictory information; they soon learn that they must evaluate all messages. One guide to credibility is the extent to which arguments are backed up by facts and research data.

A clear and straightforward presentation also suggests credibility to a receiver. However, clear presentations backed up by data are proven incorrect from time to time; therefore, government officials look to the source of the data for an additional guide. The sender's reputation for integrity and trustworthiness is often decisive in determining the credibility of communications. This point was reiterated again and again both by congressional and lobbyist respondents. Competitive organizations comb each other's communications for mistakes or misrepresentations, which they use to the disadvantage of the original sender. One lobbyist said that once he had found over fifty mistakes in a report made by an opponent; exposition of these mistakes destroyed the credibility of the writer of the report.[2] A quotation from a lobbyist respondent emphasizes the necessity for credibility:

A reputable lobbyist must be very careful whom he represents. He may lose a great deal of prestige if he represents cases or clients that may come into conflict. It is extremely important that a congressman think of a lobbyist as a kind of doctor that he can depend on. Unless a congressman has real confidence in a lobbyist, that lobbyist simply does not have much influence. The greatest compliment one can get is for a member of Congress to say, "whatever that fellow tells you, you can depend on it."

Officials emphasize that information must be reliable not only because they need it for their own decisions, but also because they use this information in communications with other officials and with the public. An official who has committed himself using information supplied by a lobbyist which is later proved incorrect will be seriously embarrassed and will cut off further access for that lobbyist. Practically, the interdependence of lobbyist and governmental decision-maker requires that their relationship be built on trust and integrity.

To surmount these barriers lobbyists use both direct and indirect methods to communicate with governmental decision-makers. Some direct methods are personal presentations of viewpoints and research findings, and testimony at hearings. Some indirect methods are approaches through constituents and friends, letter and telegram campaigns, public relations campaigns, and the publicizing of voting records; these will be discussed in the next chapter. Both kinds of communications contain arguments

---

[2] *Methods for building a reputation for integrity and trustworthiness will be discussed at the end of Chapter XIII.*

and supporting facts; they differ only in the distinction between the lobbyist's speaking directly to the decision-maker or through an intermediary.

Lobbyists have personal predispositions or preferences for either direct or indirect methods. Respondents were initially asked an open-ended question: "What approach do you generally follow to try to get a member of Congress or other public official to agree with your point of view?" About 80 per cent of the respondents said they prefer direct methods. Next, respondents were asked to rate fourteen possible techniques for bringing home a point to a public official. They were asked to use as a guide a scale running from 0 for not effective at all to 10 for very effective; the scale was presented visually in this form:

0	1	2	3	4	5	6	7	8	9	10

The techniques to be rated were listed below it. The ratings of the direct methods correlate positively with an indicated preference for direct methods in the open-ended question. Ratings of direct methods generally correlate negatively with ratings of indirect methods. For example, respondents who rate "personal presentation of viewpoints" high tend to rate "communication through a constituent" low.

Why the general preference for direct methods? Assuming equal receptivity, direct communications are simpler, less dangerous, and less expensive. Using indirect methods, there is some danger that an intermediary will garble the message, and it is certainly more trouble to work through someone else. As pointed out previously, receptivity for a direct message cannot be assured, and when direct methods fail, lobbyists turn to indirect communications. However, lobbyists can turn to constituents to convey the message only if the membership is substantial and willing to act on signal from Washington. Moreover, lobby organizations must have large staffs to be able to convey messages through intermediaries. As a consequence, it is likely that only lobbyists for large-membership or rich organizations can effectively utilize indirect methods. Even in these cases, lobbyists sometimes emphasize and prefer direct methods and utilize indirect methods to supplement and amplify the direct messages.

Three sets of ratings for methods of direct communication

TABLE XI–1

Ratings of Direct Personal Communication by Washington Lobbyists, Michigan Lobbyists, and Congressional Respondents

MEANS OF DIRECT COMMUNICATION	PERCENTAGE SELECTING EACH RATING											Median*	Mean*	Number
	0	1	2	3	4	5	6	7	8	9	10			
Personal Presentation of Viewpoints														
Washington lobbyists	2	1	3	1	2	7	2	1	15	7	58	9.15	8.43	99
Michigan lobbyists	0	0	0	0	0	3	3	3	15	6	69	9.24	9.24	33
Congressional respondents	0	0	0	0	0	3	10	14	7	14	52	9.03	8.72	30
Presentation of Research Results														
Washington lobbyists	5	2	1	7	2	9	5	3	17	13	35	7.91	7.40	99
Michigan lobbyists	3	0	6	6	0	21	9	3	12	3	36	7.12	7.00	33
Congressional respondents	0	0	0	10	4	10	4	18	14	25	14	7.25	7.29	30
Testifying at Hearings														
Washington lobbyists	3	3	3	6	3	24	9	3	15	6	24	5.83	6.55	99
Michigan lobbyists	3	6	3	0	3	30	6	6	6	3	33	5.75	6.64	33
Congressional respondents	4	0	4	11	4	15	15	7	22	7	11	5.88	6.26	30

*Neither measure of central tendency is quite suitable. One cannot assume equal distance between intervals as required for the mean; yet the median ignores the distance of extreme ratings from the central point. The full distribution of the ratings is the best guide to the data.

are included in Table XI–1: using the rating scale mentioned above, lobbyists rated and commented on the tactics they use; congressional respondents rated and commented on the same set of fourteen techniques; and respondents from a similar study by Walter DeVries of Michigan lobbyists reacted to this identical rating method.[3] The ratings of congressional respondents and Michigan lobbyists are introduced only for comparative purposes. These respondents were not randomly selected, and their ratings should not be taken as closely representative of their groups. Thirty of the thirty-eight congressional respondents took time to make these ratings. The frequencies for the Michigan lobbyists and the congressional respondents have been converted to percentages to facilitate comparison with the Washington lobbyists.

Although the respondents in each group are by no means unanimous, the group ratings (mean and median) are strikingly similar for each of the three tactics. Not only do lobbyists and their congressional targets have similar evaluations of these tactics, but lobbyists operating in a separate setting also roughly agree. This similarity suggests both that lobbyists and officials are plugged into the same communication network and that the system develops a set of norms recognized by both officials and lobbyists.[4] The relatively high ratings of direct communication methods is consonant with the preference for direct methods indicated in the replies to the open-ended question.

PERSONAL PRESENTATION OF VIEWPOINTS

Lobbyists normally present their views personally by paying visits to governmental decision-makers and delivering their messages in face-to-face conversation. They sometimes deliver messages over the phone or via written letter or memo. Many messages are received first by staff assistants who may or may not pass them on to the official. A puristic definition would require transmission through staff assistants to be considered in-

[3] *DeVries (1960, chap. v).*
[4] *DeVries (1960, pp. 148–49) had sixteen legislative leaders and eleven news reporters make the same ratings. Their median ratings were strikingly close to those reported in Table XI–1.*

direct communication. For our purposes, however, we shall make no distinction between messages transmitted through staff and those received personally by the decision-maker. Staff members are usually very close to their superiors and know in advance how the officials would deal with messages if they received them personally. It is highly realistic to consider staff members as integral parts of the official decisional units.

As groups have set up lobbying operations over the years, they seem to have operated on the following assumptions: a direct personal visit by an envoy is more effective than a written communication in gaining access; a message delivered in person can be more fully elaborated; a personal message is more likely to reach a decision-maker when he is in a receptive frame of mind.

A group with a personal envoy is thought to have a competitive advantage over a group without an envoy; consequently, an ever-increasing number of groups have sent such envoys. Now, however, the number and variety of lobbyists competing for the limited personal attention of decision-makers is so great that the Washington atmosphere is filled with noise. Having a personal envoy no longer assures a hearing. Lobbying resources have increasingly been diverted from direct communication to communication through intermediaries who are presumed to have better access. Data presented in Chapter VI indicated that lobbyists spend relatively little time in direct conversations with officials. Members of Congress with some years of experience, and other observers as well, have noted the shift from direct to indirect methods of communication.[5]

Despite this shift to indirect communication, lobbyists still believe that their most effective tactic is the personal presentation of their case to the official. In response to the open-ended question about their preferred method, sixty-five respondents say they prefer and generally use personal presentations; fifty-eight rate the tactic at 10 on the rating scale. Table XI–1 shows the full distribution of ratings on the tactic; the mean and the median ratings are higher than for any other tactic. The same is true of the ratings by the Michigan lobbyists and the congressional respon-

---

[5]*The Buchanan Committee hearings and reports (U.S. Congress, 1950a) note this fact many times. See Chapter I for a description of this committee.*

dents. The Michigan lobbyists, in fact, are somewhat more unanimous in giving the tactic a top rating probably because access to Michigan legislators is easier to obtain. One can safely say that the tactic is universally employed.

When the Washington lobbyist sample is broken down by the type of group represented and the various tactics are then ranked by each type of group, personal presentation of viewpoints is given top ranking by all except lobbyists for farm groups, church and humanitarian groups, and foreign governments or firms. Even if not ranked at the top, personal presentation is given a high ranking.[6] When the sample is broken down by lobbyist roles, only public relations counselors fail to give the tactic first or second ranking. Ex-journalist respondents tend slightly more than others to give personal presentation less than a top rating. Perhaps experience in journalism and public relations inclines persons toward sending messages via the public rather than directly. With these minor exceptions, we can readily say that personal presentation of viewpoints is the most preferred method of communication used by lobbyists.

When lobbyists make personal presentations, they do not aim their messages indiscriminately. For each problem there is a key man or group of men to whom others will look for guidance; it is especially these men whom the lobbyists try to persuade. In Congress, the members of the committee handling a given bill are the special targets of lobbyists concerned with that bill. The chairman of the committee is usually the key decision-maker and therefore draws the heaviest flow of lobby communications. If the committee has a particularly able and respected staff member (whom the members of the committee look to for guidance), he often becomes the target for heavy lobby communications. In the executive branch, lobby messages generally are directed to the top decision-maker or the particular staff assistants on whom he leans most heavily for advice. Lobbyists, then, must locate the key people—those who are so well respected that their decisions are likely to be influential to many others. Failure to locate such key persons may result in the sending of many superfluous mes-

---

[6]See Milbrath (1960a) for detailed tables breaking down the sample by type of organization and relation of lobbyist to his employer.

sages, and if the key persons cannot be persuaded, there is a high likelihood that the decision will go adversely.

Some lobbyists direct their messages to persons who are undecided on a given question. When lobbyists have scarce resources, this is most economical. Some find it wise also to communicate briefly with decision-makers favorable to their point of view to encourage them to vote according to expectation. Most lobbyists do not bother to communicate with those they know are opposed; this is both painful and thought to be a waste of time.[7] A few lobbyists, however, deliberately call on the opposition; a well-executed visit may reduce animosity even if it changes no votes.

Usually a single lobbyist calls on a single decision-maker, but this is not universally true. Some lobbyists prefer to call as a delegation; this is more likely if several groups are collaborating. Another tactic is a conference attended by several lobbyists and several decision-makers through which the group process is used to try to convince the decision-makers. Conferences are also useful in finding compromise solutions when persistent differences make that necessary. They are, however, rather cumbersome and difficult to manage; they may even have results contrary to the wishes of the organizer. Since decision-makers have tight and varied schedules, finding a convenient time for all concerned is nearly impossible unless the participants place very high priority on the meeting. Conferences, then, can be used only on very important questions.

Some lobbyists spoke of a necessity for securing a champion for their cause in Congress. This is important for relatively minor bills, since issues of major public importance tend to attract their own champions. A champion is needed to introduce the bill, call for hearings, see that the bill is voted on in committee, see that it is called off the calendar and voted on by the house. These are tasks that only a member (usually a key member) can perform; therefore, if a lobbyist fails to enlist a champion, he has

---

[7]This communication pattern is rather typical of most political behavior. Party canvassers at election time very seldom contact or attempt to convert voters identified with the opposition party. For a summary of findings on this point, see Lane (1959, pp. 304–5). Robinson (1962, pp. 152–58) also found State Department liaison officers reluctant to contact known opposition in Congress.

little chance for success with a bill. A bill that has no member or members pushing for it (there are hundreds of them each session) will be by-passed, languish, and die.

At each legislative stage, key people must be convinced to allow the bill to pass to the next stage. Bills must be passed by subcommittees, full committees, often by the Rules Committee in the House, and the full house in each house of Congress. If the versions of the two houses differ (they usually do), the bill must go to conference committee and then back for approval to each house before being submitted to the President for approval. At each stage, there are different key people. The lobbyist must time his messages to reach the appropriate key people at the right time. A message that comes too soon may be wasted and may foreclose entree for later messages. Timing is one of the main reasons that knowledge of the legislative and political process is so important for lobbying. One lobbyist respondent explained the problem rather well:

It is important to direct the legislative effort at the level where a bill is . . . When a subcommittee is considering a bill, it's useless to turn one's energies to the full committee, and it is too early to alert the membership of the association to contact the entire House. A great deal of effort is wasted and it even tends to dry up possible sources of support if one pushes the wrong action at the wrong stage and before the thing is ready to be voted on. In order to avoid this, we withhold all bids for support until the proper time. Occasionally we get caught short and have to send out five thousand telegrams in a hurry to get the support rolling in, but this cost is worth it to avoid wasting our efforts before the time is ripe.

Another reason that timing is important is that entree must be saved for a time when lobbyists have something very important to discuss. Lobbyists who do not go to decision-makers until they definitely need to not only do the decision-makers a favor but help their own cases. One respondent uses infrequent visits to dramatize the urgency of his coming when he does have a problem to discuss. Smart lobbyists do not dissipate good will on any but the most important matters. This, then, is another reason why lobbyists spend so little time talking to members of Congress.

Appointments with senators are more difficult to obtain than appointments with representatives, but there is no automatic entree even with the latter. Successful lobbyists are resourceful and imaginative in discovering techniques for gaining entrance to see officials.[8] Methods must be varied with the target and some require considerable time and energy for execution. Friends and constituents are regularly used to get appointments. The following quotation illustrates the mood and approach of many lobbyists:

I'm in the business of communicating with these people, and if they don't have an open mind, I don't get to first base. I understand perfectly well that members of Congress are busy people, and I have a great deal of sympathy for that problem, but I can't be stopped by that. If a member tells me that he is too busy to see me, I find someone who is not insulated from the member, and I ask him to contact the member. I ask him to get my point of view over to the member, or I ask him to make an appointment so that I can get it across.

The comments of both lobbyists and congressional respondents on the kind of lobbying approach they consider effective are so similar that they shape into a set of norms. Not all actors fully perceive all of the norms, but the more effective lobbyists follow them rather closely. Decision-makers are in a position to enforce these norms because they can cut off access to those who do not conform. Even if they grant an audience, they sometimes fail to listen or they may vote against the transgressing lobbyist. So many compete for a decision-maker's attention that he can readily justify setting down conditions for giving his attention and applying sanctions to those who fail to comply.

[8]*Some of these techniques will be discussed in more detail in Chap. XIII.*

ELEMENTS OF A SUCCESSFUL PRESENTATION

The series of dos and don'ts that follow are collated and condensed from extensive comments by both lobbyists and congressional targets of lobbying.[9] Some of the points may seem rather obvious, but they were stressed very strongly by many respondents, and supposedly they are violated from time to time.

1. BE PLEASANT AND NON-OFFENSIVE

Since decision-makers must meet with many people every day, it eases their burden considerably if these associations are pleasant. Congressional respondents say they prefer visitors who have: sincerity, enthusiasm, energy, patience, a nice appearance, and confidence. One staff assistant said, "I just hate to see the shy ones come in." Officials prefer lobbyists who do not act arrogantly, antagonistically, or disagree vigorously. One congressman said he likes to deal with lobbyists when "I don't feel like a target." Just as lobbyists should not attack, they should not be thrown off balance by opposition; they need a thick skin. They apparently should not start a fight but should not shun one if it does start.

Pleasantness is probably the most important factor in obtaining and maintaining access to decision-makers. Harried officials naturally defend themselves against lobbyists, and it is up to the lobbyists to overcome that barrier. One clever respondent uses the tactic of asking members of Congress to tell him their troubles. The troubles elicited generally relate to the lobbyist's own area and help to drain off some latent resentment against the organization he represents. This deliberate "tripping of their mechanism" serves as a novel introduction and helps to bring the conversation around to the subject of the visit in a smooth and unobtrusive way.

2. CONVINCE THE OFFICIAL THAT IT IS IMPORTANT FOR HIM TO LISTEN

Some officials appear to listen to whomever is talking to them, but in many cases audiences with lobbyists are *pro forma*

---

[9]*In his study of Michigan lobbyists and their effectiveness, DeVries (1960, chap. vi) found many of these same points. He did find somewhat more emphasis on the lobbyist's personality and on the use of entertainment than seems to be characteristic of Washington lobbying.*

occurrences which have little impact. Lobbyists must convince the official that he has something at stake. Since elected officials are nearly always concerned with constituent interests, a demonstration of constituent interest is one of the best ways to insure attention. Whenever possible, lobbyists try to show members how certain behavior will help them in their districts. To do this, lobbyists must be aware of political pressures and have a realistic knowledge of the legislative process. Demonstration of constituent interest is even more important if the projected measure is not particularly just or in the public interest. Power at the grass roots is so important that its promise can enlist support even for these measures. Conversely, members often resist supporting meritorious proposals if they know their constituents are opposed (or even uninterested). Most lobbyists realistically recognize this:

> We cannot get anything done against the interests of the people on the Hill. We can seldom talk anybody out of one position and into another. A member of Congress is not going to do anything that is contrary to the interests of his constituents; at least not for us. Our job is to keep him informed of the interests we have in common with him and his constituents.

Demonstration that a given measure is in the public interest or would serve the cause of justice also stimulates attention and concern. Most officials feel that lobbyists do them a service if they help them to estimate all the consequences of a given proposal.

In addition, the very manner in which a lobbyist approaches an official affects his reception. His very bearing should convey the weightiness of the matters he wants to discuss.

3. BE WELL PREPARED AND WELL INFORMED

This is by far the most important aspect of a successful presentation. Respondents in Congress and lobbyists mention it repeatedly. Some respondents use the phrase "having a good case," which to them means essentially the same thing. Capable lobbyists are well informed not only in their own fields but on a broad range of other issues as well. They know the appropriate phrases and words to use; they know when and with whom to communicate. They know not only when and how to act but also where to get the inside information they need to do their jobs.

Lobbyists lacking a broad range of information and capabilities are revealed rather quickly as incompetent. A staff assistant to a Senate committee made this point and several others relevant to this general topic:

> If he wishes to be successful with me or the Senator, he has to be informed. I often know more about the subject than the lobbyist, so I can tell whether he is informed or not. If he isn't well informed, he just isn't effective at all. The next most important thing is being able to present the case in a succinct fashion. He's got to be able to handle ideas in an orderly way. If he just runs off at the mouth, you just want to shut him off. The first thing you do is to try and figure ways to get out of it. A good lobbyist should be able to cover the subject in twenty minutes or less, and probably in ten minutes. If he is really good he sends some of the material ahead of time and this can be read before you talk to him orally; at the very least, he ought to have something written that he can leave with you. It is comparable to filing a brief before a court and then having oral arguments. Other than that, of course, the lobbyist should possess the obvious things like good manners and a pleasant appearance.

Officials require lobbyists to be knowledgeable because they need information and want something in return for the time and attention they give. Some lobbyists try to meet this need by operating service offices to assist officials on any problem for which assistance is requested. They give reliable expert information on short notice; thus they must have a highly capable staff. An office which establishes a reputation for reliable information and assistance on a variety of subjects is in a peculiarly strong position to affect governmental decisions. Speaking generally, one staff assistant to a congressional committee said:

> Most lobbyists are very honorable and very helpful. Any member of Congress who doesn't have his door open to the lobbyists just isn't a good member. I learn a hell of a lot from them.

4. BE PERSONALLY CONVINCED

The legal profession has a tradition that the guilty as well as the innocent have a right to advocacy; accompanying this is the notion that an advocate need not believe in the truth of his case. It is the responsibility of the adversary to expose falsity; full exposure and truth are supposed to derive from the clash of the adversaries. There is a natural tempation to transfer such ideas to lobbying and conclude that lobbyists personally need not believe in what they are advocating. In lobbying, however, the advocate who is not personally convinced is less successful in pleading a case. The advocate in the court room does not personally have to withstand cross-examination; in lobbying he does. Officials opposed to a lobbyist's pleas may deliberately expose his insincerity (questioning the witness in a congressional hearing where penalties for perjury apply, for example). The lobbyist who is interested only in his fee has a difficult time justifying himself and his argument. In the competition for attention, the sincere voice is more easily heard.

Lobbyist organizations recognize this problem and "sideline" members of the staff who cannot agree with the organization point of view. Sometimes working members of the industry testify before congressional committees instead of the lobbyist staff employees. A working member may not be as skilled in testimony, but his personal involvement with his industry's problems and his knowledge in depth of those problems are often more likely to impress the committee than smooth testimony, and his statement will stand up better under cross-examination.

Advocacy is also reported to be generally more successful if it is well balanced. Many lobbyists deliberately present arguments on both sides. They do this partly to suggest fair-mindedness but mainly to strengthen their own side. The rationale for this is that an official listening to a one-sided argument says to himself, " This fellow has thought about only one side of this issue; he might think quite differently if he heard the other side. I will take his argument with reservations until I can hear the other side." In contrast, the lobbyist who presents both sides of the story leaves the official with the impression that he has looked at all sides of this question and then arrived at his conclusion. The advocate who has presented both sides leaves his listener in a better position to evaluate his presentation.

5. BE SUCCINCT, WELL ORGANIZED, AND DIRECT

Time is a precious commodity in Washington. The challenge to the lobbyist is to communicate the greatest amount of relevant information in the shortest possible time. Presentations should not only be short but simple, well organized, and direct. Simplification should not take the form of talking down to the official, but the message should be carefully drawn so that it is easy to grasp. The lobbyist who violates this norm challenges his listener to devise ways to dismiss him; he stands to lose the official's attention for not only this but also future presentations. Several officials made this point strongly:

> All they need to do is tell me exactly what they are endeavoring and then leave me alone. If they dog me by calls and pester me, it might affect me adversely.

* * *

> The man who keeps his appointment, presents his problem or proposal, and lets the congressman get on with his other work, comes to be liked and respected. His message has an excellent chance of being effective. The man who feels that it somehow adds to his usefulness and prestige to be seen constantly in the company of one legislator or another, or who seeks to ingratiate himself with congressional staffs, gets under foot and becomes a nuisance. He does his principal and his cause no good. Every Congressman receives many visits from both kinds of callers. He can only hope that the first kind will increase and that the second kind will gradually disappear.[10]

* * *

> A lobbyist should be able to get quickly to the matter at hand without presuming on the time of the person he is contacting. Any person coming in here is in a very competitive situation; there are lots of other demands on our time. When they get an opportunity to present their story, they ought to

[10]*Celler (1958, p. 8).*

take advantage of it and do their job concisely without being either too brief or too discursive.

* * *

The lobbyists who make the most difficult time demands are inexperienced ones. The good lobbyist is sensitive to the demands he makes on the people he is contacting. The bird who bends your ear for an hour and wants to buy you a beer is hopeless. A guy should be able to say in fifteen minutes what it is he wants.

6. USE THE SOFT SELL

Some lobbyists make the mistake of pushing their case too hard. They ask for the whole pie and accept nothing less than everything they have asked for. This is foolhardy in the atmosphere of compromise that inevitably prevails in legislative decision-making:

If you insist on it being all or nothing, you usually get nothing. We look for a language in a bill which will help us to get all we can out of a situation. We try to write the bill so that it pleases as many people as possible and yet gives us as much as we feel we can get.

The sensitive lobbyist pleads but does not demand. He does not pressure the official to commit himself to a definite line of action. Above all, he does not threaten—that would only create antagonisms which would destroy his case and cut off access. Present-day lobbyists are more inclined to use the "soft sell" than lobbyists of bygone days. Several old-timers in Congress reported this:

There now seems to be a lot more emphasis on working through the people back home and not so much emphasis on personal contact. I probably don't see a lobbyist a week here. The present-day lobbyists are cuter, too. They don't come around and try to pressure you, they just drop in and present their case. You get the impression they are afraid you won't understand their case.

* * *

I've been very much impressed with the low pressure sell. We don't get any of this brashness or pounding on the table or threats not to deliver votes or anything like that. There are some exceptions, but usually those are people who are not well qualified.

* * *

If he says to me, "Here's our story; here's the way our people feel about it. I would like you to think it over and see if you can go along with us." The fellow who has approached it from that angle has left a good impression and is much more likely to be influential with me than if he approaches it in a demanding way or threatens some damage to me in a campaign. I know more about my state than most people do, so that doesn't scare me. A member of Congress bitterly resents someone who thinks he can own him or vote him.

7. LEAVE A SHORT WRITTEN SUMMARY OF THE CASE

Most officials prefer to have something in writing to relieve them of the necessity of taking notes and to insure correctness of information and interpretation. They often file this for consultation when the official makes his decision or talks with others about the issue. Some lobbyists send this written summary in advance of the oral presentation; then when the official or his staff man talks to the lobbyist, he can ask questions in areas or topics that need clarification or amplification. Written statements from lobbyists are used by officials in speeches to other officials (on the floor of the House or Senate, for example) or to the public. Sometimes campaigning officials contact lobby organizations for arguments justifying stands they have taken.

One respondent prepares his statements in question-and-answer form. He thinks this simplifies the presentation and has the greatest impact in the shortest space. The officials sometimes use these questions to probe witnesses at hearings or fellow members in floor debate. Officials who have been primed on the relevant questions in advance are better prepared to defend their position before fellow officials.

One additional quotation about preferred presentations rounds out this topic:

First of all, I prepare myself factually on the subject that I'm to talk about. Then I go to him and I make my point — one, two, three, four, five, in that order. I prepare a memo on the information, and I leave it with him. Sometimes he may ask for more data, which of course I will be glad to send him, or he may ask if I know someone who can give him specific information on the subject. Usually I will recommend someone who can give him that information, preferably someone from his home state. I operate in this way because that's what I wanted when I was on the Hill. Now when I talk to these people I put myself in the position of the guy I am talking to. Many lawyers try the method of threatening the guy, "If you don't go along with us, it will be too bad for you." From my own experience that is a very wrong approach. It immediately queered me with such fellows; they lost all their influence right away.

PRESENTATION OF RESEARCH RESULTS

Most lobbyists consider research results to be integral components of their presentations. The ratings of the two tactics of research and personal presentation were highly correlated. Lobbyists give research a mean rating of 7.4—higher than that given any other tactic except personal presentation of viewpoints. Michigan lobbyists and congressional respondents also rate research second. As with presentation of viewpoints, the rating of research results correlates negatively with preference for indirect methods of communication. Lobbyists for organizations with a specialized subject matter emphasize research more than others. And lobbyists for small organizations emphasize research more than those from large organizations. Large organizations are less inclined to be specialized, and they generally have greater political resources to throw into the battle.

Lobbyists in most roles rank research second or third among the fourteen tactics. Legislative staff persons are notable exceptions, however; they rate research high but rate other tactics such as collaboration, constituent contact, hearings, and letters, higher. This exception is not clearly explicated by the data, but the data do suggest some hypotheses. Since legislative staff persons generally work more closely with Congress than other lobbyists, they may reflect feedback from Congress. Research has become honorific in modern American society; members of Congress are bombarded with research results. In many cases, the findings are not in agreement; they may, in fact, point to diametrically opposite conclusions. Recipients of conflicting research results are forced to the realization that the quality of research depends very much on the quality of the researcher and his methods. Most of these people know that statistics can be found to support almost any view. Consequently, every research report must be carefully evaluated in terms of the method, the reputation of the researcher, and the strength of the impact of the findings. In certain instances, facts may be dramatic, irrefutable, and point to an obvious conclusion—as such they have tremendous power. When they are not, however (as is the usual case), they must be evaluated personally by each decision-maker; such judgments sometimes develop into bitter disputes over method and reputation. Congressional respondents also appear to reflect an ambiguous attitude toward research; very few give it a top rating, but most rate it highly.

Some persons, of course, have little or no respect for research of any kind. They believe that science (especially social science) can never be sufficiently precise to be informative and prefer to depend on their own limited observations and experiences as a basis for deciding what they will believe and disbelieve. The presentation of research results to such an official has little or no effect. Most officials, however, are pleased to have information and ideas supported by research. Some lobbyists confine their presentations almost totally to research findings; they leave persuasion to the constituents of the official. Few lobbyist roles are so narrow, however.

TESTIMONY AT HEARINGS

Hearings are a formal communication procedure provided by congressional committees and some independent regulatory commissions. They are available to nearly anyone wanting to present his point of view. Not only do congressional committees feel compelled to hold hearings on every major bill, but all lobby groups concerned feel compelled to testify. Committees fear criticism from groups and individuals if all are not allowed to be heard at open hearings. Similarly, lobby groups fear criticism from officials—especially committee members and committee staff—and from their own members if they do not take the opportunity to testify. Congressman Celler gives the rationale for hearings:

> A number of the modern lobbies operating in Washington are of the highest quality. With plenty of money to spend, they spend it on qualified analysts and advocates and provide Congressional committees with lucid briefs and technical documentation in support of their positions. Nothing is more informative and helpful to a legislative committee than to hear the views of competent well-matched advocates on the opposite sides of a legislative issue.[11]

Testifying at hearings (going on the record) is often seen as a defensive action that dare not be neglected. Hearings, requiring only a single presentation which then becomes available to all concerned, appear to be an efficient means of communication. Yet both lobbyists and congressional respondents rate hearings considerably below personal presentation of viewpoints and equal to contact by constituent and public relations campaigns. Congressional respondents also rate friend contact and campaign work equally high. The rating of hearings does not significantly correlate with preference for direct communication or with rating of personal presentation of viewpoints.

There are several reasons for the imperfection of hearings as a communication device. Although messages are transmitted both orally in the hearing room and later in writing via hearing reports, there is no guarantee that the intended receivers are listening. Hearings are often held with only one member of Congress present. Even if members are present, they may not be listening. They are frequently called out of hearings to attend to something more urgent. Most members have somewhat fixed opinions about the topics on which hearings are held; thus their predispositions are likely to screen out non-congenial messages. If a member serves on a committee for several years (a common practice), he will probably have attended several hearings on the

[11]Celler (1958, p. 7).

same subject. He is certain to become bored listening to the same people repeatedly saying more or less the same thing:

Sometimes we in Congress prolong hearings unnecessarily in order to hear all the lobbyists that want to be heard. Every time we hold hearings on tariff legislation, for example, we have the same people coming up and saying the same things over and over again. A lot of this could be dispensed with. In Britain they don't have the tradition of open hearings. If they want to hear someone in testimony before one of their committee meetings, they invite them to come. They don't hold committee meetings in such a way that practically everybody who wants to be heard has to be heard.

Several respondents think that hearings on new bills or problems are efficient and useful but that the repetitious regular hearings on all bills should be dispensed with. Some repetition of testimony can be avoided by the collaboration of several groups on a joint presentation.[12]

A message on the hearing record is available in print to officials (and to the public) at no cost to the lobby group. But again, there is the problem of the overload of messages. It is simply impossible for officials to read transcripts of all hearings relevant to the decisions they must make. Most volumes of hearings are unduly long and difficult to sift through. Committees try to circumvent this by asking their staffs to present résumés of the hearings as they meet in executive session. In this process, however, the lobbyist's most important point is sometimes dropped out altogether. The function of preparing summaries makes committee staffs as much a target of lobbying as the members themselves.

Some lobby groups try to meet the problem of overload of messages by having their witness submit a written statement for the record, then briefly summarize the main points orally and submit to questions. This saves the committee from having to listen to a long statement intended only for the record. This

[12]*See Chapter VIII.*

lengthens the printed hearings, however, and the message overload for those not present at the hearings is not at all reduced.

It is important that, although the lobbyist dare not pass up an opportunity to testify, he also cannot count on hearings to get his message across to officials. He must use other methods as well. Some lobbyists do not expect to change the minds of any officials by testifying at hearings, but they think that hearings are useful in "strengthening the backbones" of persons who might be wavering. They also provide questions, information, and arguments that can be used by the committee members in floor debate. One lobbyist reported that he uses every opportunity to testify not because he hopes to change anyone's mind, but rather because his performance on the witness stand might fix an impression of him as a person in the minds of his listeners. This impression is useful in gaining access and rapport when he later contacts the official for a personal conference.

Gaining attention at a hearing may partly make up for sparse attendance by members; reporters are generally assigned to cover hearings, and one of the Washington newspapers occasionally picks up a bit of a lobbyist's testimony. In fact, lobbyists sometimes play to the mass media rather than to the committee members at hearings. Some, perhaps many, members read the newspapers more carefully than they read hearings. Seeing an issue or a lobbyist's testimony spotlighted in a newspaper may raise that point higher on the member's agenda of attention.

Since hearings must be used, most lobby groups are careful to appear at their best. One recurring dilemma is whether to put the lobbyist skilled at communication or a working member of the lobby group on the stand. Generally, the working member is asked to speak. He is usually carefully briefed, and his testimony usually is written by the lobby staff. One staff member to a senator contributed the following remarks to the controversy:

From the standpoint of speed, committees of Congress probably get more information from the expert counsel of an organization than they do from the rank and file. On the other hand, we feel we get a better impression if we hear from people in the field; that way we get some idea of how they really feel about the issue out in the constituency. The witness who is a paid expert just doesn't make the same impression as a person who has taken the trouble to come in from outside of Washington.

COLLABORATION BETWEEN GOVERNMENT OFFICIALS AND LOBBYISTS

Communications and influence attempts flow in both directions between officials and lobbyists. Matthews, in writing about the Senate, makes this same point:

> It is a mistake, then, to think of lobbying in terms of influence from the lobbyist to the Senator. Lobbying is a matter of bargaining. The Senator is far from a passive puppet manipulated from afar.[13]

In this section we will look briefly at communications flowing from officials to lobbyists and at collaborative relations between the two types of political actors.

Officials often initiate communications with lobby groups to gather basic intelligence about their environment. They need to know where various groups—especially those which are powerful politically—stand on issues. Usually these stands are so public and visible that the official need not inquire; sometimes, however, he must make a special investigation. A member of Congress planning to introduce a bill for example, sometimes checks with groups likely to be affected to see what they think about it. Intelligence gathering is basically defensive; it is only good sense to be well informed before exposing oneself.

Occasionally officials initiate communications with lobbyists to promote a bill or policy. Certain kinds of bills require considerable external pressure on members of Congress, and interested officials may set up a super-lobby group (usually called a "citizens committee") to stimulate and organize the support of lobby groups. Nearly all congressional respondents report that they collaborate with lobbyists in this fashion from time to time.

[13]*Matthews (1960, p. 190).*

As one vigorous old warrior in the House expressed it: "Yes I do. I think every member who is worth a damn does that kind of thing." A similar comment came from a senator:

> I would not hesitate to spur on a pressure group in an activity directed to my colleagues. I might contact some farm groups or some business groups and say to them, "You know, you have been very silent on this tax proposal; I wonder why you haven't spoken up on it."

Sometimes members collaborate with sympathetic lobby groups in staging hearings. They review the testimony of witnesses in advance so that the witnesses can prepare answers. They also plan the order of witnesses to maximize the impact on the public of the desired viewpoint. Such collaboration promotes a policy and stores up good will on behalf of officials with lobbyists. A smoothly staged hearing impresses the officers and members of the pressure group. Conversely, an embarrassing hearing may lead a testifying officer to conclude that the lobbyist staff is inadequate.

Officials also store up good will with lobbyists by holding hearings on bills that really have no likelihood of passage, giving the lobbyist an opportunity to appear to defeat the bill. Officials want to "make points" with lobbyists to gain leverage for use in controlling lobbyist behavior. An official who has a store of good will can more freely vote against the desires of a pressure group. The lobbyist who is a close friend of an official finds himself identifying with the official's problems and career; he may therefore restrain his own behavior and that of his group so as not to embarrass or hurt the official.

Other favors are available to officials for building good will with lobby groups. Officials "leak" advance information to interested lobbyists—usually not improperly, for the lobbyist would hear about it in due time. The speed with which the lobbyist is informed constitutes the favor. Lobbyists who were former staff members on the Hill often receive their "leaks" from congressional staff persons. Officers and executives of lobby groups, who generally operate on a somewhat higher level, usually learn advance information from members of Congress themselves.

Members also assist lobby groups and lobbyists to get publicity. A favorite device is to praise a group's stand or activity on the floor of the House or Senate. Members also insert speeches or statements in the *Congressional Record*. The relevant material can then be reproduced at low cost exactly as it appears. Some enthusiastic members distribute the material postage free under their own franks. Even if publicity does not directly allude to the lobby group, a public endorsement of the group's policy stand is considered a favor. These gestures not only promote the policy of the group, they may also enhance the standing of its leadership with the group's membership.

Members of congress contact lobbyists for such services as speech-writing, preparing reports, answering correspondence, writing legislative bills, entertaining out-of-town visitors, and so forth. Some lobbying offices are, in effect, adjuncts to certain members' offices. This is seldom pushed too far because members generally keep close control of things going out over their name, but greatly overworked congressional offices welcome the free services of lobby groups in time of need. Lobbyists, for their part, are delighted to provide these services; they know no better way to affect policy than to be in on its creation. These relationships develop only when there is very close agreement on policy between the member and the lobby group; therefore, the relationship is not invidious or an abdication of functions by the member. Each participant does what he would do in any case; their cooperation merely increases their efficiency.

SUMMARY

Lobbyists were asked to choose a preferred tactic and to rate several tactics for gettings messages through to officials. They generally prefer either direct or indirect methods. Most lobbyists prefer direct communication tactics, and these are rated most effective by the recipients of lobbying as well. The effectiveness of personal presentations is limited, however, by the fact that officials are overloaded with visitors. Visits by lobbyists must be saved for important problems.

Lobbyists try hardest to see the key people at each stage of the development of the issues and vary the manner of presentation according to several factors; they generally include research results as an integral part of their presentations. Their use of research depends on the nature of the issue and their estimation of the reaction of the intended receiver.

Congressional committees feel obliged to hold hearings and lobbyists feel compelled to testify at them for public relations reasons. Although hearings appear to provide an efficient communications channel, lobbyists cannot rely on hearings alone to get their messages across; hearings are used only to supplement other methods of communication.

Communications flow in both directions over the direct channels between lobbyists and officials; collaborative relations between these two sets of actors are frequent. These relationships are important in making the policy process more efficient and in enabling officials to control the functioning of the process.

CHAPTER XII

LOBBYISTS APPROACH GOVERN-MENT — COMMUNICATION THROUGH INTERMEDIARIES

Several intermediary routes are used by lobbyists to supplement direct communications. These routes are intermediary only from the perspective of the lobbyists. When lobbyists ask constituents to write letters to their representatives in Congress, they are using an intermediary communication route. The constituent, on the other hand, is using a direct communication method.

The governmental communication network sketched in Chapter IX indicates the various routes that intermediary communications take. Some messages flow from lobbyists to the body politic and then back to officials, either directly or through another institution such as a political party. Lobbyists also stimulate actors in other institutions—such as the mass media or political parties—who, in turn, exhort the people to communicate with their representatives.

Although both lobbyists and officials rate direct communications higher than indirect methods, they do not agree that they are preferable. Most lobby groups use both means of transmission of messages; it is difficult, then, to attribute success or failure to either method. This accounts in part for the inability of respondents definitively to evaluate the methods. The high competition of lobbyists trying to deliver direct messages to officials[1] encourages lobbyists to seek alternative transmission routes which have better access. The shift toward stirring up the public at the grass roots has been noted by many observers.[2] The Buchanan Committee especially dramatized this shift:

> If lobbying consisted of nothing more than the well-established methods of direct contact, there would have been relatively little need for our investigation. . . . Ever since President Wilson's first administration, however, the ever-growing army of pressure groups has recognized that the power of government ultimately rests on the power of public opinion. This simple discovery lies at the root of the evolution of lobbying techniques since 1913. The extensive use of franked releases antagonistic to the chief aims of the Underwood tariff bill of that year was probably the first large-scale effort to bring public opinion to bear on legislation. In this sense, the use of highly charged franked releases as an instrument of pressure was the bridge between the old lobbying and the new. It opened the way to the development of entirely new dimensions in the theory and practice of lobbying. Today, the long-run objective of every significant pressure group in the country is and must inevitably be the creation and control of public opinion; for, without the support of an articulate public, the most carefully planned direct lobbying is likely to be ineffective, except on small or narrow issues.
>
> If a descriptive label is needed, this new emphasis in pressure tactics might best be called "lobbying at the grass roots." What it amounts to is this: Rather than attempt to influence legislation directly, the pressure group seeks to

[1] *Current journalistic reports often exaggerate the number of Washington lobbyists. James McCartney of the* Chicago Daily News Washington Bureau, *for example, reported that registered lobbyists outnumber members of Congress eight to one. (*Chicago Daily News, *March 18, 1961, p. 7.) This figure probably was the result of careless double counting. A more realistic ratio is about two to one.*

[2] *E. Pendleton Herring is generally credited in academic circles with being the first to note the shift from the "old" to the "new" lobby — which stirs up grass-roots sentiment. See Herring (1929).*

create an appearance of broad public support for its aims, support which can be mobilized when the legislative situation demands it. The general premise underlying this effort is that if people are made to feel deeply enough about an issue they will translate their feelings into action which will affect that issue's resolution by the Congress. This expression of public opinion may be genuine in the sense that the views expressed are expressed spontaneously and with conviction. Or, on the other hand, such expression may be artificial and contrived. In either case, the process is one which has been deliberately and specifically instigated by one group or another having a particular stake in legislative issues. This process may bear little resemblance to the lobbying of 1880, but the intent behind it and the end results are unquestionably the same; namely to influence the determination of legislative policy.[3]

* * *

Realization that ultimate power to affect legislation resides in the people has given a significant new direction to pressure group activities, which now seek to influence legislation by remote control. The new profession of public opinion engineers is engaged in creating public sentiment in favor of or opposed to particular policies. The though is that once the desired public climate is achieved, the people themselves will do the work. . . . For Congress to attempt to control the formulation of public opinion would be to throw out the baby with the bath. The constitutionality of such an attempt would be highly dubious and the cure would be worse than the disease.[4]

Here is a comment from a lobbyist:

I'm convinced that the grass-roots support is the important thing rather than my contacts. I know this from my experience on the Hill where I have been on the receiving end. I can go up and explain the technical end of the

[3]U.S. Congress (1950b, pp. 28–29).
[4]Celler (1958, p. 8).

thing, but it's the grass roots that lets the member of Congress know who is behind it. I would give 75 per cent to the grass roots.

The competition for the attention of officials has taken a new turn, however. Decision-makers, especially members of Congress, are deluged with messages from constituents. To be sure, some of these messages come spontaneously and with genuine conviction, but officials know that many others have been inspired by lobbyists and pressure groups. The net effect is that no single type of message or source can be assured attention. The competitive clamor of lobbying carries its own control. The legislator drowned in a Babel of voices is probably more free to consult wise counsel or his own conscience than one who receives only a few messages. Members must, of course, heed genuine ground swells of public opinion, which they have always done, but ordinary messages tend to cancel one another out.

Lobbyists react to this situation in several ways. Some are shifting back to direct communication. This is especially true of lobbyists for groups with specialized or technical policy concerns or with little power at the polls. Indirect communication methods are generally more time-consuming and costly. Lobbyists make tactical decisions when they allocate their resources. Smaller and poorer organizations concentrate primarily on direct methods; larger and richer organizations utilize both indirect and direct methods. Direct methods are not likely to be neglected even if indirect methods are used. A comparison of Tables XII-1 and XI-1 shows that both lobbyists and congressional respondents rate direct methods higher than indirect methods, but they vary widely in their ratings of indirect methods.

When Washington lobbyists, Michigan lobbyists, and congressional respondents are compared, they differ more in their ratings of indirect methods (Table XII-1) than in their rating of direct tactics (Table XI-1). Michigan lobbyists rate all indirect tactics lower than do the Washington respondents. DeVries ascribes this difference to the unlimited access Michigan lobbyists have to Michigan legislators[5]. Michigan lobbyists have little need to resort to indirect transmission routes.

[5]*DeVries (1960, p. 181).*

TABLE XII–1

Ratings of Communication through Intermediaries by Washington Lobbyists, Michigan Lobbyists, and Congressional Respondents

TYPE OF COMMUNICATION THROUGH INTERMEDIARIES	PERCENTAGE SELECTING EACH RATING RATING											Median*	Mean*	Number
	0	1	2	3	4	5	6	7	8	9	10			
Contact by Constituents														
Washington lobbyists	14	3	6	8	2	11	7	4	8	12	24	5.79	5.90	99
Michigan lobbyists	21	3	24	9	0	12	9	3	9	3	9	2.17	3.84	33
Congressional respondents	3	0	7	17	10	21	3	3	17	3	14	5.10	5.62	30
Contact by a Close Friend														
Washington lobbyists	26	5	8	13	3	15	6	6	6	5	5	2.77	3.76	98
Michigan lobbyists	30	15	15	15	0	6	3	0	9	0	6	1.30	2.73	33
Congressional respondents	7	0	7	7	7	11	4	15	11	15	15	6.87	6.19	30
Letter and Telegram Campaigns														
Washington lobbyists	20	6	6	5	7	19	1	7	17	4	7	4.29	4.55	99
Michigan lobbyists	54	12	6	3	0	12	9	0	3	0	0	.92	1.73	33
Congressional respondents	17	10	13	3	27	10	0	0	13	0	7	3.75	3.87	30
Public Relations Campaigns														
Washington lobbyists	21	2	2	3	2	15	2	11	17	5	17	6.14	5.55	97
Michigan lobbyists	24	9	3	3	0	18	3	9	6	9	15	4.58	4.79	33
Congressional respondents	4	0	4	22	19	11	7	7	11	7	7	4.67	5.30	30
Publicizing Voting Records														
Washington lobbyists	49	8	12	5	4	8	2	4	2	2	2	1.00	2.05	98
Michigan lobbyists	78	6	3	3	0	3	3	0	0	0	3	.63	.84	33
Congressional respondents	35	8	4	15	11	11	0	8	8	0	0	2.75	2.73	30

*Neither measure of central tendency is quite suitable. One cannot assume equal distance between intervals as required for the mean; yet the median ignores the distance of extreme ratings from the central point. The full distribution of the ratings is the best guide to the data.

Most respondents rate constituent contact and public relations campaigns highest among the indirect methods. Congressional respondents give an equally high rating to contact by a friend, but neither set of lobbyists does; this is striking because the ratings of lobbyists and congressional respondents are quite similar for the other tactics. A possible explanation for this will be suggested in the more detailed discussion of the tactic to follow.

The indirect communication methods discussed in this chapter are not necessarily the only ways in which lobbyists use intermediaries to communicate. It was noted in Chapter IX that lobbyists might use members of Congress as intermediaries in attempts to communicate with administration officials. Political party officials are sometimes intermediaries in channels to administrative officials or legislators. Administration officials who handle personnel appointments and party affairs are also favorite points of access to administrative decisions.

APPROACHES THROUGH CONSTITUENTS AND FRIENDS

From time to time lobbyists fail to get appointments with offiicials or a favorable reception for their messages. If it is important, they must find another means of gaining acceptance of the message. A favorite tactic is having the message conveyed by someone to whom the official is more sensitive, such as a constituent or a friend; if constituent and friend are combined in the same person, so much the better. At times messages are conveyed in writing; sometimes the intermediary pays a personal visit or calls the official on the phone.

Table XII-1 shows that lobbyists clearly prefer constituents as intermediaries; while congressional respondents rate friend contact just a little higher than constituent contact. Lobbyists were asked to rate the tactics according to the way they use them in their work; whereas congressional respondents were asked to rate tactics in terms of their effect on themselves. From the perspective of the recipient of lobbying, contact by a friend is just as impressive as a contact by a constituent. Lobbyists, however, have discovered it is much easier to find constituents who will contact an official than to find a friend who will do so. Officials have only a limited circle of intimate friends. Also, constituents are generally less reluctant than friends to use the power of their relationship to influence the official. An official is less likely to resent being importuned by a constituent than by a friend.

Constituents are not always available as intermediaries either. Table XII–1 shows that respondents vary greatly in their evaluation of constituent contact. Representatives of groups with large memberships rate this tactic higher than representatives of small membership groups. Representatives of farm groups, big labor organizations, and church and humanitarian groups rate this tactic quite highly. Some farm and labor groups bring their members to Washington by the busload ("bus trippers" they are called), give them some hasty training in lobbying techniques, and send them out to call personally on governmental decision-makers. Each man focuses most heavily on his own representative and senators.

Constituent contact is also rated higher highly by persons who have observed closely the way officials react to constituents. Lobbyists who have had experience on the Hill or who are on a legislative relations staff rate constituent contact higher than other lobbyists. Some respondents even go so far as to use constituent contact exclusively. One lobbyist who has a rather weak case to sell says he never attempts to promote his proposal on its merits. The only point he brings up in personal visits to officials is the power of the constituents; he then stimulates constituent contact in an effort to drive his point home.

Most lobbyists use constituent contact rather carefully. They use it more for gaining access than for "making the pitch" to officials. It is common practice for the constituent and the lobbyist to call jointly on an official. The constituent has the entree and can answer questions about his personal situation; the lobbyist usually presents the main argument with the broader picture. Constituents who call on officials alone must be carefully chosen for their knowledge in depth and their ability to communicate. They are usually thoroughly briefed. Officials are themselves usually well informed, and they are not likely to be impressed by a poorly informed constituent. Some members of Congress report that they like to have constituents call on them even if they hold opposing views; this gives the member an opportunity to try to talk the constituents out of their positions.

Some members feel that pressure groups overstep the bounds of propriety in utilizing constituent contacts from time to time. One member reported an instance in which lobbyists for a certain group called on him but failed to convince him of their case. Their proposal was voted down in committee. The lobbyists next hired an attorney from the member's home town to present the case once more. The member considered the maneuver deceptive, was angered, and stiffened his opposition.

Personal friends of officials are utilized similarly—except that the difficulties are even greater. All officials have a few friends whom they respect so highly that they will always listen to them. Such close associations can only be built up gradually on the basis of reciprocal obligations, mutual respect, and non-exploitation. The relationship carries its own control, for few friends would endanger a relationship by exploiting it. One senator said, "A friend that contacts me should be doing it to help me, not someone else. If he is being used by someone else and I discover it, he is no longer a friend."

On the other hand, friendships can arise from relationships between lobbyists and officials:

> Political collaboration far more often leads to friendship than the other way around. Once established senator-lobbyists friendships also tend to reinforce the Senator's commitment to a particular group and line of policy. Perhaps on minor bills, friendships are important. "You can't go far on friendship alone. Oh, maybe once a Senator would push a little bill for you because you were his friend. But a Senator is like a well—you can only draw on it so many times. And if he does anything for you on that basis that proves to be politically unwise, he won't do it again. Chances are he won't do *anything* for you again."[6]

One lobbyist told a fascinating story illustrating how a friend of an official can be used to transmit a communication. A lobby group some years ago wanted to amend some legislation that was before the Senate Finance Committee. It had tried and failed to convince committee members or staff. They needed an alternative means of communication. There was a law firm in Washington headed by an ex-senator who was a close personal friend of

[6]*Matthews (1960, p. 191). Italics in original.*

the chairman of the committee. This same firm had a brilliant young expert on taxation and financial matters on its staff. The lobby group, believing that the combination of access plus expertise was just right for their purposes, asked the firm to assist in the attempt to pass the desired amendment. The group was told that the fee charged would be $5,000—win, lose, or draw. After hesitating over the high fee, the lobby group decided to proceed. The ex-senator entertained the committee chairman and his wife at a football game and a dinner party in his home. At the conclusion of the evening, he called the lobby group to say that their lobbyist and the young tax expert could have half an hour with the chairman and committee counsel the next day. This time they succeeded in persuading these two men of their point of view, especially of the extent to which their industry would be hurt if the amendment was not passed. The chairman called the committee into executive session, the tax expert testified, and the amendment was passed. The respondent considered the $5,000 fee well spent because the damage to his industry would have been many times greater. At the conclusion of this story, the respondent made this amazing statement, "Of course this was not lobbying, we were just honestly trying to do what we could to get good legislation."

In summary, it is fair to say that in many instances constituents or friends have better access to an official than do lobbyists. Lobbyists try to send messages through these intermediaries. They use constituents more than friends primarily because constituents are more readily available. Officials seem to be about equally sensitive to either intermediary. Neither friends nor constituents are particularly easy to find, and trying to manage communications through these intermediaries complicates the lobbyist's task. The very closeness of the relationship between official and his friend may preclude the friend's being used as an intermediary.

LETTER AND TELEGRAM CAMPAIGNS

One of the surest ways to influence an elected official is to convince him that a given proposal has strong or overwhelming support among his constituents. Deluging the official with letters and telegrams is frequently presumed to convince him of this fact. In fact, most letter and telegram campaigns have little impact on the decisions of officials. To be effective, a campaign must be very large and weighted to one side of the issue or it must appear to be spontaneous. A campaign which is both large and genuine in appearance is most potent.

The official cannot ignore a big campaign because of the sheer political weight which it represents. Some respondents characterized it as a "hurricane warning." Often, officials simply batten down for the storm and wait for it to pass. Members of Congress philosophically wait for the public to move from one wave of sentiment to another. While the interviewing for this study was being conducted, Congress was flooded with letters in favor of an "economy drive"; legislation which might have been adversely affected by the drive was simply postponed until it could be considered in a more favorable climate.

Leter campaigns have an irritation value, since the overworked staffs of members must respond to the letters. Sometimes the mere threat of such a campaign accomplishes the lobbyist's purpose. Another result of a big campaign is that it actually stimulates closer scrutiny of the proposed legislation.

It would, however, be inaccurate to say that petitions, form letters, chain telegrams, and other forms of mass propaganda are discounted entirely. Pressure mail forces a member to find out what the legislation is about, to give it some study, and to inform himself on both sides of the issue. And by study of the forces behind a pressure campaign, he may get considerable light on the real purposes of the legislation. We do not imply that all propaganda tactics are used for selfish interests. However, an alert member will do his own investigating.[7]

Lobbyists know that members of Congress try to distinguish between pressure mail and letters that are written spontaneously from a genuine concern in the minds of constituents. It then becomes a game in which the lobbyists try to launch a campaign

[7]*Kefauver and Levin (1947, pp. 180–81).*

which does not look like one, and the members try to spot a campaign and discount it. Smart lobbyists do not prepare mimeographed messages for members to sign and mail to members of Congress; neither do they supply suggested wording for messages. It may even be dangerous to supply points or topics to be mentioned in the letters. Lobby groups find the best tactic is to try to teach their members how to write messages to officials and trust them to make relevant points.

A great many cards may impress a member of Congress with the fact that you could get that many people to sign cards, indicating a powerful organization. But most congrassmen are pretty wise at figuring out what such a campaign really means. They can gauge fairly well if there is a real ground swell of sentiment back in the constituency. When we send out information, we just ask our people to write their own letters. I try to refrain from giving them any language in a memo that they could then transfer to the letter and make it look like a put-up job. Sometimes you can't help this on pretty technical questions, but I always attempt not to do so.

Some groups print pamphlets showing how to write spontaneous letters, or hold short courses on stimulating spontaneous grassroots sentiment.

The difficulty with this game, from the lobbyist's point of view, is that it depends too much on untrained, unskilled persons. Often members are tipped off because some constituent has been sloppy. One member told of a local club that, not wishing to waste postage, put all their letters in a hosiery box and mailed them to the member. Sometimes a constituent sends the bulletin giving instructions for letter-writing to the congressman. Members spot campaigns from similarities in envelopes, stationery, stamps, postmarks, even the special characteristics of certain typewriters. Occasionally an overzealous constituent sends messages on behalf of his friends without consulting them. Such a tactic is generally uncovered when the letter or telegram is answered and the unconsulted constituent communicates his surprise to his representative. Because of these kinds of difficulties, letter and telegram campaigns are less frequently used now than in the recent past.

Another reason members of Congress discount letter and telegram campaigns, even the spontaneous ones, is that they realize that only a small portion of the population will take the trouble to write. If a congressman should get thirty thousand letters on an issue, this would be considered a great number; yet it would account for no more than 10 per cent of his constituency. The persons who do write may well feel more strongly on an issue than those who are silent, but the views of the writers should not, for that reason alone, be given preference. Writers tend to be drawn from the upper socio-economic strata of the population; persons who perceive themselves as poorly educated or of lower status are hesitant to approach officials, even by letter. Persons of lower status are less likely to be alerted to impending legislation that affects their interests; this does not mean their interests ought not to be protected.

> The average citizen who does not have any peculiar interest in a measure is not apt to be vocal. The people who do not write expect their Senator or Congressman to "do the right thing," and it doesn't occur to them to lend a helping hand with an encouraging letter.
>
> At one point in the 1946 OPA fight, congressional mail was running eighty percent *against* OPA extension, yet a Gallup poll showed the public was more than seventy percent *in favor of* extension. Proposals for extension of Selective Service brought a ten to one ratio of opposition mail, yet all polls showed a majority of the people felt that the draft should be continued.[8]

An official generally welcomes floods of letters if they support the position he has already taken; it helps him to realize he is not battling alone:

> When one's vote on a national issue is challenged, it is comforting to be able to tell disgruntled constituents that "I

[8] *Kefauver and Levin (1947, pp. 183–84). Italics in original.*

had twenty letters sustaining my vote to every one I received against it."[9]

As was noted earlier, members of Congress deluged with letters to take a stand they do not want to take may ask an opposition group to produce an equal or greater number of letters on the other side so that they will be left free to vote their convictions. Members differ in their reaction to mail; some readily conform to the pressure; some react strongly against it; others react mildly or not at all. Some members like the attention of letter or telegram campaigns; these are known as members who "court mail." Some need to lead their constituents, and respond to a mail campaign with a communication of their own setting forth their reasons for taking their own position. They sometimes also use the mass media to educate their constituents.

Because of these variations and uncertainties, lobbyists vary widely in their ratings of letter and telegram campaigns (Table XII–1): twenty rate the tactic 0, and seven rate it 10. Congressional respondents somewhat consistently rank the tactic low, and Michigan lobbyists quite consistently rank it low. Lobbyists for big labor and farm organizations give it higher ratings than do other lobbyists, probably because their mass membership enables them to turn out thousands of letters. Lobbyists for organizations with low mass membership rank letters lower. Lobbyists identified closely with a particular organization (officers and staff) rank letters higher than those in a more peripheral relationship (lawyers, public relations men, etc.).

Even if an organization has the membership to stage mass letter or telegram campaigns, several other factors are considered when the group is deciding on use of this tactic. Certain subject matters of technical or narrow interest are not adaptable to broad pressure tactics. Also, the campaign may backfire if it is poorly executed. Most important, it is difficult for any organization to stimulate its membership to send messages to officials; they can call on the membership only a limited number of times (perhaps three per session). Therefore, letter campaigns must be saved for the most important issues. One lobbyist for a mass organization says he does not expect letters to accomplish much toward

[9]*Kefauver and Levin (1947, p. 181).*

influencing the decisions of officials, but he thinks they are useful in stimulating the political interest of the membership. Any member of his organization who writes a letter is likely to watch the performance of his congressional representative more closely; if the official does not perform to expectations, the letter-writer is more likely to retaliate at the polls.

These summary comments might be made about letter and telegram campaigns. Officials appreciate thoughtful well-reasoned letters: "One thoughtful letter is worth five hundred uniform ones." Therefore, letters generally are superior to telegrams. Campaigns are discounted when officials know that someone is turning a crank. Even tremendous campaigns may well not accomplish their purposes. One committee staff member reported that eighteen sacks of mail piled up in the committee office during one campaign, but the legislation still did not pass. It is almost impossible to disguise a letter campaign so that officials will not detect it as such. Lobbyists vary considerably in their rating of letter campaigns. The organizations that use them think of letters from the grass roots as a reinforcing tactic to back up other methods of communication.

PUBLIC RELATIONS CAMPAIGNS

Public relations campaigns are much more indirect than letter campaigns; therefore they are less efficient and more costly. On the other hand, they are not so likely to be detected as a pressure tactic. One supposition behind such campaigns is that if enough people can be convinced to favor a given viewpoint, this viewpoint and the power behind it will be communicated in various ways to government officials. Another supposition is that such campaign will have long-range effects on the voting behavior of the public and thus will find policy expression through the selection of governmental decision-makers. Successful public relations campaigns set the stage or create the climate within which governmental decisions are made. Any given climate will facilitate certain decisions and exclude others. The climate created by a successful "PR" campaign also sets the limits for the transmission and acceptance of messages. A message that might have been ignored in one climate may be favorably received in another.

Public sentiment is everything. With public sentiment nothing can fail. Without it nothing can succeed. Consequently, he who molds public sentiment goes deeper than he who enacts statutes or pronounces decisions. He makes statutes and decision possible or impossible.[10]

A PR campaign can be partially effective even if the people send only a few communications to officials. Officials are more likely than voters to perceive public relations campaigns. If they begin to think that the views of the public are indeed being affected, they may begin to adjust their behavior even before they hear from the constituents.

Lobbyists report that the effects of PR campaigns are so diffuse and delayed that they are difficult to evaluate. This is one reason for the wide variance in the lobbyists' rating of the tactic: seventeen rate it 10; twenty-one rate it 0 (Table XII-1). Michigan lobbyists also give it widely varied ratings, but over-all, their ratings are higher for this tactic than for any other indirect method of communication. Congressional respondents do not give the tactic such extreme ratings, but the mean for the entire group is close to the mean for the lobbyists. This suggests that another reason that PR campaigns are rated so unevenly by lobbyists is that these campaigns must be very large and expensive to be successful. Therefore only a few organizations can afford to use them. Organizations that cannot afford PR campaigns naturally rate it very low. Congressional respondents rate the effect of the tactic on themselves, and are not concerned with ability to use the tactic.[11]

The PR campaign of the margarine manufacturers to abolish the federal tax on margarine and the campaigns of the American Medical Association to defeat Presidents Truman's and Kennedy's health insurance programs are notable postwar examples of successful public relations campaigns.[12] Each cost several million dollars. Less ambitious campaigns have effects so

[10]*Abraham Lincoln, quoted in Celler (1958, p. 8).*
[11]*Michigan legislators also tended to give middle ratings to the tactic.* DeVries (1960, p. 148).
[12]*See Kelley (1956) for a description of the 1949–50 AMA campaign.*

diffuse that the public may not be visibly moved. If officials do not perceive that the public is actually manipulated, they are less likely to respond.

All three groups of respondents rate PR campaigns higher than letter and telegram campaigns; yet reactions to the two types of campaigns are similar. There is a .38 tau beta correlation of the ratings of the two types of campaigns by Washington lobbyists. As is true of letter campaigns, lobbyists for large labor and farm organizations rate PR campaigns higher than other lobbyists; lobbyists for organizations with high power at the polls rate PR campaigns higher than those with low power at the polls; lobbyists closely affiliated with an organization (officers and staff) rate PR campaigns higher than those with peripheral affiliations (lawyers and consultants). Both letter campaigns and PR campaigns take more total group effort than does the transmission of direct messages from lobbyists to officials.

Although PR campaigns are so expensive that only certain organizations can use them, some of the costs are passed on to the public or consumers. Advertising expenses, even for institutional advertising which is often semi-political, can be deducted from corporation income tax as a business expense; therefore, PR campaigns are partially publicly supported. PR campaign costs are also passed on to consumers as higher prices for products and service. Indirectly, this is true of all lobbying expenses; consumers ultimately pay for all lobbying.

Public relations campaigns that are big enough and clever enough to establish a climate of opinion are very effective for influencing governmental decisions. Such campaigns are not widely used, however, because they are so costly. They may also stimulate counter-campaigns by opponents, the two campaigns cancelling each other. Moreover, the public is not passively pushed hither and yon by PR campaigns. A public discussion, once begun, carries its own momentum. People have their own ideas on public policy which they communicate with one another. The total political climate resulting from this multitude of interactions may have much wider ramifications and results quite different from those anticipated by the planners of the PR campaign.

PUBLICIZING VOTING RECORDS

Roll-call votes in both houses of Congress are part of the public record available to anyone who is interested. A few lobby organizations give roll-call votes wide publicity, so that many more voters know the voting records of officials than would otherwise be the case. Curiously, the wide publicizing of a public record is rejected and resented by most lobbyists and officials. Half of the lobbyists rate it 0, and the mean rating is only 2.05. Michigan lobbyists even more unanimously reject the tactic. Congressional respondents rate it somewhat higher than do lobbyists, but they also are not enthusiastic. The major reason for the difference in ratings and for the low rating given by most lobbyists is that publicizing voting records is a powerful and dangerous political tactic open only to groups with considerable power at the polls. The rating of this tactic was very significantly correlated (TBr .37) with the power at the polls of respondent's organization and with his rating of such other political tactics as contributing money to parties or working in political campaigns. Lobbyists for groups without power at the polls naturally rate the tactic 0; whereas congressional respondents perceive that the tactic generally has an effect on them.

The tactic is dangerous because most members of Congress perceive it as punitive and sometimes unjust; they may retaliate against the organization or lobbyist who uses it. Members quite accurately feel that pressure is being applied to force their vote in a certain direction. Many also object because they think that the particular combinations of votes published by some organizations present unfair pictures of their voting records. Quotations from congressional and lobbyist respondents make this point. One senator said, "It makes you feel adverse—a sort of kick-back." As a staff assistant to a senator expressed it:

> They are very deceptive since the organization that publishes them picks the issues, and they usually pick and interpret them from their own viewpoint. They can be very misleading because sometimes the key vote on an issue is on a procedural matter. There are very few objective voting record jobs. Of course, they do help to maintain support for an organization.

A lobbyist and former congressional staffer said:

Publication of voting records is a sneaky kind of thing. People can get the records if they want them. It is best to evaluate a man on the basis of his over-all record. It is just not honest to pick out a certain group of votes and evaluate a man on the basis of that selection.

In an effort to set the record straight, some members have publicized a voting record compiled by themselves which they feel is more fair than that circulated by the lobby group.

Publicizing voting records has been pursued most diligently by labor and other large membership groups. Most labor lobbyists are convinced of the wisdom of the tactic:

I think it's important. Of course we make people mad at us at times. Bill———is sore as hell at me now because we published his records. But I think we are going to make up—I kind of like Bill and I think he kind of likes me. I really don't get particularly bothered if they do explode. We find this especially valuable in the case of a congressman who comes from a very close district. He's got to have labor votes in order to win, so he will certainly come around. The reason I am so convinced that they are helpful is that I get many calls from members saying, "Couldn't you keep that vote off the record?" and "Do you have to have this vote on the record." I reply that the record is purely objective and we've got to report whatever they do.

Although most labor lobbyists agree with the above point of view, a few do not totally concur.

I have quite mixed feelings about this. You incense as many people as you please when you publicize these records. Some members of Congress have come to me and said, "You didn't tell me you were going to put that particular vote in the record." Usually they are pretty angry about it. I am not so convinced it is useful. This is all confidential, isn't it? No one in the organization is going to see this are they?

The vulnerability of a member to pressure arising from publicizing his voting record depends on his strength in his constituency. A man who is fairly certain of re-election is not very concerned if his record is published. If his re-election is doubtful, he is not in a position strong enough to protest vigorously to a politically powerful organization which has published his record. He can, however, end all the future access for which a group with little power at the polls publishes his record; that is why such organizations do not use the tactic.

In summary, we can say that the tactic has some power to influence a vote if the publicizing organization has a large and faithful membership. Most congressional respondents rate the tactic above 0. A staff assistant to one of the labor committees in Congress reports that he has seen committee members switch their vote according to whether it was a voice or a roll-call vote. He rates the tactic 6. He also reports that he uses the AFL-CIO record in his own work in the committee. If a member of the committee calls up and wants to know his voting record on certain bills, the staff assistant finds it easier to consult the AFL-CIO record than to dig back through the official records.

CHAPTER XIII

KEEPING COMMUNICATION
CHANNELS OPEN

Open and free communication is of paramount importance to the lobbyist. To the extent that certain channels of communication are closed to him, he is impaired in doing his job. Even the closing of a mind constitutes the shutting off of a channel. It is essential, therefore, that the lobbyist be sensitive to the problem of open communication.

The lobbyist must keep all types of channels clear; the main types are sketched in Figure I, page 181. Since the direct channels from lobbyist to decision-maker are in the most danger of being closed, they are the ones to which lobbyists devote the most attention. The decision to open or close the direct channel lies almost exclusively with the governmental decision-maker; he can decide to whom he will listen. The decision to listen or not to listen enables officials to prescribe the conditions for access and indirectly to control the behavior of lobbyists.[1] Lobbyists use several methods to ensure open channels.

The tactics discussed in this chapter have been categorized

[1] See the discussion at the end of this chapter and in Chapter XVI.

as primarily designed not to transmit messages but simply to keep channels open; however, such a classification is not neat and definitive. Certain of these tactics, such as contributing money to a political campaign, both keep channels open and convey messages. Entertaining an official for an evening may be primarily designed to ensure open channels between the participants, but many messages will also pass on such an occasion. A certain ambiguity of classification is unavoidable.

Table XIII-1 reports the ratings that Washington and Michigan lobbyists and congressional respondents give to tactics for keeping communication channels open. The two groups of lobbyists are fairly similar in their ratings of these five tactics; the tactics, as a whole, are given little importance. Congressional respondents give similarly low ratings to entertainment, parties, and bribery, but their ratings of the political tactics are somewhat higher than the lobbyists' ratings.[2] The main reason for this difference is essentially the same as that given in Chapter XII for different ratings of indirect methods: not all lobby groups can use political tactics. If a lobby group does not use political tactics at all, its lobbyist rates the tactics 0; more than half do. Congressional respondents, however, rate the tactics for their effect on their own behavior; very few of them dismiss the political tactics as having no effect.

Obtaining and maintaining contacts are also important in keeping communication channels open. Since contacts were given special attention, they were not included as a tactic to be rated by lobbyists and do not appear in Table XIII-1.

THE IMPORTANCE OF CONTACTS

The well-worn cliché claims that lobbyists succeed because they have contacts or were hired on this basis. Some men presumably have more contacts or are better at forming them than

[2]*Michigan legislators also rate political tactics higher than do lobbyists; the legislators' ratings are, in fact, quite close to those of congressional respondents. See DeVries (1960, p. 145). Another curious finding from the DeVries study shows that state-house reporters in Michigan rate all five of the access tactics discussed in this chapter much higher than either lobbyists or legislators (pp. 149–50). Journalists traditionally emphasize these tactics when they report on lobbying; apparently they believe their own writing.*

TABLE XIII-1

Ratings of Methods of Keeping Communication Channels Open, by Washington Lobbyists, Michigan Lobbyists, and Congressional Respondents

METHOD OF KEEPING CHANNELS OPEN	PERCENTAGE SELECTING EACH RATING — RATING											Median*	Mean*	Number
	0	1	2	3	4	5	6	7	8	9	10			
Entertaining														
Washington lobbyists	47	15	14	7	4	4	1	5	2	0	0	1.17	1.59	99
Michigan lobbyists	30	18	15	9	0	18	6	0	0	0	3	1.10	2.33	33
Congressional respondents	50	30	13	7	0	0	0	0	0	0	0	.50	.76	30
Giving a Party														
Washington lobbyists	56	14	11	3	5	7	0	1	2	0	0	.88	1.24	99
Michigan lobbyists	45	12	9	9	0	12	3	0	3	0	6	.75	1.91	33
Congressional respondents	47	33	13	3	0	3	0	0	0	0	0	.60	.70	30
Bribery														
Washington lobbyists	98	0	0	0	0	0	0	0	0	0	1	.01	.10	99
Michigan lobbyists	100	0	0	0	0	0	0	0	4	0	0	.00	.00	33
Congressional respondents	96	0	0	0	0	0	0	0	4	0	0	.04	.31	30
Contributing Money														
Washington lobbyists	58	5	5	8	7	4	2	1	3	4	2	.85	1.88	99
Michigan lobbyists	69	6	12	3	0	6	3	0	0	0	0	.42	.87	33
Congressional respondents	30	11	7	15	4	11	7	4	11	0	0	2.62	3.00	30
Campaign Work														
Washington lobbyists	54	6	7	6	3	5	1	5	5	1	6	.92	2.28	99
Michigan lobbyists	66	0	18	6	0	3	0	3	0	0	3	.45	1.21	33
Congressional respondents	21	4	14	4	4	7	11	14	7	7	7	5.00	4.50	30

*Neither measure of central tendency is quite suitable. One cannot assume equal distance between intervals as required for the mean; yet the median ignores the distance of extreme ratings from the central point. The full distribution of the ratings is the best guide to the data.

TABLE XIII–2

Uses for Contacts

SECOND MOST IMPORTANT USE FOR CONTACTS	MOST IMPORTANT USE FOR CONTACTS (Same as 1-7 left)								TOTAL
	1	2	3	4	5	6	7		
1. Transmitting tips and information		7	4	3	1				15
2. Gaining access or arranging appointments	19		2	4	1				26
3. Facilitating collaboration on problems	13	2		1	2				18
4. Learning where to get information	15		1						16
5. Influencing decisions	8	3	1			1			13
6. Miscellaneous	5				1				6
7. No use for contacts							1		1
No response	1	1	1	1		2		13	19
TOTAL	61	13	9	9	5	3	1	13	114

others. Lobbyists were asked for general and evaluative comments about the role of contacts in their work; they were not asked about specific contacts.

Table XIII–2 reports a cross-tabulation of the first and second most important uses of contacts mentioned by respondents. Most emphasize the utility of contacts for keeping communication channels open and aiding the speedy transmission of information. Well over half of the respondents say that contacts are most important for the passing of tips and information. Gaining access or arranging appointments is the next most important use. The other categories also deal with the free flow of information. According to one very active lobbyist, "Contacts are used mainly for information; that is the most important thing." When the interviewer inquired about additional uses, the respondent thought for a moment and then said:

> It really all comes under information. For instance, I might be up on the Hill and somebody will come along and say, "You think that you've got Brown in Line? Well, you better check up on him because he is slipping away." Basically, it is just information.

Less than one-fifth of the respondents mention that contacts are useful for influencing decisions. If one analyzes the meaning of such an answer, he must conclude that contacts per se do not produce influence; they are a channel or a means to obtain a channel. If any influence is transmitted over the channel, it is probably a function of the respective roles of the contacting individuals within the political system. If information does flow freely over a contact point, the parties probably do have a set of reciprocal obligations, but the obligations are usually oriented toward keeping the channel open rather than toward transmitting influence.

When does a contact become a communication channel? The mere fact that one man is acquainted with another does not mean the contact is an effective channel of communication. The possessor of the relevant information must be aware of the potential receiver's need for that information. In addition, the sender must think it is worth his while to transmit the information.

Generally he expects some kind of reciprocal action: a favor, the transmission of relevant information in the other direction, appreciation, etc. Further, the sender must not feel that transmission of the information will endanger himself, his position, or those to whom he is responsible. Therefore, a trusting relationship must exist before information will flow freely over the contact channel. A couple of respondents discussed this point:

Contacts are useful in getting the information that you need. They are also useful in getting an opportunity to talk to a particular individual. If you are favorably known, you don't need to qualify yourself whenever you want to see somebody. My personal feeling is that a great deal of the success of any man in lobbying is dependent on the character that he has got: his reputation for telling the truth and the facts as he knows them. Once you have developed this reputation, you have gone a long way toward getting unsuspicious consideration from the man that you are talking to. You may not get favorable consideration, but at least they won't suspect everything that you say.

* * *

I think I was hired because they figured I could get information. They thought I had a lot of contacts and knew where to get information. A lobbyist is not so much a doer as he is a receiver of information. It is his job to find out what's in the wind, and if he can do this, he is performing well his task as a lobbyist . . . My contacts trust me, and I think their trust is well placed. Most of the things they tell me are not of a secret nature; it's just a development that they have discovered which they think I would be interested in. It is very difficult to get information if you go out digging for it, especially if you do it in a surreptitious way that arouses suspicion. Actually, you get much better information from people who know you, know what your interests are, and know that they can trust you. Sometimes you need to dig for information, too, but you should do this directly. Just follow your lead and approach it in a straightforward manner. You are more likely to get a response that way than if you try to do something circuitous.

A good contact not only increases the likelihood that relevant information will flow over the channel, it also speeds up the flow of information and saves time for the participants.

> Good contacts help direct my activities to get fast results; they can keep me from opening too many side doors and spending time in ineffective places. When I have a new problem, I work through old contacts to reach and make new ones. The people you contact must accept your confidence, and you must be fair and reasonable.

The receipt of confidential or inside information is not an unmixed blessing:

> I don't have any sources of inside information, and I don't want any. I would rather not be told things in confidence. About everything that is going to happen in this town I found out yesterday at Burning Tree Country Club. Then, if I have been told this thing in confidence and it leaks out, the person who has told it to me calls me and accuses me of having let it go. Actually, it is almost impossible to keep things quiet in this town. Those lobbyists who pretend they have inside information in order to try and get clients are 99 per cent bluff. Anybody who hires them is likely to get disappointed because there is very little inside information in this town. A contact is useful only to the extent it gets you a hearing. I have a thousand people I can call, and if a phone call is put through, they will listen.

How do lobbyists develop and maintain their contacts? Table XIII-3 reports a classification of the answers to this question. A majority of them report that contacts develop naturally as they work with or meet people. One respondent says he has developed his contacts "by being a human being over the years":

> You develop a circle of contacts just by doing your business. People that you deal with get to know you; eventually you get on a first-name basis; you invite them out to the house, and you develop them because they are friends. You don't

TABLE XIII-3
Ways of Developing Contacts

SECOND BEST WAY TO DEVELOP CONTACTS	BEST WAY TO DEVELOP CONTACTS							
	Working Together on Problems	Calling on Them on Own Initiative	Through Friends or Co-Workers	Parties, Gifts, Favors	Miscellaneous	Do Not Develop Contacts	No Response	Total
Working together on problems		13	2	1	2			18
Calling on them on own initiative	18		1	1				20
Through friends or co-workers	18	8		1	2			29
Parties, gifts, favors	2	2	1		1			6
Miscellaneous	5	1	2					8
Do not develop contacts						4		4
No response	8	6					15	29
TOTAL	51	30	6	3	5	4	15	114

develop a friendship purely because it might help you in your lobbying activities. Another way I have been able to develop my contacts is by hearing about a tremendous number of job openings. Maybe I know someone on the Hill who wants to move out of his position; then, on the other hand, I may know of some trade association which needs someone. I will get the two of them together, and maybe a guy has found a new job and will be very grateful. I keep on the lookout for opportunities to help friends. I don't snoop to get this information; people just tend to come to me with these situations.

If a lobbyist happens not to possess a contact in a certain problem area, it is relatively easy for him to call on the indicated persons on his own initiative. Most lobbyists do not consider lack of a contact in a particular area to be a great barrier to action. Table XII–3 shows that initiating one's own contacts is the second most frequently selected method. Large labor organization lobbyists prefer this method. One lobbyist for a minority group has his own studied way of making contacts which merits quotation, though his tactics are not widely used:

Very few of our better contacts were introduced to us by others; we would rather develop them ourselves. We try to find out the eating habits of the person we want to meet, or his barber habits, or some other kind of habitual activity. We then try to catch the member of Congress at an informal time and see if we can get an opportunity to chat with him. Most offices try to overprotect their senator or representative, especially if they think the group trying to see him might want a favor. It is much better if you run into the guy in the washroom or meet him in the elevator. The elevator is especially good because he is captive there for a while and can't get out for at least one floor. These are dodges that a minor league lobbyist has to adopt; lobbyists from big constituency groups like labor can be sure of getting in to see a member of Congress because he wouldn't dare refuse. Another reason for meeting congressmen in this informal fashion is to avoid going first to the staff people in the office.

If I can meet the congressman in an informal way and then go and talk to him and later be introduced by the congressman to the staff, the staff will get the impression that this is an important person in the eyes of the congressman. Then, whenever there is a letter from me, or a report, or a memo, it will get put on top of the pile as it goes to the congressman's desk.

There are, of course, highly-placed individuals who simply are not accessible to an ordinary lobbyist. Personal initiative is not enough; the lobbyist without contacts may hire one who has them:

If I tried to see Harry Byrd, I would get nowhere. But if a former colleague calls him up and says "Harry, I've got something here I think you ought to see. Can I have half an hour?" he'll say, "yes," even though he knows the former Senator is a registered lobbyist.[3]

Contrary to popular belief, entertainment, parties, gifts, and favors are of little importance in developing or maintaining contacts. Only nine respondents think this kind of tactic is important. The lobbyists that Matthews interviewed had similar reactions.[4] Curiously, however, lobbyists do entertain despite their belief that it is not beneficial. This topic is discussed more fully later in this chapter.

Once made, contacts require at least minimum maintenance. Lobbyists must seek a delicate balance between coming around often enough to be remembered but not so much as to exhaust the welcome. Lobbyists who take the maintenance of their contacts seriously (not all of them do), must devote a good deal of time to it—so much that they can keep up only a small circle of contacts. Large lobbying staffs share the burden by having different men cultivate sets of contacts:

I do not attempt to contact a large number of congressmen and senators. I concentrate on a few men strategically

[3]*Quoted in Matthews (1960b, p. 180).*
[4]*Matthews (1960b, p. 180).*

placed on the Appropriations committees. These men are economy-minded and are generally in sympathy with our political outlook. I restrict my efforts for several reasons. Over the years, I develop friendships with these men. You know they are all—well, almost all—exceptional men, the kind you would like to know even if you didn't have any business reason for doing so. To keep these friendships alive and genuine, I have to stop around to see them quite often just to say hello. For example, if I don't see————at least once a week, he'll say, "Where the hell have you been? You only stop around when you want something from us." Even a few contacts on the Hill require a good deal of time and attention.

And when I stop around to see these men, they always ask me to do something for them—you know how overworked and understaffed most of them are. I can't afford to let them down.[5]

Not only can too frequent attention wear out a welcome, but if a lobbyist develops too close a friendship with a contact, he may find it interferes with his purposes:

I find that a close friend may bend over backwards to avoid favoritism. It is a mistake to say that you have a good friend who will do anything you want him to. Usually everybody knows who your close friends are, and if such a friend did you a favor, he would jeopardize his own position; you just can't risk that kind of thing. I would much rather go before a person who is in the impartial category. Those persons who think they can accomplish a lot by having lots of close contacts actually get into difficulties.

* * *

Very good friends are often more skeptical that a mediocre friend might be when you are trying to convince them of your position. The close friend is so intimately acquainted with you he often wonders why you are trying so hard to get his vote.

[5]*Quoted in Matthews (1960b, p. 181).*

TABLE XIII—4

Preferred Loci for Contacts

SECOND BEST LOCUS FOR CONTACTS	BEST LOCUS FOR CONTACTS						
	Members of Congress	Staff Assistants to Members	Congressional Committee Staffs	Executive Agency Staffs	Miscellaneous	No Response	Total
Members of congress		3	8	6			17
Staff assistants to members	3		5	2	1		11
Congressional committee staffs	13	4		16			33
Executive agency staffs	8		14				22
Miscellaneous			1				1
No response	2			3	11	14	30
TOTAL	26	7	28	27	12	14	114

These comments support the point made earlier that contacts facilitate the flow of information but are not particularly useful for the exertion of influence.

Another reason that contacts require constant attention is that the key men in Washington are always changing. Voters retire some and replace them with others. Men shift or are shifted from job to job. The grim reaper takes his annual toll. Political parties lose elections. No lobbyist can confine his contacts to persons of one political party. "No political party has enough discipline in Congress to get any new legislation through." The alert lobbyist is busy making new contacts every day.

Where do lobbyists prefer to have their contacts? The obvious and oversimplified answer is everywhere, especially with top decision-makers. It is simply impossible, however, for the average lobbyist to make contact with top decision-makers. Furthermore, we have already seen that the costs are high, especially in time. The more realistic question, then, is: Where do lobbyists expend their scarce resources in attempting to establish and maintain contacts?

Lobbyists were asked where they try to establish contacts and what their most important sources of inside information are. The cross-tabulations of the first and second answers to each of those questions are reported in Tables XIII–4 and XIII–5. As expected, respondents pick their most important source of inside information as their preferred locus for contacts, but this was true of only 45 per cent of the sample.

Looking at the table showing preferred loci for contacts, one can see that respondents were about equally likely to choose members of Congress, congressional committee staffs, and executive agency staffs as their first choice. For the second choice, however, staff persons, especially committee staffs, were most frequently selected. Committee staff persons were selected as important (first or second choice) contacts by 61 per cent of the respondents. Executive agency staff persons were selected by 49 per cent, and members of Congress, by 42 per cent. Staff assistants to members were not selected as frequently, probably because they generally are less directly involved in the decision process.

The table showing sources of inside information again indicate that congressional staff persons are given the most first and

TABLE XIII-5

Sources of Inside Information

SECOND MOST IMPORTANT	MOST IMPORTANT							
	Members of Congress	Congressional Staff	Staff in Executive Branch	Journalists	Other Lobbyists	Miscellaneous Sources	No Response	Total
Members of congress	13	11	2	1	2	1		17
Congressional staff		10	8	2	1	4		28
Staff in executive branch	4	2			1	3		18
Journalists	1	2						3
Other lobbyists	2	5	4	1	1	1		6
Miscellaneous sources	2	3	2		2	3		15
No response	1					4	15	27
TOTAL	23	33	16	4	7	16	15	114

second choices (61 per cent). Members of Congress are next (selected by 40 per cent) followed closely by executive agency staff (selected by 34 per cent). Journalists and other lobbyists are also given occasionally as important sources of inside information, but the frequency of selection is rather low.

Lobbyists' preferences for various loci of contacts depend partly on their roles. Members of large staffs concentrating primarily on Congress prefer congressional committee staff contacts. Trade association executives and representatives of big corporations, who are interested in decisions on business regulation, prefer contacts with executive agency staffs. Washington representatives and representatives for farm and civic groups prefer contacts directly with members of Congress. Lobbyists in the last category generally belong to small staffs, and they prefer that the few contacts they can maintain be directly with decision-makers.

It is evident that most respondents would prefer to attempt to contact staff assistants than to try to reach the decision-makers directly. Why? There are several intertwined reasons mainly related to the difficulty of communicating directly with decision-makers. Usually lobbyists can get longer and more relaxed appointments with staff assistants. Also, busy decision-makers must turn over the investigation of problem areas to staff assistants. The assistants will eventually gather the relevant information—so why not talk to them at the beginning? Third, staff assistants often become expert in a given subject area; therefore, they are more likely to understand and correctly evaluate lobbyists' pleas than the not-so-expert decision-makers. Fourth, lobbyists want to receive information from their contacts, and staff assistants are more likely to have time to pass along tips to lobbyists. Finally, decision-makers and assistants are so interdependent that talking to staff is almost equivalent to talking with an official.

A senator has so many problems and they are so varied that it is unfair to him to press him personally on an issue. It is much better to get to his immediate assistant. It is also unfair to the assistant not to be alerted if I am going to talk to the senator. No senator makes a dent in a problem without an assistant to keep him in line. Also an assistant can do you a great deal of harm if he is not on your side.

The transmission of information is so important in the governmental system that a shadowy specialized role of "finder" has developed. "Finders" are persons who, appearing anonymous and vacant, wait and watch at places of high communication activity such as halls of the capitol building. They hope to pick up inside information to sell to groups or individuals interested enough to pay their price. They try to earn a living as a broker of information. Information from these sources is reputed to have doubtful reliability, and lobbyists seldom use such persons. None of the respondents mention "finders" as important sources of inside information.

Staff employees who do not agree with the policy followed by their bosses are special sources of inside information. Such employees sometimes leak information to the opposition in the hope of defeating the policy of the superiors. Lobbyists, of course, welcome this kind of inside information, but it comes their way so seldom that the total impact is relatively slight.

Here are a few summary generalizations on the role of contacts in the governmental communication network. First, contacts are important communication channels, and every lobbyist uses them. Second, contacts are relatively easy to obtain, and, therefore, the possession of a circle of contacts is not a crucial consideration in the recruitment of lobbyists. Third, although influence can be transmitted over a contact channel, the contact per se is not a significant factor influencing decisions. Fourth, lobbyists playing different roles need contacts in different places; they are rather selective in deciding where to have contacts. Fifth, most lobbyists jealously protect and keep their contacts. They are reluctant to reveal specific contacts both because they want to protect their sources from abuse, and also because they want to preserve the special advantage that their more-or-less exclusive communication channel gives them.

ENTERTAINMENT AND PARTIES

This study questions the time-honored belief that lobbyists accomplish their purposes by softening up their marks with liquor, food, and entertainment. Although an unlimited expense account is said to be one of the lobbyist's best tools, both Washington lobbyists and congressional respondents (see Table XIII–1) rate the tactics as of little or no importance. Michigan lobbyists, who operate under somewhat different conditions, rate them slightly higher, but even they rate them rather low.

Why does the myth persist? Perhaps the major reason is that charges of lobbyist entertainment are frequently made by opposing sides in policy battles to discredit the opposition and improve the position of the challenger. Another reason is that it is more psychologically satisfying to a lobbyist to believe that the opposition forces won because they "wined and dined" officials than to admit that the opponents had a better case or that the voters preferred the opposite side. A defeated person can self-righteously maintain his position if he believes he was defeated because the opposition used entertainment, which is extraneous to the merits of the case.

Another reason is that colorful charges of lobbyist entertainment are disproportionately publicized in the press. The stories in the average newspaper about lobbying are generally about entertainment, parties, and bribery. Such stories are both colorful and believable. Every person has felt grateful to persons who have presented him with gifts, entertainment, and other rewards; surely officials would feel grateful, too. Entertainment is widely used in business and diplomacy, so it is presumed to be very useful in lobbying also.

Yet the fact is that those in the best position to know say entertainment has almost no effect in lobbying. Why is this so? The implicit assumption about entertainment and parties is that they are rewarding; the persons being entertained are supposed to feel goodwill and gratefulness toward those who entertain them. Washington, however, is a city where entertainment has been carried so far that another invitation becomes a punishment instead of a reward. The decision-maker, who is required by his position and role to attend a large number of functions, treasures most highly the freedom to spend an evening at home with his family. The more important the person, the more overburdened he usually is by obligatory parties and entertainment. This surfeit of entertainment extends even to clerks of committees and staff assistants to decision-makers; for them, too, an evening at home is a matter of rejoicing. Lobby groups and lobbyists recognize this desire and do not press entertainment on unwilling invitees. A few groups now turn their entertainment efforts to the secretaries and minor clerks, the only ones who might appreciate them. The point that entertainment is not a reward was made by many respondents. A committee clerk said:

> I give entertainment a zero. I have a feeling that when they take me out it's either to fill a seat or get a free meal themselves. I don't want to go most of the time, it's no treat for me. I don't feel obligated at all because most of these guys are on an expense account and get a free meal themselves. . . . the inviting is much more important than the fact one attends a party or not. If you get overlooked on a guest list, and you think you ought to get invited, then I would give that party a minus ten.

A lobbyist who has worked as an assistant to a senator remarked:

> I only entertain friends, and when I do, we never talk business. I soon got over the idea that it's necessary to entertain people. When I worked as ———'s assistant, I was invited to a lot of functions, but I soon discovered that I was invited because I was ———'s assistant and not because these persons were interested in me as a personal friend. Most members of Congress are so fed up with all these invitations that it is pitiful. Generally, they try to think up good excuses so they don't have to go. Some lobbyists get so enamored of the idea that they have to entertain people that they will call up somebody in the home state of the congressman or senator and ask the constituent to invite the member to a function in Washington, even though the constituent won't be there himself. This is just a waste of time and money; experience on the Hill taught me that.

A few lobbyists do not see that entertaining is generally considered a burden and feel obliged to do it. Some despise having to entertain without realizing that it may not be welcome to those they invite:

I have no real enjoyment in lobbying; I dislike the amount of entertaining that goes along with it. I despise the necessity to drink a lot of liquor and associate with wearisome people. My home is a semi-club; people come at all hours and get food and drink. Yet I can't see how I can avoid it. I can't avoid buying food and liquor for these people, and I can't be antisocial and not eat and drink with them when they come. Many times I would prefer not to take another drink, but because I am entertaining I feel I have to do so. I entertain important people at least 80 per cent of my evenings. I sometimes go thirty days without eating a meal alone.

Entertaining and giving a party are rated as separate tactics by the respondents, but the two tactics are appraised so similarly that they may well be considered as one. The ratings of the two tactics are significantly correlated. Those who spend the most time entertaining rate parties higher. Table XIII–1 shows that some lobbyists think that these tactics are rewarding to a certain extent. They apparently do not use parties as occasions to convince decision-makers of policies; however, they do use them to open doors or keep them open. One respondent who spends 10 to 15 per cent of his time entertaining reports, "I think entertaining an official for an evening is important in opening a door for me the next day or the next week. We never talk business on those occasions." This same respondent rates several other tactics much higher than entertaining.

Respondents who take a long-range view of their lobbying find entertainment a "door-opener." Those who plan to make lobbying a career rate entertainment higher. Those who sought their lobbying jobs rate it higher than those pressed into lobbying by circumstances. Those who are strongly committed to the policy of their organization rate it higher than those not so heavily committed.

Generally, a lobbyist's evaluation of entertaining does not vary significantly with the type of organization he represents or with his role toward his employer. There were a couple of exceptions: lobbyists for organizations with high power at the polls rate entertainment higher than lobbyists for organizations with less power. High poll power organizations have wider interests, and their lobbyists knock on the doors of decision-makers more often; thus they must avoid wearing out their welcome. In addition, these organizations have more resources to devote to entertainment and parties.

Officers of organizations, who have more responsibility for representation, rate entertaining higher than respondents in other roles. Interestingly, lobbyists with higher incomes do not rate entertaining higher; there was, in fact, a reverse relationship. The higher-income respondents rate entertaining lower than the lower-income respondents. The data do not suggest an explanation for this relationship.

One congressman thinks that communications passed on entertainment occasions are almost useless for exerting influence:

> I haven't been to a cocktail party or a banquet in the last ten years. Those things are a waste of time. If someone does try to influence you at one of those things and gets you off in a corner and starts to talk to you, why you know what he is up to. You realize that he is trying to pull something, at least trying to press something, and you begin to resent it. It puts your guard up, and you are likely to react against them instead of in favor of them.

Although the general opinion of entertainment is low, lobbyists have not given up entertaining, and decision-makers and staff assistants still accept invitations. But entertainment, at best, helps a little to keep communication channels open; however, that will be accomplished only if the recipient of the invitation feels rewarded and honored by the inivitation. In the rush of Washington entertainment and parties, even that essential condition is often unfulfilled.

DIRECT AND INDIRECT BRIBERY

Another popular belief is that lobbyists use bribery to accomplish their ends. But bribery was almost universally rejected by both lobbyists and congressional respondents as an effective lobbying tactic. Evidence gathered for this study suggests that this rejection is not mere lip-service to public concepts of morality.

The myth about bribery persists for many of the same reasons that the myth about the value of entertainment persists. Bribery charges are weapons of political battle, and belief that opponents use bribes is a psychologically acceptable excuse for defeat. The most important reason for the myth is that stories of lobbyists who have tried to bribe officials have always been headlined and given extensive play in the press. Many citizens read about lobbying only in connection with bribery.

Some confusion arises from the careless use of the term "bribery." Many activities looked upon as normal in certain settings are called bribery by political opponents in a public setting. There is, first, a difference between direct and indirect bribery—though the distinction is somewhat arbitrary and is not adhered to in ordinary public discourse. Direct bribery is the receipt by a decision-maker of personal favors or rewards specifically in return for a pattern of behavior expected by the donor. (It is this kind of bribery that is rated in Table XIII-1.) The specific quid pro quo distinguishes direct from indirect bribery. Indirect bribery is the receipt by a decision-maker of favors or rewards— without any specific behavior change expected or communicated by the donor. The reward is given the recipient just for doing what comes naturally. Subtle behavior changes might result from the reward (they are usually hoped for), but the donor expresses no clear indication of expectations as a condition of the reward. If one looks at real cases, indirect bribery becomes more difficult to distinguish from ordinary human relationships than from direct bribery.

Flagrant direct bribery is almost never used in the influence process in Washington—according to virtually all the participant-observers interviewed for this study. The major reason for this is that bribery is a terribly dangerous tactic which has little likelihood of producing policy influence even if it goes undetected. Given a sensation-hungry press corps and alert opposition, bribes are likely to be exposed. One clerk of a congressional committee said, "I've never seen it up here. I just can't feature it. Over the long pull, any time bribery would help them there would be a thousand times that it would hurt them."

In addition to the danger of exposure by press and opponents is the risk that the proferred bribe will be looked upon as an insult by the intended receiver. It may destroy any possibility for favorable consideration. The few experiences with bribery in Washington proved to have been mainly unsuccessful. There is a consensus that members of Congress, with very rare exceptions, are simply unbribable. One long-time member of the House of Representatives said:

> I have served with twenty-five hundred members since I have been in Congress, and all of them are honest and honorable people. The incidence of bribery and bad conduct is lower among congressmen than any other group of people in America. The amount of bribery is so small in that whole group that it is next to nothing.

A lobbyist who is a former clerk of a congressional committee made the same point:

> In all of my experience here in Washington, and I have been around here for fifteen years, I have never seen an instance where bribery entered the picture. Most persons in Congress are definitely above that sort of thing. You couldn't bribe them if you tried. . . . I have made political contributions ever since I can remember, and I intend to continue to make them, but this doesn't enter one iota into my lobbying activities. Campaign contributions and political activity are a part of my citizen's duty and have no role at all in lobbying. They are two separate segments of my life.

Another lobbyist reported:

> I have never met a member of Congress whom I felt I could bribe with any amount of money. I do know of a member I can get so drunk that he can't appear on the Hill the next day.

A lobbyist who thinks about using bribery must consider the enormous cost of switching even a few votes; furthermore, he has no assurance that the bribed officials will stay bought. Men who can be bribed can be bribed by both sides or treacherously turn upon the briber:

Bribery could only be effective to buy one or two individuals. One always wonders about such a guy: does he stay bought? Persons that can be bribed can be bribed either way.

* * *

I don't use bribery, nor do I think it is effective. The member of Congress who is so lacking in character that he would accept a bribe certainly would not have any influence in Congress anyway. He couldn't change any votes, and it would be a waste of money to get his particular vote.

The perception that lobbyists use bribery may stem in part from activities in state legislatures.[6] Several respondents who have had experience both with the national Congress and various state legislatures refer to a difference in atmosphere between the national and state legislative bodies:

Bribery and such things never happen in Congress; members of Congress are much too smart to get mixed up in that kind of thing. It does happen fairly often, however, before state legislatures. I never engage in bribery, and I resent it very much when members of state legislatures come up and ask, almost straightforwardly, for a bribe in order to back a certain bill.

* * *

State legislatures are a horse of another color. There is none of this petty venality around Congress that one finds in the state legislatures.

These comments should not be taken to mean that bribery is common in all state legislatures. DeVries (1960, p. 178) found no evidence whatsoever of bribery in Michigan lobbying.

The occasional lobbyist who decides to try bribery usually tries to disguise his bribe as something else. A bribe disguised as a gift or a campaign contribution is considered to be more acceptable to the self-image of the recipient. Even so, the recipient

Fowler (1957), and see Lester Velie (1949).

sometimes sees through the disguise and reacts against the donor. Two interesting examples of this were picked up in the congressional interviewing. One respondent, an assistant to a senator, was approached by a group in the watch industry; they wanted the senator to insert a speech in the *Congressional Record*. The lobbyist subtly suggested to the assistant that he wear a $250 wrist watch for a few days and then tell them how he liked it. The assistant almost agreed to do so until he realized he was being bribed; he quickly escorted the lobbyist from the office. Another assistant to the senator was less suspicious and accepted a watch; however, when the implications were explained to him, he returned it posthaste by registered mail. When the speech arrived for consideration for insertion in the *Congressional Record*, the respondent found it so bad that he declined even to show it to the senator.

A member of Congress related that on a particular day crowded with appointments one fellow was admitted without an appointment and stayed only a short time. As he left, he dropped an envelope on the desk, announcing, "This is something for your campaign." The busy member slipped the envelope in his drawer without looking at it. When he opened it at the end of the day, he found $500 in $20 bills. Since the "donation" was made far in advance of the election and the member had not even decided to run again, he could only conclude that this was a bribe. He immediately sent the money to the Sergeant-at-Arms office and notified the Department of Justice to investigate whether a criminal act had been committed. There were no witnesses, however, and no indictments were ever brought (making a campaign contribution is a legitimate act). One other member of the same congressional committee reported receiving the same kind of envelope on the same day. The incident was picked up by the press and widely publicized, much to the chagrin of the members who received the envelopes, for they felt it projected an unfavorable image of them. The respondent wondered if some members quietly keep or return bribes rather than force prosecution and risk unfavorable publicity. The respondent eventually voted against the donor of the bribe.

Indirect bribery is a much safer, although not necessarily more effective, tactic than direct bribery. Indirect bribery takes many subtle forms that are common in many segments of our society. Most instances of conflict of interest found in government might be called indirect bribery. In each Congress a few individuals utilize their congressional positions to maximize their personal incomes. This can be done in many ways: a member is "let in on" special high-profit business deals; he or his law firm is given a handsome retainer by an individual or firm; or he is paid large fees for private consulting. These same tactics are used with officials in the executive branch and with staff assistants to officials. Subtle influence arises because the recipient knows that the rewards may well be withdrawn if he acts contrary to the interests of the donors. One clerk of a congressional committee commented:

> The great majority of people up here will have no truck with that kind of thing; however, there are also some unscrupulous people up here. There are some who are just here to make the most out of their position. We have one senator up here who won't leave town till he has three or four persons or firms paying for his trip and providing him with other kinds of services. This is far the exception, however.

Campaign contributions have already been mentioned as a legal means used by lobbyists to ingratiate themselves and keep communication lines open. They also offer small gifts, usually at Christmas time, to officials and their staffs. Offices differ on whether or not the staff may accept small gifts. The careful lobbyist checks in advance to see whether gifts can be received:

> Our gifts are small because we don't have enough money; we try to give small and unique things that will stand out; usually they are made by our own people. These things usually go to the secretaries and the staff assistants to members of Congress. Many members of Congress personally would not accept gifts, and many even have rules for the gifts that their staff might accept. Some say they won't accept gifts above a certain value; these limits go as high as $25 or as low as $5. We have to get intelligence on this before we send the gift so as not to embarrass the recipient. We find generally that it helps in getting us an opportunity to have a member look at our stuff.

Congressional respondents gave differing reports on practices in their offices:

> We discourage anything like gifts; we don't want to be in a position where anyone might say we were influenced. We can accept lunch in order to talk business, but that's all. This wasn't always the rule with this committee; but we have tightened up; we are much tighter than anyone on the Hill on this. If I received a gift, it wouldn't necessarily mean I was influenced, but it creates an impression, and I don't want anyone getting the wrong impression. We send a lot of stuff back; it is kind of embarrassing, too, because we don't like to offend people. Most of the lobbyists around town know our ruling or they check in advance to see if a gift can be accepted. Our ruling applies only to the professional staff, not to the clerical staff. The staff of this committee is pretty familiar with most . . . problems, and a smooth approach will not necessarily get a man a better hearing.

* * *

> It is always a problem to figure out how far you can go on these things. Every year someone on the staff will get three fifths of liquor instead of one; our rule says we can accept one fifth but not three. A lot of times they will call and ask how many people are on the staff and what their names are. They will send all the girls a box of hose and all the boys a fifth of whiskey. Whether or not you think it is bad depends on the person who is behind it. If it is a borderline case, we turn it down just to be safe. Of course the staff doesn't vote, so there are no bribes for us. We do, pretty much, decide what goes into the reports, but we decide on the merits of the case; whether or not we have gotten a little gift doesn't make any difference.

One member of Congress related:

> I have never had a fellow try to bribe me in the fourteen years I have been here. Occasionally, they come in and make some kind of inference implying maybe a campaign contribution will be forthcoming, but there is not even much

of that. We also have very little indirect giving through gifts. We might get a bottle of whiskey or something like that, but there is very little of that, too.

One congressional staff person who formerly worked in the executive branch contrasted the two:

> The lobbyists tried to cultivate us more in the Department of Interior than up here on the Hill. When I was in Interior, the Shell Oil Co. would send a crate of pears every Christmas. One of the fellows in the division got a case of minced clams one time. That kind of gift is hard to deal with because it is perishable. You can't send it back, and you don't want to throw it away, so you have to use it up or give it away.

Another form of indirect bribery consists in inviting officials on weekend cruises ("inspection trips") or to speak at conventions. The latter tactic is very subtle. Often the convention is held at a nice resort, and the official spends a few days enjoying himself. During his stay he makes a speech for which he receives a $500 or $1,000 honorarium. The official may think that he has earned his reward and that acceptance is perfectly legitimate. Still, one guesses that after such a pleasant experience the lobbyist for the group holding the convention will always find the official's door open.

One cannot decide a priori that any or all tactics of indirect bribery are bad. All of these methods are used in ordinary human relationships, frequently without any intent to influence. Quid-pro-quo relationships, too, are found everywhere in human society. Usually indirect bribery tactics are used merely or solely to keep communication channels open, an uncensorable motive. Ultimately, however, this activity is kept within bounds only by the strength of character of persons in decision-making positions. Officials of high character refuse bribes and do not allow favors to influence their decisions. One member of Congress discussed this problem:

> There are not many bribes offered either directly or indirectly. We may be glad to get the calendars and the ash

trays and the flags that they send to us, but very little of any value is offered. Most of the congressmen have judgment about this, and so do most of the lobbyists. I think perhaps the rule that the President has in the White House is a very good one. He says it's all right to accept anything that will go into a deep freeze but not the deep freeze itself. That goes for anything else of importance such as an automobile. If someone sent me a brace of birds that I could put in my freezer, I would be glad to have it, and I wouldn't think it would be improper. I think a good rule here would be comparable to the rule ladies use; they can accept anything in the way of jewelry that is small but nothing that is big. Much the same thing should be true of members of Congress; they shouldn't be accepting any engagement rings from lobbyists.

One curious consequence of the popular image that lobbyists use bribery to accomplish their purposes is that lobbyists often must go to some lengths to explain to naïve clients that bribery is not necessary:

> They came to me with the idea that we had to do something under the table or something dirty to get what they wanted. They asked, "Where do we put the fix in?" Such persons are often taken in by unscrupulous lobbyists who probably pocket the money they have been given to bribe officials.

Free-lance lobbyists with many clients encounter this image more often than the staff persons hired by associations.

CONTRIBUTIONS OF MONEY AND WORK IN POLITICAL CAMPAIGNS

The political party activity of Washington lobbyists was discussed in Chapter IV from the perspective of the individual lobbyist. In this chapter, contributions of money and work will be examined for their utility as tactics employed by lobby groups. Groups generally have two motives for contributing money and work. They want to place persons who are favorable to the policy they propose into decision-making positions in the government. Also, they want to keep communication channels to decision-makers open.[7] Actually, the two purposes are intertwined; the power to place a man in office most certainly forces decision-makers to keep lines of communication open to groups with political power. Only the most foolhardy elected officials would close off communication to groups with substantial political power. Lobbyists commented that political action is most viable in providing access:

> I don't think contributing money to a campaign has much purpose for lobbying. Of course, if a man contributes year after year, he can get in to see his congressman. Contributing work is much the same, the hard worker is the nearest and dearest person to a member of Congress.
>
> * * *
>
> A political contribution is not ever likely to change a vote or get a vote from an official, but it does get you a sympathetic audience. If you have made a contribution, the fellow looks on you with favor, and he will give you a chance to be heard. Contributing work in a campaign is even better to accomplish this.

Contributions of campaign money and work are much more welcome and acceptable to elected officials than are gifts, favors, and bribes. Generally, political contributions are not forthcoming unless there is already considerable similarity in outlook and interest between donor and recipient. The official can accept without feeling pressured because he is being supported for doing what he wanted to do all along. One senator said:

> A contribution by a lobbyist or a lobby group usually backs the same thing you are interested in; this common interest comes as an appreciation of past work. Where common interest brings contributions of work, the candidate is even more grateful and feels confident that he can go along with that person or group.

[7] *Participants in the Brookings' round table of business representatives also thought of political action primarily as a device for keeping communication channels open. Cherington and Gillen (1962, p. 57).*

The above point of view is not shared by all officials; some of them think that any contribution restricts their freedom of action:

A contribution by a lobbyist or lobby group makes one suspicious. You get to feeling you don't want to accept the money even though you might need it. You don't want to get obligated. Most members of Congress want to be in a position where they can change their mind if they want to. Of course, money and work are important in being re-elected, but I prefer not to get obligated if I can help it.

Congressional respondents report that they cannot always do something positive for their political contributors but that at least they do their best not to hurt them. Naturally they find it difficult to deny someone who has been generous. Some decision-makers try to protect themselves from influence by deliberately not knowing who contributes to their campaigns. Candidates commonly appoint a finance chairman or campaign treasurer to handle contributions and expenditures; sometimes these men are instructed not to tell the candidate who his contributors are. It is more difficult for a candidate to ignore those working on his behalf; workers are more visible than monetary contributors.

Most political contributions by lobbyists or lobby groups go to individual candidates rather than to political parties. Most lobbyists believe that political parties are relatively unimportant in the policy-making process. In addition, lobby groups do not want to be known as aligned with one party or another. Generally they must secure support from persons in both parties to produce passage of specific legislation. Should they develop too close a relationship with the party in power, and the majority should shift after the next election, they might be frozen out. Groups that do not become identified with parties can "reward their friends and punish their enemies" regardless of party.

The initiative in making political contributions often comes not from the pressure groups but from campaign treasurers. Some groups and individuals find it difficult to resist requests for campaign funds, especially if they want easy access to the official in the future. Other groups take a firm position against all such requests. A president of a relatively poor organization explained that they simply do not have the money to make many contributions. If they were to make one contribution, they would be pressed to make many more; thus they have a rigorous rule against any contributions at all.

From time to time, lobbyists threaten not to make political contributions if officials do not cooperate. Both lobbyists and congressional respondents report that such threats are totally ineffective. Public officials, especially members of Congress, have a sense of their own importance and their own integrity; a threat not to contribute is an insult to those two aspects of their self-image. The result is more likely to be action against the interests of the threatening lobbyists than cooperation.

Table XIII-1 displays the ratings of campaign work and partisan political contributions by lobbyists and congressional respondents. Campaign work is generally rated higher than contributing money, especially by the congressional respondents; however, those who give one tactic a high rating also give the other quite a high rating. Washington lobbyists show a .60 tau beta correlation between ratings of the two tactics. It makes sense, then, to regard the two tactics as very similar.

Lobbyists and congressional respondents rate these tactics differently because many lobby groups simply cannot use political tactics. Political tactics are "hot potatoes," and only organizations with considerable power at the polls can use them without being burned. Lobbyists from organizations with high power at the polls rate both tactics higher. Lobbyists from organizations with high poll power also make more political contributions at more levels of government and raise more political funds than lobbyists from other groups.

Support from an organization with considerable power at the polls can be decisive to the election of a candidate; when he assumes office, he is not likely to forget that support. Furthermore, even when a powerful organization backs a losing candidate, its power is often sufficient to prevent the winning candidate from retaliating against it. The plight of the organization with little power at the polls is quite different. Its impact in a given campaign is much less likely to be decisive and thus much less likely to be remembered. Most important, should it back a losing candidate, it is likely to find access to the winner cut off. Rather than risk such an outcome, most small organizations completely abstain from political tactics.

Some lobbyists give political tactics 0 ratings because they represent clients with very narrow specific interests which are outside political contention. Such lobbyists have no use whatsoever for political tactics.

Ratings of the two tactics also vary with the lobbyist's own experience in politics. Chapter IV shows that lobbyists differ in their involvement in politics and that this difference stems primarily from personal rather than occupational factors. A relevant finding is that lobbyists with experience in partisan politics rate these two political tactics higher than lobbyists without experience. A syndrome of evidence corroborates this: contributors rate the tactics higher than non-contributors; those who contribute to persons at three levels of government rate them higher than those who contribute at only one level; those who have raised political money rate them higher than those who have not; political campaigners rate them higher than non-campaigners; those more active in all kinds of groups (high group activity is nearly always positively correlated with political activity) rate them higher than those less active in groups. It is an accepted generalization of psychology that persons value the things they do. Psychologically, we expect lobbyists who participate in politics to value political tactics more highly than those who do not.

To summarize, the tactics are most effective in keeping access doors open and communication channels clear. They are also important in placing decision-makers in office. There are both high rewards and high costs involved in their use. Only organizations with high power at the polls can safely employ them. Familiarity with political methods mitigates some of the fear lobbyists might have about their use. Lobbyists for organizations with little power at the polls, or clients with special non-political problems will not use the tactics. Moreover, if lobbyists are unfamiliar with partisan politics, they are disinclined to use them.

BUILDING A TRUSTING RELATIONSHIP

It was explained in Chapter IX that one of the lobbyist's major tasks, perhaps his most important one, is to insure favorable reception of his messages by the persons he desires to influence. Easy access and clear communication channels are essential to this. Perhaps the surest way the lobbyist can achieve these goals is by developing a trusting relationship between himself and the decision-makers. Decision-makers also want such relationships because they need the reliable information, services, and pleasant trusting associations they can find with lobbyists.

Trusting relationships are so important in government because all of the actors in the government policy-making process are potentially vulnerable. Vulnerability is built into the system because it is the way in which government is made responsible to the wishes of the governed. Elected officials are vulnerable to voters. Appointed officials are vulnerable to elected officials. Lobbyists are vulnerable to clients and to governmental officials who can cut off access. Reporters are vulnerable to newsmakers, who may or may not give them stories, and to their publishers. Political party officials are vulnerable to voters and to officials who hand out patronage and other favors. All actors keep their eyes on the voters because they are the ultimate source of power setting the tone for the system. Between elections, power centers in the elected officials. Any other actor who wants to exert power on elected officials must ultimately use the threat of a diminished vote.

In a system where every actor leans on other actors, rules must be devised for the mutual protection of all. The most basic rule is that the various actors must be able to trust one another. Many subrules are designed to assist the fulfillment of this basic condition. They will be discussed briefly here as a summary of the communication relationships between lobbyists and officials.

The actors enforce the system of trust. No one is admitted to the decision-making circle until he proves he can be trusted. Formal appointment to a position, even an elected position, does not insure admission to the "inner club," as it is sometimes called. Any violator of the rules finds himself ostracized cold-bloodedly and unforgivingly. The point soon comes clear: if one wants influence, he must behave so that people can trust him. The words of two staff assistants in Congress emphasize this point:

> Oftentimes I take liberties with my position of trust by depending on lobbyists. When you do that with a lobbyist, he just doesn't dare let you down. Up here you depend pretty much on the grace of your patron, and if you violate

his trust, you are dead. If you let a lobbyist get a shot at you, you're done because you showed up your patron. The lobbyist feels this, too; he has a future in this, too; and he mustn't let himself be made the sucker. If you let someone down and you get caught, everyone looks on you with a jaundiced eye. We have the biggest daisy chain in the world up here. . . . We play footsie with all lobbyists, and we play favorites with none. Those who want to stay on build a reputation for honesty, integrity, and dependability.

* * *

You not only find this code as between lobbyists and members of Congress, but you particularly find it among members of the House. Every member of the House has two constituencies—one is the folks back home and the other is his fellow members. Lobbyists are required to follow the same rules; if one tries to sell an untrue bill of goods, he gets the brushoff. No man stands alone.

Analysts of the political process often overlook the fact that the elected officials have the upper hand in setting up and enforcing the rules. This is especially true in the relationship between lobbyists and officials. Officials can make decisions without consulting or depending on anyone else—except the voters at the next election. They can neutralize the lobbyists by cutting off access or neglecting to listen. They have many alternative sources for the information they seek. Lobbyists have much less power; they can accomplish their ends only by reaching officials; they have no alternative target. It is the officials who admit the lobbyists to the trust relationship—not vice versa. Lobbyists can try to exert power on officials by attempting to manipulate the popular vote, but that is difficult and costly. Thus, lobbyists have influence only through conformity with the rules. The lobbyist's worst fate is to be ostracized, especially if his opponent continues to have access. Officials lay down the rules under which they will welcome lobbying messages; sometimes they are very explicit. One lobbyist reported that a senator told him, "If you make a reputation for honesty and never give me a wrong steer, I will welcome that kind of lobbying."

To discover what these trusting relationships are and how lobbyists go about building them, dozens of interview responses were analyzed. A set of rules or precepts relevant to building a trusting relationship was compiled. A trusting relationship is built on deeds or behavior, not simply on words. Its construction is laborious and time-consuming. The "fly-by-night" lobbyist can and does come to Washington, but his influence is seriously limited. One lobbyist said, "We are just getting to the point where members of Congress and agency officials come to us and seek information. This office is only ten years old, and you know it takes time to establish a reputation."

To be trusted, the lobbyist must appear to be concerned with the public welfare in addition to the advantage of his own special group. Very narrow special interest pleading conveys the impression that the pleader does not have a balanced view of the world and his client's place in it. Many lobbyists try to convey a broader and more balanced view by presenting, or at least admitting that there are, two sides to the argument. Listeners know that almost all questions have two sides; only naïve lobbyists pretend there is only one.

Second, the lobbyist must build a reputation for complete dependability, honesty, and sincerity. The actors cannot lean on one another unless the support is reliable. Respondents make this point again and again. Their own words best convey the thought; one of the oldest and wisest men in Congress related:

> If a lobbyist misrepresents something, he is through. Then there are those who don't know very much, too. Those are soon dismissed, and we pay little attention to them. Maybe birds-of-a-feather flock together, but not one human in my life—and I have been holding public office since I was twenty-five and I am now seventy-five—has ever asked me to do an indecent thing. The fellow who does differently from this just doesn't have a chance up here.

A senator said:

> If he doesn't have enough information, he should get accurate information and know when it is accurate. Above all, he should be honest. It is just as easy to recognize a

faker in Washington as it is in any other place; a faker
can't cover up in this community better than in any other
place. If I know him to be honest and he knows his subject,
if I can call him and get reliable information, it puts him
in an excellent position. A lobbyist should also not become
a nuisance; he should recognize that time is important and
should assume the role of a cheerleader at a football game
[encourage support from the people back home]. . . . In
my experience, the notion that lobbyist entertaining gets
votes isn't so. A member of Congress has got to do what his
people want; he certainly isn't going to try and please a
lobbyist.

An old-time member of the House confirmed:

A lobbyist should be rigidly honest and tell the truth.
Beyond that he should have the same virtues that would go
well in other occupations and professions. One thing a
lobbyist can't do is to afford to deceive members. Nobody
expects him to come up here and spill his entrails; he can
keep his little secrets; but he does not dare deceive anybody.
The most successful lobbyists are quite outstanding people,
and they will tell the truth about something if you press
them, even if it is against their own interest.

A clerk of a committee reported:

You can spot a phony pretty quickly and especially you
can spot a curve. One lobbyist lost a vote on this committee because he misrepresented something to one of the members. Sometimes a fellow might more or less inadvertently
mislead, but sometimes it is also deliberate. If that is the
case, the people just don't listen anymore.

A lobbyist:

If one wants to have influence with members of Congress, the members must trust him. Therefore, I always
keep all my cards on the table so everything is clear and
open to them; they must feel at any time they can depend

on what I say. . . . It is most important for a lobbyist to be a man his contact can trust; that is important above all else. If a lobbyist is not that kind of person, he is no good at all.

Third, the actors must be very careful to respect sources and confidences. Revelation of a source or confidence punishes the one who has proffered the information; if this happens, all future access will be cut off.

A lot of people, even our own members, do not understand that we are unable to betray the confidence of the persons that tell us things. If we do, we have lost our source. A lot of this stuff is not secret information, but at the same time, if you betray the fellow's confidence, he is not going to stand by you next time.

Fourth, lobbyists must stand ready to provide information and other services when officials request them. Officials habitually turn to certain sources they know they can trust.

I never initiate anything or assert myself in any way. We operate on the principle that if we produce a good product, the members of Congress will learn to depend on us. We operate on the same code as the doctor and the lawyer, we do not advertise and we do not solicit. I am a fanatic on accuracy and truthfulness of whatever we supply to the people in Congress. The mills of the gods grind slowly, but they grind exceedingly fine. I never take a momentary advantage to win a momentary prize. I avoid all kinds of slick tricks and similar subterfuge that might, in the long run, spoil my effectiveness. Congress has no place for people who try to pull slick tricks. I have watched persons who operate that way come and go; it eventually boomerangs on all of them.

* * *

The people in Congress have confidence in our proposals. They feel they are carefully studied, thoroughly prepared, and backed by sound legislative history. I try very hard to develop this confidence in the association. It does not come from going up there and demanding, and it does not come from getting into political issues; rather we go up there and present only our own case.

Fifth, the lobbyist who hopes to get respect, confidence, and trust must present a consistent image. He cannot talk on one side of an issue one week and on the other side the next—even if he is representing different clients. Most lobbyists try to project a consistent image of expertise and personal conviction. The lobbyist who does not speak from personal conviction is weaker and is likely to be uncovered and discounted.

There is not much log-rolling in lobbying; that does not set well with Congress. Congressmen have expectations about lobbyists. If a lobbyist comes up to the Hill and talks about tariff problems, he should not come up to the Hill to talk about income tax problems. If he advocates something he is supposedly not concerned with, they will suspect there is a quid pro quo. This tends to destroy one's reputation for integrity and to destroy the confidence that one might get with members of Congress. . . . As you become more acquainted with members of Congress, they begin to feel that you are an expert and they pay more attention to you. The standing you get from what you write and say is very important. The most important thing is to develop this feeling of confidence; once you have achieved that, they even call you up for an opinion or a view.

* * *

It is pretty difficult to put much over on Congress. One time I turned down a client who was offering a $25,000 fee because I did not honestly feel I could represent the fellow. If I had accepted that fee and represented him, I would have ruined my reputation as a lobbyist.

Sixth, the trusting relationship that is built up over time generally has a personal component. There is a genuine attraction between the parties which is more than the result of a professional relationship or entertaining and favors. Such an attraction cannot be abused. An old patriarch of Congress reported:

> One time I was talking to a lobbyist who said he envied another lobbyist we both knew. This other fellow had a lot of personal friends and would invite them out to small intimate dinners. Actually, they never talked business at these dinners, and they had no relation to his lobbying, but the first lobbyist said he would like to give dinners like that. I told him, "When you become personal friends with those people, you can invite them to dinner—but not before."

A committee clerk commented:

> Some of the boys that come around seem to think that if they wine you and dine you, take you to lunch two or three times a week, they more or less think they can buy you. This does them more harm than good; all we do is resent them.

A few additional "don'ts" related to the building of a trusting relationship: Lobbyists should not bluff or act all-knowing. One committee clerk said:

> There are some lobbyists here who, instead of coming around and asking us what is going to happen, they call the shots and tell us what is going to happen. Some guys came in here a while ago and told us we were going to hold hearings on a topic. That was the first we had heard about it. We hadn't even discussed it, and yet they were telling us what we were going to do. That type of person shouldn't hold a lobbying job.

Lobbyists should not make constant requests. This practice can shut off the entire supply of goodwill and helpfulness. Another committee clerk said:

> Take———who lobbies for———; he never asks me to do anything. I like him better for it. It is easier to buddy up to a guy who isn't constantly asking you to do something.

Respondents' own words have explained the rules and procedures by which a lobbyist attains a reputation for reliableness and service. Such a reputation is a lobbyist's most prized asset; in a sense it is his union card. Lobbyists, as well as other actors in the system, who violate the rules are ostracized. The system exposes and forces out the fraudulent and the treacherous; that is the only way the honorable actors can protect their careers. The lobbyist who wants open channels and influence soon learns he must play according to the rules.

Part Four

Lobbying in
American Democracy

THIS study was designed to examine the individual lobbyist, his roles, and his methods. It was not projected as an over-all evaluation of lobbying in the United States, or even in Washington. Therefore, what can be said here is limited. In any case, at this stage of the development of the social sciences it would be impossible to gather data which would enable one to provide a conclusive evaluation of lobbying. This study of individual lobbyists does, however, disclose information which furthers our understanding and evaluation of the role of lobbying in the political process. The remarks of the next four chapters derive from impressions gathered in the course of this study. The author has attempted to be cautious because the data are not conclusive, but also to speak forthrightly. These impressions are not proven facts but the opinions of an informed observer.

The interviews with congressional respondents clarified many impressions gained from the lobbyist interviews and constitute important data for this section of the book.

The United States Constitution guarantees that individuals and groups may petition their governors for redress of grievances. This *assumption, that all individuals and groups are entitled to representation in the making of public decisions, forms the background for Part Four.*

A quotation from a lobbyist respondent provides perspective for observing lobbying in American democracy:

> *Sure lobbying is healthy for our democracy; it is a part of life. It's like the weather; it exists whether it is good or bad. The founding fathers were quite effective lobbyists, too; the Federalist Papers are a good lobby document. You have good and bad lobbying; sure there is some bribery and some subversion, but most of it is good lobbying. It is very necessary to have good lobbying; in a complex society, everyone can't come to the town meeting. People need to organize; they need representation—which means they need a person to act as a proxy. There also needs to be division of labor. Only a few people can be in the position of representing great numbers of people.*

CHAPTER XIV

HOW "CLEAN" IS THE LOBBY PROCESS?

Most persons, without being very precise about the meaning of the term, already seem to know that lobbying is "dirty." To be somewhat more precise about the meaning of "clean" and "dirty," "dirty" connotes corruption. We shall use "dirty" to mean violation of the rules of the game for personal or private ends.[1] Since rules of the game are defined socially (legal prescription is only a specific statement of a social rule), the specific behavioral content of dirty or corrupt acts may vary over time or from setting to setting.

In the context of American politics, certain broad rules of the game, the violation of which constitutes corruption or dirt, can be stated. One broad rule is that public decisions shall be taken in full public view so that the decision-makers may be held accountable. An effort to work secretly or behind the scenes to steal a decision for private gain is considered dirty or corrupt. Another broad rule is that each man shall have one vote which is counted equally. A man who has more money or property is

[1]Banfield (1961, p. 315) defines corruption as a violation of a rule forbidding the use of certain kinds of power for private ends.

not to be given special consideration. If money or favors predominate over votes in weighing decisions, we believe there is corruption. A corollary is that decision-makers may consider the merits of the case and the desires of their constituents as they arrive at decisions, but they may not consider personal pecuniary factors. There are many other rules of the game, but these are the main ones relating to the meaning of dirt and corruption.

THE WIDESPREAD DISTRUST OF LOBBYING

It is curious that lobbying, which is protected by the constitutional right to petition, should be so thoroughly distrusted by the press and the public. Many lobbyists are sensitive to the stigma attached to their profession and try to avoid being labeled as lobbyists. They believe, however, that the public impression of lobbying is unjustified. Several factors contribute to the public disapprobation of lobbying. Most are subsumed under the fact that the public generally receives only negative information about lobbyists.[2]

The press plays up the unsavory and sensational aspects of lobbying, printing very few stories about the ordinary, honest lobbyist and his workaday activities—presumably because they would not "sell." Further, reporters often become victims of the public's, and their own, preconceptions of lobbying; they look for evidence to prove what they already believe. In seeking to interpret a particular political outcome, it is simple and believable to place the blame on the unsavory activities of lobbyists; it is difficult to search out the true complexities of the situation.[3]

The press is aided in the misinterpretation of lobbying by the reckless charges of political opponents. The defeated party in a policy battle often charges that his opponents won because of the nefarious activities of lobbyists. The motives for such charges were mentioned in Chapter XIII: discrediting the opposi-

[2]See the studies and articles cited in note 3, Chapter I.
[3]As reported in the previous chapter, DeVries (1960, p. 150) found that state-house reporters rate the stereotyped tactics of lobbyists (entertaining, parties, favors, campaign contributions) as much more effective than do the legislators or the lobbyists.

tion and face-saving. Such charges are easily accepted by the public because they are consistent with its preconceptions.

Some of the unsavory characteristics attributed to lobbying, such as widespread entertaining, money "under the table," and other forms of venality, were more widely practiced thirty or forty years ago. There are still a few governmental units where such practices are found today, but for the most part they have passed away. Observers and students of lobbying talk about the "old" lobby and the "new" lobby. Respondents in this study repeatedly pointed out that lobbying has moved into a new phase which is more open.[4] The public, as usual, has not caught up to the new state of affairs.

Some might argue that suspicion serves the public well; if people continue to believe the worst about lobbying, they will be alert for transgressions, forcing lobbyists to behave more circumspectly. However, does a person perceived as a scoundrel act more correctly than one perceived as a decent man? Furthermore, a correctly informed public presumably would be in a better position to make policy on lobbying.

CAN A DECISION BE STOLEN OR BOUGHT?

There have been instances when decisions have been bought or stolen, but most careful observers would probably agree that in Washington they happen very rarely. A brief look at the enormous complexity of governmental policy-making may help to place this question in perspective. Nearly every governmental decision must have the consent of many decision-makers. In turn, each decision-maker must have the tacit consent of a great number of other people to maintain his position and his decision. A new law, for example, must have the consent of about 218 representatives, 50 senators, the President, and sometimes 5 members of the Supreme Court. It is easier to veto or stop a proposed policy than to pass it, but even the veto or pigeonhole must be tacitly assented to by a large number of decision-makers.

4*Academic students of politics and pressure groups also have noted the change. See, for example, Blaisdell's (1958) foreword to the special issue of the* Annals *dealing with pressure groups and lobbies.*

An executive decision, or a decision by a regulatory agency, also follows certain procedures and characteristically involves at least ten or twenty persons, usually many more. Important executive decisions involve as many persons as legislative decisions. In addition, the checks in the separation-of-powers system enable actors in other branches to keep decision-makers within bounds.

It is virtually impossible to buy a decision and *make it stick;* someone else somewhere along the line will have the power of veto or reversal. All decision-makers are sooner or later replaced and may be reversed. The Miami TV channel 10 case before the Federal Communications Commission is a good example of a decision that was supposedly bought but later was reversed and the careers of the culprits ruined.[5] It is equally impossible to steal a decision; there are too many steps in the process for them all to be carried out in secrecy. Respondents repeatedly said it is impossible to keep a secret in Washington. The likelihood of disclosure is so high that secret decisions or agreements are not worth the risk. The only kind of decision that could be bought or stolen in Washington would be so insignificant and so specialized that it would have little or no impact on the public welfare. One respondent had some interesting comments on this topic:

> As far as I know, there certainly isn't enough money to buy Congress. If it was a very close fight, you might be able to switch two votes by bribes, but I certainly wouldn't want to try it. There isn't one lobby in town big enough to do something with Congress by themselves, especially if someone is watching; that is why we try to obtain assistance from other organizations. Perhaps if an organization went about something very quietly, nobody was watching, and the bill was small with small stakes, they might put it through. Any organization that wants to work alone must either be very big or very shrewd and careful.

Though it is virtually impossible to steal or buy a governmental decision in Washington, occasionally a decision-maker's vote is bought or enticed from him. To the extent that this happens, there is dirt in the process. It is impossible to say with precision how much dirt is present. We can, however, note the judg-

[5] *See Rosenblum's (1962) study of this case.*

ments of observers on the scene. Respondents were asked, "Do you think lobbying as we see it today is healthy for our democracy?" None of the respondents thinks lobbying as a whole is bad. About 33 per cent admit there are a few bad elements in lobbying, but generally they believe it is healthy; 7 per cent give other qualified approval, and 61 per cent give unqualified approval to lobbying. Most congressional respondents also believe that lobbying is healthy: 50 per cent give unqualified approval; 44 per cent give qualified approval; and 6 per cent think it is more bad than good.[6] Their reservations about lobbying generally relate to possibilities for abuse if the process is not kept under careful surveillance. Not one respondent thinks that lobbying, on the whole, is corrupt or dirty.

Most lobbyists are aware that their profession attracts a few corrupt individuals and regret this blight on their collective reputation. It is relevant to ask whether the system unearths, exposes, and rejects such individuals before they can do much damage. The weight of evidence suggests that most corrupt lobbyists are quickly and definitely dealt with. Chapter XVI examines some reasons for this.

Such "dirty" tactics as entertainment, parties, and bribery discussed in Chapter XIII are rated by both lobbyists and congressional respondents as virtually useless. Such tactics have not declined because lobbyists are more moral than previously. This has occurred because the system and its decision-makers punish instead of reward the use of such tactics. The key to a clean lobbying process is the election of honorable public servants and constant vigilance by the people. A decision-making system which is responsive to the needs and desires of the voters cannot be bought or stolen and offers no rewards to those who try to get special privilege or gain by not playing according to the rules.

FEDERAL AND STATE LOBBYING CONTRASTED

From time to time respondents commented that in general lobbying is "cleaner" in Washington than in most state capitals.

[6]DeVries (1960, chap. vii) found that his Michigan lobbyists almost universally approved of lobbying and that his legislator and newsmen respondents generally approved of it.

This study has little to contribute on the subject of state lobby-ing.[7] Nevertheless, a few of the respondents' insights might be passed on. A leader in the Senate reported, "There is very little corruption at the federal level; we have more reason to suspect it at the state level." Some of the Washington lobbyists who had earlier worked at state capitals made the same point.

Lobbying is very different before state legislatures; it is much more individualistic. Maybe this is the reason they have more bribery and peddling of influence in state legis-latures than in Congress. Most state legislators take it as a part-time job and don't have the feeling that their future and career is tied up with it, certainly not to the extent that this is true of members of Congress. It is easier to get a bill through a state legislature than through Congress, too.

* * *

In the state legislatures, lobbying is definitely on a lower plane. The lobbyists are loose and hand out money and favors quite freely. Lobbyists excercise more influence on the regulatory agencies at the state level, too. Here in Washington, however, no man is a real power in himself.

Respondents seem to be saying that the difference between Washington and the state capitols is that the policy-making proc-ess in the state capitals is more informal; there is less structure, less rigid adherence to rules, and less permanent record-keeping. There also seems to be less personal commitment by the actors to the success of the system and to the building of long-range personal reputations.[8] A congressional committee staff member related:

[7]*Those interested in state lobbying should consult, in addition to DeVries' (1960) work, Belle Zeller (1937); McKean (1938); and Wahlke et al. (1962). Schriftgiesser (1951) contains an appendix on state lobbying. Information on state lobby laws has been collected by two recent congressional committees: Belle Zeller's statement in U.S. Congress (1950a), and U.S. Congress (1957, pp. 69–71, 222).*
[8]*Wahlke et al. (1960a) found they had to distinguish the political cultures of the four state legislatures they studied.*

Lobbying at the state level is cruder, more basic, and more obvious. The system is better at the federal level; the rules are good, and we do things according to the rules. Everything that is done is in the record, and printing the record is very important. We continually consult the old record around here, and that is why printing the record is so important. It is quite costly and requires a big staff. At the state level you oftentimes can't get a copy of a bill or you can't get committee hearings. Lobbying at the state level is faster and more freewheeling and less visible; that is why it is more open to corruption. The slowness, the rules, and the methodical recording of everything here at the federal level makes it less possible for corruption to creep in.

Another reason for the difference arises from the fact that state legislators are more readily accessible than federal officials. Entertainment, parties, and favors apparently are more effective at the state level. Michigan lobbyists rate entertaining slightly higher and devote considerably more time to it.[9] Most state legislators are away from home during the legislative session and thus may be more inclined to welcome entertainment; members of Congress, on the other hand, maintain permanent homes in Washington. The difference in access to officials between the state and federal levels is reflected in the evaluation of lobbying tactics. Michigan lobbyists place relatively more emphasis on direct personal communication, but Washington lobbyists place relatively more emphasis on communication through intermediaries.

DeVries, as well as some of the Washington respondents, described a tactic called "sandbagging" that is occasionally employed at the state level. A legislator introduces a bill which is injurious to a certain pressure group in the state. He actually does not intend passage of the bill; he wants to threaten the group in order to receive a reward.[10] After the group gives him a retainer or some other suitable reward, he kills the bill or arranges to have it killed. Lobbyists have also been known to practice this tactic. A lobbyist will have a friendly legislator introduce a bill

[9]*DeVries (1960, p. 117 and chap. v).*
[10]*For an example in Texas, see Fowler (1957, pp. 21 ff.).*

injurious to his own group. After a display of great activity and prowess by the lobbyist, the friendly legislator kills the bill and the lobbyist reaps the rewards for his effectiveness.[11] "Sandbagging" is nearly impossible at the federal level; no legislator or lobbyist has enough control of the process to attempt such a manipulation. There is no way of knowing how prevalent it is at the state level, but observers indicate that it happens only occasionally.

There seems to be little movement of methods and personnel between state and national lobbying. Very few of the Washington lobbyists have worked as state lobbyists, and very few move from Washington to a state capital. Probably the main reason for this is that effective lobbying requires the establishment of a reputation, and that reputation is good in only one setting. A lobbyist who may be very valuable in a state capital because of his experience, reputation, and contacts would have considerably less value in the national capital—at least at first. The policy-making machinery at each level of government is run by an inner leadership clique, and it is simply a fact that it takes a long time to win confidential access to that leadership. As a consequence, each setting has its own set of actors, and there is little movement from setting to setting.

SUMMARY

The points relevant to the cleanliness of lobbying can be summarized in this way: There are a few corrupt individuals in lobbying, and, therefore, a little dirt is present. The whole process, as a whole, however, is remarkably clean; the system provides few rewards for dirthy methods. It is virtually impossible to steal or buy a public policy decision of any consequence in Washington. The actors on the Washington scene effectively eject violators of the rules from the system. At the state level, the system seems less tight, and a somewhat greater incidence of venality and corruption seems to creep in. More adequate studies of state lobbying must be made to confirm the latter generalization.

[11]*DeVries (1960, pp. 108–9).*

CHAPTER XV

THE VALUE OF LOBBY SERVICES

Most lobbyists think lobbying is a healthy influence within the political system. Their reasons for this conclusion have been coded into the first and second most important benefits of lobbying. A cross-tabulation showing those reasons is reported in Table XV-1. The two most frequently enunciated reasons are that Congress benefits from the presentation of different arguments and viewpoints and that lobbying provides essential information to Congress. A few also think that lobbying insures a fair hearing for all sides; officers of organizations are especially prone to pick this reason.

Since the beliefs about information and other service benefits of lobbying are so widely held by the lobbyists, it seemed necessary to ascertain whether lobby services are also highly regarded by the recipients of lobbying. Congressional respondents were asked the following questions: "Lobbyists tell me that they supply invaluable information to Congress. To what extent do you depend on information from lobbyists to inform yourself about most issues or bills?" "Do you feel confident in using their information?" "Do you get a lot of information you don't use?"

TABLE XV–1

Benefits of Lobbying

SECOND MOST IMPORTANT BENEFITS	Provides Information to Congress	Congress Benefits from Arguments and Viewpoints	Insures Fair Hearing for All Sides	Other Benefits	No Response	Total
			MOST IMPORTANT BENEFITS			
Provides information to Congress		24	1			25
Congress benefits from arguments and viewpoints	25		3			28
Insures fair hearing for all sides	2	13				15
Other benefits	6	1				7
No response	3	9		5	22	39
TOTAL	36	47	4	5	22	114

"Is there a better or more efficient way to get the information?" "Political writers generally give the impression that they think lobbying is a bad thing. Do you think lobbying as we see it today is healthy for our democracy?" The responses to those questions serve as the major basis for the discussion to follow.

Lobbyists prefer a service role. This probably arises in part from a psychological need to give in order to receive. The lobbyist is essentially a pleader, and he may find it uncomfortable always to ask and never to give. Giving helps him to justify his role and existence. He may also feel that he is likely to receive more if he gives in return.

> Our approach is to give as well as to receive; and if we need help, we will go and ask for it; but in turn we will indicate that we would be very glad to help them. We have gotten and we have given help many times.

INFORMATION

What kinds of services do lobbyists provide to decision-makers? The most widespread and tangible service is providing information. So much information is offered to decision-makers that they have a considerable administrative task sorting, sifting, and evaluating the constant inflow. They must employ staff assistants to process the information. An administrative assistant to a senator reported:

> We get reams and reams of this stuff. It is a considerable operation just to see it all. You sift most of the material over a period of time, but you never have the opportunity to really read it all. We of this office keep more material in the research files than most other offices do. Things that are readily available in Congress, such as committee reports, we don't always keep because we know we can get them on a few moments' notice.

Staff members evaluate all information from lobbyists and lobby groups with the knowledge that it might be slanted. They consider the motives and the special interest of the organization in making their judgment. In addition, decision-makers use the differing views and facts from opponents on an issue to bring out the truth:

> We use the information from lobbyists that is presented to us quite extensively. We very carefully check it, however; we do this primarily by using alternate sources.

* * *

> The information we get from lobbyists is appreciable but not substantially important. . . . I like to get lobbyist information through hearings and get it on the record. Then people can see the information and put it to the acid test. The opponent is especially important here; he checks the information and challenges it once it is on the record. An opponent is likely to quickly catch an error and call it to account.

The reputation of the sender is also very important to persons attempting to evaluate information. If the sender has an unknown or a poor reputation, the information is likely to be dismissed. If the sender has a reputation for accuracy, brevity, and the ability to get to the crux of the matter, the information is likely to be welcomed and carefully read.

> After you are up here a while, you learn who is reliable and who is not. We especially welcome lobbyist information on issues that we don't know anything about; we try to make full use of the knowledge and skills available here on the Hill. We go to specialists we have learned to rely on.

Many times lobby groups can obtain the most expert information, and they have first-hand knowledge of the practical effects of legislation. Thus, they are natural sources. In addition, they tend to have information instantly available when a decision-maker needs it.

> There are certain subject matters that are completely new, and probably the only, or ready, source of information

is the lobbyist. He is closest to it and, therefore, the most worthwhile source. Committees need practical as well as theoretical knowledge and oftentimes a lobbyist, at least one close to the problem, can give this practical knowledge.

* * *

One generally gets all the information he wants from groups voluntarily. Lobbyist organizations tend to anticipate further in advance than government agencies. If you go to them, you don't have to wait for your information. Of course you can get the information from the Legislative Reference Service of the Library of Congress, but oftentimes with that service, or from the executive departments, you have to wait for an answer. Most lobby organizations have developed as much factual information on their particular area as it is possible to have, and you can get this stuff pretty quickly.

Congressional respondents were asked how much they depend on lobbyist information to acquaint themselves with issues. Committee clerks and staff assistants report more dependence on lobbyist information than do members of Congress. There seem to be two reasons for this difference. Decision-makers rely on their staff to sift, organize, and condense information for their consumption. The staff may well use considerable information from lobbyists mixed with the information from other sources; thus lobbyists' data are not detectable as such by the decision-makers. The second reason is that most decision-makers think of themselves as self-sufficient and independent of mind. They are reluctant to admit that they depend on lobbyists for anything.[1] In addition, members of Congress have relatively fixed ideas on most political issues and thus listen selectively to the information thrust at them. Here are the comments of two congressmen:

I don't depend on them at all. You get to know pretty well who the lobbyists are, and you judge from whence the

---

[1]*Congressional respondents to a* Redbook *survey exhibited this pattern:* "The net impression arising from the survey is that Congress members are reluctant to credit any lobby with much power. Frequently in marking a lobby 'high influence,' the Senator or Representative would write next to it 'but not with me.'" *Toffler (1962).*

information comes. I use some of their stuff on occasion if it is literature that contains some points that I want to use, but I do it to a very limited extent. I get just lots of literature. I know where it comes from, and if the views are generally opposed to mine, I just toss it aside.

* * *

I don't know if I depend on it at all. If I am really concerned about something and I want to find out which of two or three viewpoints is correct, I may do some research on my own. . . . I place the same confidence in lobbyist information as in information coming from my colleagues; I presume I know their prejudices and can judge accordingly. If I really need to sort it out, I can use some limited objective research and arrive at a better answer for myself. . . . Sometimes I get saturated, and I just can't assimilate all the information coming in.

ALTERNATIVE SOURCES FOR SERVICES

The likelihood of dependence by decision-makers on lobbyists for information is considerably lessened by the fact that there are many alternative sources for the information that decision-makers need. An assistant to a senator discussed the alternative sources rather fully:

We use all types of sources—executive departments, the legislative reference service, alternative lobby sources. I personally use the executive branch a lot where I have lots of contacts. We also use the academic world a good deal, but but there are certain drawbacks such as the fact that they don't like to work on time schedules and deadlines. Thank God for that; they take time to reflect on things; but it does make our work more difficult. I don't think much of the Library of Congress; they are too sterile. I'm not sure that in every situation there are better sources than the lobbyists. It's mighty nice to know that if you need some dope pretty fast you can call them up. Of course, the executive branch has experts on practically anything provided you can find them. Sometimes you need to do a little searching.

A congressman had this to say about alternative sources:

> Sure, we have a better and more efficient way to get the information, but we haven't done it. We in Congress are very reluctant to staff the members and the committees adequately. Obviously you have to have quality people to make a staff operation work. If I were king and able to call the tune, I would really do something. Take for example the dispute between the executive and legislative branch about who should prepare and evaluate the budget. In order for the Congress to compete adequately in such a fight, it needs staff. I would hire a hundred good staff people to go over the budget.

The mere availability of research and information does not guarantee that all possible points of view will be brought out, however. New points of view and new ideas often have to be thrust upon a man before he will consider them. The more firmly a decision-maker holds an opinion on a topic, the greater the likelihood that new points of view will have to be forcefully presented. Challenge is an important source of creativity, and it is as a challenge to creativity that the constant barrage of lobbyist communications toward decision-makers performs its most useful function. Officers of lobby organizations and others involved in making organizational policy are especially likely to thank this is the most important benefit of lobbying. In addition, the constant barrage of ideas and points of view helps to inform decision-makers about the desires of the people; of course officials use many additional sources to learn what the people want. Another consideration is that if Congress did not use lobbyist information it would be even more dependent on the executive branch to inform itself.[2] This would enable the executive branch to seize the policy initiative even more decisively than at present.

[2]*Taylor and Christian (1958, p. 37), quote a lobbyist as saying, "A congressman would be completely at the mercy of the damn bureaucrats if it wasn't for us furnishing him with information."*

Decision-makers customarily request a variety of services from lobbyists. Lobbyists write speeches, write reports, draft answers to letters from constituents, draft bills, and so forth. Very close working relationships sometimes develop between lobbyists and decision-makers, especially when they collaborate in pushing a piece of legislation. In such instances, the lobbyist becomes, in effect, another staff assistant to the decision-maker. Matthews calls this "backstopping" and suggests that senators make widespread use of such lobbying services.[3] Sometimes a lobbyist has the skill and connections to solicit publicity for a decision-maker or for an issue that he supports. Many members of Congress consider it a service if lobbyists can build public support for legislation they are trying to get through Congress. Lobbyists can also be very helpful in keeping track of particular bills and alerting members to appropriate times for action. Members are so busy that they can give detailed attention to only a relatively narrow range of public policy.

Lobbyists often claim that the public should appreciate them because their services are free. This argument is specious because the costs of lobbying, like the costs of advertising, are passed on to the consumer in one way or another. The public pays for lobbying services to decision-makers as surely as if taxes were used to pay the salaries of staff assistants to provide the same services. Considering that alternative sources for the services are also available and that decision-makers are flooded with much more information than they can possibly consume, one is forced to conclude that lobbying is actually wasteful to the public. Thousands of laboriously prepared communications are never heard or read by the intended receivers. Many congressional respondents are surfeited with information:

I get ten to twenty times as much information into my office as I can get time to look at personally. My staff looks at a lot of it but only about one-tenth ever gets to my desk.

* * *

They have a lot of statistical information available, but I suppose I could have someone dig it up for me instead. It's

[3]*Matthews (1960b, pp. 183–84).*

my impression, however, that there is more money wasted on lobbying than most any other thing around Congress.

*   *   *

I have heard lobbyists say that they supply such important information that Congress really couldn't get along without it. I don't agree with them; I think we could get along without it. There is no doubt that in many instances they do help, but we certainly don't have to depend on it. . . . I don't know if lobbying is really helpful or harmful. The reason is that lobbyists really don't have much effect. Two-thirds of lobbying is wasted. I don't want my views known on this. I don't want any of those fellows thrown out of their jobs because of what I am saying. You can report this if you don't identify me, however.

SUMMARY

Returning once more to the question of the value of lobbying services, lobbyists do contribute many useful services which many decision-makers seem glad to use. Many of these services could be obtained from alternative sources, however, and probably at a lower net cost to the body politic. The present system provides much duplication and is clearly wasteful and time-consuming. Yet no responsible official is inclined to forbid or severely restrain lobbying. Dispensing with lobbying services would make Congress even more dependent on the Executive.

There is no substitute for one service—the clash of viewpoints. The creative function this serves in alerting decision-makers to all possible alternatives outweighs all the waste and frustration involved in lobbying. This one function is also most clearly protected by the constitutional right to petition. Officials might find other sources for most services lobbyists provide, but they could never find a substitute for the essential representational function that the spokesmen for organized interests provide. Congressman Emanuel Celler sums up this point rather well:

It is true that the cost of effective lobbying is ultimately borne by the people. It is also true that the pressures generated by a well organized interest group can become irritating. But despite this cost and irritation, I believe that too much lobbying is not as dangerous to the quality of the resulting legislation as too little. It is disturbing to sit through legislative hearings at which the conflicting interests which should be heard are unequally represented in the presentation of their views. Worst of all, from the standpoint of a Congressman's desire to legislate intelligently, are those situations in which only the proponents of the suggested legislation are heard from. The Congressman may know or suspect that there are serious opposing considerations, but they are simply not presented. He is faced with a dilemma as to how far he should go to supply the omission.[4]

'Celler (1958, p. 7)

CHAPTER XVI

CONTROLLING THE LOBBY PROCESS

Nearly everyone who thinks seriously about lobbying confronts the question of how it can be controlled. Implicit is the assumption that if the process is left uncontrolled, the public good might not be served. In the past, there have been enough instances of venality and subversion of the public good to make that assumption credible.

STANDARDS FOR CONTROLS

There is widespread agreement on two standards to guide the choice of controls of lobbying. It is almost universally agreed that no control of lobbying should infringe on the constitutional right to petition. This right is so fundamental to the process of democracy that it would be better to suffer some abuse of lobbying than to infringe on it. Thus, any proposal to forbid or outlaw lobbying is automatically out of the question. Second, there is widespread agreement that the lobbying process should be made visible. If citizens are to participate adequately in their own governance, they must know what is happening in the policy-making process. If lobbying takes place in darkness or without full disclosure, subversion of the process is possible. Most attempts at regulation have aimed at making the process visible without infringing on the right to petition.

Certain obviously wrong behaviors such as bribery, giving false information, conflict of interest, and other corrupt practices can be and are forbidden by law. Additional standards beyond these are hard to find. Looking beyond regulation to positive fulfillment, the process should be as free and accessible as possible so that every citizen who wants a hearing can have it. This means the process should not allow money to become a criteria for access or to guarantee a preferred hearing. In American democracy, we have decided to count heads (votes) when making decisions—not money, property, guns, or other sources of power. Positive fulfillment of a right is generally more difficult to achieve than prohibition against infringement of the right.

LEGAL CONTROLS

The problem of legally controlling lobbying has been given a great deal of attention both by congressional committees and by academic students of the subject.[1] It would be a duplication of effort and an excursion far afield to give full attention to the subject in this volume. A brief look at the subject might be of some help to the casual reader, however; and notation of a few relevant

[1]*Two recent congressional investigating committees have examined the subject thoroughly and made specific recommendations for legal controls. U.S. Congress (1951a, 1957). The 1957 report summarizes much of the past work on lobby regulation and contains a section by George B. Galloway on the operation of the Federal Regulation of Lobbying Act. Among academic students of lobbying, the most sustained attention to this problem has been given by Belle Zeller. One of her articles (1958) summarizes the history of regulation attempts, analyzes recent proposals for regulation, and briefly summarizes state legal controls. See also the Zeller appearance before the House Select Committee on Lobbying. U.S. Congress (1950a, pp. 58–97, 116–21) and Belle Zeller (1948). And see Graves (1949). Dorothy C. Tompkins (1956) contains citations to all hearings and reports on the subject, a section on experience with the Federal Regulation of Lobbying Act, and citations to many articles and books on the subject.*

findings from this study might be useful to the more serious student.

Concern with the control of lobbying developed about 1900. The first bills to control lobbying were introduced in Congress in 1907, and in 1913 the first extensive investigation of lobbying was held. Effective regulation was long in coming, however. Various bills attempting regulation did not clear all the legislative hurdles. A few bills such as the Public Utility Holding Company Act of 1935, the Merchant Marine Act of 1936, and the Revenue Acts of 1938 and 1939 contained peripheral provisions affecting lobbying. The Foreign Agents Registration Act of 1938 required persons representing foreign principals to register with the Department of Justice. Not until 1946 did Congress pass a general Regulation of Lobbying Act as Title III of the Legislative Reorganization Act. This lobby law is still on the books virtually unchanged and is the major legal control of federal lobbying today. Over time, legislative enactments to control state lobbying have gradually been adopted; as of 1958, thirty-one states had some sort of lobby registration provision.[2]

The 1946 Federal Regulation of Lobbying Act is unchanged not because it is perfectly drawn; it has, in fact, been called one of the most poorly drawn laws of all time. There have been many serious studies of its performance and recommendations for changes,[3] but Congress apparently does not consider that changes are urgently needed. Congressional respondents in this study show almost no serious dissatisfaction with lobbying and no disposition to do something further about legal regulation. This finding is doubly interesting since many of the persons interviewed were members of the special committees investigating lobbying and/or sponsors of bills to revise the lobby regulation provisions. One cannot escape concluding that many investigations and bills recommending changes are instigated by public distress with the highly publicized malfeasance of occasional lobbyists. Decision-makers realize that the unethical behavior of an occasional lobbyist is by no means characteristic of the entire group; therefore, they demonstrate righteous indignation publicly, start an investigation, introduce reform bills, and wait for the

---

[2]*Belle Zeller (1958, p. 95).*
[3]*See citations in note 1 above.*

public clamor to die down. When the committee report is finally written, the public is concerned about something else, and no one has the time and energy to push the reform bill through.

The 1946 act has been most seriously criticized for its vague definitions. Many persons in borderline positions simply cannot determine whether they are required to register; they can avoid prosecution by registering, and many seek safety in this fashion. The provisions requiring the reporting of income and expenditures are so vague and so laxly enforced that the resulting information is almost meaningless. Lobby groups and lobbyists literally define for themselves what is lobbying and what is not. One-third of the respondents report no fees for lobbying whatsover; yet it is clear from the interview materials that they are engaged in lobbying at least part of the time. The lower the percentage of a respondent's income that comes from lobby clients, the less likely he is to report any fee at all. Respondents were asked to disclose their personal income; there is no correlation between this personal income figure and the amount of income reported on the lobby reports. For example, five respondents in this study have personal incomes above $50,000; four of these report no lobby income whatsoever; one reports a fee in the $15,000 to $19,999 bracket. Twenty-four respondents have personal incomes ranging from $25,000 to $49,999; nine of these report no lobby income at all; six report lobby income of less than $5,000; other figures range upward, but only three report lobby income commensurate with personal income. The Supreme Court in the Harriss case[4] was confronted by the law's ambiguity; it narrowed the definition of lobbying to direct communication with members of congress, and essentially invited Congress to rewrite the act.

Although the 1946 federal act contains criminal penalties for non-compliance, no special enforcement procedures are provided. The Clerk of the House and Secretary of the Senate are mere depositories of the reports; no systematic check is made to see whether lobbyists are registered, and no attempt is made to summarize or analyze the reports other than to list registrations and reports quarterly in the *Congressional Record*.[5] A private publi-

[4]*347 U.S. 612 (1954), p. 633.*
[5]*The new act recommended by the McClellan Committee in 1957 would have placed enforcement with the Comptroller General and would have given him broader powers to analyze the reports and to require compliance.*

cation, the *Congressional Quarterly*, has over the years conducted a simple periodical analysis of the reports; however, this endeavor is seriously limited by the unevenness of the data in the reports. Congressional respondents almost universally report that they do not bother to check to determine whether a person approaching them on legislation is registered. Belle Zeller reports that strict enforcement is also the exception rather than the rule in most states.[6]

Congressional respondents were asked whether they had specific recommendations for changes in the law, and occasional lobbyist respondents volunteered suggestions for changes. This fishing expedition turned up very few new ideas. Most frequently, respondents requested a clearer definition of lobbying and greater precision in the reporting requirements. Several lobbyists, objecting to the connotations of the word lobbying, suggested that the word be dropped from the title of the act. The act recommended by the McClellan Committee was to have been called the Legislative Activities Disclosure Act. Although this change might please some lobbyists, it is doubtful that a title change would have any noticeable impact on the nomenclature used by the public; the word lobbying is too deeply ingrained in our political culture. It could conceivably reduce the trauma of registration for some lobbyists who personally have a high negative attachment to the word lobbyist.

Provisions for checking compliance, analysis of data reported, and stricter enforcement would strengthen the act for its intended purpose of revealing lobby activity to the public. Some suggestions were made that, where applicable, the act should require lobbyists to list contributors to their committees or organizations. In the case of lobbyist entrepreneurs, who collect contributors and subscribers who support them in what they already intend to do, this would be highly informative. It would, however, be difficult to draw the act so as to catch those cases without making such reports a tremendous chore for mass membership organizations.

The present act does not cover lobbying before executive agencies; yet this study shows that executive lobbying is given as

[6]*Belle Zeller (1958, p. 95).*

much attention as congressional lobbying. The act recommended by the McClellan Committee would partially cover executive branch lobbying. Such a change should cover especially all attempts to influence the decisions of independent regulatory commissions; the McClellan Committee act is a little vague on this. The need to cover regulatory commissions was pointed up by the scandal attending the decision of the Federal Communications

"You Got Elected, Didn't You?"

from Herblock's Special for Today (Simon & Schuster, 1958).

Commission to award television channel 10 in Miami to National Airlines.[7] This study indicates that industries, pressure groups, and lobbyists try very hard to influence the decisions of regulatory commissions.

It is more difficult to suggest changes to insure that the policy-making process responds to votes and not to money. Improved methods for financing political campaigns would alleviate the dependence of elected officials on pressure groups and private interests for campaign funds. This study disclosed that monetary contributions to parties by lobbyists are more frequent than participation in any other partisan political activity. More important, many lobbyists and pressure groups work actively to raise funds for candidates. Such activity is not illegal and is not necessarily bad; but the public has a right to know about it and, if possible, to find a way to free candidates from their dependence on it. A special commission appointed by President Kennedy to study this problem has recommended that tax credits and deductions be granted as incentives to broaden the base for campaign contributions, that contribution and expenditure ceilings be abolished, and that further specific measures be taken to facilitate full disclosure of campaign finance.[8]

Laws cannot necessarily be depended upon to control a process, and changes in laws do not necessarily produce changes in society. Evildoers can usually find ways to evade a law, and the behavior of moral persons does not change very much when controlled by law. As one senator put it:

> I can't see much difference in the way lobbying is conducted since the law was passed and reports filed. Whenever something is done that's not right, it is certainly not going to be reported. I realize there are abuses, but there is very little one can do. We can do something by our personal conduct; it takes two people for a public official to be improperly influenced.

Laws can also produce humorous and unanticipated results. The intention of the federal lobby law was to make lobbyists known to the public. Sometimes enterprising souls have used

[7]*Rosenblum (1962).*
[8]*President's Commission on Campaign Costs (1962). See also Heard (1960).*

registration to become known and to attract clients. According to one story circulated in Washington, a lobbyist came in to register with the Secretary of the Senate explaining that he had no clients as yet but hoped to soon. The secretary thought this unusual and passed it on to a senator who indignantly publicized the action through the *Congressional Record*. A few weeks later the lobbyist returned to register several new clients and thanked the secretary for the free advertising. Other stories claim that some lobbyists wrote letters seeking clients and offered their registration as a credential, almost as if they had been certified "O.K." by the federal government. Reportedly, some clients have been taken in by such false claims of certification.

Many lobbyists, realizing that executive branch officials are often their strongest competitors in trying to influence Congress, indignantly suggest that administration officials should also be required to register as lobbyists. There is no doubt that officials of one branch often try very hard to influence decisions made by officials of the other branch; by some definitions of the term, they could even be called lobbyists. There would, however, be little purpose in requiring them to register, since most interagency contacts are part of the official role of the participants. When an official of one branch importunes an official of another branch, there is no difficulty in identifying the pleader and the group or the organization on behalf of which he speaks. The salary supporting an official is part of the public record; thus, there would be little point in requiring reports of income and expenditures.

Even at present, some laws do govern relations between branches of the government. The Bureau of the Budget coordinates all departmental requests for money from Congress. Executive departments are forbidden to use public funds to hire "publicity experts" or to launch pressure campaigns against Congress. These laws have mainly been declarations of rules of the game; no prosecutions have been brought under them. Departments hire "liaison," "information," "education," and "publication" officers but are careful not to call them publicity experts.[9]

Some communications flowing from officials of one branch to those of another are made part of the public record. The policy-

[9]*Freeman (1958, p. 12). See also Freeman (1955). Dorothy C. Tompkins (1956) lists many references to articles and hearings on the subject.*

making process would become more visible if this were done more regularly. The public record can also be used to diminish pressure effects. One lobbyist respondent who is a former chairman of an independent regulatory commission related:

> When I was chairman of ————, I would get many calls from members of Congress, and they quietly tried to pressure me to get a decision in favor of some constituent of theirs. I would always insist that their request be made a part of the public record; generally they would refuse, saying that they didn't want it public. Members are bothered a lot to plead for constituents with administration officials. In fact, one time I had a letter from Senator George, followed up by a phone call, saying that he wanted to go on record automatically vouching for the good character and need of any of his constituents that might approach the commission. He was apparently rather peeved at the constant pestering for recommendations.

While officials are occasionally incensed at pressures from the other branch, generally the communications flowing between branches are welcomed. Members of Congress welcome the information and research findings they receive from the executive branch; they almost invariably request the department concerned to comment on proposed legislation.[10] When asked how they felt about lobbying from the executive branch, only a few congressional respondents complained, and none suggested legal controls.[11] The most effective controls are already built into the reciprocal relations of the actors. This is the topic of the next section.

BUILT-IN SYSTEMIC CONTROLS

The diagram set forth in Figure I (page 181) illustrates some of the interrelationships tying several sets of actors into a policy-

[10]Communications between officials of different branches were discussed more fully in Chapter IX.

[11]The Buchanan Committee held hearings on the subject but found little trouble with executive agency lobbying and did not recommend additional controls. U.S. Congress (1951a, pp. 35–36).

making system. No one man in the system has sole power of decision; not only does each decision require the acquiescence of many decision-makers, but these decision-makers must depend on many other actors in the system for support, information, advice, and so forth. Interdependence gives men power over one another and forces them to be responsive to one another's needs.[12] In an interdependent system, the goals and rules of the system become more important than the needs and desires of any individual actor. Actors in the system deal ruthlessly with those who violate the rules or who jeopardize the welfare of other actors; the preferred penalty is ejection from the system.

Rules of the game for the Washington policy-making system have been alluded to at various places in the book. Since the policy-making system is essentially a communication system, the most important rules relate to communication. False or spurious messages ("throwing curves") are forbidden. Sanctions are simple to apply; the intended rece‸ver ceases to listen and passes the word to other intended receivers; when everyone of importance has stopped listening, the offender has literally been ejected from the system. Messages should be short, easily understood, and to the point; this helps to protect actors from a persistent overload of messages. When an actor must decide which of many messages to attend to and accept, the reputation of the sender becomes a crucial variable in the decision; a sender favorably known to the intended receiver has the best chance of message acceptance. The sender keeps the needs and responsibilities of the intended receiver in mind if he hopes to have his message accepted.

Demands and sanctions keep the actors in the system responsive to one another. If one actor leans on another (e.g., uses a speech another has written) and suffers damages because of failure of the other, penalties will be severe. Advancement in the system depends on playing along with the team. Interdependence stimulates bargaining, and bargains, once made, must be kept. Actors are careful not to make demands on other actors which the latter's system responsibilities (roles) will not allow them to fulfill.

In such a system, any given actor wants things from other

[12]Banfield (1961, esp. chaps. ix, xi) has a good theoretical discussion of an interdependent political system.

actors, but the balance between any two actors may be quite unequal. If B wants more from A than A wants from B, A has power over B.[13] This point is especially important when thinking about lobbyists vis-à-vis officials. Lobbyists want the most valuable product of the system, the favorable decision of the decision-maker. In most cases, this is much more valuable than anything the lobbyist can offer the official in return, except in the extremely rare case where the lobbyist can offer a decision-maker his official position itself. Officials having power superior to lobbyists have relatively greater freedom of action and can set the rules by which they may be approached. One lobbyist said a senator told him:

> If you make a reputation for your honesty and never give me a wrong steer, I will welcome that kind of lobbying. I want good factual information; don't come in and try to sway me emotionally; if you do, you are wasting your time. I especially don't want you to preach at me.

In addition to cutting off access, officials can refuse to cooperate in other ways or, in extreme cases, they can attack or instigate an investigation. Considering the public suspicion of lobbying, nearly all the advantages are with the official vis-à-vis the hapless lobbyist should their relationship come to open conflict. One of the greatest concerns of lobbyists is to avoid drawing the anger of decision-makers.

Officials may build up their power vis-à-vis the lobbyists by positive actions as well as negative sanctions.[14] Officials can store up credit with lobbyists by doing various favors: collaborating in their campaigns, helping them get publicity, making them appear to be successful to their clients or members, passing them vital information, and so forth.[15] In addition, officials may bind lobby-

---

[13]*James A. Robinson (1962, p. 179), in discussing the communications network between Congress and the State Department, reported a general rule that the person who wants something makes himself available to the person who holds that which he values. Banfield (1961, p. 312) defines power as the ability to establish control.*

[14]*Matthews is one of the few academic analysts to see this vital point (1960, chap. viii).*

[15]*Banfield (1961, esp. chap. xi) points out that all the actors in the political game have a limited supply of power which can be expended in a variety of ways. Conserving, investing, and increasing one's power is a major motivation for playing the game.*

ists to them with friendship. The lobbyist who is friend begins to identify with the causes and career development of the official. The lobbyist often is more loyal to his friend than to the cause of the organization he represents in case they conflict. Many lobbyists report that they find it more difficult to lobby their personal friends than to lobby strangers or mere acquaintances.

The interdependence, rules of the game, power relationships, and threat of sanction against offenders that characterize the Washington policy-making system operate rather effectively to control the behavior of the actors. In the writer's judgment, these factors are much more important than legal controls in keeping Washington lobbying as clean as it is. But is this enough? Can we be assured that the system will continue to function well? The system handles occasional offenders, but it would not be adequate to handle widespread collusion for evil. If large numbers of officials and lobbyists conspired secretly to steal decisions or to turn the government sharply against the welfare of the public, the system controls would break down.[16] The likelihood of such an occurrence is extremely small, but one must keep the possibility in mind. Only eternal vigilance by the citizenry and responsible exercise of the vote can prevent such an occurrence.

The most effective control of lobbying, and perhaps all that is really needed, is the election of highly qualified responsible persons to public office. Votes guide the direction of the system and insure that it operates honestly and fairly. Officials have so much power over lobbying and lobbyists that they can determine how the lobby system shall work. By their personal behavior they can require conformance to certain rules for the system. They can make it clear that they will accept communications only from persons who build a reputation for honesty and integrity. They can demand short businesslike relations with lobbyists, refusing entertainment, favors, and bribes. They can refuse to bow to drummed up pressure, yet remain sensitive to genuine voter demands. They can arrange to inform themselves adequately so that they are not dependent on lobbyists for information and advice. "Congress lessens its dependence upon pressure groups by improving its own procedures and by supplying itself with

---

[16]*This is one danger the Buchanan Committee was alarmed about in its investigation of lobbying during the Eighty-first Congress.*

competently professional assistance for committees and individual members."[17] Wrongdoing can be exposed on the floor of the House or Senate or probed by investigation. Elected officials should keep the actions of appointed officials under constant surveillance and should be concerned about the relations between appointed officials and lobbyists. The morality of lobbying is, in the final analysis, dependent on the morality of elected officials.

Such moral judgments constitute the real answer to the existence of lobbyists. No registration law, no listing of connections and salaries in the *Congressional Record,* no system of party responsibility, by itself, can scratch the surface of the problem of controlling pressure politics. In the long run, a civilized morality is the sole key to the survival of democracy.[18]

[17]*Belle Zeller (1958, p. 103).*
[18]*Stephen K. Bailey, testifying before the Buchanan Committee. U.S. Congress (1950a, p. 45).*

CHAPTER XVII

THE IMPACT OF LOBBYING ON GOVERNMENTAL DECISIONS

Perhaps the most difficult question about lobbying is that of the extent of its influence or impact on governmental decisions. No one has a definitive answer to that question. Yet an understanding of the influence of lobbying is essential to a full perspective on the topic. This study was not designed to measure the impact of lobbying and can offer only partial answers. Still, quite a number of observable facts contribute some enlightenment. Some have been alluded to previously. In this chapter, all findings relevant to the impact of lobbying will be reviewed to provide as broad a perspective as possible.

Inquiring about the influence of lobbying is not the same as inquiring about the influence of pressure groups. Admittedly, the factors are highly related, but they are not identical. Some lobbying is carried out on behalf of individuals or corporations as well as groups. On the other hand, some of the influence of pressure groups is not exerted through lobbying (using a special envoy at the seat of government) or lobbyists. It will not be necessary to maintain a clear distinction between lobbying and pressure groups, but the reader should be aware that the primary purpose of this chapter is to evaluate the influence of lobbying, not that of pressure groups.

SOME CHARACTERISTICS OF INFLUENCE

Several approaches to the study of influence were noted in Chapter IX.[1] Some characteristics of influence are relevant to the query of this chapter. First, influence is not an absolute quantity of which an individual or an institution has a certain measurable amount. One can speak about influence in comparative terms (e.g., A has more influence than B) but even that can be done only with reference to a given issue or decision (B may have more influence than A on another decision). Influence, then, varies with the decisional setting, the roles of the actors, the diligence with which goals are pursued, and the tactics employed, as well as with the assets available to each contestant.

Second, influence does not automatically make itself felt; it must be exerted. Moreover, exertion entails some costs (time, money, attention, etc.) on the part of the influencer. The costs of exerting influence must be weighed relative to the value of the anticipated reward. Banfield (1961) thinks of influence as analogous to money; it is a scarce resource which can be saved, invested, and spent. Some political actors have more influence assets than others, but assets must be carefully managed to avoid influence bankruptcy. It is "rational" for political actors to try to maximize their influence just as it is "rational" for economic actors to maximize their monetary assets or gains.

Third, political influence is necessarily focused on the decisional processes of authoritative decision-makers (government officials). Influence can be achieved only by affecting the perceptions of officials (short of replacing one official by another), and it must be conveyed via some kind of communication.

The perceptions of the policy process held by the official decision-makers and the values they try to achieve are of central

[1] *See works cited in notes 2–6 of Chapter IX.*

importance. The problems involved in measuring the perceptions and values of officials, even assuming they would remain constant enough to be measured, are so great that one can make only very general statements. Some generalizations made in Chapter IX bear brief repetition here: (1) The basic goal of officials is to maintain and enhance their position; achieving a "good record" is usually essential to that. (2) Assuming position can be maintained, officials tend to decide policy questions in accordance with their political philosophy. (3) Motivations of friendship, having a good time, making money, and so forth will generally be of lesser importance than the first two.

One could push to a more abstract analysis of influence by dealing with such questions as free will versus determinism, but that would take us far afield. In the other direction, one could press for a more specific level of analysis, but that would require dealing with many specific issues and actors and would not readily lead to a general understanding of the process.

Because influence takes place only in the decisional process of human beings, it is extremely difficult to measure. Most humans could not report accurately, even if they sincerely desired to, the proportionate weight they assign to various influences as they make a decision. Influence is generally measured by some less direct method. March (1955) says three general ways to measure influence have been widely used: measuring attributed influence, measuring changes in opinions, and measuring interaction between actors. This study contains only measures of attributed influence and some measures of interaction between lobbyists and officials.

In this discussion of the influence of lobbying, three kinds of evidence relevant to the point will be presented. First is an analysis and pinpointing of where and how influence can be exerted; some supposed methods of influence fall by the wayside because they are too difficult or too costly to employ. For example, it is virtually impossible to steal or buy governmental decisions of any consequence in Washington. In seeking points at which influence may be exerted, it is relevant to examine the factors that officials consider as they make their decisions. Second is an analysis of lobbyists' evaluations of their personal success and the success of their organization and their selections of the most effective lobby organization in Washington; these are taken as partial evidence of attributed influence. Third, the influence of lobbying is compared to other forces also attempting to influence policy. Some lobbying cancels out other lobbying because groups oppose one another; some lobbying is simply overwhelmed by the power of non-lobbying forces.

FACTORS CONSIDERED BY OFFICIALS WHEN MAKING DECISIONS

We noted the general motivations of officials as they carry out their roles in Chapter IX and briefly in the section above. From the time the interview schedule was written to the present, the conceptualization of the decision process implicit in this study changed. Therefore, the question put to congressional respondents was phrased in conceptual terms different from those given in Chapter IX. Even so, the data give strong support to the generalizations made in Chapter IX. Moreover, no executive branch officials were interviewed for this study. The pre-eminent motivation to maintain or enhance one's position is probably characteristic of both elected and appointed officials. However, for elected officials, it is oriented toward pleasing constituents; whereas for appointed officials, it probably is oriented toward following the directions of and attempting to please elected officials. This study has no data relevant to the latter generalization.

Congressional respondents were asked the following question:

> Whenever a person must decide how he will vote on an issue or a bill, he must take several factors into account, such as: the wishes of his constituents, the views of interest groups, the recommendations of his colleagues and friends, and his personal feelings. Which of these kinds of factors are uppermost in your mind as you arrive at your decisions?

Members gave complicated and varied answers reflecting different backgrounds and different situations. Before discussing each factor more fully, some quotations from members will point up the complexity of the interrelationships:

That is the sixty-four-dollar question to ask a member of Congress. I think it varies. If it is a question which affects the national security, why I invariably vote the way the best information for me indicates I should vote regardless of the constituents.

*   *   *

I take them all into account, but I almost always vote the way I personally decide. I don't make this decision naïvely, by the way. My own view is that it is good politics to take a personal position, and that is the way representative government should function. However, it is not as simple and clear-cut as that. Many times you may see an issue very clearly at the beginning of a session, and you know how you are going to stand on that issue, but by the time you get to the end of the session, it may become confused because there are so many compromises and changes. You wonder if the problem is being evaded and how you should really stand on it. . . . I would say by and large I have a view of my own before I am approached by an interest group. The lobbyist may bring me the first information on a "cat and dog bill"; those are bills without much consequence for the public. I don't remember a time when a position I had was changed by a contact. I do recall making at least one recognizable mistake each year I have been in Congress. The only one that ever upset me was one time when I voted on both sides of an issue; I voted for the bill and then voted to sustain the President's veto. I tried to explain it to the people in the next campaign and discovered it had no effect on my election; since then I haven't been too worried about making a mistake once in a while.

*   *   *

You haven't listed the most important one—that is, the merits of the legislation. There is an interaction in the mind of the legislator which considers all those factors. The attitude of every member is influenced by his over-all background and the nature of his constituency. Members are either born economizers or born spenders, and this is influenced by the nature of his constituency. Most members are more or less predisposed toward an issue before they get to it. We take a pretty common sense approach to the views of interest groups: Are they selfish or unselfish? How does opinion run in one's district? Is there undue advocacy or undue advantage? How the views are presented is a lesser factor but still a factor.

*   *   *

Your first claim is to your district or you won't be here next time. Second comes the desires of the President; I am his leader in the House, and I wouldn't desert the President or the aims of the administration unless there were a mighty weighty reason. I am a member of the team, and this is uppermost in my mind on most questions. I don't take the views of interest groups too seriously. Actually, I don't get too much pressure; I have a very good district in that respect. Maybe it is because I have been here thirty years; they know what to expect. Either they have confidence that I will do the right thing, or they figure it is hopeless—either way I don't get a lot of letters.

*   *   *

The number one factor is that you make sure it doesn't adversely affect the people you represent. If it doesn't hurt your people or you feel it might be good for them, you also try to weigh the public or the national interest and try to decide what the legislation will do over a long pull. If you decide it is a good bill and it is lasting, why this is a very persuasive factor in one's decision. What your colleagues think about an issue or a bill doesn't enter into your decision. All of these people have their own problems, and just because one guy is in favor of a bill doesn't mean you should be. He may have different problems with his constituency. What shall it profiteth a man if he vote to save the country and lose his own seat? . . . I do discuss certain problems with other members; these are men I have come to know and trust over the years.

It can be seen from the quotations that the wishes of a member's constituents are an omnipresent factor, and, in a broad sense, they are decisive. The desires of constituents might be conceived of as boundaries beyond which a member dare not step without suffering dire consequences. These boundaries might be very wide on certain questions and very narrow on others. If a constituency is vitally interested in a question—for example that of segregation (for a southern district)—the boundaries are very tight, and the representative can take only one action if he hopes to be re-elected. The folkways of the Congress recognize these restrictions, and a member who breaks with the leadership to please his constituency on such a tight matter will be forgiven. If a constituency is not so vitally interested, the boundaries are broader, and on some questions there are no boundaries at all. Lobbying has greater opportunities for influence when the constituency is not very interested and the decision-maker has greater decision latitude. If the constituents are interested and aware, their desires are undoubtedly the most important factor. A congressman put it this way:

> Well, of course the views of the constituents are always uppermost in the politician's mind. We jokingly make a distinction between a politician and a statesman, but we are all politicians, too. As statesmen, we are delegated to represent not only the views of our constituents but also their best interests. If we could count on the people being properly informed, well then, their views would be all that is necessary, but unfortunately that cannot always be counted on. When you come up here they expect you to study and advise them, and I try to do so. I lead them a little bit, but in the end, their views tend to be uppermost.

A clerk for a congressional committee said:

> If I had to select one as the most important day-in-and-day-out, I would say it is the appraisal of the member of what his constituents think. He may not know what his constituents think; he has no really good measure; but it is what he thinks they think that is important. Even if he believes his constituency is not too interested in a bill, he may try to

parlay his vote on that bill into an advantage for him in his constituency on some other kind of issue. Ninety-nine per cent of the money spent on lobbying falls short because it ignores that fact. . . . To the extent lobbying can influence public opinion, it has some impact because voter reaction is the most important thing in Congress.

Most lobbyists also recognize the predominating influence of voter desires:

> Most of what happens in the legislative area is at least 80 per cent determined on the day of election; in addition, much of the legislative activity throughout a session of Congress is actually a setting of the stage for the next election It is impossible for a lobbyist "to make a silk purse out of a sow's ear." . . . You do not change a member of Congress by buying him or browbeating him or otherwise attempting to change him.

The smart lobbyist tries to demonstrate to a member that following a particular course of action will help him in his constituency. The member usually listens attentively to such information, but he also learns that he must view claims of constituency support with some skepticism. Reliable information about constituent desires is difficult to obtain. The leaders of large membership organizations generally claim that they speak for all their members, but this is a claim they can hardly substantiate.

> You can't be a public official without having considerable knowledge in your own right, and you learn to discount what these groups say. I come from a farm district, and it makes a difference if the Farm Bureau is for or against a piece of legislation. But I have learned that the top people in these organizations often have views that are different from their members down below who are my constituents; therefore, I discount what they say a little.

Following constituent desires too closely can be harmful in certain cases. Constituents generally do not and cannot follow the development of information and arguments on an issue. The complexion of the issue may change, and the available alternatives may shift to such an extent that constituent desires provide little or no guidance. Many members also take the traditional Burkean perspective that constituents really elect a man's judgment and that it is proper to vote according to their own judgment even if it goes against the desires of the constituents. Members report that they feel compelled on occasion to vote against their constituents, especially if they believe it is for the good of the country:

It so happens that practically all of my votes are the way that the prevailing opinion is in my district. This is probably because my own philosophy of government is the same as that of the people in my district. However, there are times when we differ, and in such cases I vote the way my best judgment indicates. In the long run, this is in the interests of the people, and they do have an opportunity to express approval or disapproval at the next election. The Lend-Lease and defense acts early in World War II were opposed by 75 per cent of the people in my district; yet I voted for every one of them and in so doing I was performing my representative function.

* * *

There are two types of issues. When it doesn't involve a profound decision or doesn't strongly affect the government or there will be no great disparity in cost, I give the weight to what the people feel strongly about. There are other kinds of decisions that are weighty and will affect the security or solvency of the country. On those kind your own convictions are dominant. The people are very understanding even if you go against their wishes. If you frankly tell them that it wasn't wise for the country, they are not going to turn against you. You can try to educate them, but generally you can't make them change their mind. They may still be against you, but they will realize there are two sides to the question, and they will not turn against you.

If boundaries set by the constituents on an issue have left some decision latitude to the member, the next most important factor is likely to be his personal convictions about the issue. Most members have a long-established political philosophy which guides their decisions. Through their political philosophy they "know" what is good and bad for the country and the people. Furthermore, a man who has served in public office for some time has had to take a stand on most issues in the past. A prior stand tends to freeze his current position. A change from a past position can easily be interpreted as a tacit admission that the prior position was incorrect or possibly that undue influence was used.

On broader legislation which affects the lives and future of the people, I vote according to my philosophy of government. Some people in government stress the money values and some stress the human values. Without disregarding money values, my emphasis is on the human values.

* * *

When lobbyists work on broad national policy, their effect is very minor. Lobbyists are effective when they are urging what you are for and not effective when they are urging what you are not for. I have watched people come and go on the Hill here for fourteen years, and I have seldom seen a change in a fellow's basic philosophy even though he has been subject to all sorts of pressures.

* * *

Everyone has a political philosophy and is seldom talked out of it. If they have been re-elected, they feel it has paid off in getting them re-elected. Lobbying might have some effect on insignificant facets of legislation, but it doesn't have much effect on the philosophy of a senator. The longer a senator has been here, the more he is convinced the people back home like his philosophy and the less susceptible he is to lobbying. . . . You can pretty well judge in advance how a senator will vote on something because he has been voting that way for years. You really can't get them out of their rut, and the pressure groups tend to freeze them this way; they feel they must hold these people within the traces. If a senator kicks over the traces, the pressure groups generate indignation all over the country.

It is important to keep in mind that simple "yeas" or "nays" are not the only alternatives open to a member when an issue is up for decision. A wide range of actions is possible—from campaigning on the issue, to mere voting, to abstaining. Matthews (1960b, p. 192) diagrammed nine alternative positions that a member might take on an issue. Most lobbying effort, then, is aimed not at conversion but at activating the favorable member or at least at ensuring that he remains committed and votes "correctly."

Every public official is interested in making a "good record." A "good record" is instrumental in maintaining and enhancing his position. It brings increased influence, which is important to all public officials. Further, when an official pursues policies that fulfill his political philosophy, he thinks that he is making a "good record"; this is important in satisfying his ego needs (his conception of himself). But no public official can make a "good record" by himself. He must have the cooperation of other officials. To obtain this cooperation, he must be prepared to bargain and must learn to play as a "member of the team." Former Speaker Rayburn is reputed to have said, "The way to get along is to go along."

The organization of a majority to get a bill passed requires some minimum amount of discipline and compromise. Once the "team" position on a given piece of legislation has emerged, the pressures for the members of the team to "go along" become rather intense. Failure to "go along" lowers one's standing within the team and lessens one's chances for advancement in the system; it may even result in negative sanctions such as withdrawal of campaign support or loss of preferred committee assignments, although Congress is generally reluctant to apply such severe sanctions. The major penalty for not playing as a member of the team is loss of reputation or standing, which provide influence or power. Certain members can be characterized as very powerful; their power generally derives from the respect they have gained from their fellow members as they have played by the rules on the team over the years. A non-team player never gains that respect and influence.

When a member's political party holds the Presidency, his team grows to include the presidential office and even the executive departments. His leader becomes the President, and much of the policy initiative flows from that quarter. Presidential and departmental recommendations become important influences on his voting decisions. These recommendations are backed by superior information and research as well as all of the influences associated with the team effort.

Officials cannot avoid making decisions though they generally must make them on the basis of somewhat imperfect information. To fill the gap, they usually welcome or actively seek out information. The need for facts provides lobbyists with their best opportunity to influence decisions. But even here, lobbyists must compete with many other sources of information and advice. Information and recommendations of colleagues are very important in this process. Officials are inclined to accept information and advice from a colleague if they respect his integrity and wisdom and believe that he has superior knowledge. The complexity of modern legislation and the norms of the institution encourage members to develop knowledge in depth in only a few legislative subjects.[2] In subjects about which they are not so well informed, members lean heavily on committee recommendations or on the advice of a member of the relevant committee.

Informal circles of friends with similar political philosophies spring up in Congress. Information on forthcoming developments is exchanged within them. Respect for one another's specialties within such a circle can be so great that the recommendation of the specialist in a certain policy area can determine the votes of the entire friendship circle. One lobbyist said that at the time when he was a member of Congress he belonged to a circle of friends with similar political philosophies. Each member of the group served on a different committee, and they met weekly at lunch to report to one another on developments in their respective committees. Asked if he accepted the recommendations of his colleagues without further investigation, the respondent rocked back in his chair, thought for a full minute, and then said quite decisively, "Yes, by God, I did."

Staff assistants to decision-makers also exercise an important influence on the information and advice accepted by officials. Staffs not only process incoming information, they also take the initiative in digging out information. Staff persons are appointed by their superiors and are supposed to be alter egos for them, but

[2]*Matthews (1960b, pp. 95–97).*

since staff members are individuals, they may have some political convictions which intrude into the performance of their tasks. It is impossible to say with any precision how much decision-makers lean on their staffs; some are probably much more dependent than others. Dependence on staff recommendations probably increases if decisions involve technical or specialized questions and as decision-makers become more rushed.

Since officials have several alternative sources for information and advice, it is difficult to measure how effective lobbyist messages are. Chapter XV demonstrated that officials do attend to lobbying information; they welcome it even if they do not feel very dependent on it. A rough indication of the value decision-makers place upon messages from lobbyists also can be derived from answers to the question of how often decision-makers come to lobbyists for information and advice.

Table XVII–1 shows how often lobbyists have been solicited for their views and the kind of views sought. Twenty-four per cent report that they have never been solicited; 44 per cent say it has happened no more than ten times a year; 18 per cent say it occurred eleven to twenty-five times a year; and 14 per cent say it has been continual. Most lobbyists report that communications initiated by decision-makers are confined to requests for information to which the lobby organization has unique access or to views on issues on which the organization has strong and established opinions. A prime aim of most lobbyists is to develop confidential relationships with decision-makers which will provide regular opportunities to exert influence. These data suggest that no more than 10 per cent of the lobbyists achieve this with even one official; only 9 per cent are consulted frequently on a wide range of policy issues. There is no evidence in this table that lobbying messages are widely sought after by decision-makers.

The representatives of large organizations with considerable power at the polls, such as labor and farm groups, report being solicited for their views more often than other lobbyists. This again reflects the power of the constituents; the stand of an organization with power at the polls may be important information when an official is making a decision. Organizational executives and officers who are the spokesmen for their organizations are solicited more often for their views than lobbyists in other roles. Lawyers in private practice are seldom solicited. Lobbyists who

TABLE XVII–1
Decision-Makers' Solicitation of Policy Views from Lobbyists

TYPE OF VIEWS SOLICITED	FREQUENCY OF SOLICITATION					
	Never	2 Times a Year or Less	3–10 Times a Year	11–25 Times a Year	On-going Activity	No Response	Total
None	24						24
Inquiry confined to organizational views or information		13	25	15	8		61
Wide range of issues		2	2	3	3		10
Confidential conversations		1	1		3		3
No response						14	16
TOTAL	24	16	28	18	14	14	114

have previously had confidential relationships with decision-makers tend to carry part of that confidence over to their new role; former office-holders, those with Hill experience, and those who are very active in groups, tend to be solicited more frequently. Political activity also seems to be rewarded by increased solicitation of one's views; political contributors, especially political fund-raisers, are solicited more than those who do not so participate.

These data do not precisely indicate the extent to which lobbyists are heard. However, where lobby groups have useful information, it is heeded; and when their stand has important political implications, it is heeded. But we must also say that many lobby messages fall on deaf ears. Decision-makers occasionally seek information and advice from lobbyists, but very few of these interchanges are on a confidential and wide-ranging basis. Very few lobbyists report, and none of the congressional respondents report, having such confidential relationships.

Looking back now on the factors that decision-makers consider as they make their decisions, we can more clearly evaluate the range of lobbying influence by inquiring into the probability that lobbying or lobbyists can affect these factors. Lobbyists and lobby groups have a very limited ability to control the selection of officials or to affect the likelihood that an official can keep or enhance his position. Data presented in Chapters IV and XIII show that lobbyists and lobby groups are reluctant to become involved in partisan politics. They also find it difficult and very expensive to try to manipulate public opinion; many of them have great difficulty manipulating even the opinion of their own membership. This is not the same as saying that groups have little influence on politics; they obviously do have considerable influence; however, the influence of groups is derived from the fact that members of groups are citizens and the political system is designed to respond to the influence of their votes.

In similar vein, lobbyists and the leaders of lobby groups cannot, by themselves, make an official look good or bad. They have little to say about whether an official makes a "good record" or not. They can, of course, offer support to or oppose an official, and that may have some little impact on his public image; but they do not have votes on bills that they can use to bargain with officials in the way officials bargain for one another's votes. They are not members of the team and do not have team norms and sanctions to use to control the behavior of officials. They have little or no success in changing the political philoscphies of officials. Even their impact from supplying information and suggested policy alternatives to officials is diluted by the many alternative sources officials have for information and ideas.

The kinds of rewards and punishments that lobbyists are in the best position to offer have relatively low priority for the officials. It has been shown that entertainment and parties are not even considered a reward by most officials. Favors and bribes are not highly valued and are considered very dangerous by both officials and lobbyists. Lobbyists do have a kind of nuisance impact. They can make life somewhat unpleasant for officials who do not go along with them: It is embarrassing to vote against someone who is watching; it is difficult to vote against a group that has sent six thousand letters; it is hard not to listen to someone who is very persistent; it is hard to stand up to scorn by the public media. On small matters these nuisance factors may have considerable impact; they may even be decisive; but on matters of large public import such factors are rarely, if ever, of any great importance.

It has been suggested that the impact of lobbying on governmental decisions varies with the nature of the issue. On broad political issues commanding considerable public attention, the major determinant is the desire of the public. Lobbyists can do very little to affect the outcome, though they may influence the details of the bill or the specific language of small sections. If the legislation is specialized and affects only a small segment of the population, lobbyists are more likely to play a larger role. A member of the Ways and Means Committee of the House told a story about representatives of two large whiskey distilleries who came before the committee to argue about when the tax on whiskey should become due and payable. Each was seeking a competitive advantage over the other. There was no governmental or public interest to be served or disserved. The issue received no attention in the press. The committee listened quietly to the pleas from both sides and then made its decision (handed down its judgment). Lobbying may have been important on this bill, but was the bill really important?[3]

It is the demands of the people that start the country on a certain broad road policy-wise. Lobbyists may affect the language of the bills and legislation that come out in conformity with this broad policy, but they have little influence on the general outcome. They may not have any influence about the choice of the road to drive on, but they do have something to say about the way we drive on the road once we are on it.

* * *

I think lobbying plays a role in shaping the final content of a piece of legislation. We went out and slugged for an amendment to the highway act and got it tacked on. We couldn't affect the outcome of the bill very much, but in this technical way lobbying plays its role.

* * *

I think over the long haul that lobbying hasn't too much influence. I think they do have some impact on the details, and considerable impact on specialized legislation.

* * *

The lobbyists are really interested in the details, and this is where they have their effect. On over-all policy, however—the 1954 tax code for example—I don't think they are particularly effective. I suppose on broad policy if you get enough lobby organizations heading in the same direction, it has some effect. But once a coalition is built up on one side, it stimulates an opposing coalition on the other side, and Congress is caught in the middle.

Some observers argue that lobbyists have their greatest power when the issue is closely contested and switching a few

[3]*Eckstein (1960, p. 167), speaking of his own study of pressure groups, said, "In a nutshell, the study suggests (to me, at any rate) that the influence of private groups is greatest when, from the standpoint of demorcatic values, it matters least whether it is great or small."*

votes here or there may turn the tide. It is rather superficial, however, to give lobbyists credit for the outcome if they have switched a few votes in a close contest. It ignores all the factors that originally made the contest close, the influences that created the firm stands of the persons lined up on both sides of the issue. In legislative votes, the factors that determine one vote are as important as those that determine any other vote. If two hundred House members, acting on their political beliefs, were to line up on each side of a bill and the tide were turned by a dozen votes that were influenced by lobbying, would it be correct to say that the votes of four hundred persons acting on political conviction were outweighed by the dozen acting on pleadings from lobbyists?

THE BALANCE OF POWER IN LOBBYING

An important factor attenuating the impact of lobbying on governmental decisions is the fact that nearly every vigorous push in one direction stimulates an opponent or coalition of opponents to push in the opposite direction. This natural self-balancing factor comes into play so often that it almost amounts to a law.[4] The great numbers of lobbyists in Washington may actually be a blessing instead of a threat to the governmental system. When groups push on both sides of an issue, officials can more freely exercise their judgment than when the groups push on only one side.

The theory that countervailing power will cancel out some of the one-sided strength and evil effects of lobbying is an old one in Washington and is criticized vigorously by some persons. One criticism is that certain interests, such as consumers, have no one to represent them and that, therefore, any pressure against the welfare of these weakly organized interests is not resisted adequately. Although there is some truth to that criticism, the point is often overstressed.[5] From time to time, consumer representa-

[4]*In each of the six case studies of decisions in Chicago described by Banfield, one group or coalition was opposed by another (1961, chaps. ii–vii). Subsequently, he searched for an "underlying logic" for the decisions and felt that there must have been some "invisible hand" at work (pp. 327–28). These notions are not far from the concept of a natural self-balancing factor.*
[5]*Truman (1951, p. 519) also questions the assumption in the argument and calls for further research.*

tives are placed on boards and other decision-making bodies. More important, consumers, and any other poorly organized group, have a voice through constituent pressures and the vote. In addition, it is common for one of the organized interests to have an interest coinciding with unorganized interests.[6] For example, in the struggle over the tariff, the direct interest of the consumer is in free trade; the goods he purchases will be cheaper. Every time tariff decisions must be made, some organized interests lobby vigorously in favor of free trade.

A more telling criticism of the theory of countervailing power is that there is some danger that such an overwhelming coalition of groups may be organized on one side of an issue that the beneficial effect of competition may be outweighed by the irresistible force of combination.[7] This criticism can be overemphasized, too. If an overwhelming combination of powerful groups were on one side of an issue, the public would probably also favor that side of the issue. In such a case, the outcome would be completely in accord with our beliefs about how the political process should work. If the public were not behind the coalition of groups, the decision-makers would have sufficient public support to decide without being irresistibly influenced by the coalition.

When thinking about the theory of countervailing power, it is important not to think of decision-makers as inanimate objects which are manipulated by group pressures. Officials have beliefs and values of their own which are important guides to their decisions.[8] The group or coalition with the greatest numbers, or the most money, or the loudest noise will not necessarily prevail, especially if their prevailing is not in the public or national interest. As we saw above, the pressures of groups are but one of the factors considered by decision-makers—and by no means the most important one.

Another false notion in thinking about the impact of lobbying is the condemnation of all pressure as bad. It is a fact that life, especially organized community life, does not exist without

[6]*Even disfranchised, unorganized groups may find some representation because they are potential groups. Truman (1951, p. 511). This point is also made in Key, Jr. (1949, p. 235) and in Bentley (1908, pp. 314–15).*

[7]*This argument is made in the General Interim Report of the Buchanan Committee. U.S. Congress (1950b).*

[8]*Wahlke et al. (1960a) categorize legislators as facilitators, neutrals, and resistors with respect to their role toward pressure groups.*

pressure of one kind or another. Pressure is effective when it is backed by sanctions. The sanction with the greatest impact on the public official is the decision of the voters to support him or not. Every vote is a unit of pressure on a representative. Every communication from a constituent to his representative is a pressure. Our political system was designed to register those pressures, and we consider it proper when public officials respond to them.

All other forms of pressure derive meaning only as they are converted into voter pressure. If a lobby group can use money and other resources to convince the body politic that a certain policy should be followed, that conviction will be registered in pressure at the polls, and it will be proper for the system to respond to that pressure. We would not, in fact, want public officials who were insensitive to pressures at the polls. The only feasible and legitimate way to counteract political pressures is to form opposing groups and to try to convince the public that the original pressure group is wrong. If a group can sway the body politic, that is exactly what our system responds to and should reward.

ESTIMATIONS OF LOBBYING SUCCESS

Lobbyist respondents were asked to make several subjective evaluations of their success and of the contribution of lobbying to the policy-making process. In addition, they were to name the most successful lobby organization in town. Some consensus in this selection was expected. Lobbyists do not agree on the most successful lobby group in Washington; no organization received more than eight or ten choices. One reason for this is that judgments of success are very subjective. Different lobbyists use different standards. Some evaluate the percentage of bills passed that a group supported. This fails to come to grips with the question, however; one does not know whether the same bills would have passed if the lobby group had done nothing. Others use a broader criterion of long-range progress toward a distant goal. The subjective component of this kind of appraisal is readily apparent. Still others use a negative criterion of a group's ability to prevent potential damage to its interests.

Another reason for the lack of agreement on the most successful lobby group was that lobbyists naturally tend to choose a recent opponent as the strongest or most successful group.[9] Psychologically, one enjoys believing that one's opponents are strong. Like anyone else, lobbyists need to believe they are succeeding. The feedback from their activities, however, is very ambiguous and difficult to interpret. They naturally interpret their progress as favorably as possible; this helps to maintain their self-respect. Believing that one's opponent is very strong, a lobbyist who wins a point scores a striking success in his own mind. Even if he should be defeated, his deflation is minimized because one could not really expect much more when opposing such a strong adversary. About 15 per cent of the lobbyists choose a major opponent as the strongest group in town. There are also psychological rewards for believing that one's own organization is the strongest in town; about 14 per cent of the lobbyists believe that.

Despite the subjective difficulties in estimating group success, lobbyists tend to pick large membership organizations—like farm groups, veteran groups, and labor organizations (especially the railway labor unions)—as the most successful. About one-third of the lobbyists choose a large membership organization as the most successful.[10] This is consistent with the contention that power at the polls is the greatest power in lobbying. The American Medical Association and the oil and gas lobbies are the specialized groups most often listed as quite powerful.[11] The reputation of the AMA stands out quite sharply and stems largely from their successful public relations campaigns to label proposed national health insurance plans as "socialized medicine." Another

[9]*Most members of the group of business representatives in Washington who participated in the round-table conference at The Brookings Institution perceived labor unions as their main opponents; they also considered them to be very strong. Cherington and Gillen (1962, chap. v).*

[10]*The business representatives mentioned in note 9 apparently felt weak and unsuccessful compared to labor; they reasoned thus partly because they did not mobilize votes the way labor did and partly because they had difficulty agreeing among themselves on policy and tactics. Cherington and Gillen (1962, p. 46 and chap. v). Redbook sent a six-page questionnaire to 537 members of Congress in the fall of 1961; 174 replied. Members were asked to rate the influence of twenty-eight lobby groups as low, moderate, or high. To only one group was high influence attributed by a majority of those responding; the AFL-CIO was rated high by 58.6 per cent, moderate by 36 per cent, and low by 5.4 per cent. Al Toffler (1962).*

[11]*White (1956) picked the farm lobby and the AMA as the strongest in Washington.*

source of the AMA's strength is their firm policy that the organization shall take public stands only on medical matters.

On the whole, lobbyists rate the success of their own organizations rather highly. None calls his own organization a failure, and only six report that they do poorly. About one-fourth think they have moderately good results, and about one-half say their results are good; only one-sixteenth think they are resoundingly successful. Respondents tend to estimate that the odds against great success are rather high. They made such statements as, "Considering the odds against us, I think we did rather well." Estimations of success vary with the kinds of goals the group sets for itself; usually these goals are broad and long-range—more than simply a successful outcome on particular bills. Naturally it is easier to obtain specific limited objectives than to realize broad long-range goals.

These varying goal standards for measuring organization success produced interesting results in the data. Most observers would agree that organizations with great power at the polls generally have lobbying power superior to those with little power at the polls. High-poll-power organizations, however, tend to set broad, long-range goals which are difficult to attain. Thus, representatives of organizations with high power at the polls are no more inclined to claim high success for their organization than representatives of organizations with less power at the polls. Rather significantly, few lobbyists claim outstanding success. If the total lobby setting results in a balancing of groups, we should find, as we do, that groups claim moderate success against strong odds. If a substantial percentage claims resounding success, it would signal that a balancing process might not be functioning.

It is a truism that it is easier to stop a bill at some one hurdle in a legislative passage than it is to get it over all the hurdles (eight or ten in a two-house legislature) and signed into law. From this observation it is often suggested that "defensive organizations" (those trying to maintain the status quo) will generally be more successful in lobbying than "offensive organizations" (those trying to change the status quo).[12] The organizations represented by respondents in this study were categorized according

[12]DeVries (1960, p. 221) makes such a claim for lobbying in Michigan. Eckstein (1960, p. 37) makes a similar generalization.

to whether the policy of the group was primarily designed to preserve the status quo in society or to change the status quo.[13] The results show no relationship between these categories and respondents' appraisal of the organization's success.[14] This suggests that the generalization that defensive organizations find more success than offensive ones must be examined more rigorously.[15] The lack of correlation between defensive-offensive postures and appraisal of organization success probably results from several factors. Group success depends on many factors in addition to defensive and offensive posture; it is also appraised by varying goal standards. In addition, the legislative process is not so neatly arranged that defensive organizations will nearly always attempt to defeat bills while offensive organizations will nearly always attempt to pass them. Both types of organizations attempt to pass some bills and to defeat others. This results mainly from the fact that numbers of bills are introduced on all sides of questions in each Congress.

One lobbyist for a deprived minority group attributes much of his organization's considerable success to the fact that there is basic and clearly recognizable justice in his pleas. He believes that decision-makers recognize this fundamental justice and that this prevails as they make their decisions. Yet, careful examination of the data does not show that organizations trying to correct a basic injustice have any more success at lobbying than other kinds of organizations. The success of this respondent's lobby group probably stemmed more from the fact that the rationale for the original injustice had disappeared and that no organization is pushing on the other side. In many other cases of injustice, the organization, or organizations, benefitting from the injustice is still active on the other side.

Lobbyists' estimations of their personal success are highly

---

[13]*This is not a liberal-conservative, welfare state vs. free enterprise distinction; nor is it related to defense and offense on specific bills. It is whether the organization in its broad policy is trying to change or to preserve the status quo in society.*

[14]*Four of the six respondents who report poor success for their organizations represent groups attempting to defend technologically obsolete industries. The decline of such industries probably cannot be stopped by even the most energetic lobbying activity.*

[15]*The business representatives at the Brookings round table did not think they were very successful; yet it was clear from their remarks that they were primarily defending the status quo. Cherington and Gillen (1962, chap. v).*

correlated with estimations of their organization's success (see Table VI–8). Most lobbyists report moderate or good results from their personal efforts; only two report poor results; and only three report resounding success. Most lobbyists take a rather long-range view of their efforts. One reports, "I have only been on this job for five years, and that's not long enough to find out how successful I will be." Lobbying success is very much dependent on tenure, since acceptability of messages from lobbyists by officials can be gained only if the lobbyist builds a reputation for reliability. Most lobbyists hold their job for some time and plan to make a career in lobbying. Feeling successful goes along with liking the work and planning to make a career of it. The lobbyist's feeling of personal success shows no relationship to the poll-power of his organization. This finding was not unexpected; lobbyists for weak organizations take that fact into account as they appraise their personal success, and lobbyists for strong organizations realize that organizational success is due to many other factors in addition to their personal efforts. It also seems to be generally true that every lobbyist aspires to more than he achieves; he must then decide what he might reasonably expect to achieve.

EVALUATIONS OF ALL POLICY INFLUENCES

In attempting to make an over-all evaluation of lobbying impact on governmental decisions, it is important to place lobbying within the setting of all the factors influencing public policy. The final question of the interview with respondents was:

> We all know that lobbying is just one factor in making public policy. The President, Congress, executive agencies, political parties, opinion leaders, and voters also participate in policy-making. How would you appraise the relative influence of these various forces as they operate in making policy?

More than half of the respondents pick the President or the executive branch as the most important factor in making policy; even lobbyists with experience on the Hill and congressional respondents tend to give first rank importance to the executive branch. About 20 per cent of the lobbyists give the voters first rank importance. (These people tend to give unqualified approval to lobbying.) Many congressional respondents also rate voters first. Approximately 10 per cent of lobbyists give first rank importance to Congress. Congress is most often named second (about 35 per cent) and is followed closely by the executive branch (30 per cent). Opinion leaders and political parties are named relatively few times.

Most important for our purposes, only one lobbyist gives first rank importance to lobbying, and only five rate it second. Congressional respondents also accord very slight importance to lobbying in making public policy; about half of them, in fact, place lobbying at the bottom of the list. It is rather striking that both the practitioners and the recipients of lobbying think that lobbying is of so little importance in making public policy. One lobbyist struggling with this question said:

> I don't know where in the world I would fit the lobbyists as a group. Some of them have been up here for years battling for lost causes. On the whole, and speaking of all lobbyists in general, I think they are a lot less effective than most people believe.

The tendency of the public to overestimate the impact of lobbying on public policy is curiously seductive. If one assumes that lobbying is bad and ought to have little or no influence on policy and then discovers that lobbying does have some influence, it is easy to leap to the conclusion that lobbying is powerful and exercises inappropriate influence. If, on the other hand, one assumes that lobbying is legitimate and then evaluates all the other influences on public policy, he concludes that lobbying has relatively little impact on policy when compared with the other factors. Persons who believe human nature is essentially evil seem to be able to find sinister influences everywhere; finding a few sinister influences in lobbying, they are overeager to condemn all lobbyists.

The strong influence of the President and the executive branch on public policy is attested to by some very knowledgeable leaders in Congress:

You would almost have to put the President number one. He has such a tremendous command of the sources of information, this automatically gives him an advantage. Next I suppose you would put the sources of information such as the press, mass communications, political commentators, and other opinion leaders. The public opinion they create is reflected from the districts back into Congress. Congress has some leadership in policy but it is more difficult to pinpoint than the leadership of the President.

* * *

Policy is made largely by the executive and the legislative party leaders; these two most important factors are somewhat influenced by the other factors. Lobbyists have very little to say on legislation so far as I can see. . . . I have known lots of party chairmen and the party, on the national scene is not very effective. I never saw a chairman who would swear he had any effect on policy whatsoever. Any attempts to influence policy would be instantly resented either by leaders in the executive branch or leaders of the legislative party in Congress.

* * *

There is just no way of getting around it, the President is the dominant force in policy-making. The President is one man, and when he speaks he has the attention of the world. He can mold public opinion, and he also tends to have the confidence of all the people. There is no one member of Congress who has that much respect. If it should become a popularity contest, the President will always win out. All policy is made from a view of what the public demands; political figures orient to it. I doubt if the lobbyist has much to say except when he gets down to specific language of particular sections of bills; he is not very effective on broad policy.

The lobbyist-son of a former President said:

The President is certainly the most influential—this is without any question. Second I would put the head of an executive department who is putting up a real fight and is backed by the President. The most important single element is the President's backing up of a fighting cabinet officer.

THE DANGERS OF LOBBYING

The weight of the evidence that this study brings to bear suggests that there is relatively little influence or power in lobbying per se. There are many forces in addition to lobbying which influence public policy; in most cases these other forces clearly outweigh the impact of lobbying. Voters set the broad trends of public policy which all the other influences on policy must follow. It is for this reason that so many forces battle to manipulate public opinion. Public opinion is a factor which sets the boundaries for the policy struggle. On certain questions the boundaries are closely restricted, and the policy decisions of officials must closely follow public demands. On other questions, the boundaries may be broader, leaving wider discretion to decision-makers and more possibility for lobbyists to influence their decisions. Questions of large public attention and import are chiefly determined by considerations of political success and winning the next election. The chief executive, through his political leadership, his ability to mold public opinion, and his command of the resources and imagination of the executive bureaucracy, has the greatest single impact on the shape of public policy. Questions of small technical nature, which attract little public attention, are more subject to lobbying influence. The growth of one lobby group or coalition generally stimulates the development of an opposing group. Most careful observers of governmental decision-making have concluded that the over-all impact of lobbying is relatively minor. This point was made by both lobbyist and congressional respondents and agrees with the observation of other writers on the subject.[16]

If the conclusion that lobbying has a relatively weak impact on policy is added to the conclusions that system controls and legal controls are adequate, that public decisions cannot be

---

[16]*White (1956, pp. 145, 149); Matthews (1960b, pp. 195–96); Key, Jr. (1961, chap. xx).*

bought or stolen, and that the lobbying process is relatively clean, the result is clear: lobbying as we see it today in Washington presents little or no danger to the system. This does not mean that a dangerous situation could not arise or that lobbyists would not engage in unethical or unfair tactics if they believed these would be to their special advantage. The best insurance against

"It's Terrible How the Big Money Guys Run Politics"

Herblock in the Washington Post.

danger and corruption in the process is an alert citizenry which elects responsible officials to public office. A wide-open communications system and viable and responsible public media are important preconditions to maintaining public alertness.

THE CONTRIBUTIONS OF LOBBYING

Eckstein raises the most fundamental question about lobbying and pressures groups: "What contributions do pressure groups make to the political system as a whole, and do these contributions tend to make the system more or less viable (stable and effective)? Are their consequences 'dysfunctional' or 'eufunctional' for the larger systems in which they operate?"[17] Though this study focuses on lobbying rather than pressure groups, the question is essentially the same; however, the contribution of these data to an answer is relatively limited.

In this context it is relevant to point out again that lobbying is inevitable and is likely to grow in scope. One lobbyist says it is analogous to automobile drivers: there are a few bad drivers, but people continue to drive, and more cars are added to the road each year. Lobbying is protected by the First Amendment to the Constitution, and government officials are not disposed to hamper its growth or activities.

Granted the inevitability of lobbying, what are its positive contributions to the political process? Lobbyists provide information and other services which are welcomed by governmental decision-makers. These services are costly and somewhat wasteful; the public or the consumer pays for them ultimately; congressional officials even claim they could function quite adequately without them. In another sense, however, they are indispensable. If information from lobbyists and lobby groups was, for some reason, unavailable to government officials, they would be largely dependent on their own staff for information and ideas. Since the Congress is reluctant to staff itself adequately, it would have to turn primarily to the Executive for information. This would create an even further imbalance between Congress and the Executive in policy-making.[18] More important, cutting off

[17]*Eckstein (1960, p. 152).*
[18]*The author is indebted to James A. Robinson for suggesting this point.*

lobbying communications would eliminate a valuable, even indispensable, source of creativity. There is no assurance that government institutions can turn up all the possible alternative solutions to policy problems. A decision-maker who has his mind made up may well have to have new points of view forcefully thrust upon him before he can perceive and accept them. The clash of viewpoints between contesting groups is not only informative; it also is creative. Formerly unperceived alternatives may arise from the challenge to previously accepted possibilities.

Eckstein (1960, p. 162) suggests that lobby groups perform two other indispensable functions in the political system: integration and disjunction. Officials must know very specifically what the effects of a given policy will be and how citizens will react to that policy. Lobby groups and lobbyists define opinion for government with a sense of reality and specificity which political parties, the mass media, opinion polls, and staff assistants seldom, if ever, can achieve. Aggregating and defining specialized opinions have both integrative and disjunctive aspects. The function is integrative in that persons with special interests or problems need group action to aggregate their views and communicate the positions to officials. The aggregation process requires some compromise on the part of group members and therefore is integrative. Group opinion is a more manageable consideration for officials than scattered individual opinions.

Specialized opinion is disjunctive as well, in that it encourages multiple group demands. Political parties (especially in a two-party system) strive for a very broad integration in order to win elections. That kind of integration can be achieved only by reaching a very low and vague denominator which may not be very functional for making policy. If special interests were confined to vague representation through political parties, they might begin to feel alienated from a political system which persistently distorts their goals.[19] Affording disparate interests special representation through their own lobby group probably con-

[19]*The Washington representatives at the Brookings round table all represented corporations. They expressed dissatisfaction with general business organizations such as the National Association of Manufacturers and the National Chamber of Commerce and even with their own trade associations for compromising too much on policy, being too vague, and being too slow to take action. Cherington and Gillen (1962).*

tributes to the stability of the system. There is reason to suppose, then, that the policy-making system produces wiser or more intelligent decisions and functions with more stability than might be the case if lobby groups and lobbyists were not present. If we had no lobby groups and lobbyists we would probably have to invent them to improve the functioning of the system.

APPENDIX A

Lobbyist Interview Schedule

Code No.:

Name:
Address: Office:
Home:

Data from the Report:
Organizations or Clients Represented:
Salary or Fee:
Expenses:

Observation by the Interviewer:
Sex: Race:
Impression of R's SES: High____ Upper Middle____ Lower
Middle____ Low____
Impression of R's dominant interests and artifacts of significance:

Interview
1. One of the things we are most interested in is how the people who register as lobbyists happen to get into this line of work. Could you briefly recount your occupational history since the completion of your formal education?
2. What were the major influences that developed your interest in public affairs and legislation?

3. How did you happen to become a lobbyist?

4. Were you selected for your position as a lobbyist because of some special skill or knowledge?

5. To what degree were you selected because of your circle of contacts?

6. Speaking generally, is a man considered valuable for lobbying because of his circle of contacts?

7. What features of your work appeal to you the most?

8. What features of your work appeal to you the least?

9. Would you like to continue in this type of work for the rest of your professional life?

   a. Why?

10. If you had a perfectly free choice, and without considering any lack of talent or training on your part, which of the jobs or professions listed on this card would be your first five choices? (Hand card to R.)

   ＿＿＿Administrative assistant to senator

   ＿＿＿Attorney

   ＿＿＿College professor

   ＿＿＿Congressman

   ＿＿＿Corporation executive

   ＿＿＿Government agency head

   ＿＿＿Journalist

   ＿＿＿Judge

   ＿＿＿Legislative representative for an organization

   ＿＿＿Physician

   ＿＿＿Proprietor of small business

   ＿＿＿Public relations counsel

   ＿＿＿Realtor

   ＿＿＿Sales representative

   ＿＿＿United States senator

11. How much formal education have you had?

   None＿＿ Elementary＿＿ Some high school＿＿ Finished high school＿＿ Some college＿＿ Finished college＿＿ Graduate or professional training＿＿ Professional degree＿＿ Ph.D. or equivalent＿＿

12. In which of these four socio-economic classes would you place yourself: (1) lower class; (2) lower-middle class; (3) upper-middle class; (4) upper class?

13. What year were you born?

14. I have a list here of different kinds of clubs and organizations that people can belong to. I would like to go over this list with you. Please tell me if you belong to any organizations in these categories, and whether or not you hold an office and are active or inactive in the organization.

Business	Labor
Professional	Veterans and patriotic
Fraternal	Charitable and welfare
Civic and service	Farm
Informal social	Neighborhood
Clubs with permanent facilities	Political
School and education	Governmental
Religious	National origins

   a. Can you think of any organizations that you belong to that are not on the list?

15. What is your religious preference?

16. How large is your immediate family?

17. Now I would like to get a little information about your political activities. Generally speaking, do you usually think of yourself as a Republican, a Democrat, an Independent, or what?

   a. (If R or D) Would you call yourself a strong (R) (D), or a not very strong (R) (D)?

   b. (If I) Do you think of yourself as closer to the Republican or Democratic party?

18. Are you active in a political party now or have you been active in a party?

   a. Active from_____ to_____

   b. At what level of political organization were you active? By that I mean local, state, or national.

19. (If yes to 18) What positions have you held in the party, if any?

   a. When?

20. Have you ever held a public office?

   a. What? b. When? c. Was it elective or appointive?

21. Have you ever been a candidate for public office?
    a. When? b. What office?
22. Have you ever campaigned for a candidate or a party?
    a. When? b. Where? c. How much time did you give?
23. How often do you ordinarily attend party meetings or other political rallies?
    a. At what level of politics usually?
24. Do you attend meetings with party leaders on things like strategy, nominations, candidates, etc.?
    a. How often? b. At what level of politics usually?
25. How many political contributions would you estimate you personally have made in the past five years from 1952 to 1956? This covers two presidential elections and three congressional elections.
    a. To whom did you generally make them? (Get this in specific detail, if possible.)
    b. What was the average amount of your contributions?
26. Have you ever assisted in the raising of political funds?
    a. Have you solicited political funds from others?
       (1) How many people did you generally contact?
       (2) How do you ordinarily come in contact with these people?
27. In general, what does your organization expect its representative to do?
28. What is your specific job in this organization?
29. How do you report back to the organization you represent?
    a. Do you write a newsletter?
30. How are you paid for your services? In other words, do you have a contract, a fee, or a salary?
    a. About how much has your average yearly income been for the past three years? (Present card with income categories on it if R is hesitant to name a precise figure.)
       (1) Does that figure report your income before or after taxes?
31. (Ask only of people not working full-time at lobbying.)
    On the average, about what per cent of your income comes from clients on behalf of whom you register?

_____Less than 5 per cent   _____51 to 65 per cent

_____5 to 20 per cent   _____65 to 80 per cent

_____20 to 35 per cent   _____80 to 95 per cent

_____35 to 49 per cent   _____Above 95 per cent

_____About 50 per cent

32. How is general policy made for your organization?

   a. Are your personal recommendations on policy adopted frequently, occasionally, seldom, or never?

33. How is strategy on specific problems mapped?

34. Do you have freedom to determine your own tactics on most problems?

35. What are your most important sources of inside information?

36. In what ways are contacts useful to you?

37. How do you develop a circle of contacts?

38. Generally, where do you try to establish contacts?

   a. Do your contacts include officials of either of the political parties?

   (1) Does your organization present its views before the platform committees of the parties?

   (2) How important are the political parties in creating public policy?

   (3) Do you find it necessary to work both sides of the aisle on most issues?

39. How important is joint activity with other lobby organizations on certain problems?

40. What group or groups of people do you generally consider to be your opponents on most issues?

   a. How do you estimate the strength of your opponents?

   b. Do you keep close tabs on the latest alignment of important people on an issue or bill?

41. Do public policy-makers—by that I mean members of Congress or agency heads—come to you very often to solicit your views on a policy matter?

   _____Less than once a year   _____11 to 25 times a year

   _____1 or 2 times a year   _____Ongoing activity

   _____3 to 10 times a year

42. Speaking generally, about what portion of your time do you spend in each of these various activities? (Hand card to R.) Your answer need not add up to 100 per cent.

_____Working in own office _____Calling on members of Congress _____Calling on others _____Chatting with people on the Hill _____Doing research _____Traveling around at the grass-roots level _____Entertaining important people

43. What approach do you generally follow to try to get a member of Congress or other public official to agree with your point of view?

44. Several possible techniques for bringing home a point to a public official are listed on this card. Would you evaluate each of these techniques as they seem to work for you? It would be useful if you could rate them on a scale running from zero, for not effective at all, to ten, for very effective.

_____Personal presentation of arguments _____Presenting research results _____Testifying at hearings _____Having an influential constituent contact the official _____Getting close to a person who has the ear of the public official one wants to convince _____Entertaining the official for an evening _____Giving a party _____Contributing money to a political campaign, or threatening not to do so _____Contributing work in a political campaign _____Inspiring a letter-writing or telegram campaign _____Publicizing voting records _____ Instituting a public relations campaign to convince the general public of the organization's point of view _____Direct bribery _____Obtaining assistance from other organizations (Probe respondent on those techniques rated highest.)

45. Do people develop specialties of techniques or subject matter in lobbying?

46. Can you think of a group of traits that seem to characterize most of the people who become lobbyists?

47. How do lobbyists learn the skills that are necessary for their work? Are they specially trained in any way?

48. Is there a sense of belonging to a profession, or a sense of camaraderie among lobbyists?

49. Is there very much demand for professional lobbyists? By that I mean, are there more people available than there are lobby positions, or do lobby positions go begging?

50. Do you consider your relationship to the organization you represent to be like that of a lawyer to his client; that is, presenting your client's case in the best possible light without necessarily committing yourself personally to your client's position?

   a. Would you describe your commitment to your organization's policy position as strong, mild, or weak?

   b. Was the policy position of your organization a very important factor in your decision to represent it?

51. Is there any need to make a case periodically for the continuation of representation in Washington for your organization? In other words, does the organization occasionally consider withdrawing its representation?

52. How is the cost of the lobbying operation financed by the organization?

53. (If organization is a client) Is there much competition for clients among professional lobbyists?

54. To your mind, which is the most successful lobby organization in town?

55. How do you appraise the record of success of your own organization?

56. How do you appraise your personal record of success? (If necessary, inquire about his criterion for success.)

57. Political writers generally give the impression that they think lobbying is a bad thing. Do you think lobbying as we see it today is healthy for our democracy?

58. We all know lobbying is just one factor in making public policy. The President, Congress, executive agencies, political parties, opinion leaders, and voters also participate in policymaking. How would you appraise the relative influence of these various forces as they operate in making policy?

INTERVIEWERS' COMMENTS ON
INTERVIEW SESSION

Date:_____ Time:_____ Duration:_____

General receptivity of Respondent to interview
Rapport and cooperation throughout interview:
Completeness of interview:
Any interest shown in interviewer or study:

Impressions of Responses:
Sincerity?
Well-informed?
Open-minded?
Fluency?
Resentment or resistance?
Reliability?

APPENDIX B

Congressional Interview Schedule

Name: Code No.:

Office or Position:

Throughout the interview I will be using the word "lobbyist" a good deal. When I do so I don't express any judgment. It is merely a convenient and well-known term, and I use it in a rather broad sense. Some of the questions that follow ask for your general point of view toward certain aspects of lobbying; others ask specifically about ways that you deal with lobbyists. Please feel free to be completely frank with me. I would like to take notes on your answers but rest assured that everything you tell me will be held in the strictest confidence.

1. I have talked to many people who register as lobbyists, and I find a good deal of disagreement among them about who should be considered a lobbyist and who should not. The lobby registration act itself seems to have failed to clarify this vagueness. It might be helpful at the beginning, then, if you could give me your personal definition of a lobbyist.

2. Can you think of a group of traits that seem to characterize most of the people you know as lobbyists?

3. What kinds of traits or skills, in your opinion, make a lobbyist successful?

4. When a person whom you consider to be a lobbyist comes to talk with you, do you check up on him or ask him if he is registered?

5. Whenever a person must decide how he will vote on an issue or a bill he must take several factors into account, such as the wishes of his constituents, the views of interest groups, the recommendations of his colleagues and friends, and his personal feelings. Which of these kinds of factors are uppermost in your (his [member's]) mind as you (he) arrive(s) at your (his) decision?

   a. How do you decide in any particular case how seriously to take the views of interest groups?

6. I presume you know special persons with whom you like to discuss difficult problems in confidence. Are these people mainly here on the Hill, downtown, or outside of Washington?

7. In your experience, do lobbyists noticeably try to cultivate you as a person with whom it would be important for them to have contact?

8. Many lobbyists have told me that Congress is more likely to be impressed if several organizations present a united front on an issue or a bill. Does a joint presentation by several groups impress you more than separate presentations by each organization?

9. Do you ever participate jointly with the representatives of interest groups in planning strategy to get a bill through or stopped?

10. Do lobbyists very often try to poll you in advance of a vote in committee or on the floor to see which way you plan to vote?

11. As you might guess, lobbyists have varied ideas about what approach is most effective in trying to get people on the Hill to agree with their point of view. What approach is most likely to be effective with you?

12. Each of the lobbyists I interviewed was asked to rate the effectiveness of the fourteen techniques listed on this card. I would like you to rate these same techniques in terms of the effect they have in bringing a point home to you. Please rate them using the scale shown on the card which runs from zero for not effective at all to ten for very effective.

   _____Personal presentation of arguments

_____Presenting research results

_____Testifying at hearings

_____Being contacted by an influential constituent

_____Being contacted by a close personal friend or confidant

_____Being entertained for an evening

_____Being invited to a party

_____Contributions of money to a political campaign, or threats not to do so

_____Contributions of work in a political campaign

_____A letter-writing or telegram campaign

_____The publicizing of voting records

_____A public relations campaign to convince the general public of the organization's point of view

_____Direct bribery

_____Joint lobby efforts by several organizations

13. Do you receive many requests from lobbyists for special information about the status of some bill they are interested in?

14. When a bill directly affects some special interest group, do you take the initiative in trying to find out how that group feels about the bill?

15. Lobbyists tell me that they supply invaluable information to Congress. To what extent do you depend on information from lobbyists to inform yourself about most issues or bills?

   a. Do you feel confident in using their information?

   b. Do you receive a lot of information you don't use?

   c. Is there a better or more efficient way to get the information?

16. Political writers generally give the impression that they think lobbying is a bad thing. Do you think lobbying as we see it today is healthy for our democracy?

17. Some people have accused the administrative agencies of the executive branch of the government of lobbying. Do you think their kind of lobbying is different from that of private groups?

   a. Is lobbying by executive agencies healthy for our democracy?

18. Can you see specific evils in lobbying that you think can be controlled by legislation?

   a. Are there any specific ways you would change the present lobby regulation act?

   b. To what extent can members of Congress themselves control lobbying?

19. We all know that lobbying is just one factor in making public policy. The President, Congress, executive agencies, political parties, opinion leaders, and voters also participate in policy-making. How would you appraise the relative influence of these various forces as they operate in making policy?

APPENDIX C

Lobbyist Study Code
Card Number One

COLUMN NO. ITEM

1–3   Identification Code

4   Nature of Organization Represented

         (10) * 0 Labor organization—large membership (over 50,000)

         (8) 1 Labor organization—small membership (under 50,000)

         (2) 2 Farm organization—large membership

         (3) 3 Farm organization—small membership

         (9) 4 Trade association—large membership

         (43) 5 Trade association—small membership

         (17) 6 Corporation

         (6) 7 Large membership citizens organization

         (2) 8 Service or veterans organization

         (5) 9 Church and humanitarian organization

         (7) X More than one type

         (2) P Foreign government or firm

*Figures in parentheses are number of respondents in each category.

COLUMN NO.   ITEM

5   Reported Salary or Fee—Transposed to an Annual
         Basis

         (39)   0   None
         (7)   1 $1–999
         (9)   2 $1,000–2,499
         (12)   3 $2,500–4,999
         (8)   4 $5,000–7,499
         (9)   5 $7,500–9,999
         (16)   6 $10,000–14,999
         (5)   7 $15,000–19,999
         (3)   8 $20,000–24,999
         (4)   9 $25,000 up
         (2)   X   No response

6   Sex

         (107) 1   Male
         (7)   2   Female

7   Interviewer's Judgment of R's SES

         (6)   1   Upper
         (103) 2   Upper-middle
         (4)   3   Lower-middle
         (0)   4   Lower
         (1)   X   No response

8   Career Preparation

         (12)   0   No specific one
         (45)   1   Law
         (9)   2   Journalism
         (1)   3   Politics
         (11)   4   Business
         (3)   5   Governmental service
         (19)   6   Teacher or professor or researcher
         (4)   7   Labor
         (0)   8   Clerical
         (2)   9   Other
         (8)   X   No Response

9   Over-All Career Pattern

         (0)   0   None discernable
         (23)   1   Law
         (4)   2   Journalism
         (5)   3   Politics
         (10)   4   Business

COLUMN NO.   ITEM

(28)	5	Governmental service
(18)	6	Association work
(7)	7	Labor organization work
(6)	8	Lobbying
(4)	9	Other
(9)	X	No response

10   Position Immediately Prior to Becoming a Lobbyist

(2)	0	Never did anything but lobbying
(9)	1	Lawyer
(1)	2	Journalist
(3)	3	Political office
(18)	4	Business man or employee
(41)	5	Government job—administrative branch
(16)	6	Government job—legislative branch
(4)	7	Other professional
(5)	8	Labor union employee
(7)	9	Other
(8)	X	No response

11   Influences Developing Interest in Public Affairs

(3)	0	Never have been really interested
(14)	1	Father or family
(3)	2	Proximity of home environment to politics
(7)	3	Courses or teachers in school
(50)	4	Involvement in work or job
(4)	5	Involvement in civic affairs
(10)	6	Always been interested
(10)	7	Combination of home, school, and early job
(13)	X	No response

12   Primary Reason for Becoming a Lobbyist

(17)	0	Am not a lobbyist, only register to be safe
(42)	1	Requirements of job led me into it
(7)	2	Boss thought I was especially qualified
(26)	3	It was the best use to which I could put my talents
(10)	4	Promotion of some policy
(1)	5	Monetary reward
(0)	6	Enjoy working with people
(0)	7	Enjoy variety of work
(0)	8	Enjoy working on important decisions
(0)	9	Other
(11)	X	No response

COLUMN NO.   ITEM

13   Secondary Reason for Becoming a Lobbyist

(1) 0   Am not a lobbyist, only register to be safe
(25) 1   Requirements of job led me into it
(15) 2   Boss thought I was especially qualified
(25) 3   It was the best use to which I could put
          my talents
(12) 4   Promotion of some policy
(15) 5   Monetary reward
(1) 6   Enjoy working with people
(1) 7   Enjoy variety of work
(4) 8   Enjoy working on important decisions
(1) 9   Other
(14) X   No response

14   Primary Skills or Knowledge Involved in
            Recruitment

(1) 0   Can't think of any skills
(23) 1   Knowledge of the legislative and political
          process
(15) 2   Knowledge of law and legal processes
(5) 3   Ability to meet people and leave good im-
          pression
(8) 4   Ability to communicate effectively
(6) 5   Possession of a wide circle of contacts
(38) 6   Knowledge of the subject under review
(0) 7   Ability to testify before committees
(4) 8   Reputation for success
(1) 9   Other
(13) X   No response

15   Secondary Skills or Knowledge Involved in
            Recruitment

(1) 0   Can't think of any skills
(35) 1   Knowledge of the legislative and political
          process
(10) 2   Knowledge of law and legal processes
(8) 3   Ability to meet people and leave good im-
          pression
(11) 4   Ability to communicate effectively
(13) 5   Possession of a wide circle of contacts
(12) 6   Knowledge of the subject under review
(1) 7   Ability to testify before committees

(4) 8   Reputation for success
(3) 9   Other
(16) X   No response

16   Importance of Circle of Contacts in R's Case

(43) 0   Not at all
(18) 1   Minor importance—less than 25 per cent
(25) 2   Some importance—25 per cent to 50 per
            cent
(8) 3   Considerable importance—50 per cent to
            75 per cent
(7) 4   Major importance—more than 75 per cent
(13) X   No response

17   General Importance of Circle of Contacts (not asked
          of all R's)

(4) 0   Not at all
(8) 1   Minor importance—less than 25 per cent
(29) 2   Some importance—25 per cent to 50 per
            cent
(21) 3   Considerable importance—50 per cent to
            75 per cent
(4) 4   Major importance—more than 75 per cent
(48) X   No response

18   Most Appealing Features of Lobbyist Work

(5) 0   None is appealing or none stands out
(3) 1   Freedom of schedule
(7) 2   Variety of work
(16) 3   Interacting with people
(1) 4   Monetary reward
(35) 5   Sense of accomplishing something impor-
            tant—sense of mission
(9) 6   Contact with important people and
            decisions
(0) 7   Entertainment and parties
(11) 8   Preparing an argument
(3) 9   Matching wits with opponents
(11) P   Other
(13) X   No response

19   Least Appealing Features of Lobbyist Work

(16) 0   Nothing disagreeable about it

COLUMN NO.   ITEM

(7) 1 Working conditions: long or odd hours, low pay, travel

(8) 2 Approaching people who disagree with or oppose you

(8) 3 Having to be nice to people to win their favor

(21) 4 Detailed preparation of briefs or research results

(2) 5 Having to state only one side of an argument

(2) 6 Too much entertainment and parties

(3) 7 Discouraging to fail at times

(2) 8 Public disapprobation of job

(8) 9 Getting clients to understand a lobbyist's job and requirements of lobbying

(22) P Other

(15) X No response

20   Desire To Continue in Lobbying

(2) 0 Unqualified no

(1) 1 Probably not, unless situation improves

(2) 2 Haven't decided, or maybe

(7) 3 For a while, but not for rest of career

(76) 4 Hope to continue or make a career in lobbying

(13) 5 Like my job in general and will continue, but dislike lobbying aspects of it

(13) X No response

21-22   First Choice of Profession

First			Second	Third	Fourth	Fifth
(1)	01	Adm. assnt. to				
		senator 4	4	2	3	
(30)	02	Attorney 10	11	6	7	
(6)	03	College professor.. 5	8	4	8	
(3)	04	Congressman 11	8	7	5	
(7)	05	Corporation				
		executive 11	8	8	5	
(2)	06	Government				
		agency head 3	6	5	4	
(2)	07	Journalist 8	5	7	13	
(6)	08	Judge 12	8	10	3	

COLUMN NO.   ITEM

(13) 09	Legislative rep. for an org............ 10	13	5	7
(5) 10	Physician 3	4	2	2
(4) 11	Proprietor of small business .. 4	6	5	6
(3) 12	Public relations counsel 2	8	20	8
(0) 13	Realtor 0	1	0	3
(1) 14	Sales representative .. 4	1	2	0
(18) 15	United States senator 13	5	3	4
(13) X	No response 14	18	28	36

23–24	Second Choice of Profession (same code as 21–22)
25–26	Third Choice of Profession (same code as 21–22)
27–28	Fourth Choice of Profession (same code as 21–22)
29–30	Fifth Choice of Profession (same code as 21–22)

31   Education

(0) 0   None
(0) 1   Elementary
(5) 2   Some high school
(7) 3   Finished high school
(14) 4   Some college
(11) 5   Finished college
(16) 6   Grad. or professional training
(45) 7   Professional degree
(7) 8   Ph.D. or equivalent
(9) X   No response

32   R's Choice of Class

(11) 1   Upper
(77) 2   Upper-middle
(12) 3   Lower-middle
(1) 4   Lower
(13) X   No response

33   Age

(1) 1   20–29
(8) 2   30–39
(38) 3   40–49

COLUMN NO.   ITEM

(35) 4   50–59
(15) 5   60–69
(5) 6   70 up
(12) X   No response

34   Score on Occupation Groups (3 points for officer; 2, for active; 1, for inactive—business, professional, labor, farm)

(12) 0   0
(21) 1   1–3
(32) 2   4–6
(16) 3   7–9
(13) 4   10–14
(6) 5   15–19
(1) 6   20–24
(0) 7   25–29
(0) 8   30–40
(0) 9   41 up
(13) X   No response

35   Score on Political Groups (partisan, governmental— same scoring as 34)

(54) 0   0
(27) 1   1–3
(13) 2   4–6
(2) 3   7–9
(4) 4   10–14
(1) 5   15–19
(13) X   No response

36   Score on Civic Groups (civic and service, school and educational, veterans and charitable—same scoring as 34)

(22) 0   0
(39) 1   1–3
(19) 2   4–6
(11) 3   7–9
(7) 4   10–14
(0) 5   15–19
(2) 6   20–24
(0) 7   25–29
(1) 8   30–40
(13) X   No response

COLUMN NO.   ITEM

37   Score on Social Groups (fraternal, informal, club, neighborhood, national origin—same scoring as 34)

(8) 0 0
(17) 1 1–3
(24) 2 4–6
(25) 3 7–9
(23) 4 10–14
(3) 5 15–19
(0) 6 20–24
(1) 7 25–29
(1) 8 30–40
(12) X No response

38   Score on Religious Groups (same scoring as 34)

(25) 0 0
(60) 1 1–3
(11) 2 4–6
(3) 3 7–9
(2) 4 10–14
(13) X No response

39   Score on Total Groups (same scoring as 34)

(0) 0 0
(3) 1 1–3
(6) 2 4–6
(6) 3 7–9
(19) 4 10–14
(16) 5 15–19
(18) 6 20–24
(9) 7 25–29
(18) 8 30–40
(6) 9 41 up
(13) X No response

40   Experience on the "Hill"

(79) 0 None
(8) 1 Committee staff
(3) 2 House member's staff
(6) 3 Senator's staff
(3) 4 Member of House
(0) 5 Member of Senate

COLUMN NO.   ITEM

(3) 6   More than one type of position
(1) 7   General congressional staff
(11) X   No response

41   Religious Preference

(6) 0   None or no organized religion
(6) 1   Baptist
(16) 2   Presbyterian
(13) 3   Methodist
(0) 4   Lutheran
(4) 5   Congregational
(23) 6   Other Protestant sect or Protestant without designation
(12) 7   Roman Catholic
(5) 8   Jewish
(16) 9   Episcopal
(13) X   No response

42   Size of Family

(6) 1   Bachelor or maiden
(5) 2   Man and wife
(5) 3   Divorced, widowed, etc.
(20) 4   One child
(36) 5   Two children
(13) 6   Three children
(16) 7   Four or more children
(13) X   No response

43   Party Affiliation

(17) 1   Strong Democrat
(22) 2   Weak Democrat
(7) 3   Independent Democrat
(7) 4   Independent—no leaning
(12) 5   Independent Republican
(18) 6   Weak Republican
(15) 7   Strong Republican
(3) 8   Presidential Republican (Republican nationally, Democrat locally)
(0) 9   Other
(13) X   No response

44   Party Activity

(44) 0   Never active
(29) 1   Active once, not now

COLUMN NO.   ITEM

(12)   2   Active local and state level
(1)   3   Active national level
(15)   4   Active all three levels
(13)   X   No response

45   Party Position

(77)   0   Never held position
(13)   1   Local and state position once, not now
(1)   2   National position once, not now
(4)   3   Local or state position now
(2)   4   National position now
(3)   5   Positions on all three levels once, not now
(1)   6   Positions on all three levels now
(13)   X   No response

46   Holding Public Office

(69)   0   Never held public office
(8)   1   Local or state appointive office
(11)   2   National appointive office (federal)
(5)   3   Appointive office at three levels
(1)   4   Local or state elective office
(1)   5   National elective office (federal)
(1)   6   Elective office at three levels
(2)   7   Both elective and appointive office local or state level
(0)   8   Both elective and appointive office federal level
(3)   9   Both elective and appointive office three levels
(13)   X   No response

47   Candidate for Public Office, Lost the Election

(88)   0   Never been candidate
(8)   1   Candidate local or state level
(2)   2   Candidate federal level
(0)   3   Candidate all three levels
(3)   4   Won the election (see 46, categories 4, 5, 6)
(13)   X   No response

48   Campaigning

(43)   0   Never campaigned
(11)   1   Local or state campaign less than 25 hours
(4)   2   Federal campaign less than 25 hours
(1)   3   Three levels less than 25 hours

COLUMN NO.   ITEM

        (11) 4 Local or state campaign 25–100 hours
        (5) 5 Federal campaign 25–100 hours
        (11) 6 Three levels 25–100 hours
        (0) 7 Local or state campaign more than 100 hours
        (5) 8 Federal campaign more than 100 hours
        (10) 9 Three levels more than 100 hours
        (13) X No response

49   Attendance at Party Meetings

        (37) 0 Never attend
        (17) 1 Seldom (less than 1 per year) local and state level
        (5) 2 Occasionally (1 to 3 per year) local and state level
        (3) 3 Regularly (4 or more per year) local and state level
        (3) 4 Seldom federal level
        (4) 5 Occasionally federal level
        (1) 6 Regularly federal level
        (8) 7 Seldom all three levels
        (18) 8 Occasionally all three levels
        (5) 9 Regularly all three levels
        (13) X No response

50   Strategy Meetings and Caucuses

        (71) 0 Never attend
        (6) 1 Occasionally local and state level
        (0) 2 Regularly local and state level
        (5) 3 Occasionally federal level
        (1) 4 Regularly federal level
        (5) 5 Occasionally all three levels
        (2) 6 Regularly all three levels
        (11) 7 Attended once but not now
        (13) X No response

51   Political Contributions in Five Years

        (29) 0 None
        (17) 1 1–2
        (17) 2 3–4
        (14) 3 5–6
        (7) 4 7–8
        (7) 5 9–10

COLUMN NO.   ITEM

          (3) 6 11–12
          (1) 7 13–14
          (3) 8 15–16
          (3) 9 Over 16
          (13) X No response

52   Political Level of Contribution

          (29) 0 None
          (10) 1 Local and state
          (10) 2 Congressional
          (17) 3 National campaign
          (28) 4 All three
          (6) 5 Organization's own political fund
          (14) X No response

53   Average Amount of Contribution

          (29) 0 None
          (19) 1 Less than $25
          (14) 2 $25–49
          (14) 3 $50–99
          (18) 4 $100–199
          (2) 5 $200–299
          (1) 6 $300–399
          (0) 7 $400–499
          (3) 8 $500 and up
          (14) X No reponse

54   Raising Political Funds

          (59) 0 Never
          (4) 1 Finance committee, local and state level
                 (includes solicitation)
          (10) 2 Finance committee, federal level (includes
                 solicitation)
          (8) 3 Finance committee, three levels (includes
                 solicitation)
          (8) 4 Solicitation of personal acquaintances
          (1) 5 Solicitation door-to-door
          (11) 6 Money raising through own pressure group
          (13) X No response

55   Role to Government

          (0) 1 Information liaison only
          (4) 2 Information and action liaison only

COLUMN NO.   ITEM

 (18) 3 Liaison and advocate before Congress only
 (84) 4 Liaison and advocate before Congress and
      executive agencies
 (1) 5 Liaison and advocate before executive
      agencies only
 (3) 6 Strategist lobbyist
 (0) 7 Expert consultant
 (4) X No response

56 Role to Employer

 (19) 0 Trade association executive
 (9) 1 Officer of the organization
 (12) 2 Legislative relations staff
 (21) 3 Legistlative and executive relations staff
 (18) 4 Washington representative
 (10) 5 Lawyer in large law firm
 (14) 6 Free-lance lawyer
 (6) 7 General counsel in organization
 (2) 8 Public relations consultant
 (3) 9 Lobbyist entrepreneur
 (0) X No response

57 Method of Reporting to Employer

 (0) 0 No report required
 (27) 1 Informal report, signal check only
 (15) 2 Report to supervisor or staff meeting
 (8) 3 Report to board or annual meeting
 (2) 4 Write periodical newsletter
 (5) 5 Newsletter plus reports to supervisor
 (33) 6 Newsletter plus reports to board and
      meeting
 (4) 7 Reports to supervisor and board and
      meeting
 (9) 8 All three (newsletter, supervisor, board)
 (11) X No response

58 Method of Payment for Services

 (0) 0 None at all
 (31) 1 Annual salary only
 (0) 2 Monthly or weekly salary only
 (2) 3 Contract
 (20) 4 Fee only
 (0) 5 Expenses only

COLUMN NO. ITEM

       (2) 6 Fee plus salary
       (40) 7 Salary and expenses
       (9) 8 Fee and expenses
       (10) X No response

59   Income before Taxes

       (0) 0 Under $2,500
       (2) 1 $2,500–4,999
       (6) 2 $5,000–7,499
       (8) 3 $7,500–9,999
       (22) 4 $10,000–14,999
       (21) 5 $15,000–19,999
       (13) 6 $20,000–24,999
       (24) 7 $25,000–49,999
       (5) 8 $50,000 and over
       (13) X No response

60   Percentage of Income from Clients

       (1) 0 Not appropriate
       (5) 1 Less than 5
       (7) 2 5 to 20
       (8) 3 20 to 35
       (2) 4 35 to 49
       (2) 5 50 approximately
       (6) 6 51 to 65
       (7) 7 65 to 80
       (11) 8 80 to 95
       (49) 9 Above 95
       (16) X No response

61   Locus of Policy Leadership

       (10) 0 No policy leadership or not appropriate
       (5) 1 Primarily by respondent
       (3) 2 Primarily by staff
       (6) 3 Primarily by staff executive
       (21) 4 Primarily by board
       (5) 5 Primarily by executive committee
       (2) 6 Primarily by annual meeting or convention
       (10) 7 By staff plus board
       (42) 8 By board or executive committee
                      and annual meeting
       (1) 9 Policy-making diffused to several centers
       (9) X No response

COLUMN NO.   ITEM

62   R's Role in Policy-Making

(7)   0   No role in policy
(9)   1   Most important factor in policy
(41)   2   Substantial share in policy
(20)   3   Policy role confined to strategy and tactics
(28)   4   Minor role involving occasional sugges-
              tions which are sometimes followed
(9)   X   No response

63   Locus of Strategy Planning

(0)   0   No strategy mapped
(16)   1   Personal operation—strategy mapped by R
(35)   2   Strategy mapped in staff conference or
              committee
(6)   3   Strategy mapped in consultation with other
              lobby groups
(9)   4   Strategy mapped by board or committee of
              board
(4)   5   Strategy mapped by staff executive
(19)   6   Strategy mapped by staff and board
(3)   7   Strategy mapped by executive and board
(10)   8   Strategy mapped by staff and other lobby
              groups
(5)   9   Strategy mapped three or more places
(7)   X   No response

64   R's Role in Strategy Planning

(0)   0   No role in strategy
(57)   1   One of the staff in strategy sessions
(43)   2   Primary responsibility for strategy
(7)   3   Sole strategy planner
(7)   X   No response

65   Freedom to Determine Own Tactics
(2)   0   No freedom
(9)   1   Some freedom
(37)   2   Considerable freedom
(57)   3   Complete freedom
(9)   X   No response

66   Most Important Source of Inside Information

First   *Second*

(4)   0   No special sources   (1)

First			*Second*
(33)	1	Congressional staff members	(28)
(23)	2	Members of Congress	(18)
(4)	3	Journalists	(3)
(16)	4	People in administrative branch	(18)
(7)	5	Other lobbyists	(6)
(1)	6	Fellow staff members	(3)
(7)	7	Publications	(5)
(3)	8	Inside own industry	(2)
(1)	9	Fellow club members	(3)
(15)	X	No response	(27)

67   Second Most Important Source of Inside
Information (see 66)

68   Most Important Use of Contacts

First			*Second*
(1)	0	No use for contacts	(1)
(9)	1	Learning where to get information	(16)
(61)	2	Passing of tips or information (includes building a trusting relationship)	(15)
(13)	3	Gaining access or arranging appointments	(26)
(0)	4	Favors	(1)
(5)	5	Obtaining favorable decisions	(13)
(2)	6	Useful, but nothing specific mentioned	(1)
(1)	7	Advice	(4)
(9)	8	Work together to solve problems	(18)
(13)	X	No response	(19)

69   Second Most Important Use of Contacts (see 68)

70   Best Way of Developing Contacts

First			*Second*
(4)	0	Do not develop contacts	(3)
(51)	1	Working together on problems	(18)
(30)	2	Calling on them on own initiative	(20)
(1)	3	Testifying before hearings	(3)
(1)	4	Giving parties or going to parties	(4)
(0)	5	Proffering gifts	(0)
(4)	6	Common interests	(4)

COLUMN NO.   ITEM

First   *Second*

(2) 7 Doing favors   (2)
(5) 8 Through friends or co-workers   (21)
(1) 9 Fellow club members   (9)
(15) X No response   (30)

71   Second Best Way of Developing Contacts (see 70)

72   Best Locus for Contacts

First   *Second*

(0) 0 Have no contacts   (0)
(28) 1 Staffs of committees   (33)
(7) 2 Staffs of members of Congress   (11)
(27) 3 Staffs of executive agencies   (22)
(1) 4 The press corps   (0)
(1) 5 Other lobbyists   (1)
(26) 6 Members of Congress themselves   (17)
(10) 7 Everywhere (no specific location)   (0)
(14) X No response   (30)

73   Second Best Locus for Contacts (see 72)

74   Contacts among Party Officials

(58) 0 None at all
(39) 1 Yes, few
(4) 2 Yes, many
(13) X No response

75   Organization Presents Views before Platform
      Committees

(62) 0 No
(14) 1 Yes, sometimes
(15) 2 Yes, always
(4) 3 Not appropriate
(11) 4 Through joint presentation with other
         groups
(8) X No response

76   Importance of Parties in Policy (not asked of all
      R's—see 46 and 47 of Card 2)

(1) 0 None whatsoever
(31) 1 Very little importance
(8) 2 Moderate importance
(10) 3 Considerable importance

COLUMN NO. ITEM

(2) 4 Don't know
(62) X No response

77 Work Both Sides of Aisle

(1) 0 No
(1) 1 Yes, sometimes
(7) 2 Yes, usually
(93) 3 Yes, always
(12) X No response

78 Importance of Joint Activity with Other Lobby Organizations

(5) 0 None whatsoever
(9) 1 Slight importance
(16) 2 Moderate importance
(48) 3 Considerable importance
(12) 4 More important than any other factor
(10) 5 Probably important but we don't do it
(4) 6 Important on some bills, unimportant on others
(10) X No response

79 Opponents

(12) 0 Have few or no opponents
(23) 1 From competing kinds of business or union
(19) 2 From opposing economic forces
(8) 3 From an executive department
(2) 4 From members of Congress
(19) 5 From opposite political faiths
(15) 6 Shifts too much from case to case for one to stand out
(16) X No response

80 Basis of Estimating Opponent's Strength (not asked of all R's)

(16) 0 Never estimate
(4) 1 Financial resources
(3) 2 Size of membership
(5) 3 Dedication of adherents
(10) 4 Feedback from contacts
(20) 5 Votes they command in Congress
(2) 6 Newspaper reports
(8) 7 Varies too much from case to case to tell
(7) 8 Other
(39) X No response

Lobbyist Study Code:
Card Number Two

COLUMN NO.   ITEM

1–3   Identification Code

4   Checking on Alignment on Bills
    (25) 0 No, not much
    (41) 1 Yes, informally on most bills concerning us
    (6) 2 Yes, keep formal records on important bills
    (29) 3 Yes, close informal check on important bills
    (13) X No response

5   Solicitation of Policy Views
    (24) 0 Never solicited
    (5) 1 Less than once a year
    (11) 2 1 or 2 times a year
    (28) 3 3 to 10 times a year
    (18) 4 11 to 25 times a year
    (14) 5 Ongoing activity
    (14) X No response

6   Nature of Policy Views Solicited
    (23) 0 None solicited
    (13) 1 Only information to which organization has unique access
    (48) 2 Only views on issues on which organization has strong opinions
    (10) 3 On a wide range of policy issues
    (3) 4 Confidential consultation with intimate friends
    (1) 5 Occasionally ask advice on strategy or "feel you out"
    (16) X No response

8   Percentage of Time Spent Calling on Members of Congress (see 7, opposite page)

9   Percentage of Time Spent Calling on Others (see 7)

10   Percentage of Time Spent Chatting with People on the Hill (see 7)

11   Percentage of Time Spent Doing Research (see 7)

COLUMN NO.   ITEM

7   Percentage of Time Spent Working in Own Office

Office	Per Cent of Time		Members of Congress	Others	Hill	Research	Travel	Entertainment
(0)	0	None	7	5	21	39	31	32
(1)	1	1–5	50	40	48	17	21	50
(1)	2	6–10	18	32	13	11	16	9
(12)	3	11–25	20	17	15	17	24	7
(13)	4	26–40	5	6	2	11	5	2
(34)	5	41–60	...	...	1	4	3	...
(17)	6	61–75	...	...	...	1	...	...
(12)	7	76–90	...	...	...	...	...	...
(9)	8	91–95	...	...	...	...	...	...
(1)	9	96–100	...	...	...	...	...	...
(14)	X	No response	14	14	14	14	14	14

COLUMN NO.	ITEM
12	Percentage of Time Spent Traveling at Grass-Roots (see 7)
13	Percentage of Time Spent Entertaining Important People (see 7)
14	Approach Emphasized to Convince Public Officials

(0) 0 No approach emphasized
(65) 1 Personal presentation of arguments
(11) 2 Research results
(6) 3 Testifying at hearings
(16) 4 Contact by constituent or friend
(1) 5 Political activity
(1) 6 Letter-writing or telegram campaigns
(1) 7 Public relations campaigns
(13) X No response

15   Rating of Personal Presentation of Arguments (10=P)

0	1	2	3	4	5	6	7	8	9	10	X
(2	1	3	1	2	7	2	1	15	7	58	15)

16   Rating of Presenting Research Results (10=P)

0	1	2	3	4	5	6	7	8	9	10	X
(5	2	1	7	2	9	5	3	17	13	35	15)

17   Rating of Testifying at Hearings (10=P)

0	1	2	3	4	5	6	7	8	9	10	X
(3	3	3	6	3	24	9	3	15	6	24	15)

18   Rating of Contact by Constituent (10=P)

0	1	2	3	4	5	6	7	8	9	10	X
(14	3	6	8	2	11	7	4	8	12	24	15)

19   Rating of Contact by Close Friend (10=P)

0	1	2	3	4	5	6	7	8	9	10	X
(26	5	8	13	3	15	6	6	6	5	5	16)

20   Rating of Entertaining for an Evening (10=P)

0	1	2	3	4	5	6	7	8	9	10	X
(47	15	14	7	4	4	1	5	2	0	0	15)

COLUMN NO.   ITEM

21   Rating of Giving a Party (10=P)

0	1	2	3	4	5	6	7	8	9	10	X
(56	14	11	3	5	7	0	1	2	0	0	15)

22   Rating of Contribution of Political Money (10=P)

0	1	2	3	4	5	6	7	8	9	10	X
(58	5	5	8	7	4	2	1	3	4	2	15)

23   Rating of Campaign Work (10=P)

0	1	2	3	4	5	6	7	8	9	10	X
(54	6	7	6	3	5	1	5	5	1	6	15)

24   Rating of Letter or Telegram Campaign (10=P)

0	1	2	3	4	5	6	7	8	9	10	X
(20	6	6	5	7	19	1	7	17	4	7	15)

25   Rating of Publicizing Voting Records (10=P)

0	1	2	3	4	5	6	7	8	9	10	X
(49	8	12	5	4	8	2	4	2	2	2	16)

26   Rating of Public Relations Campaign (10=P)

0	1	2	3	4	5	6	7	8	9	10	X
(21	2	2	3	2	15	2	11	17	5	17	17)

27   Rating of Direct Bribery (10=P)

0	1	2	3	4	5	6	7	8	9	10	X
(98	0	0	0	0	0	0	0	0	0	1	15)

28   Rating of Assistance from Other Organizations (10=P)

0	1	2	3	4	5	6	7	8	9	10	X
(12	5	0	6	3	13	4	13	12	11	20	15)

29   R's Specialty in Lobbying

          (55) 0   None
          (0) 1   Research
          (0) 2   Preparing arguments
          (0) 3   Personal advocacy
          (3) 4   Testifying at hearings
          (1) 5   Strategy
          (2) 6   Public relations

COLUMN NO.   ITEM

         (1) 7 Knowledge of whom to see to get action
         (36) 8 Specialized subject matter
         (16) X No response

30   Trait Most Characteristic of Lobbyists (not asked of all R's)

         (31) 0 None
         (31) 1 Ability to interact well with people
         (1) 2 Knowledge of the political process
         (9) 3 Intelligence or well-educated
         (2) 4 Ability to "roll with the punches"
         (8) 5 Skill with words
         (3) 6 Manipulative ability
         (1) 7 Patience
         (5) 8 Other
         (23) X No response

31   Learning Lobbyist Skills (not asked of all R's)

         (11) 0 No training
         (3) 1 Law training
         (2) 2 Political experience
         (2) 3 Specialized knowledge of an industry or subject
         (45) 4 Experience working in Washington
         (51) X No response

32   Sense of Profession or Camaraderie (not asked of all R's)

         (53) 0 None or almost none
         (3) 1 Only as a by-product of the law profession
         (17) 2 Only among those who collaborate
         (3) 3 Feel that professional standards should be adopted
         (16) 4 General feeling of goodwill, even among opponents
         (22) X No response

33   Demand for Lobbyists (not asked of all R's)

         (13) 0 Don't know
         (23) 1 Plenty of men seeking positions
         (13) 2 Difficult to find good lobbyists
         (65) X No response

34 R's Feelings about Policy Line He Espouses

(0) 0 Don't like organization's policy line
(6) 1 It's just a job—no commitment
(9) 2 Weakly committed
(48) 3 Mildly committed
(36) 4 Strongly committed
(3) 5 R makes the policy
(12) X No response

35 Policy Position Factor in Decision to Represent

(26) 0 Not at all
(47) 1 Yes, partially
(26) 2 Yes, very much so
(3) 3 R makes the policy
(12) X No response

36 Periodic Case for Continuation Required (not appropriate for all R's)

(59) 0 None at all
(10) 1 Necessary to keep the members informed
(5) 2 Question comes up, but no difficulty in convincing
(5) 3 Considerable difficulty in maintaining position
(2) 4 Clients come and go as their cases are completed
(2) 5 Most clients satisfied but lose a few
(31) X No response

37 Financing Lobby Operation (not appropriate for all (R's)

(5) 1 Solely by contributions
(48) 2 Solely by dues
(4) 3 Combination of dues and contributions
(17) 4 Charge fees
(14) 5 Budgetary appropriation
(0) 6 Conventions or other money-raising functions
(4) 7 Combination of dues and other money-raising functions
(1) 8 Other
(1) 9 Sell subscriptions
(20) X No response

COLUMN NO.   ITEM

38   Competition for Clients (not asked of all R's)

(9) 0 None at all
(9) 1 Undercover competition—moderate
(3) 2 Overt competition—moderate
(0) 3 Desperate struggle
(1) 4 Professional ethics forbids solicitation
(5) 5 Don't really know
(87) X No response

39   Most Successful Lobby Organization

(20) 0 None
(14) 1 Own organization
(15) 2 A major opponent
(7) 3 A large membership business organization
(12) 4 A large membership farm organization
(13) 5 A large membership labor organization
(13) 6 A specialized organization
(1) 7 Other
(1) 8 Changes over time
(4) 9 Executive agencies
(14) X No response

40   Appraisal of Success of Own Organization

Organizational Success   *Personal Success*

(0) 0 Failure   (0)
(6) 1 Poor results   (2)
(25) 2 Moderate results   (30)
(52) 3 Good results   (54)
(6) 4 Resounding success   (3)
(6) 5 Can't measure   (8)
(19) X No response   (17)

41   Appraisal of Personal Success (see 40)

42   Lobbying Bad or Good

(0) 0 Usually bad
(33) 1 Some bad elements in it—generally good
(2) 2 Good if carefully controlled
(5) 3 Good, other qualified approval
(61) 4 Unqualified approval
(13) X No response

COLUMN NO.   ITEM

43   Most Important Benefits of Lobbying

First			Second
(0)	0	None	(0)
(1)	1	Provides free information to Congress	(1)
(35)	2	Provides essential information to Congress	(27)
(47)	3	Congress benefits from arguments and viewpoints	(28)
(1)	4	Prevents bad legislation	(3)
(1)	5	Educates the public	(0)
(3)	6	Insures a fair hearing for all sides	(12)
(4)	7	General (non-specific) benefits to Congress	(4)
(22)	X	No response	(39)

44   Secondary Benefits of Lobbying (see 43)

45   Evils of Lobbying (volunteered response—no specific question)

(3)	0	None
(24)	1	A few corrupt individuals
(2)	2	Pressure tactics
(1)	3	Presents biased viewpoints
(2)	4	Presents biased information
(0)	5	Great waste of time and effort
(0)	6	Prevents much good legislation
(0)	7	Misinforms the public
(0)	8	Evil could be corrected by legislation
(3)	9	Seeks the good of a few, not the many
(2)	P	Public disapprobation of job
(77)	X	No response

46   Predominant Influence in Government

First			Second
(25)	1	President	(7)
(20)	2	Executive branch	(16)
(8)	3	Congress	(19)
(3)	4	Opinion leaders	(3)
(17)	5	Voters	(8)
(1)	6	Lobbying	(5)

COLUMN NO.   ITEM

		First	Second
			Second
(2)	7	Political parties	(5)
(1)	8	Depends on issue	(1)
(37)	X	No response	(50)

47   Second Rank Influence in Government (see 46)

80   Power at the Polls (combination of three judgments of organization's size, use of money, and concern with policies affected by elections which are summed to form the over-all code)

(0)	0	(a) Membership
(1)	1	0 No voters to speak of
(2)	2	1 1–99 voters
(34)	3	2 1,000–5,000 voters
(20)	4	3 5,000–50,000 voters
(14)	5	4 Over 50,000 voters
(22)	6	
(11)	7	(b) Monetary resources for elections
(5)	8	0 Small
(4)	9	1 Ample resources but little disposition to use them
(1)	X	2 Ample resources and readiness to use
		(c) Concern with election outcome
		0 None
		1 Small
		2 Moderate
		3 Great

SELECTED BIBLIOGRAPHY

Sources that deal with the effect of special interests on public policy are so extensive as to defy a comprehensive listing in a volume such as this. In addition to the sources cited in the text, the list includes academic sources which are directly relevant to lobbying and group activity in politics.

Abernathy, Glenn. *Freedom of Association.* Columbia: University of South Carolina Press, 1961.

Acheson, Dean. *A Citizen Looks at Congress.* New York: Harper, 1957.

Adler, Kenneth P., and Bobrow, Davis. "Interest and Influence in Foreign Affairs," *Public Opinion Quarterly,* XX (Spring, 1956), 89–101.

Adorno, Theodore, *et al. The Authoritarian Personality.* New York: Harper, 1950.

Agger, Robert E. "Lawyers in Politics," *Temple Law Quarterly,* XXIX (Summer, 1956), 434–52 (a).

————. "Power Attributions in the Local Community: Theoretical and Research Considerations," *Social Forces,* XXXIV (May, 1956), 322–31 (b).

Almond, Gabriel A. *The American People and Foreign Policy.* New York: Harcourt, Brace, 1950.

————. "Comparative Political Systems," *Journal of Politics,* XVIII (August, 1956), 391–409 (a).

————. "A Comparative Study of Interest Groups and the Political Process," *American Political Science Review*, LII (March, 1958), 270–82.

————. "The Political Attitudes of German Business," *World Politics*, VIII (January, 1956), 157–86 (b).

————, and Coleman, James S., eds. *The Politics of the Developing Areas*. Princeton: Princeton University Press, 1960.

Amrine, Michael. *The Great Decision: The Secret History of the Atomic Bomb*. New York: G. P. Putnam's Sons, 1959.

Annals of the American Academy of Political and Social Science, CCCXIX (September, 1958). Entire issue devoted to pressure groups and lobbies. See also July, 1929; May, 1935; January, 1938; May, 1942; May, 1947; September, 1948.

Bailey, Stephen K. *Congress Makes a Law: The Story behind the Employment Act of 1946*. New York: Columbia University Press, 1950.

Baker, Gladys. *The County Agent*. Chicago: University of Chicago Press, 1939.

Baker, Roscoe. *The American Legion and Foreign Policy*. New York: Bookman Associates, 1954.

Banfield, Edward C. *Political Influence*. New York: Free Press of Glencoe, 1961.

Baratz, Morton. "Corporate Giants and the Power Structure," *Western Political Quarterly*, IX (June, 1956), 406–15.

Bartley, Ernest R. *The Tidelands Oil Controversy*. Austin: University of Texas Press, 1953.

Bauer, Raymond A., Pool, Ithiel de Sola, and Dexter, Lewis Anthony. *American Business and Public Policy: The Politics of Foreign Trade*. New York: Atherton Press, a division of Prentice Hall, 1963.

Beer, Samuel H. "Group Representation in Britain and the United States," *The Annals*, CCCXIX (September, 1958), 130–40.

————. "Pressure Groups and Parties in Britain," *American Political Science Review*, L (March, 1956), 1–23.

————. "The Representation of Interests in British Government: Historical Perspective," *American Political Science Review*, LI (September, 1957), 613–50.

Belknap, George M., "A Method for Analyzing Legislative Behavior," *Midwest Journal of Political Science*, II (November, 1958), 377–402.

Bentley, Arthur F. *The Process of Government*. 2nd ed.; Bloomington, Ind.: The Principia Press, 1949. (The 1st ed. is by The University of Chicago Press, 1908.)

Berelson, Bernard, Lazarsfeld, Paul, and McPhee, William. *Voting*. Chicago: University of Chicago Press, 1954.

Bernstein, Marver. "Political Ideas of Selected American Business Journals," *Public Opinion Quarterly*, XVII (Summer, 1953), 258–67.

Blaisdell, Donald C. *American Democracy under Pressure*. New York: Ronald Press, 1957.

————. *Economic Power and Political Pressures*. Temporary National Economic Committee, Monograph No. 26 (76th Cong., 2d sess.) Washington, D.C.: Government Printing Office, 1941.

————. *Government under Pressure*. New York: Public Affairs Pamphlet, 1942.

————. "Pressure Groups, Foreign Policies, and International Politics," *The Annals*, CCCXIX (September, 1958), 149–57.

Bone, Hugh A. "Political Parties and Pressure Group Politics," *The Annals*, CCCXIX (September, 1958), 73–83.

Bonilla, Frank. "When is Petition Pressure?" *Public Opinion Quarterly*, XX (Spring, 1956), 39–48.

Bonnett, Clarence A. *Employers' Associations in the United States*. New York: Macmillan, 1922.

Boulding, Kenneth. "Decision-Making in the Modern World." In Lyman Bryson, ed. *An Outline of Man's Knowledge of the Modern World*. New York: McGraw-Hill, 1960, pp. 418–42.

Brady, Robert A. *Business as a System of Power*. New York: Columbia University Press, 1943.

Brooks, Robert R. R. *When Labor Organizes*. New Haven: Yale University Press, 1937.

Brown, Bernard E. "Alcohol and Politics in France," *American Political Science Review*, LI (December, 1957), 976–94.

————. "Pressure Politics in France," *Journal of Politics*, XVIII (November, 1956), 702–19.

Brown, MacAlister. "The Demise of State Department Public Opinion Polls: A Study in Legislative Oversight," *Midwest Journal of Political Science*, V (February, 1961), 1–17.

Buchanan, William, Eulau, Heinz, Ferguson, LeRoy C., and Wahlke, John C. "The Legislator as Specialist," *Western Political Quarterly*, XIII (September, 1960), 636–51.

Bunzel, John H. *The American Small Businessman*. New York: Knopf, 1962.

————. "The General Ideology of American Small Business," *Political Science Quarterly*, LXX (March, 1955), 87–102.

Burdette, Franklin L. "Influence of Noncongressional Pressures on Foreign Policy," *The Annals,* CCLXXXIX (September, 1953), 92–99.

———. *Lobbyists in Action: How Strings are Pulled.* Manassas, Va.: National Capitol Publishers, 1950.

Calkins, Fay. *The CIO and the Democratic Party.* Chicago: University of Chicago Press, 1952.

Carey, James B. "Organized Labor in Politics," *The Annals,* CCCXIX (September, 1958), 52–62.

Cater, Douglas. *The Fourth Branch of Government.* Boston: Houghton Mifflin, 1959.

Celler, Emanuel. "Pressure Groups in Congress," *The Annals,* CCCXIX (September, 1958), 1–9.

Chafee, Zechariah, Jr. *Government and Mass Communications.* 2 vols. Chicago: University of Chicago Press, 1947.

Chamberlain, Lawrence. *The President, Congress, and Legislation.* New York: Columbia University Press, 1946.

Chase, Stuart. *Democracy under Pressure.* New York: Twentieth Century Fund, 1945.

Cherington, Paul W., and Gillen, Ralph L. *The Business Representative in Washington.* Washington: The Brookings Institution, 1962.

Childs, Harwood L. *Labor and Capital in National Politics.* Columbus: Ohio State University Press, 1930.

Christie, Richard. "The Likertization of Machiavelli: A Progress Report." Mimeographed, Bureau of Applied Social Research, Columbia University, 1956.

———, Havel, Joan, and Seidenberg, Bernard. "Is the F Scale Irreversible?" *Journal of Abnormal and Social Psychology,* LVI (March, 1958), 143–59.

Christie, Richard, and Merton, Robert K. "Procedures for the Sociological Study of the Values Climate of Medical Schools." In *The Ecology of the Medical Student.* Evanston: Association of American Medical Colleges, 1958. The book also appeared as Part II of the *Journal of Medical Education,* XXXIII (October, 1958).

Cleveland, Alfred S. "NAM: Spokesman for Industry," *Harvard Business Review,* XXVI (May, 1948), 353–71.

———. *Some Political Aspects of Organized Industry.* Unpublished Ph.D. dissertation, Harvard University, 1948.

Cohen, Bernard C. *The Influence of Non-Governmental Groups on Foreign Policy-Making.* Boston: World Peace Foundation, 1959.

Committee on Congress, American Political Science Association. *The Reorganization of Congress.* Washington: Public Affairs Press, 1945.

Committee on Political Parties, American Political Science Association. "Toward a More Responsible Two-Party System," *American Political Science Review,* XLIV (1950), Supplement.

Congressional Quarterly News Features, XV (January 11, 1957).

Congressional Quarterly Weekly Report, XVIII (March 11, 1960).

Cooper, Kent. *The Right to Know: An Exposition of the Evils of News Suppression and Propaganda.* New York: Farrar, 1956.

Coyle, David C. *Conservation: An American Story of Conflict and Accomplishment.* New Brunswick: Rutgers University Press, 1957.

Coyle, Grace L. *Social Process in Organized Groups.* New York: Richard R. Smith, 1930.

Crane, Wilder, Jr. "A Caveat on Roll-Call Studies of Party Voting," *Midwest Journal of Political Science,* IV (August, 1960), 237–49.

_____. "A Test of Effectiveness of Interest-Group Pressures on Legislators," *Southwestern Social Science Quarterly,* (December, 1960) 336–40.

Crawford, Kenneth G. *The Pressure Boys: The Inside Story of Lobbying in America.* New York: Julian Messner, 1939.

Curley, James M. *I'd Do It Again.* Englewood Cliffs: Prentice-Hall, 1957.

Dahl, Robert A. "Business and Politics: A Critical Appraisal of Political Science," *American Political Science Review,* LIII (March, 1959), 1–34.

_____. "The Concept of Power," *Behavioral Science,* II (July, 1957), 201–15.

_____. "A Critique of the Ruling Elite Model," *American Political Science Review,* LII (June, 1958), 463–69.

_____. *Who Governs?* New Haven: Yale University Press, 1961.

_____, and Lindbloom, Charles. *Politics, Economics, and Welfare.* New York: Harper, 1953.

_____, March, James G., and Nasatir, David. "Influence Ranking in the United States Senate." Paper prepared for the annual meeting of the American Political Science Association, Washington, D. C., September, 1956.

Davis, Morris. "Some Neglected Aspects of British Pressure Groups," *Midwest Journal of Political Science,* VII (February, 1963), 42–53.

Dearing, Mary R. *Veterans in Politics: The Story of the GAR.* Baton Rouge: Louisiana State University Press, 1952.

De Grazia, Alfred. "Nature and Prospects of Political Interest Groups," *The Annals,* CCCXIX (September, 1958), 113–22.

Derber, Milton, and Young, Edwin, eds. *Labor and the New Deal.* Madison: University of Wisconsin Press, 1958.

Derge, David. "The Lawyer as Decision-Maker in the American State Legislature," *Journal of Politics,* XXI (August, 1959), 408–33.

De Roos, Robert, and Maass, Arthur A. "The Lobby That Can't Be Licked: Congress and the Army Engineers," *Harper's Magazine,* CXCIX (August, 1949), 21–30.

Deschler, Lewis, Parliamentarian. *Rules of the House of Representatives.* Washington, D. C.: Government Printing Office, 1953.

Detzer, Dorothy. *Appointment on the Hill.* New York: Holt, 1948.

DeVries, Walter. *The Michigan Lobbyist: A Study in the Bases and Perceptions of Effectiveness.* Unpublished Ph. D. dissertation, Department of Political Science, Michigan State University, 1960.

Dexter, Lewis. "The Representative and His District," *Human Organization,* XVI (Spring, 1957), 2–13.

———. "What Do Congressmen Hear: The Mail," *Public Opinion Quarterly,* XX (Spring, 1956), 16–27.

Djordjevic, Jovan. "Interest Groups and the Political System of Yugoslavia." In Henry W. Ehrmann, ed. *Interest Groups on Four Continents.* Pittsburgh: Pittsburgh University Press, 1958, pp. 197–228.

Drury, Allen. *Advise and Consent.* Garden City: Doubleday, 1959.

Duffield, Marcus. *King Legion.* New York: Cape & Smith, 1931.

Ebersole, Luke. *Church Lobbying in the Nation's Capital.* New York: Macmillan, 1951.

Eckstein, Harry. "The Politics of the British Medical Association," *Political Quarterly,* XXVI (October–December, 1955), 345–59.

———. *Pressure Group Politics: The Case of the British Medical Association.* London: Allen & Unwin, 1960.

Edwards, Corwin D. *Big Business and the Policy of Competition.* Cleveland: Western Reserve University Press, 1956.

Ehrmann, Henry W., ed. *Interest Groups on Four Continents.* Pittsburgh: Pittsburgh University Press, 1958 (a).

———. "Les Groupes d'intéret et la Bureaucratie dans les Democraties Occidentales," *Revue Française de Science Politique,* XI (September, 1961), 541–68.

————. *Organized Business in France*. Princeton: Princeton University Press, 1957.

————. "Pressure Groups in France," *The Annals*, CCCXIX (September, 1958), 141–48.

Eldersveld, Samuel. "American Interest Groups: A Survey of Research and Some Implications for Theory and Method." In Henry W. Ehrmann, ed. *Interest Groups on Four Continents*. Pittsburgh: University of Pittsburgh Press, 1958, pp. 173–96.

————, ed. "The Comparative Study of European Pressure Groups." Report of a conference held at the University of Michigan, February 28-March 2, 1957, mimeograph, Department of Political Science, University of Michigan.

Engler, Robert. *The Politics of Oil*. New York: Macmillan, 1961.

Eulau, Heinz. "Career Perspectives of American State Legislators." In Dwaine Marvick, ed. *Political Decision-Makers*. New York: Free Press of Glencoe, 1961.

————, Buchanan, William, Ferguson, LeRoy C., and Wahlke, John C. "The Political Socialization of American State Legislators," *Midwest Journal of Political Science*, III (May, 1959), 188–206.

Eulau, Heinz, Wahlke, John C., Buchanan, William, and Ferguson, LeRoy C. "The Role of the Representative: Some Empirical Observations on the Theory of Edmund Burke," *American Political Science Review*, LIII (September, 1959), 742–56.

Evan, W. M. "Dimensions of Participation in Voluntary Associations," *Social Forces*, XXXVI (December, 1957), 148–53.

Everest, Allan S. *Morgenthau, the New Deal, and Silver: A Story of Pressure Politics*. New York: King's Crown Press, 1950.

Farris, Charles D. "A Method of Determining Ideological Groupings in the Congress," *The Journal of Politics*, XX (May, 1958), 308–38.

Fellman, David. *The Constitutional Right of Association*. Chicago: University of Chicago Press, 1963.

Fenton, John H. *The Catholic Vote*. New Orleans: Hauser Press, 1960.

Finer, S. E. *Anonymous Empire: A Study of the Lobby in Great Britain*. London: Pall Mall Press, 1958.

————. "The Federation of British Industries," *Political Studies*, IV (February, 1956), 61–84.

————. "Interest Groups and the Political Process in Great Britain." In Henry W. Ehrmann, ed. *Interest Groups on Four*

Continents. Pittsburgh: Pittsburgh University Press, 1958, pp. 117–44.

———. "The Political Power of Private Capital," *Sociological Review,* III (December, 1955), 279–94, and IV (July, 1956), 5–30.

Fitzpatrick, Dick. "Public Information Activities of Government," *Public Opinion Quarterly,* XI (Winter, 1947–48), 530–39.

Flynn, Ed. *You're the Boss.* New York: Viking, 1947.

Foss, Phillip O. *Politics and Grass; the Administration of Grazing in the Public Domain.* Seattle: University of Washington Press, 1960.

Foster, H. Schuyler, Jr. "Pressure Groups and Administrative Agencies," *The Annals,* CCXXI (May, 1942), 21–28.

Fowler, Dan C. "How Corrupt is Texas?" *Look,* XXI (July 9, 1957), 21 ff.

Freeman, Edward M. "The Pattern of Pressure," *Sociology and Social Research,* XXXVII (January-February, 1953), 182–88.

Freeman, Howard E., and Showel, Mirris. "Differential Political Influence of Voluntary Associations," *Public Opinion Quarterly,* XV (Winter, 1951–52), 703–14.

Freeman, J. Lieper. "The Bureaucracy in Pressure Politics," *The Annals,* CCCXIX (September, 1958), 10–19.

———. *The Political Process: Executive Bureau–Legislative Committee Relations.* New York: Random House, 1955.

Futor, Norman J. "An Analysis of the Federal Lobbying Act," *Federal Bar Journal,* X (October, 1949), 366–90.

Gable, Richard W. "NAM: Influential Lobby or Kiss of Death?" *Journal of Politics,* XV (May, 1953), 254–73.

———. *A Political Analysis of an Employers' Association, the National Association of Manufacturers.* Unpublished Ph.D. dissertation, Department of Political Science, University of Chicago, 1950.

———. "Political Interest Groups as Policy Shapers," *The Annals,* CCCXIX (September, 1958), 84–93.

Galloway, George B. *Congressional Reorganization Revisited.* College Park: University of Maryland, Bureau of Government Research, 1956.

———. "The Operation of the Legislative Reorganization Act of 1946," *American Political Science Review,* XLV (March, 1951), 41–68.

Garceau, Oliver. "Interest Group Theory in Political Research," *The Annals,* CCCXIX (September, 1958), 104–12.

———. "Organized Medicine Enforces Its Party Line," *Public Opinion Quarterly,* IV (September, 1940), 408–28.

———. *The Political Life of the American Medical Association.* Cambridge: Harvard University Press, 1941.

———. "Research in the Political Process," *American Political Science Review,* XLV (March, 1951), 69–85.

———, and Silverman, Corinne. "A Pressure Group and the Pressured: A Case Report," *American Political Science Review,* XLVIII (September, 1954), 672–91.

Glaser, William A. "Doctors and Politics," *American Journal of Sociology,* LXVI (November, 1960), 230–45.

Goldberg, Arthur J. *AFL-CIO: Labor United.* New York: McGraw-Hill, 1956.

Goode, W. J. "Community within a Community: The Professions," *American Sociological Review,* XXII (April, 1957), 194–200.

Gough, Harrison G. *Manual for the California Psychological Inventory.* Palo Alto: Consulting Psychologists Press, 1957.

Graham, George A. *Morality in American Politics.* New York: Random House, 1952.

Graham, Philip L. "High Cost of Politics: Undue Influence of Special Interests," *National Municipal Review,* XLIV (July, 1955), 346–51.

Graves, W. Brooke. *Administration of the Lobby Registration Provision of the Legislative Reorganization Act of 1946.* Washington, D.C.: Library of Congress, Legislative Reference Service, Government Printing Office, 1949.

Gray, Justin. *The Inside Story of the Legion.* New York: Boni & Gaer, 1948.

Griffith, Ernest S. *Congress: Its Contemporary Role.* 3rd ed.; New York: New York University Press, 1961.

Gross, Bertram M. *The Legislative Struggle: A Study in Social Combat.* New York: McGraw-Hill, 1953.

Gross, Neal, Mason, Ward S., and MacEachern, Alexander W. *Explorations in Role Analysis.* New York: Wiley, 1958.

Guetzkow, Harold, ed. *Simulation in Social Science: Readings.* Englewood Cliffs: Prentice-Hall, 1962.

———. "A Use of Simulation in the Study of Inter-Nation Relations," *Behavioral Science,* IV (July, 1959), 183–91.

Hacker, Andrew. *Politics and the Corporation.* New York: Fund for the Republic, 1958.

Hagan, Charles B. "The Group in a Political Science." In Roland Young, ed. *Approaches to the Study of Politics.* Evanston: Northwestern University Press, 1958, pp. 38–51.

Hale, Robert L. *Freedom Through Law: Public Control of Private Governing Power.* New York: Columbia University Press, 1952.

Hamilton, Walton. *The Politics of Industry*. New York: Knopf, 1957.

Hansen, Orval. "The Federal Lobbying Act: A Reconsideration," *George Washington Law Review*, XXI (April, 1953), 585–602.

Hardin, Charles M. *The Politics of Agriculture: Soil Conservation and the Struggle for Power in Rural America*. Glencoe: Free Press, 1952.

Harding, T. Swann. "Genesis of One 'Government Propaganda Mill,'" *Public Opinion Quarterly*, XI (Summer, 1947), 227–35.

Hardy, Margaret. *The Influence of Organized Labor on the Foreign Policy of the United States*. Liege: Vaillant, 1936.

Harness, Forest A. "Federal Thought Control: A Study in Government by Propaganda," *American Affairs*, Supplement 10 (April, 1948), pp. 3–24.

Heard, Alexander. *The Costs of Democracy*. Chapel Hill: University of North Carolina Press, 1960.

Hecksher, Gunnar. "Group Organization in Sweden," *Public Opinion Quarterly*, III (January, 1939), 130–35.

———, "Interest Groups in Sweden: Their Political Role." In Henry W. Ehrmann, ed. *Interest Groups on Four Continents*. Pittsburgh: Pittsburgh University Press, 1958, pp. 154–72.

———. *Staten Och Organisationerna*. New ed.; Stockholm, 1951.

Heidenheimer, Arnold J. "German Party Finance: The CDU," *American Political Science Review*, LI (June, 1957), 369–85.

Herring, E. Pendleton. *Group Representation Before Congress*. Baltimore: Johns Hopkins University Press, 1929.

———. "Lobbying," *Encyclopedia of the Social Sciences* (Vol. IX). New York: Macmillan, 1942.

———. *Presidential Leadership*. New York: Farrar & Rinehart, 1940.

———. *The Politics of Democracy*. New York: W. W. Norton, 1940.

———, and Hansen, Elisha. "Official Publicity under the New Deal," *The Annals*, CLXXIX (May, 1935), 167–86.

Herter, Christian A. "Our Most Dangerous Lobby [federal bureaucracy]," *Tax Digest*, XXV (October, 1947), 334–35.

Hinshaw, Kenneth. *Farmer in a Business Suit*. New York: Simon & Schuster, 1957.

Hirsch-Weber, Wolfgang. "Some Remarks on Interest Groups in the German Federal Republic." In Henry W. Ehrmann, ed. *Interest Groups on Four Continents*. Pittsburgh: Pittsburgh University Press, 1958, pp. 96–116. The bibliography accompanying this work has citations to a considerable literature in German.

Horn, Robert A. *Groups and the Constitution.* Stanford University Series in History, Economics, and Political Science, Vol. XII. Stanford: Stanford University Press, 1956.

Huitt, Ralph K. "The Congressional Committee: A Case Study," *American Political Science Review,* XLVIII (June, 1954), 340–65.

————. "Democratic Party Leadership in the Senate," *American Political Science Review,* LV (June, 1961), 333–44.

————. "The Morse Committee Assignment Controversy: A Study in Senate Norms," *American Political Science Review,* LI (June, 1957), 313–29.

————. "The Outsider in the Senate: An Alternative Role," *American Political Science Review,* LV (September, 1961), 566–75.

Hunter, Floyd. *Community Power Structure.* Chapel Hill: University of North Carolina Press, 1953.

————. *Top Leadership USA.* Chapel Hill: University of North Carolina Press, 1959.

Hyman, Sidney. *The American President.* New York: Harper, 1954.

Jewell, Malcolm E. "The Senate Republican Policy Committee and Foreign Policy," *Western Political Quarterly,* XII (December, 1959), 966–80.

Jones, Charles O. "Notes on Interviewing Members of the House of Representatives," *Public Opinion Quarterly,* XXIII (Fall, 1959), 404–6.

————. "Representation in Congress: The Case of the House Agriculture Committee," *American Political Science Review,* LV (June, 1961), 358–67.

Katz, Elihu. "The Two-Step Flow of Communication: An Up-To-Date Report on an Hypothesis," *Public Opinion Quarterly,* XXI (Spring, 1957), 61–78.

————, and Lazarsfeld, Paul. *Personal Influence.* Glencoe: Free Press, 1955.

Keefe, William J. "Parties, Partisanship, and Public Policy in the Pennsylvania Legislature," *American Political Science Review,* XLVIII (June, 1954), 450–64.

Kefauver, Estes, and Levin, Jack. *A Twentieth Century Congress.* New York: Duell, Sloan & Pearce, 1947.

Kelley, Stanley, Jr. *Professional Public Relations and Political Power.* Baltimore: Johns Hopkins University Press, 1956.

Kendall, Willmoore. "The Two Majorities," *Midwest Journal of Political Science*, IV (November, 1960), 317–45.

Kennedy, John F. "To Keep the Lobbyist within Bounds," *New York Times Magazine* (February 19, 1956), pp. 11 ff.

———. "When the Executive Fails to Lead," *The Reporter* (September 18, 1958), pp. 14-17.

Kerr, Clark. *Unions and Union Leaders of Their Own Choosing*. New York: Fund for the Republic, 1958.

Kesselman, Louis C. *The Social Politics of FEPC: A Study in Reform Pressure Movements*. Chapel Hill: University of North Carolina Press, 1948.

Key, V. O., Jr. *Politics, Parties and Pressure Groups*. 4th ed.; New York: Thomas Y. Crowell, 1958.

———. *Public Opinion and American Democracy*. New York: Knopf, 1961.

———. *Southern Politics in State and Nation*. New York: Knopf, 1949.

———. "The Veterans and the House of Representatives: A Study of a Pressure Group and Electoral Mortality," *The Journal of Politics*, V (February, 1943), 27–40.

Kile, Orville M. *The Farm Bureau Movement*. New York: Macmillan, 1921.

———. *The Farm Bureau Through Three Decades*. Baltimore: Waverly, 1948.

Kornhauser, Arthur, Sheppard, A. L., Mayer, A. J. *When Labor Votes*. New York: University Books, 1956.

Krusius-Ahrenberg, Lolo. "The Political Power of Economic and Labor-Market Organizations: A Dilemma of Finnish Democracy." In Henry W. Ehrmann, ed. *Interest Groups on Four Continents*. Pittsburgh: Pittsburgh University Press, 1958, pp. 33–59.

Kuroda, Yasumasa. *Political Socialization: Personal Political Orientation of Law Students in Japan*. Unpublished Ph. D. dissertation, Department of Political Science, University of Oregon, 1962.

La Follette, Robert M., Jr. "Some Lobbies Are Good," *New York Times Magazine* (May 16, 1948), pp. 15 ff.

Lane, Edgar. "Interest Groups and Bureaucracy," *The Annals*, CCXCII (March, 1954), 104-10.

———. "Some Lessons from Past Congressional Investigations of Lobbying," *Public Opinion Quarterly*, XIV (Spring, 1950), 14-32.

———. *Statutory Regulation of Lobbying in the United States with Special Reference to the Federal Regulation of Lobbying Act of 1946.* Unpublished Ph.D. dissertation, University of Michigan, 1949.

Lane, Robert E. "Notes on the Theory of the Lobby," *Western Political Quarterly*, II (March, 1949), 154–62.

———. *Political Life: Why People Get Involved in Politics.* Glencoe: Free Press, 1959.

———. *The Regulation of Businessmen.* New Haven: Yale University Press, 1954.

Lasswell, Harold D., and Kaplan, Abraham. *Power and Society: A Framework for Political Inquiry.* New Haven: Yale University Press, 1950.

Latham, Earl. *The Group Basis of Politics: A Study in Basing Point Legislation.* Ithaca: Cornell University Press, 1952.

———. "The Group Basis of Politics: Notes for a Theory," *American Political Science Review*, XLVI (June, 1952), 376–97.

———. *The Politics of Railroad Coordination, 1933-1936.* Cambridge: Harvard University Press, 1959.

Lavau, George E. "Political Pressures by Interest Groups in France." In Henry W. Ehrmann, ed. *Interest Groups on Four Continents.* Pittsburgh: Pittsburgh University Press, 1958, pp. 60–95.

Lazarsfeld, Paul, Berelson, Bernard, and Gaudet, Hazel. *The People's Choice.* New York: Columbia University Press, 1948.

Leiserson, Avery. *Administrative Regulation: A Study in Representation of Interests.* Chicago: University of Chicago Press, 1942.

———. "Organized Labor as a Pressure Group," *The Annals*, CLXXIV (March, 1951), 108–17.

———. "Problems of Representation in the Government of Private Groups," *The Journal of Politics*, XI (August, 1949), 566–77.

Lenhart, Robert F., and Schriftgiesser, Karl. "Management in Politics," *The Annals*, CCCXIX (September, 1958), 32–40.

Lipset, Seymour Martin, Trow, Martin, and Coleman, James S. *Union Democracy.* Glencoe: Free Press, 1956.

Lockard, W. Duane. "Legislative Politics in Connecticut," *American Political Science Review*, XLVIII (March, 1954), 166–73.

Logan, Edward B., ed. "Lobbying," *The Annals*, CXLIV (July, 1929), 1–91.

Long, Norton E. "The Local Community as an Ecology of Games," *American Journal of Sociology*, LXIV (November, 1958), 251–61.

Lorwin, Lewis L. *The American Federation of Labor.* Washington: The Brookings Institution, 1933.

Lubin, Joseph D. *Legislative Oversight of Publicity and Propaganda in Selected Federal Agencies.* Unpublished Master's thesis, University of California, June, 1950.

Luce, Duncan R., and Rogow, Arnold A. "A Game Theoretic Analysis of Congressional Power Distributions for a Stable Two-Party System," *Behavioral Science,* I (April, 1956), 83–95.

Lundberg, Ferdinand. *America's Sixty Families.* New York: Vanguard, 1937.

McCamy, Joseph L. *Government Publicity: Its Practice in Federal Administration.* Chicago: University of Chicago Press, 1939.

McConaughy, John B. "Certain Personality Factors of State Legislators in South Carolina," *American Political Science Review,* XLIV (December, 1950), 897–903.

McConnell, Grant. "The Conservation Movement—Past and Present," *Western Political Quarterly,* VII (September, 1954), 463–78.

———. *The Decline of Agrarian Democracy.* Berkeley: University of California Press, 1953.

———. "The Spirit of Private Government," *American Political Science Review,* LII (September, 1958), 754–70.

McCune, Wesley. "Farmers in Politics," *The Annals,* CCCXIX (September, 1958), 41–51.

———. *The Farm Bloc.* Garden City: Doubleday, Doran & Co., 1943.

———. *Who's Behind Our Farm Policy?* New York: Praeger, 1956.

McKean, Dayton D. *Party and Pressure Politics.* Boston: Houghton Mifflin, 1949.

———. *Pressures on the Legislature of New Jersey.* New York: Columbia University Press, 1938.

Mackenzie, W. J. M. "Pressure Groups in British Government," *British Journal of Sociology,* VI (June, 1955), 133–48.

———. "Pressure Groups: The 'Conceptual Framework,'" *Political Studies,* III (October, 1955), 247–55.

MacRae, Duncan Jr. *Dimensions of Congressional Voting: A Statistical Study of the House of Representatives in the Eighty-first Congress.* Berkeley: University of California Press, 1958.

———, and Price, Hugh D. "Scale Positions and 'Power' in the Senate," *Behavioral Science,* IV (July, 1959), 212–18.

Maass, Arthur. *Muddy Waters*. Cambridge: Harvard University Press, 1951.

Macridis, Roy C. "Interest Groups in Comparative Analysis," *The Journal of Politics*, XXIII (February, 1961), 25–45.

March, James G. "Introduction to the Theory and Measurement of Influence," *American Political Science Review*, XLIX (June, 1955), 431–51.

————. "Measurement Concepts in the Theory of Influence," *Journal of Politics*, XIX (May, 1957), 202–26.

Masland, John W. "Pressure Groups and American Foreign Policy," *Public Opinion Quarterly*, VI (Spring, 1942), 115–22.

Mason, Alpheus T. "Business Organized as Power: The New Imperium in Imperio," *American Political Science Review*, XLIV (June, 1950), 323–42.

Masters, Nicholas A. "Committee Assignments in the House of Representatives," *American Political Science Review*, LV (June, 1961), 345–57.

————. "The Politics of Union Endorsement of Candidates in the Detroit Area," *Midwest Journal of Political Science*, I (August, 1957), 136–50.

Matthews, Donald R. "The Folkways of the United States Senate: Conformity to Group Norms and Legislative Effectiveness," *American Political Science Review*, LIII (December, 1959), 1064–89.

————. "Patterns of Influence in the U.S. Senate: Five Approaches." Paper prepared for the annual meeting of the American Political Science Association, New York, September, 1960 (a).

————. *The Social Background of Political Decision-Makers*. New York: Random House, 1954.

————. "United States Senators and the Class Structure," *Public Opinion Quarterly*, XVIII (Spring, 1954), 5–22.

————. *U.S. Senators and Their World*. Chapel Hill: University of North Carolina Press, 1960 (b).

Meller, Norman. "Legislative Behavior Research," *Western Political Quarterly*, XIII (March, 1960), 131–53.

Meynaud, Jean. "Contribution à l'analyse des Groupes d'intérets dans la vie Politique Française," *Revue de l'Institute Sociologique* (Solvay) (1956), pp. 225–56.

————. "Les groupes d'intéret et l'Administration en France," *Revue Française de Science Politique*, VII (1957), 573–93.

————. *Les Groupes de Pression en France*. Paris: A. Colin, 1958.

Milbrath, Lester W. "Lobbying as a Communication Process," *Public Opinion Quarterly*, XXIV (Spring, 1960), 33–53 (a).
———. "Measuring the Personalities of Lobbyists." Mimeographed, Political Science Department, Northwestern University, April, 1960 (b).
———. *The Motivations and Characteristics of Political Contributors: North Carolina General Election, 1952.* Unpublished Ph.D. dissertation, Department of Political Science, University of North Carolina, 1956.
———. "The Political Party Activity of Washington Lobbyists," *Journal of Politics*, XX (May, 1958), 339–52.
———. "Predispositions Toward Political Contention," *Western Political Quarterly*, XIII (March, 1960), 5–18.
———, and Klein, Walter W. "Personality Correlates of Political Participation," *Acta Sociologica*, VI, fasc. 1–2 (1962), 53–66.
Milburn, Josephine F., and Cole, Taylor. "Bibliographical Material on Political Parties and Pressure Groups in Australia, New Zealand, and South Africa," *American Political Science Review*, LI (March, 1957), 199–219.
Miller, Merle H. "Ethical Problems in Lobbying for Legislation," *Tax Law Review*, VIII (1952), 19–33.
Millett, John H. "British Interest-Group Tactics: A Case Study," *Political Science Quarterly*, LXXII (March, 1957), 71–82.
———. "The Role of an Interest Group Leader in the House of Commons," *Western Political Quarterly*, IX (December, 1956), 915–26.
Millis, Harry A., and Montgomery, Royal E. *Organized Labor.* New York: McGraw-Hill, 1945.
Mills, C. Wright. *The New Men of Power: America's Labor Leaders.* New York: Harcourt, Brace, 1948.
———. *The Power Elite.* New York: Oxford, 1956.
Mitchell, William C. "The Ambivalent Social Status of the American Politician," *Western Political Quarterly*, XII (September, 1959), 683–98.
———. "Occupational Role Strains: The American Elective Public Official," *Administrative Science Quarterly*, III (September, 1958), 210–28.
Monypenny, Phillip. "Political Science and the Study of Groups," *Western Political Quarterly*, VII (June, 1954), 183–201.
Nadel, S. F. *The Theory of Social Structure.* Glencoe: Free Press, 1951.
Neustadt, Richard E. "Presidency and Legislation: The Growth of Central Clearance," *American Political Science Review*, XLVIII (September, 1954), 641–71.

————. "Presidency and Legislation: Planning the President's Program," *American Political Science Review*, XLIX (December, 1955), 980–1021.

Odegard, Peter H. "A Group Basis of Politics: A New Name for an Ancient Myth," *Western Political Quarterly*, XI (September, 1958), 689–702.

————. *Pressure Politics: The Story of the Anti-Saloon League.* Boulder: University of Colorado Press, 1928.

————, ed. *Religion and Politics.* New York: Oceana, 1960.

Palamountain, J. C. *The Politics of Distribution.* Cambridge: Harvard University Press, 1955.

Patterson, Samuel C. "Patterns of Interpersonal Relations in a State Legislative Group: The Wisconsin Assembly," *Public Opinion Quarterly*, XXI (Spring, 1957), 101–9.

————. "The Role of the Lobbyist: The Case of Oklahoma," *Journal of Politics*, XXV (February, 1963), 72–92.

Perlman, Selig. *A Theory of the Labor Movement.* New York: Macmillan, 1928.

Pinner, Frank, Jacobs, Paul, and Selznik, Philip. *Old Age and Political Behavior.* Berkeley: University of California Press, 1959.

Political Quarterly, XXIX, No. 1 (January–March, 1958), "Special Number—Pressure Groups in Britain."

Polsby, Nelson W. "How to Study Community Power: The Pluralist Alternative," *The Journal of Politics*, XXII (August, 1960), 474–84.

————. "The Sociology of Community Power: A Reassessment," *Social Forces*, XXXVII (March, 1959), 232–36 (a).

————. "Three Problems in the Analysis of Community Power," *American Sociological Review*, XXIV (December, 1959), 796–803 (b).

Pool, Ithiel de Sola, Keller, Suzanne, and Bauer, Raymond A. "The Influence of Foreign Travel on Political Attitudes of American Businessmen," *Public Opinion Quarterly*, XX (Spring, 1956), 161–75.

Potter, Allen. "The Equal Pay Campaign Committee: A Case-Study of a Pressure Group," *Political Studies*, V (February, 1957), 49–64.

————. *Organized Groups in British National Politics*, London: Faber & Faber, 1961.

————. "Politics, Pressure Groups and Public Relations," *Public Relations*, X (July, 1958), 22–30.

President's Commission on Campaign Costs. *Final Report, Financ-*

ing Presidential Campaigns. Washington, D.C.: Government Printing Office, April, 1962.

Quisenberry, Bruce. "What's Wrong with Government Information?" *Public Personnel Review,* XIII (April, 1952), 60–65.

Rice, Stuart A. *Farmers and Workers in American Politics.* New York: Columbia University Press, 1924.

Riggs, Fred. *Pressures on Congress. A Study of the Repeal of Chinese Exclusion.* New York: Columbia University, King's Crown Press, 1950.

Riker, William H. "A Test of the Adequacy of the Power Index," *Behavioral Science,* IV (April, 1959), 120–31.

———. "The Paradox of Voting and Congressional Rules for Voting on Amendments," *American Political Science Review,* LII (June, 1958), 349–65.

Robinson, James A. *Congress and Foreign Policy-Making.* Homewood, Ill.: Dorsey Press, 1962.

———. "Decision-Making in the House Rules Committee," *Administrative Science Quarterly,* III (June, 1958), 73–86.

———. *The Monroney Resolution: Congressional Initiative in Foreign Policy Making.* New York: Henry Holt, 1959.

———. "Survey Interviewing among Members of Congress," *Public Opinion Quarterly,* XXIV (Spring, 1960), 127–38.

Rolih, Max F. *The St. Lawrence Seaway and Power Project: A Study of Pressure Groups in Action.* Unpublished Master's thesis, University of California, 1954.

Rosenblum, Victor G. "How to Get into TV: The FCC and Miami's Channel 10." In Alan Westin, ed. *The Uses of Power* New York: Harcourt, Brace, 1962.

Rossiter, Clinton. *The American Presidency.* New York: Harcourt, Brace, 1956.

Rosten, L. C. *The Washington Correspondents.* New York: Harcourt, Brace, 1937.

Rothman, Stanley. "Systematic Political Theory: Observations on the Group Approach," *American Political Science Review,* LIV (March, 1960), 15–33.

Rutherford, M. Louise. *The Influence of the American Bar Association on Public Opinion and Legislation.* Philadelphia: The Foundation Press, 1937.

Schattschneider, E. E. *Party Government.* New York: Farrar & Rinehart, 1942.

———. *Politics, Pressures and the Tariff.* New York: Prentice-Hall, 1935.

———. "Pressure Groups vs. Political Parties," *The Annals,* CCLIX (September, 1948), 17–23.

————. *The Semi-Sovereign People*. New York: Holt, Rinehart & Winston, 1961.

Schettler, Nancy F. *The Influence of an Interest Group on Federal Appropriations: A Case Study of the American Farm Bureau Federation*. Unpublished Master's thesis, University of California, 1950.

Schlesinger, Joseph A. "Lawyers and American Politics: A Clarified View," *Midwest Journal of Political Science*, I (May, 1957), 26–39.

Schmidhauser, John R. *The Supreme Court: Its Politics, Personalities, and Procedures*. New York: Holt, Rinehart, Winston, 1960.

Schriftgiesser, Karl. *The Lobbyists: The Art and Business of Influencing Lawmakers*. Boston: Little, Brown, 1951.

Selznick, Philip M. *T.V.A. and the Grass Roots*. Berkeley: University of California Press, 1949.

Shils, Edward A. "The Legislator and His Environment," *University of Chicago Law Review*, XXVIII (1951), 571–84.

Silverman, Corinne. "The Legislator's View of the Legislative Process," *Public Opinion Quarterly*, XVIII (Summer, 1954), 180–90.

Smigel, E. O. "Interviewing a Legal Elite: The Wall Street Lawyer," *American Journal of Sociology*, LXIV (September, 1958), 159–64.

Smith, T. V. *The Legislative Way of Life*. Chicago: University of Chicago Press, 1940.

Somit, Albert, and Tanenhaus, Joseph. "The Veteran in the Electoral Process: The House of Representatives," *Journal of Politics*, XIX (May, 1957), 184–201.

Sprout, Harold H. "Pressure Groups and Foreign Policies," *The Annals*, CLXXIX (May, 1935), 114–23.

Stedman, Murray S. "The Group Interpretation of Politics," *Public Opinion Quarterly*, XVII (Summer, 1953), 218–29.

————. "Pressure Groups and the American Tradition," *The Annals*, CCCXIX (September, 1958), 123–29.

Steiner, George A. *Government's Role in Economic Life*. New York: McGraw-Hill, 1953.

Stephan, Frederick F., and McCarthy, Philip J. *Sampling Opinions: An Analysis of Survey Procedure*. New York: Wiley, 1958.

Stewart, J. D. *British Pressure Groups: Their Role in Relation to The House of Commons*. New York: Oxford University Press, 1958.

Surrey, Stanley S. "The Congress and the Tax Lobbyist—How

Special Tax Provisions Get Enacted," *Harvard Law Review*, LXX, No. 7 (May, 1957), 1145–82.

Sussman, Leila. "Mass Political Letter Writing in America: The Growth of an Institution," *Public Opinion Quarterly*, XXIII (Summer, 1959), 203–12.

Sutton, Francis X., Harris, Seymour E., Kaysen, Carl, and Tobin, James. *The American Business Creed*. Cambridge: Harvard University Press, 1956.

Taft, Philip. *The Structure and Government of Labor Unions*. Cambridge: Harvard University Press, 1954.

Taylor, Richard W. "Arthur F. Bentley's Political Science," *Western Political Quarterly*, V (June, 1952), 214–30.

Taylor, Tim, and Christian, Frederick. "Rumors, Gossip and Lobbies," *Cosmopolitan* (May, 1958), 35–39.

Toffler, Al. "How Congressmen Make Up Their Minds," *Redbook* (February, 1962), pp. 56–57, 126–31.

Tompkins, Dorothy C. *Congressional Investigation of Lobbying*. Berkeley: Bureau of Public Administration, University of California, 1956.

Townsley, W. A. "Pressure Groups in Australia." In Henry W. Ehrmann, ed. *Interest Groups on Four Continents*. Pittsburgh: Pittsburgh University Press, 1958, pp. 9–32.

Truman, David B. *The Congressional Party: A Case Study*. New York: Wiley, 1959.

————. *The Governmental Process*. New York: Knopf, 1951.

————. "The State Delegations and the Structure of Party Voting in the United States House of Representatives," *American Political Science Review*, L (December, 1956), 1023–45.

Tsuji, Kiyoski. "Pressure Groups in Japan." In Henry W. Ehrmann, ed. *Interest Groups on Four Continents*. Pittsburgh: Pittsburgh University Press, 1958, pp. 145–53.

Turner, Henry A. "How Pressure Groups Operate," *The Annals*, CCCXIX (September, 1958), 63–72.

Turner, Julius. *Party and Constituency: Pressures on Congress*. Baltimore: Johns Hopkins University Press, 1951.

Ulman, Lloyd. *The Rise of the National Trade Union*. Cambridge: Harvard University Press, 1955.

U. S. Congress. House, Select Committee on Lobbying Activities. *Hearings Part I, The Role of Lobbying in Representative Self-Government*, March 27–30, 1950 (81:2). Washington, D.C.: Government Printing Office, 1950 (a). Statement by Belle Zeller, "The Role of Lobbying in Representative Self-Government," pp. 58–97, 116–21.

————. House, Select Committee on Lobbying Activities. *General Interim Report* (81:2, H. Rep. no. 3138). Washington, D.C.: Government Printing Office, October 20, 1950 (b).

————. House, Select Committee on Lobbying Activities. *Report and Recommendations on Federal Lobbying Act* (81:2, H. Rep. no. 3239). Washington, D.C.: Government Printing Office, January 1, 3, 1951 (a).

————. Senate, Special Committee on the Organization of Congress. *Legislative Reorganization Act of 1946,* report to accompany S. 2177 (79:2, S. Rep. no. 1400). Washington, D.C.: Government Printing Office, May 31, 1946, Title 3: Lobby Regulation.

————. Senate, Committee on Expenditures in the Executive Departments. *Legislative Reorganization Act of 1946; Hearings on Evaluation of . . . Act,* February 2–25, 1948 (80:2). Washington, D.C.: Government Printing Office, 1948.

————. Senate, Committee on Expenditures in the Executive Departments. *Organization and Operation of Congress; Hearings on Evaluation of the Effects of Laws Enacted to Reorganize the Legislative Branch of the Government,* June 6–27, 1951 (82:1). Washington, D.C.: Government Printing Office, 1951. Statement of Belle Zeller on Lobbying, pp. 220–27; "Operation of the Legislative Reorganization Act of 1946" by George B. Galloway, pp. 627–43 (b).

————. Senate, Special Committee to Investigate Political Activities, Lobbying and Campaign Contributions (McClellan Committee). *Final Report* (85:1, S. Rep. no. 395). Washington, D.C.: Government Printing Office, May 31, 1957.

Van Deusen, Glyndon G. *Thurlow Weed: Wizard of the Lobby.* Boston: Little, Brown, 1947.

Velie, Lester. "The Secret Boss of California," *Colliers* (August 13, 1949,) pp. 11 ff. and (August, 20, 1949), pp. 12 ff.

Vose, Clement E. "Litigation as a Form of Pressure Group Politics," *The Annals,* CCCXIX (September, 1958), 20–31.

Wahlke, John C. "Behavioral Analyses of Representative Bodies." In Austin Ranney, ed. *Essays on the Behavioral Study of Politics.* Urbana: University of Illinois Press, 1962, pp. 173–90.

————, Buchanan, William, Eulau, Heinz, and Ferguson, Leroy C. "American State Legislator's Role Orientations toward Pressure Groups," *Journal of Politics,* XXII (May, 1960), 203–27 (a).

————, and Eulau, Heinz, eds. *Legislative Behavior.* Glencoe: Free Press, 1959.

———, Eulau, Heinz, Buchanan, William, and Ferguson, LeRoy C. *The Legislative System.* New York: Wiley, 1962.

Walker, Harvey. *The Legislative Process.* New York: Ronald Press, 1948.

Warner, W. Lloyd, and Srole, Leo. *The Social Systems of American Ethnic Groups.* New Haven: Yale University Press, 1948.

Watkins, Charles L., and Riddick, Floyd M. *Senate Procedures: Precedents and Practices.* Washington, D.C.: Government Printing Office, 1958.

Watson, Richard A. "The Tariff Revolution: A Study of Shifting Party Attitudes," *Journal of Politics,* XVIII (November, 1956), 678–701.

Weiner, Norbert. *Cybernetics.* New York: Wiley, 1948.

———. *The Human Use of Human Beings: Cybernetics and Society.* 2nd rev. ed.; Garden City: Doubleday Anchor Books, 1956.

Wengert, Norman. *Natural Resources and The Political Struggle.* Garden City: Doubleday, 1955.

White, William S. *Citadel: The Story of the U.S. Senate.* New York: Harper, 1956.

Whyte, William H., Jr. *Is Anybody Listening?* New York: Simon & Shuster, 1952.

Wilson, H. H. *Congress: Corruption and Compromise.* New York: Rinehart, 1951.

———. *Pressure Group: The Campaign for Commercial Television in England.* New Brunswick: Rutgers University Press, 1961.

Wirtz, W. Willard. "Government by Private Groups," *Louisiana Law Review,* XIII (March, 1953), 440–75.

Wolfinger, Raymond E. "Reputation and Reality in the Study of Community Power," *American Sociological Review,* XXV (October, 1960), 636–44.

Wright, C. R., and Hyman, Herbert H. "Voluntary Association Memberships of American Adults," *American Sociological Review,* XXIII (June, 1958), 284–94.

Wyant, Rowena. "Voting Via the Senate Mailbag," *Public Opinion Quarterly,* V (Fall, 1941), 359–82.

Young, Roland. *The American Congress.* New York: Harper, 1958.

Zeigler, Harmon. *Interest Groups in American Society.* Englewood Cliffs: Prentice-Hall, 1963.

Zeller, Belle, ed. *American State Legislatures.* New York: Thomas Y. Crowell, 1954.

SELECTED BIBLIOGRAPHY   421

_____. "The Federal Regulation of Lobbying Act," *American Political Science Review*, XLII (April, 1948), 239–71.

_____. *Pressure Politics in New York*. New York: Prentice-Hall, 1937.

_____. "The Regulation of Pressure Groups and Lobbyists," *The Annals*, CCCXIX (September, 1958), 94–103.

INDEX